Dedicated to

loving memory of my father

(who was also my teacher) late

Prof. R.R. Deshpande, Former Head,

Department of Sanskrit, Ramnarain

Ruia College, Matunga, Bombay

## Preface

As a student of Sanskrit, I had studied some religious texts and as a student of sociology I knew that religion and society always interact with each other. The change in one of these two brings about change in the other. That is why I found the topic of my research work 'Religion in Social Flux (as seen in the main *purāṇa*-s) very fascinating. The work was submitted in the from of a thesis to the University of Bombay, for which I was awarded Ph.D. degree. I am very much thankful to the authorities of Bombay University for granting me permission to publish this thesis in the form of a book.

As I went on studying the various component parts of Puranic religion, I came to know that it was a product of changing social circumstances. It was also responsible for bringing about changes in society. Manu stated that the entire Veda is the first source of the sacred law, next the tradition and the virtuous conduct of those who know the Veda further, also the customs of holy men and finally self-satisfaction. (*Manusmṛti* II. 6). This can very well be the description of the Puranic religion. The study of religion is the study of faith of various beliefs which culminate into different practices, of various symbols of religion and of the thought of the Supreme Being conceived by people. This thought is bound to have its impact upon the members of society. This is true especially regarding Puranic religion. The authors of the *purāṇa*-s popularised religion by incorporating as much as they could and by appealing to as many people as possible. It is my endeavour to demonstrate the changes in religion during the Puranic age in relation to social changes.

I consider it my first and foremost duty to thank my guide Dr. Smt. S.S. Dange, R.G. Bhandarkar Professor of Sanskrit and Head, Department of Sanskrit University of Bombay for her valuable guidance and suggestions. Their influence on the way this work has taken shape has been decisive. My sincere thanks are also due to the Library staff or three libraries - Ramnarain Ruia College Library, Matunga, Bombay 400 019, Jawaharlal Nehru Library, Kalina, Bombay 400 098 and Fort Library, Bombay 400 032 of the University of Bombay.

I am extremely thankful to Dr. S.A. Dange, Ex. R.G. Bhandarkar Professor of Sanskrit and Head, Department of Sanskrit, University of Bombay for being extremely kind in sparing his valuable time in going through the present work and for wholehearted appraisal of the same in his foreword.

I owe a considerable debt of gratitude to various scholars whose names and the titles of the books have been enlisted by me in the bibliography and who have provided significant guidelines for the present study.

I shall consider myself to be fortunate if this study can be of some use on understanding Hindu religion.

Varsha Pratipadā
1995

**Smt. A. Bakre**

## Foreword

The Purāṇas are known in the tradition as the fifth Veda. In other words, we could say that it is the *laukaika veda*. While the Vedic literature is believed to be *a-pauruṣeya*, the Purāṇas are perfectly *pauruṣeya*, and they are meant for the people at large. However, both have been accepted as the source of Dharma. It is clear form the Atharvaveda (xv. 6.11-12) and the later Vedic texts (Śat. Br. XI. 5.7.9) that a student's daily *svādhyāya* comprised not only the Vedic branch of his own family or other Vedic texts but also Itihāsa and Purāṇa, though the concept of Purāṇa, then, was not of individual texts. Purāṇa was the name of a class of floating 'knowledge', which was the proto-type of Smṛti, as against the sacred knowledge of Vedic ritual and philosophical concepts called Śruti. Both these formed parts of the ancient Hindu tradition, each influencing the other and getting influenced. When we arrive at the stage of the individual Purāṇas (the time span being from 200 A.D. through 1000 A.D., not to speak of the Upa-purāṇas), we find a happily interesting blend of the ancient sacerdotal and the comparatively new (at the turn of that particular century) rituals and customs. Purāṇas, thus, stand as avowedly preserved records wherein social realities and historical facts are present, many times in the garb of myths.

A number of scholars has studied the Purāṇa texts as one unit, while others have studied individual texts, from various angles, which include the socio-religious and sociomythical. R.C. Hazra's book, *Studies in the Purāṇic Records on Hindu Rites and Customs* (University of Dhaka, 1940) served as an impetus for the studies of Purāṇas from the social and religious points of view, and a good number of such studies followed.

The present study by Dr. (Smt.) Bakre is not merely one such attempt. It is a fresh and well guided methodological approach to mark the gradual evolution of religious concepts with the bearing on social normative change.

Here we have deliberation on the concept of Dharma from various angles, more specifically from the socio-anthropological (cultural), all of which are shown to be mutually interdependent. The modification, which the Purāṇas reflect, in the ancient monistic and the polytheistic concepts to suit the later period in an effort to wean away people from the impending influence of Jainism and Buddhims is convincingly shown. While doing so, the various behavioural patterns that differentiated various *varṇa*-s and the Purāṇic record of opening avenues for the Śūdra-s and women are very well shown. The complex polytheistic nature of the span of the period covered by the Purāṇas introduced many new gods and goddesses in the Hindu pantheon. There clearly appears to be a conscious effort towards fusion of various cults to evolve a consolidated whole during this period. -- a trait that continued for centuries later on. One of the most prominent of such cults was that of the Devī, which absorbed various local goddesses as aspects of the Mother goddess, whose popular name was Durgā, or Kātyāyanī. These and many such important points have been dealt with by Dr. Bakre in this book, which is well written, giving also information regarding the emergence of a number of holy places to mark the directions of social flux and the status of Hindu religion in its progress.

The information is painstakingly collected and methodically presented. There is no doubt that the book is a welcome addition to the literature on the Hindu religion, and particularly on the Purāṇas. I congratulate Dr. Bakre for this very useful accomplishment.

**Sadashiv A. Dange**

## CHRONOLOGICAL TABLE

(of important works and authors referred to in this book)

N.B. Some dates, particularly of ancient works, are conjectural and only tentative.

| | | |
|---|---|---|
| 4000 B.C. — 1000 B. C. | — | The period of the Vedic Saṁhitās, Brāhmaṇas and Upaniṣads. It is possible that some hymns many go back to a period even earlier than 4000 B.C. and the some Upaniṣads (even out of those that are regarded as the principal and the earliest ones) are later than 1000. B.C. |
| 800 B.C. — 400 B. C. | — | The Principal *śrauta sūtra*-s (of Āpastamba, Āśvalāyana, Baudhāyana, Kātyāyana, Śāṅkhyāyana and some of the *gṛhyasūtra*-s (Āśvalāyana, Āpastamba & C.) |
| 600 B.C. — 300 B. C. | — | The *dharmasūtra*-s of Āpastamba, Gautama, Baudhāyana, Vasiṣṭha and the *Gṛhyasūtra*-s of Pāraskara, Baudhāyana and some others. |
| 500 B.C. — 200 B.C. | — | Jaimini's Pūrvamīmāṁsā-sūtra |
| 300 B.C. — 100 A.D. | — | Kauṭilya's Arthaśāstra |
| 200 B.C. — 200 A.D. | — | Manusmṛti |
| 100 A.D. — 200 A.D. | — | Viṣṇudharmasūtra |
| 100 A.D. — 400 A. D. | — | Nāradasmṛti |

| | | |
|---|---|---|
| 200 A.D. — 500 A.D. | — | Śabara, Com. of Jaimini |
| 200 A.D. — 600 A.D. | — | Some of the extant *purāṇa*-s viz. Vāyu, Viṣṇu, Mārkaṇḍeya, Kūrma, Matsya. |
| 788 A.D. — 820 A.D. | — | Śankarācārya, the greatest Advaita philosopher. |
| 600 A.D. — 900 A.D. | — | Most of the other *Smrti*-s and some of the *purāṇa*-s |
| 900 A.D. | — | Medhāththi, Com. of Manu |
| 1000 A.D. | — | Mitākṣarā of Vijñāneśvara |
| 1150 A.D. — 1300 A.D. | — | Kullūka. |

These dates of the above works have been given by Kane P.V. (History of Dharmaśāstra, Vol, II, Part I, Bhandarkar Oriental Research Institute, Pune 1941) pp. x 1.3 XII they are regarded as the standard dates and the same have been accepted by me.

For other details regarding the dates of the Purāṇas see appendix at the end.

## TABLE OF CONTENTS

# LIST OF ABBREVIATIONS

| | | |
|---|---|---|
| **AV.** | : | *Atharvaveda* |
| **Ait. Br.** | : | *Aitareya Brāhmaṇa* |
| **Agn. P.** | : | *Agni Purāṇa* |
| **Aṅgiraḥ S.** | : | *Aṅgiraḥ-saṁhitā* |
| **Atri S.** | : | *Atri-saṁhitā* |
| **Āp. Gr. S.** | : | *Āpastamba Gṛhyasūtra* |
| **Baudh. Dh. S.** | : | *Baudhāyana Dharmasūtra* |
| **Bh. Gītā** | : | *Bhagavadgītā* |
| **BORI** | : | *Bhandarkar Oriental Research Institute* |
| **Bar. P.** | : | *Brahma Purāṇa* |
| **Brahmāṇḍa P.** | : | *Brahmāṇḍa Purāṇa* |
| **Br. V.P.** | : | *Brahmavaivarta Purāṇa* |
| **Br. up.** | : | *Bṛhadāraṇyaka upaniṣad* |
| **Ch. up.** | : | *Chāndogya upaniṣad* |
| **Dakṣa S.** | : | *Dakṣa-Saṁhitā* |
| **Devī Bhāg.** | : | *Devī Bhāgavata Purāṇa* |
| **Gaut. Dh. S.** | : | *Gautama Dharmasūtra* |
| **Gobh. Dh. S.** | : | *Gobhila Gṛhyasūtra* |
| **Hārita S.** | : | *Häritā-Saṁhitā* |
| **H. of Dh. S.** | : | *History of Dharmaśāstra* |
| **Jaimini** | : | *Pūrvamīmāṃāṁsāsūtra by Jaimini* |
| **Kaivalya up.** | : | *Kaivalya upaniṣad* |
| **Kāt.Gr.S.** | : | *Kātyāyana Gṛhyasūtra* |
| **Kūr. P.** | : | *Kūrma Purāṇa* |
| **Kauṣ. Gr. S.** | : | *Kauṣītaki Gṛhyasūtra* |
| **Lin.P.** | : | *Liṅga Purāṇa.* |
| **Likhita S.** | : | *Likhita-saṁhitā* |
| **Mbh.** | : | *Mahābhārata* |
| **Mbh. Anu.** | : | *Mahābhārata Anuśāsana Parva* |
| **Mbh. Ādi.** | : | *Mahābhārata Ādi Parva* |

| | | |
|---|---|---|
| **Mbh. Vana.** | : | *Mahābhārata Udyoga Parva* |
| **Mān. Gr. S.** | : | *Mānava Gṛhyasūtra* |
| **Manu S.** | : | *Manusmṛti* |
| **Mārk. P.** | : | *Mārkaṇḍeya Purāṇa* |
| **Mat.P.** | : | *Matsya Purāṇa* |
| **Muṇḍ. up.** | : | *Muṇḍaka upaniṣad* |
| **Nār.P.** | : | *Nārada Purāṇa* |
| **Pad. P.** | : | *Padma Purāṇa* |
| **Par.S.** | : | *Parāśara-saṁhitā* |
| **Pār. Gr. S.** | : | *Pāraskara Gṛhyasūtra* |
| **RV.** | : | *Ṛgveda saṁhitā* |
| **Saṁvarta S.** | : | *Saṁvarta-saṁhitā* |
| **Ska. P.** | : | *Śkanda Purāṇa* |
| **Śaṅkha. S.** | : | *Śāṁkhya-saṁhitā* |
| **Śat. Br.** | : | *Śatapatha Brāhmaṇa* |
| **Śātātapa S.** | : | *Śātātapa-saṁhitā* |
| **Śvet.up.** | : | *Śvetāśvatara upaniṣad* |
| **Tai. Saṁ.** | : | *Taittirīya Saṁhitā* |
| **T.D.S.** | : | *The Dharma Shāstra* |
| **Uśanaḥ S.** | : | *Uṣaṇaḥ-saṁhitā* |
| **Vaikh. Dh. S.** | : | *Vaikhānasa Dharmasūtra* |
| **Vāj. S.** | : | *Vājasaneyi Saṁhitā* |
| **Var. P.** | : | *Varāha Purāṇa* |
| **Varāha Gr. S.** | : | *Varāha Gṛhyasūtra* |
| **Vedānta S.** | : | *Vedāntasūtra* |
| **Viṣṇu P.** | : | *Viṣṇu Purāṇa* |
| **Vyāsa S.** | : | *Vyāsa-saṁhitā* |
| **Yāj. S.** | : | *Yājñavalkyasmṛti* |

CHAPTER — I

# INTRODUCTION

Religion is a universal social phenomenon. Some relate it with the feelings of wonder, awe, fear, ecstacy, reverence or admiration which man entertained when he was helpless before the caprices of nature, while some others hold that it is an outcome of some psychical tendencies that are universally found among human beings. It is based upon supersitious belief — the belief in the existence of superhuman beings and supramundane abstract principle. It indicates the sense of yearning or craving, an urge to unite with that Supreme Transcendental Relaity. It is characterised by two aspects—

(i) The psychological one in the form of various feelings entertained by man and

(ii) The physiological one in the form of the manner of approaching that Reality which is revealed in propitiating it.

These two aspects together have their impact upon human life. Religion is a means to an end, a sheet anchor, which gives solace to its followers.

## Radhakrishnan's Explanation of the Term *Dharma*—

As Radhakrishnan has aptly explained, the basic urge in man is to live nobly. We have the feeling of amazement at the mystery of the universe, faith in its adoration and endless quest for awareness to the personal riddles, an eager longing to discover, the truth of things, the truth which is universal and absolute in the sense that it is valid for all men, in all places at all times. The experience of the mysterious is the fundamental quality of all religions.[1] While explaining the functional aspect of religion, he has further stated that religions teach that God is in man and the unique discriminating ability of man to choose

1. Radhakrishnan S., *Religion and Society*, London, 1948, p. 44.

between good and evil distinguished him from the animal and lends sacredness to human life.[2]

According to him, *dharma* is a word of protean significance. It is derived form the root ***dhṛ*** used in the sense of upholding, sustaining, nourishing.[3] It is the norm which sustains the universe. While pointing out the various senses in which the word *dharma* occurs in ancient Indian texts, Radhakrishnan has stated that in the Vedas, this word is used in the sense of religious rites. The *Chāndogya up,* speaks of the three branches of *dharma (trayo dharmāḥ)* relating to the duties of householder, hermit and student.[4] the *Tait. Up*[5]., the *Bh. Gītā*[6] and the *Manu S.*[7] use the word in the sense of the duties of persons. In the eyes of the Budhists, *dharma* is one of the three jewels i.e. *triratna*-s, the other two being, the *Buddha* and *Saṅgha.* The Pūrvamīmāṁsā uses it in the sense of the object defined by a direction.[8]

He has further observed that human beings have diverse interests, various desires and conflicting needs which grow and change and to round them off into a whole is the purpose of *dharma.* The principle of *dharma* rouses us to a recognition of spiritual realities not by abstention from the world but by bringing to its life its business *(artha)* and its pleasures *(kāma)* the controlling power of spiritual faith, thus, in his view, supplement and supplant *dharma.* Life, he has remarked, is one in which there is no distinction between sacred and secular. *Bhakti* and *mukti* are not opposed. *Dharma, artha* and *kāma* go together.[9]

---

2. *Ibid,* p. 55.
3. *Mbh. śānti* 109.11. Also Radhakrishnan, *op. cit.*, p. 107
   धारणात् धर्ममित्याहुः धर्मेण विधृताः प्रजाः।
4. *Chā. Up.* II. 23. Also Radhakrishanan S., *op.cit.*, p. 107 -
5. *Tait. Up.* I.II - धर्मं चर।
6. *Bh. Gītā* III.35.
7. *Manu S.* I. 108[a] - आचारः परमो धर्मः।
   *Ibid,* I.110[d] - आचारं जगृहुः परम्।
8. *Jaimini,* I. 1.2
9. Radhakrishnan S., *op. cit.*, p. 105.

While explaining the importance of *dharma* in human life, Radhakrishnan has pointed out that the supreme aim of social order is to train human beigns for a state of spiritual perfection and sanctity. Its essential aim, he believed, is the development of social conditions in such a way that as they would enable every individual to the basic principle of *dharma* i.e. the realisation of the dignity of the human spirit which is the dwelling place of the supreme.[10] With an apt quotation from the *Mbh.* 'He who by his action, mind and speech is continually engrossed in the welfare of others, knows the meaning of *dharma*',[11] he has rightly explained the noble aspect of *dharma*.

While expounding the concept of *dharma* in general and Hinduism in particular,[12] Radhakrishnan has glorified Hindusim stating that religions divide humanity into hostile camps instead of uniting it. They emphasize the individual, rather than the social side of life. Hinduism, however, represents an effort at comprehension, and co-operation. It recognises the diversity in man's approach towards and realisation of the Supreme Reality... All creeds are attempts of the finite mind to grasp the infinite. They are valuable in so far as they help us to reach the ultimate goal. They are different because they are adapted to the different needs ot the people. Hinduism, however, is not bound up with a creed or prophet, a book or a founder, it is a persistent search for truth on the basis of a continouously renewed experience. Hinduism is human thought about God in continuous evolution.[13]

Religion being a broad and multifaceted concept can be thought of from various aspects. *In Eastern Religions and Western Thought*, Radhakrishnan has taken some of

10. *Ibid*, p. 107.
11. *Mbh. śānti* 261. 9
    सर्वेषां यः सुहृन्नित्यं सर्वेषां च हिते रतः।
    कर्मणा मनसा वाचा तं धर्मं वेद जाजले।।
    Also Radhakrishnan, *op. cit.*, p. 107
12. *Ibid*, pp. 107-108.
13. *Ibid*, pp. 51-52

these aspects into consideration.[14] He has classified religions of the world into two categories, viz., those that emphasize the object and those that insist on experience. As for the first category, he has stated, religion is an attitude of faith and conduct directed to a power without and for the second one, it is an experience to which the individual attaches supreme value. Hindu religion, he believed, belongs to the second category and philosophy and religion are two aspects of a single movement. Real religion, he holds, can exist without a distinction between the spiritual and profane, the sacred and secular. Religion, according to him, is the conquest of fear, the antidote to failure and death and to be religious is to apprehend the reality of other souls.[15]

**Kane's Exposition on the Theme *Dharma*—**

In Vol. I of the *History of Dharmaśāstra,* Kane has shown that the term *dharma* is used in different senses in different works.[16] At the very outset, he has pointed out that *dharma* is one of those Sanskrit words that defy all attempts at an exact rendering in English or any other tongue. The word has passed through several vicissitudes. Like Radhakrishnan, Kane also has stated that the term *dharma* is derived from the root ***dhṛ***, used in the sense of upholding, supporting, nourishing. In the Ṛgvedic hymns,[17] it is frequently used in the sense of "religious ordinance" or rites, though at times, it is used in the sense of "upholder, supporter or sustainer.[18]" In some passages[19] it seems to have been used in the sense of 'fixed principles' or 'rules of conduct'. In the *AV.*,[20] it appears that the word is used in the sense of merit acquired by the performance

14. Radhakrishanan S., *Eastern Religions and Western Thought*, London, 1949, pp. 20ff.
15. *Ibid*, p.45
16. Kane P.V., *History of Dharmaśāstra*, Vol. I, Part-I, Pune, 1968, pp.1-3.
17. *RV.* I.22.18; V. 26.6; VIII.43.24.
18. *RV.* I. 187.1$^{ab}$, X. 92.2$^{cd}$.
19. *RV.* IV. 53.34; V. 63.75.
20. *AV.* X.9.17.

of religious rites. In the *Ait. Br.*,[21] it is used in the sense of the whole body of religious duties. The *Chān. Up.*[22] speaks of '*trayo dharmaskandhāḥ*', i.e. three branches of *dharma*, one study and charity, representing the stage of a hermit and the third that of a *brahmacārin*, dwelling in the house of his teacher. Dharma, here, thus stands for the peculiar duties of āśrama-s. In the famous *anuvak* from the *Tait. Up.*[23] meant for the disciples who have satisfactorily completed their course of study, *i.e.*, *satyam vada, dharmam cara* etc., it is used in the sense of privileges, duties and obligations of a man, his standard of conduct as a member of the Aryan community, as member of one of the castes, as a person in a particualr stage of life. *Bh. Gītā* also uses it in the same sense. *Manu S.*[25] speaks of the *dharmas* of all the *varṇa-s* and the *Yāj s.*[26] also employs it in the same sense. Medhātithi[27] commenting on Manu speaks of fivefold *dharma*, viz., *varṇadharma, āśramadharma, varṇāśramadharma, naimittikadharma* and *guṇadharma*. Kane has further drawn the attention of the readers towards several definitions of *dharma* such as a desirable goal or result that is indicated by injunctive Vedic passages.[28] that from which result 'happiness or final bliss'.[29] According to Kane other definitions where *dharma* is equated with non-violence or *ānṛśaṁsya*,[31] good behaviour or conduct are one-sided.

## Dange's Exposition on *Dharma*—

Dange has elucidated the meanings of the term *dharma*

---

21. *Ait. Br.* VII.17.
22. *Chā.Up.* II.23.
23. *Tait. Up.* I.II.
24. *Bh.Gītā* III.35.
25. *Manu s.* I.2.
26. *Yāj.S.* I.1.
27. Medhātithi on *Manu S.* II.25.
28. *Jaimini* I.1.2. चोदनालक्षणो धर्मः।
29. *Vaiśeṣika S.* I. 1.2. यतो ऽभ्युदयनिःश्रेयससिद्धिः स धर्मः।
30. *Mbh.* Anu. 115.1- अहिंसा परमो धर्मः।
31. *Ibid,* Vana, 373.76. आनृशंस्यं परो धर्मः।

by citing a number of appropriate examples.[32] He has stated that the Ṛgvedic term *dharma*[33] when used in neuter gender denotes various constituents of the 'whole', known as *dharma*, wherein the 'whole' stands for a sacrifice. The *Pūrvamīmāṁsākāras* use the term in the sense of sacrificial activities, whereas, the *Uttaramīmāṁsākāras* use in the sense of fundamental philosophical doctrines. In Jaimini's definition,[34] the word *codanā* stands for the earnest injunctions meant for performing various sacrificial activities such as throwing oblations into sacrificial fire, payment of sacrificial fees etc. and *dharma* stood for the achievement of goal in the form of sacrifice. Dange believes that sacrifice or *yajña* itself was a *dharma* which was supposed to support the concept of *ṛta*. Dange has further shown as to how *dharma* was dynamic and how it became more and more comprehensive in the course of time with the changing social conditions and customs. At times *dharma* stood for the act of sticking to traditional *saṁskāras*[35] or activities one intends to do *(ācāradharma)* or the activities that one is supposed to carry out in keeping with one's own *āśrama*, while on other occasions, it comprised various ideal principles such as self-control, non-violence, the act of bestowing gifts *(dāna)* etc. Each *yuga*, Dange has observed, had its own ideal *dharma* and as such sacrifice was the most significant *dharma* of *dvāpara*, while *dāna* was that of *kali*. Dange has defined the term *dharma* as a tradition of customs, beliefs and duties of a particular group of society which is useful to it in maintaining or supporting themselves. He has further remarked that *dharma* as a *puruṣārtha* was so significant in ancient India that even the pursuit of *artha* and *kāma* was supposed to be in consonance with *dharma* and an abandonment of *dharma* was frowned upon by people. In fact, non-abandonment of *dharma* was a highly cherished religious norm. While ex-

32. Dange S.A., *Hindu Dharma āṇi Tattvajñāna*, Pune, 1975, pp.1-15.

33. *RV.* X. 90.16 - तानि धर्माणि प्रथमान्यासन्।

34. *Jaimini* I. 1.2- चोदनालक्षणो धर्मः।

35. *Bh. Gita* III. 35 - स्वधर्मे निधनं श्रेयः परधर्मो भयावहः।

plaining the special feature of Hindu *dharma*, Dange has remarked that even though Hindu religion was based on traditions, it was not characterised by traditionality. Hindu religion, according to him, was never static. It was always dynamic and comprehensive. It underwent several transitions along with the changing conditions and customs. The ancient Vedic religion incorporated several non-Vedic ideas and customs and the synthesis of these two brought about transformation of the Vedic religion into Hinduism and soon it became the religion of the masses.[36]

### Views of Joshi J.V.[37]

Joshi has taken into consideration several meanings of the term *dharma* explained by various Indian and Western scholars and has elaborately dealt with the concept of *dharma*.

His views and explanations of the term *dharma* or religion given by other scholars which he has discussed could be summarised as follows—

The term *dharma* is defined and explained variously by various people and each one of these explanations is representative of the peculiar outlook of the explainer. A thorough analysis of these definitions and explanations throws light on the comprehensive nature of religion.

Joshi has stated that according to the explanations stated in *Mahārāṣṭra Śabdakośa* :

i) *Dharma* enables human beings to follow good conduct, to think about the Supreme Reality.
ii) The term *dharma* can stand for a means to an end, *i.e.* religious rites or propitiatory activities which enable the *sādhakas* to reach the Supreme Reality.
iii) It also denotes Śāstric and traditional customs, sacred rites etc.

---

36. Dange S.A., *op.cit.*, p.13.
37. Joshi J.V., *Hindu Dharmāche Tattvajñāna*, Pune, 1975, pp.2ff.

iv) The term represents moral qualities, excellent conduct developed by following a given religion.

v) The term stands for propitiatory and religious activities.

vi) It signifies the principles of social justice, social system and law.[38]

vii) It represents the relationship between the god and human beings, a combination of *karmakāṇḍa*, Vedānta and Nīti which includes customs, rules and duty.[39]

According to Mure, *dharma* has three consitituents[40]—

i) Recognition on the part of some higher, unseen power as having control of his destiny and being entitled to obedience, reverence or worship.

ii) The general mental and moral attitude resulting from the belief with reference to its effect upon the individual and the community.

iii) Personal or general acceptance of this feeling as a standard of spiritual and practical life.

*Dharma* represents—

i) Belief in supernatural and sacred beings.

ii) Ceremonial rites and prayers in honour of sacred beings.

iii) Mode of life shaped by that belief system.

iv) Institution of religion which guides and regulates social behaviour.

According to William James, human beings think about divine beings and their feelings, experiences and activities with reference to them culminate into religion.

According to Gallove, religion represents man's faith in the Highest Power through which he fulfils his emotional needs and achieves stability in life, the faith which is

---

38. Date Y. R., *Mahārashtra Śabdakośa*, IV, Pune, 1935 p. 1726.
39. Opinion of Kulkarni K.P., *Vyutpattikośa* (in Marathi), q. by Joshi J.V., *op.cit.*, p.3.
40. For the views of Mure J.A.H., see Joshi J.V., *op.cit.*, p.3.

manifested in the form of prayers, devotion and service.[41]

According to Indian tradition, *dharma* denotes —

i) The Highest Knowledge leading to salvation and

ii) The behavioural patterns of the followers of religion.

The term *dharma* represents two different outlooks —

i) The lore of the Upaniṣadic doctrines aiming at the Highest Welfare, Eternal Bliss, Self-realisation, the knowledge of the Highest Reality which lead to salvation.

ii) The behavioural code *(ācāraśāstra)* that in the *Śrutis*, the *smṛtis*, the *sūtra* literature, the Purāṇas and such other works contain.

**Explanation of the term *Dharma* given in Bhāratīya Saṁskṛtikośa[42]:**

The term *dharma* is to be derived from the root *dhṛ* which means to support and *dharma* is *dharma* worth the name because of its ability to sustain, maintain and support people. The connotation of this term went on changing from time to time. In the Ṛgvedic hymns, sometimes it is used in the sense of supporting, uplifting, preserving[43] or protecting[44] whereas at some places,[45] it denotes moral law and custom. Sometimes, it also stands for moral rule or order and elsewhere[47], it is also used in the sense of Varuṇa's moral order or ordinance. In *Vāj. Sam.*,[48] it represents a definite code of conduct, principles or rules of behaviour and in one of the *atharvanic mantras*,[49] it stands for the

41. For the views of James William and Gallove G., see Joshi J.V., *op. cit.*, pp.21-22.
42. *Bhāratīya Saṁskṛti Kośa*, Vol. IV, ed. by Joshi Mahadevashastri and Hodavar Padmaja, Pune, 1967, pp. 558-587.
43. *RV* I. 187.1.
44. *RV*. X. 92.2
45. *RV*. I. 22 18; V. 26.6; VIII. 43.24
46. *RV* III.17.1; III.3.1.
47. *RV*. VI. 70.1.
48. *Vāj. Sam.* II.3. ध्रुवेण धर्मणा धर्मः।
49. *AV*. XI.9.17.

merit acquired by performing religious activity. Joshi has also drawn the attention towards the reference to three *dharmaskandhas* that the *Chān. Up.* contains;[50] which stand for different stages of life. *Dharma* finally came to mean definite rights and duties, responsibilities of people as also various rules of conduct to be followed by various members of society. *Manu S.* states ten excellent qualities to be the characteristic features of *Dharma*.[51] *Yāj. S.* regards *śrutis*, *smṛtis* and good conduct to be the cornerstones of *dharma* and explains the concept of *mānavadharma* as self-realisation by concentration of mind, meditation etc.[52] Definition of *dharma* in the *Mbh.*[53] stresses the importance of protection of subjects, upliftment of society. In this connection, Joshi has remarked that the discussion of the topic *dharma* was a means to an end in the form of upliftment of society. *Dharma* denoted moral rules, bringing about the betterment of society or nation. He has further stated that according to the Purāṇic account, *dharma* originated roughly 12,000 years ago, at the beginning of Tretāyuga, Brahmā induced *Saptarṣis* and Manu to narrate *śrauta* and *smārta dharma* whereupon while narrating the *śrauta dharma*, *saptarṣis* stessed the importance of marriage and *agnihotra* and while preaching the traditional *smārta dharma*, Svāyambhuva Manu emphasized the importance of *varṇāśramācāra*.[54]

**Various Standpints to study the Concept of *Dharma* : —**

The concept of *dharma* can be studied from various points of view, *i.e.* historical, sociological, anthropological, psychological and philosophical.

---

50. *Chān. Up.* II.23.
51. *Manu S.* VI.92-
    धृतिः क्षमा दमो ऽज्ञस्तेयं शौचमिन्द्रियनिग्रहः।
    धीर्विद्या सत्यमक्रोधः दशकं धर्मलक्षणम्।।
52. *Yāj.S.* I.7.
53. *Mbh. Śānti* 109.11.
    धारणाध्दर्ममित्याहुः धर्मो धारयते प्रजाः।
    स स्याध्दारणसंयुक्तः स धर्म इति निश्चयः।।
54. *Vāyu* p. 57.39-41.

**Historical Standpoint —**

Historically speaking, like any other social phenomenon, *dharma* also has its roots in the past. Each succeeding event is shaped by the preceding ones and the study of history enables one to have the knowledge of the evolutionary process which culminates into a definite result. Changing circumstances have their direct and indirect impact upon every social phenomenon and religion is not an exception to this rule. Historical study of religion is the study of various beliefs, customs, theologies, traditions, institutions, myths, creeds in relation to time factor.

**Sociological Standpoint —**

From sociological point of view, religion is a "system of beliefs and practices by means of which a group of people struggles with the ultimate problems of human life.[55] According to Durkheim, religion is essentially a social phenomenon in the sense it can be explained only in terms of social facts. It is the social environment that produces religious ideas.[56] The forces at work within the institution of religion are not spiritual in the orthodox sense nor material, but we might say between the two. They are normal and social.[57] The powers before which the believer prostrates himself are not simply physical forces, such as are given to the senses and imagination : they are social forces, which are the direct product of collective sentiments that have clothed themselves in a material covering. .....All that goes by the name of religion — gods, rites, beliefs, religious objects arises out of man's social life, from his interrelationship with other people. Religion is a product of society.[58] It is unique to man only and it is never found except where a collective organisation exists.[59] Durkheim

55. Yinger Milton, *The Scientific Study of Religion*, London, 1970, p.9.
56. Durkheim's views; q. by Pickering S.T., Routledge and Kegen Paul : *Durkheim's Sociology of Religion*, London, 1984, pp. 193-204.
57. *Ibid*, p.195.
58. *Ibid*, p.195.
59. *Ibid*, p. 264.

believes that like any other social institution, religion is born, grows and dies. Religion which is a queen of institutions supports all other institutions. It pervades everyting, embraces the entirety of life. It directly cultivates and mobilizes attitudes of respect, submission, willingness to sacrifice oneself etc. It exercises at all times, a constraint upon the individual. It leads to social solidarity and cohesion.[60]

It has also been observed that wherever there is a man there is religion. Manifestations of it are found universally[61] and it can be defined as "the belief in and an attempt to relate favourably to (a) values of thought to have some transcendental importance and/or (b) ultimate power or powers thought responsible for all, or some significant aspect of the fundamental order of the universe."[62] Such beliefs in transcendental values and ultimate powers tend to become systematised and the upshot is religion.

According to Parsons Tolcott, from empirical point of view, religious phenonmena are dictated to man by the stresses and strains of life, the necessity of facing heavy odds and every religion presents three main aspects dogmatic, ritual and ethnic which are interrelated with each other.[63]

Sociologists are concerned with religion as an aspect of group behaviour and the role religion has played through ages. The socioligist is committed to the attempt to study religion objectively. Religion, from sociological point of view, is a product of culture. It may be regarded as a cultural tool by means of which man has been able to accommodate himself to the total environment.

---

60. *Ibid*, pp.263-265.
61. Hault Thomas Ford, *The Sociology of Religion*, New Yourk, 1958, p.3.
62. *Ibid*, p.9.
63. Parsons Tolcott, *Theories of Society : Foundations of Modern Sociological Theory*, "Introduction", by Parsons T., New York, 1961, pp. 1092-1094.
64. Nottingham Elizabeth, *Religion : A Sociological Review*, New York, 1971, pp.37-59.

Religion being an established way, repeatedly resorted to by people over a period of time is firmly rooted in the structure of society and, thus, is an institution in itself. As an institution, it carries out several important functions. It gives meaning and cohesion to the society's value system.... provides values that serve to channel the attitudes of the members of society, ... supplies ideal standards of behaviour, i.e. "oughts" or norms. Being backed by sacred sanctions, religion has a special constraining force upon the members of society and thus can bring about social control.[64]

**Anthropoligical Point of View—**

From anthropoligical standpoint, religion relates a view of the ultimate nature of reality to a set of ideas of how man is well advised even obligated to live. Religion tunes human actions to a view of the cosmic order onto the plane of human existence.[65]

Anthropologically, Geertz Clifford, has defined religion as—

1) A system of symbols which acts to
2) established powerful, pervasive and longlasting moods and motivations in men by
3) formulating conceptions of a general order of existence and
4) clothing these conceptions with such an aura of factuality that
5) the moods and motivations seem uniquely realistic.[66]

Religion is an integral part of our culture. According to the classic definition of Edward Tylor, culture is... "that complex whole which includes knowledge, belief, art, morals, law, custom and any other capabilities and habits acquired

65. Geertz Cifford, *International Encyclopaedia of Social Sciences*, Vol. XIII, U.S.A., 1968, pp.398-406.
66. Geetz Cifford, *Anthropological Approaches to the Study of Religion*, London, 1965, p. 101.
67. Tylor's definition q. by Horton Paul and Hunt Chester L., *Sociology*, Tokyo, 1976, p. 76.

by man as a member of society"[67] which is received by the members of society as a part of social heritage. Religion is an outcome of peculiar belief system arising out of various emotional and psychic states such as fear, wonder, joy, reverence which induce people to have faith in supernatural powers and/or beings and think of various mental or varbal symbols to enable them to focus their attention on the supernatural and to express their feelings and attitudes about them.[68]

**Psychological Standpoint—**

From psychological point of view, religion as an inner subjective experience of man is "something natural to man and is not imposed upon him by an extraneous authority or device. It belongs to the very constitution of his nature that his reaction to the universe should find expression in forms which we can call religious."[69] It is his distingushing characteristic to react to the universe in a religious way. Man's subjective experience is the form of feelings such as wonder, awe, fear or admiration resulting into tendencies or impulses which react to his surroundings which are found to be meaningful and whereby he seeks to adjust himself to them. He starts personifying and propitiating this mysterious power or superhuman element. Religion, thus, is a propitiatory means of securing the goodwill of the Supreme Power. It helps man to overcome his tension and strains.[70]" Religion appears to be a peculiar attitude of mind which could be formulated in accordance with the original use of the word *religio* which means a careful consideration and observation of certain dynamic factors that are conceived as "powers": spirits, demons, gods, laws, ideas, ideals or whatever name man has given to such factors in his world as has been enough to be taken into careful consideration or grand, beautiful and meaninful

68. Gillin J.P., *An Introduction to Sociology*, New York, 1963, p.455.
69. Selbi, *The Psychology of Religion*, Oxford, 1924, p.2.
70. *Ibid*, pp. 22ff.
71. Jung C.G., *The Collective Works of C.G. Jung*, Vol. II, "Psychology and Religion", London, 1958, p.8.

enough to be devoutly worshipped and loved.[71]

**Philosophical Standpoint —**

Philosophy is based on assumptions rather than scientific investigations. It deals with two aspects, the material and spiritual. Philosophically speaking, man as a self-conscious being craves for rising above the material and finite and achieving knowledge of the infinite. Philosophy concerns itself with the answers to the questions such as what is the cause of the world, how is the world originated, maintained and destroyed. According to philosophical perspective, finite consciousness tries to unite with the infinite and phiolosophy aims at unfolding these relations and tracing out the process tending to communion with the infinite and attainment of Eternity."[72]

Almost every religion is characteised by philosophical or metaphysical principles and doctrines. Philosophical thought forms an integral and vital part of religion. Philosophy, however, is purely speculative in nature, whreas religion goes a step further. It is practical, its essential is worship and it is animistic in nature, that is, it is based on the belief in souls and spirits, agencies of personal nature which are propitiated by man. In this connection, it is interesting to take into consideration the controversial issue discussed by Max Weber, i.e., whether philosophy would have sprung from religion or whether philosphy may have been the parent and religious doctrine the offspring. It is true, Max Weber has opined, religion would be regarded as a popular philosophy.[73]

Religion, thus, being a multifaceted notion can be studied from these different standpoints. Interestingly, they are neither dimetrically opposed to each other, nor mutually exclusive in nature, on the contrary, they are collectively exhaustive. All of them together shape the phenomenon of

---

72. Caird John, *An Introduction to the Philosophy of Religion*, Glasgo, 1910, pp. 55ff.
73. Weber Max, *Religion of India : The Sociology of Hinduism and Budhism*, Illionois, 1958, p. 51.

religion and hence an integrated analysis based on the synthesis of these various angles would throw light on the true nature of religion.

Moreover, no element of society is static. Change is inevitable, unavoidable. The phonomenon of religion also is constantly in the state of incessant flux. It can be studied in the light of the phenonmenon of social change. Sociologists have rightly taken into consideration the longstanding and much debated questions such as whether "society" changes "religion" or vice versa, whether religion is the prime mover in history or whether religion is a mere reflection of other changes in history and society, whether society is responsible for bringing about changes in religion or whether religion leads to changes in society and have tried to conclude that such questions are misleading since both religion and society interact with each other and are brought about by a "chain of causation."[74]

## Puranic Religion

"Various writers have emphasized three modes of relationship between religious and social change — ....religious change as a result of social change, religion as a barrier to change, religion as an initiator of change."[75] Puranic religion also can be studied in the light of these statements.

Sociological analysis of the Puranic religion throws light on the fact that like any other social phenomenon, Puranic religion also

i) is a product of an interaction of certain antecedent forces.
ii) It is characterised by functional aspect and
iii) It could be studied in the light of the concept social change.

"A new religion comes into existence in response to certain felt needs of its would be followers..... when a society

74. Nottingham Elizabeth, *op.cit.*, pp. 142, 182.
75. Yinger Milton, *Religion, Society and the Individual*, New York. 1957, p.265.

is in a stable state, its members find their inherited religion statisfactory on the whole. However, in periods of rapid transition the existing system of thought and values no longer serves its needs. A significant number of persons may develop new aspirations, new view of life and look for new thought and values. Religion appears as a harbinger of change. It meets the challenge of change."[76] Puranic religion is characterised by some of these features.

Religious works and society are seen to act and react with each other and the Purāṇas do bear out testimony to this observation. "The *Purāṇas* set about their task of reorientation of earlier religious concepts, ideologies and doctrines.[77] Moreover, as stated by Chowdhari N., according to the reforming view regarding Hinduism, it "was a pure monotheistic religion whose doctrines were to be found in the Upaniṣads, but after being swamped by Buddhism it reappeared in the 7th or 8th century A.D. in grossly polytheistic from.[78]

On the one hand, the Puranic religion was a continuation of earlier traditions. Thus, e.g., the earlier popular religious doctrines such as the doctrine of unity in diversity, *Karman* doctrine, the doctrine of rebirth were retained by the *Purāṇakāras*, and on the other hand, very consciously and cleverly, they gave a new turn to the old principles and doctrines in order to preserve and protect their own religion whose existence was threatened by the rise and popularity of Budhism and Jainism. They had realised that the ritualistic *(karmakāṇḍātmaka)* aspect of Vedic religion stressed the importance of ritual activities to be performed with utmost rigidity, complexity and elaborate procedure, involving a great amount of expenditure and the philosophical *(jñānakāṇḍātmaka)* aspect of the Vedānta doctrines emphasized the importance of the acquisition of

76. Shah A.B., *Religion and Society in India*, Bombay, 1981, pp.13-14.
77. Kane P.V., *History of Dharmaśāstra*, Vol. V., Pt. II, Pune, 1962, pp.912-913.
78. Chowdhari Nirad, "History of Hinduism, Its Methodology", *Hinduism*, New Delhi, 1979, p. 29.

the knowledge of the Supreme Reality which was purely abstract in nature and therefore, the vast bulk of people who were eager to free themselves from the cycle of births and deaths and the sufferings of the mundane existence were unable to pursue *dharma*, the first goal of human life. They could neither achieve merit *(puṇya)*, nor salvation *(mokṣa)* and hence were likely to deviate from the then existing religious norms and get attracted by the teachings of Jainism and Buddhism. The authors of *purāṇa-s*, therefore, simplified religion by eulogising personified gods such as Śiva or Viṣṇu. They also tried to synthesize various conflicting cults such as Śaivism, Vaiṣṇavism and preached unity in diverstiy. At the same time, they also tried to synthesize the popular systems of philosophy such as Vedānta or Sāṅkhya and correlated them with the concept of personification of gods. Purāṇas have simplified the physiological aspect of religion, as a means of approaching the Ultimate Reality by laying down the earliest practices such as *dāna, vrata-s*, visits to holy places, *japa, pūjana, nāmasmaraṇa* creating thereby a new belief system which though superstitious in nature could appeal to all the sections of society, irrespective of caste, creed, sex or sex differences existing among them. On the one hand, Puranic religion, thus, was a transformation of the earlier religion brought about by the changing circumstances and the changing needs of society and on the other hand, by changing the belief system and behavioural patterns of people, it further brought about change in the structure of Indian society. People who were groping in darkness because of the lack of some concrete ideal in the form of *dharma* were naturally inclined to follow this new religion which represented common man's ideas, thoughts, feelings and activities, a religion which was definitely more cohesive and comprehensive in nature and which would appeal to various sections of society. In the words of Surabhi Seth, "If the basic objective of the Purāṇas was to produce cultural cohesion, by creating a belief system in which every group of people could recognise something of special appeal to itself, they succeeded well"[79]

As for the old, popular doctrines, it is quite wellknown that the *karman* doctrine and the doctrine of rebirth or transmigration of soul or self were inextricably woven together. They had formed a significant part of the belief system of ancient Indian people. These doctrines were easy to comprehend. The authors of Purāṇas, therefore, neither felt any need to introduce any change in these doctrines nor to dispose them of completely. That is why the *purāṇas* also stress their importance. *Śrāddha* ceremonies or *tarpaṇa* rites had for several years been a charactristic of *smārta* religion. The authors of the *purāṇas* retained their importance as well. Puranic religion reflects a conscious attempt to attract all the sections of society including the Śudras and women and gain popularity which is revealed by the statements such as, "If *dāna* and *yajña* enable men to reach the auspicious world, women can attain the same by waiting upon their husbands and Śūdras by serving other classes of society."[80]

The cosmogonic and philosophical contents of the *purāṇas* reveal a tendency to effect a synthesis of various systems of philosophy such as Vedānta system, Sāṅkhya system and to corelate them whith personified gods. In their attempt to simplify and popularise religion, the authors of the *purāṇas* passed on from monotheism to polytheism but although these authors glorified various personified gods, they were fully conscious of the fact that the plurality was more apparent than real. Thus, when Viṣṇu's greatness was extolled,[81] he was identified with the Supreme Brahman, the credit of the functions of creation, protection and destruction was attributed to him[82] and at the same

79. Seth Surabhi, "Introduction" to *The Religion and Society in the Brāhmaṇa Purāṇa*, New Delhi, 1979, p.4.

80. *Viṣ.P.* VI.II.28.23.

81. *Kūr. P.* I. 16, 220, 221.

82. *Ibid*, I. 15. 95[cd] - अहं हि सर्वभूतानामन्तर्यामीश्वरः परः।
96[ab] - सर्गस्थित्यन्तकर्तृत्वं प्रवृत्तिर्मम गीयते।

time it is stated that those who distinguish between Śiva and Viṣṇu go to hell or Viṣṇu, Rudra and Janārdana, in reality, are the same.[83] Undoubtedly, this is in consonance with the Ṛgvedic statement that *sat* is one, but is designated as many.[84]

## The Theory of Incarnation

It is but natural if the theory of incarnation which has its roots[85] in the Ṛgvedic hymns and in the legends given in the Brāhmaṇa texts,[86] which is further developed in the verses of the Gītā[87] which manifests the Lord of the universe as regulating the course of the world through his omnipotence attracted the authors of the *purāṇas* to suit their purpose of simplifying religious principle through manifest *(vyakta)* form of the Supreme Reality. According to this theory, (i) The various incarnations *(avatāras)* are the manifestations of the same Reality, (ii) one *avatāra* is followed by the next one and the theory is related to the theory of rebirth and (iii) The Highest Lord manifests himself in different forms and different *yonis* so as to appeal to different kinds of people.

Moreover, according to the Purāṇas, *dharma* was not just an ideal to be preached, it was also a matter to be practised and in a much wider sense, it stood for virtuous conduct, righteous attitude, in fact, *mānavadharma* itself.

---

83. *Ibid*, I. 15. 96[cd]-
यो विष्णुः स स्वयं रुद्रो यो रुद्रः स जनार्दनः।
84. *RV* I. 164.46-
एकं सद्विप्रा बहुधा वदन्ति अग्निं यमं मातरिश्वानमाहुः।
85. *RV*. VI. 47.18.
रुपं रुपं प्रतिरूपं बभूव
तदस्य रूपं प्रति चक्षणाय।
इन्द्रो मायाभिः पुरुरूप ईयते
युक्ता ह्यस्य हरयः शता दश।।
86. Devasthali G.V., *Religion and Mythology of the Brāhmaṇas*, Bhau Vishnu Ashtekar Vedic Research Series, Vol. No. 1, Pune, 1965, pp.8-10.
87. *Bh. Gītā* IV. 34, 35.

As is rightly pointed out by Akhtar J. in his introduction to the edition of the Viṣṇu P. "At a time when the existence of the Hindu society was threatened by internal blickerings and foreign invasions, the authors of the Purāṇas struggled for the formation of a united front.... created a sense of religious toleration among the followers of different religious sects." Puranic religion was the need of the time and the same was very ably fulfilled by the transformation of the earlier religion into the religion of the masses."[88]

88. Akhtar J., "Introduction" to the *Viṣṇu Purāṇa* (ed.) by M.N. Dutt, Delhi, P. xvii.

CHAPTER — II

# COSMOGONY, COSMOLOGY AND PHILOSOPHY IN THE PURĀṆAS

As is rightly pointed out by Clifford Geertz, "In the development of such an analysis, historical, pshycholcgical, sociological and what has been called here semantic considerations are all necessary, but none is sufficient. A mature theory of religion will consist in an integration of them all into a conceptual system whose exact form remains to be discovered".[1]

The term cosmogony consists of two Greek terms *kosmos*, meaning the order of the universe and *genesis* which means the coming into being. Origin and development of cosmogony have their roots in the universal tendency on the part of human beings to narrate the myths and stories of creation and to propound the theories relating to it.[2] The term cosmology represents the religious views of cosmos and thus comsmology is a study of cosmic views in general and the specific view concerning the universe held in a religion or cultural tradition.[3]

H. Jacobi has pointed out that cosmological specultions were in India, as elsewhere, the first manifestation of philosophical thought which are already met with in the Ṛgveda. According to him, these speculations are based on differeing ideas about the creation which represent a progress from crude and unconnected notions to more refined ideas, but development, Jacobi holds, did not lead to a well established comsmology.[4]

Religion and philosophy are closely related to each

1. Clifford Geertz, "Anthropological Study", *Encyclopaedia of the Social Sciences*, Vol. XIII, Ed. by David Sills, Macmillan Co. and Free Press Inc, 1968, p. 407.
2. For more details see : Charles H. Lang, "Comogony" *The Encyclopaedia of Religion*, Vol. IV, New York, 1987, p. 94.
3. For more details see : Kees W. Bolle, "Cosmology", *op. cit.*, p. 100.
4. Jacobi H., "Cosmogony and Cosmology (Indian)", *Encyclopaedia of Religion and Ethics*, Vol. IV, Ed. by Hastings James, New York, p. 155.

other. Philosophical concepts always form an integral part of every religon. It is, however, difficult to know whether religion preceded philosophy or whether philosophical dogmas led to the development of religion. Hence the issue regarding the priority and posteriority of philosophy and religion is controversial in nature. Some hold that religion is the source and philosophy is its outcome, whereas according to some others religion has sprung from philosophy. This issue has been discussed at full length by Tiele in his *Elements of Science of Religion.* The discusion can be summarised as follows —

If philosophy, or at least its theosophic part is regarded as merely a more precise and scientific form of religious doctrine, it indicates that it would then have sprung from religion and would satisfy those who are more intellectually developed and who desire finite declarations instead of the parables and allegories. Or another possiblility is that philosophy may have been the parent and religious doctrine the offspring and if so, the religious doctrine would be regarded as a popular philosophy, rendered accessible to the masses and in that case religion would strive to build its practical system on a theoretical foundation. This practical aspect of religion culminates into worship and the theoretical speculations regarding the Highest Reality, the origin and future of the world and humanity form the constituents of the sphere of philosophy.

However, besides these two views, there is one more i.e. the third one, according to which even though religious doctrine and philosophy are definitely related with each other, it is quite likely that they might have originated independently and have entirely different objects in view.[5]

## Univesality of Philosophical Concepts

The issue whether religion was the source and philosophy was its outcome, or it was just the other way round, or whether these two originated independently is undoubtedly

5. Tiele C.P., Elements of Science of Religion, Pt. II, Edinburg, 1898, pp. 51-55.

controversial in nature. However, the intimate relationship between these two connot be gainsaid. Moreover, philosophical speculations are characterised by universality since 'every man..... philosophizes in his own way and in all ages and among all peoples, at least some people have always felt the necessity of reflection more than their fellow beings as a result of which spiritual aspect is formed.[6] It is always observed that every system of mythology possesses its legend of creation and tries to account for the origin of the universe. Of course, these could just be the beginnings of philosophy in the form of half-mythical and half-dogmatical conceptions, which are yet be reduced to the unity of a symmetrical system of philosophical or religious doctrine. Still they definitely indicate that philosophy and faith existed before they were reduced to systems or were arranged in the form of dogmas.[7]

As is rightly pointed out by Radhakrishnan, Religion as the way of life is the seeking of the eternal. If we believe in God, we must act in the light of that faith. Religion begins for us with an awareness that our life is not ourselves alone. There is another greater life which enfolds and sustains us. Religion is a man's search for this greater Self. It will be evolutionary, moving onward.[8] This onward movement is full of philosophical speculations and hence these speculations form an integral part of religion.

Charlesworth regards religion to be different from philosophy because the latter is concerned with speculations for speculations sake, whereas religion is preeminently concerned with action and practice.[9] Still in his introduction, he has specifically stated that the Eastern thinkers such as Śaṅkara and Rāmānuja are concerned to speculate about

6. Ibid, p. 53.
7. *Ibid*, pp. 55-57.
8. Radhakrishnan S., *Eastern Religions and western Thought*, Oxford, 1939, pp. 61-62.
9. Charlesworth M.J., *Philosophy of Religion*, London, 1972, p.3.

religious themes in a quasi philosophical fashion and what is more important is the generalisation he has made, *i.e.* religious speculations are tinged with a more or less philosophical colouring, though according to him this philosophical conception being highly intellectual in nature leads to a kind of religious elitism or esotericism and only the few intelligent or philosophically wise can assert to the truth of a philosophical system.[10]

Claton Feaver has remarked that many definitions come to mind as one considers the meaning of the term philosophy. He has further stated that according to Socrates, philosophy is the love of wisdom, whereas according to Cicero it is the pursuit of wisdom, wisdom being "the knowledge of things both divine and human together with the causes on which they depend. Philosphy according to Cicero, Feaver remarks, is the knowledge of Reality; it is a concern with rational presentation, a discernment of relationship, an inquirty into presuppositions whereas according to Aristotle, philosophy seeks the cause of perceptible things and it should be called the knowledge of truth".[11]

Feaver C. is of the opinion that philosophy and religion are closely related with each other as is clear from his statement that philosophy and religion are both committed to the pursuit of truth and hence there can be no ultimate dichotomy in their respective conclusions. As is further rightly remarked by him, it is an historical fact that virtually every living religious tradition is permeated from the beginning with philosophical components.[12]

Man as an intelligent self-conscious being is interested in rising above what is material and finite and in reaching the infinite. This attempt on his part is at two levels, *i.e.*

---

10. *Ibid*, pp.1-43.
11. Claton Feaver, "Philosophy and Religion", *Religion in Philosophical and Cultural Perspective : A new approach to the philosophy of religion through cross-disciplinary studies*, ed. by Claton Feaver *and Horosz Williams*, Inc. 1967, p.3.
12. *Ibid*, p.6.

theoretical and practical. Metaphysical speculations regarding the Highest Reality and the knowledge regarding the same constitute the theoretical level which leads to the origin and development of philosophy and man's actions such as prayers, meditation etc. constitute the practical level which gives rise to religion and these two levels are undoubtely in close relationship with each other.

Max Müller also has stated that religion covers at least two very different things, a body of doctrine handed down by tradition and a faculty of faith in man independent of all historical religions... a mental faculty... which enables man to apprehend the infinite under different names and under varying disguises... as struggle to coceive the unconceivable, a longing after the infinite.[13] This conception of the unconceivable and a longing after the infinite undoubtedly consititutes the field of religion. These two, thus, being two different aspects of the same phenomenon are intimately related with each other.

Radhakrishnan S. also has explained the concepts of religion and philosophy. Religion according to him is not a creed or code but an insight into Reality[14] and the aim of philosophy is to elevate man above worldliness, of making him superior to circumstances of liberating his spirit from the thraldom of material things.[15] Obviously, when man tries to elevate himself superior to circumstances through philosophical speculation, he probes into Reality which according to Radhakrishnan is the field of philosophy and hence his implication also is the same, i.e, religion and philosophy are closely associated with each other.

Philosophy always aims at finding out the mataphysical truth which forms the source of religion. The task of philosophy is limited as it only tries to give a reasonable explanation

---

13. Max Müller K.M., *Introduction to the Science of Religion*, London, 1897, pp. 13-14.
14. Radhakrishnan S., "My Search for Truth"; *Religion in Transition*, ed. by V. Ferm, London, 1937, p. 36.
15. *Ibid*, p. 43.

of the phenomena of nature and set up cosmology. Religion, on the other hand, goes a step further. It reconciles human beings with the world and tries to establish their relationship with the Supreme Being. The beginning of religion is marked by emotional conceptions which produce definite sentiments which at a later stage are manifested in actions. The study of religion, thus, is the study of its three constituents, viz., abstract speculation, sentiments and actions and the first out of these three constitutents, viz. abstrct speculation culminates into philosophical notions and thus always forms an inseparable part of religion.[16] Hence, philosophical speculations form an integral part of the Puranic religion as well. The *sarga* protions of the *Purāṇa-s* form the essential components of the *pañcalakṣaṇa-s purāṇas*. The study of Puranic religion should, therefore, begin with the study of cosmogonic, cosmological and philosophical speculations.

Man does not just want to live in this world. His urge is always to live nobly. 'There is an elemental urge in man not only to live but to live nobly'[17] Hence the questions as to 'who am I ? how have things and beings originated ?' have always been arousing curiosity in the minds of all human beings. The attempts to find out answers to these questions led to the origion and development of various systems of philosophy such as Vedānta, Sāṅkhya, Nyāya, Vaiśeṣika, Yoga etc. These systems already had a large number of followers before the Purāṇas were composed.

Moreover, the seers of the Ṛgvedic age already had started giving thought to the concept of the origin of the world and have presented different accounts of creation. These accounts are not homogenous in nature, but they throw light on the conscious effort on the part of the composers of these hymns to know and describe the nature of the cause of the world and the process of creation. The composer of the famous Puruṣa-sūkta regarded Puruṣa, as having

16. For more details see, Tiele C.P., *op; cit.*, pp. 59-73.
17. Radhakrishnan S., *Religion and Society*, London, 1948, p. 43.

one thousand heads, one thousand eyes, one thousand feet and transcending it by a space of the fingers. Puruṣa, according to him, is the whole i.e. whatever has been and whatever shall be. At the same time he believed that Puruṣa is greater than his greatness.[18] This hymn throws light on the unsurpassable greatness of the Highest Cause. at the same time indicates the origin of the world through sacrifice wherein the Puruṣa born from the Great Puruṣa was sacrificed by the gods Sāndhyas and Ṛsis as their offering.[19] Another seer has imagined the world to be an outcome of unborn[20] and yet another one considers Prajāpati to be the creator who initially created the primeval waters as the Golden germ (Hiraṇyagarbha) and then created the world.[21] Yet another composer of hymn has expressed his inability to state precisely the nature of the cause of the world through the Nāsadīyasūkta.[22] The composers of the Atharvaṇic hymns described the First Cause and designated it variously in various hymns. Thus the Highest Cause is termed as Rohita[23] (the red one), Anaḍvān (the ox)[24], Vaśā (the cow).[25] Kāla (time)26 etc. The authors of the Brāhmaṇas also narrated creation-accounts, sometimes holding Prajāpati to have entertained desire to become many, performed austerities and created the world[27] or at times regarding waters to have entertained desire to reproduce performed penance, given rise to a golden egg and then created the world.[28]

The Upaniṣadic authors have replaced the cosmogonic myths by philosophical doctrines of the transcenden-

18. *RV.* X.90.1-3.
19. *RV.* X.90.16.
20. *RV.* X.81.
21. *RV.* X. 121.
22. *RV.* X. 129.
23. *AV.* XIII.3.
24. *AV.* X.10
25. *AV.* XI. 5.
26. *AV.* XIV. 53.
27. *Tait.* S.V.6.4.2, VII. 1.5.1.
28. *Śat. Br.* XI. 1.6.1ff.

tal oneness of the omnipresent, omniscient and omnipotent Highest Cause which creates, maintains and dissolves the world. At times, these authors also present the creation-accounts describing the order of creation. Thus, e.g. according to the author of the *Tait. Up.*, the Self has produced Ether, Ether the wind, the wind Agni, Agni waters and waters the Earth[29] or refer only to the three elements[30] and this reference, according to some, is responsible for the development of the theory of the Sāṅkhya system of philosophy.[31]

The *Manusmṛti* has laid down several theories of creation. Thus, according to one account, the universe existed in the form of darkness. At that time, it was unperceived, destitute of distinctive signs, unknowable and the divine Self-existent appeared with irresistible power afterwards and dispelled darkness whereby everything became discernible.[32] According to another account, Brahmā divided his own body into two halves, a male one and a female one, who together gave rise to Virāj who practised penance and created Manu and Manu further created other beings.[33] According to the third account, Brahmā awakened from sleep created mind which impelled by Brahmā's desire to create. He then produced Ether, wind, refulgent light, water, earth,[34] According to the *Yāj.S.*, Paramātman created five elements - Ether, Vāyu, Tejas, water and Earth, each succeeding one possessing a rising series of qualities. While appearing as individual Self, it received for its body the same elements. The whole world proceeded from Paramātman.[35]

---

29. *Tait. Up.* II.1.
30. *Chān. Up.* VI.2.2ff.
31. For more details see H. Jacobi, "Cosmogony and Cosmology (Indian)", *Encyclopaedia of Religion and Ethics*, Vol. IV, New York, 1935, p. 157.
32. *Manu S.* I.5-19.
33. *Ibid*, I. 34-41.
34. *Manu S.* I. 74-78
35. *Yāj. S.* III.67.70.

## The Creation Accounts of the Purāṇas

It is very interesting to know how the authors of the *purāṇa-s* compiled these widely accepted philosophical doctrines existing at that time and sythesized them in their works. The accounts taken here for consideration stand as representative of all such accounts. Hence, similar accounts from other *purāṇa-s* are not taken into consideration.

### Creation-account from the Brahmāṇḍa Purāṇa -

Thus, according to the creation-account of the *Brahmāṇda Purāṇa*, the eternal Brahman which is the source of the universe is without a beginning and without an end. The same is the place of the ultimate merging. This incomprehensible Being which is beyond Sat and Asat has pervaded the entire world. It was unmanifested during the state of equilibrium of the constituents *(guṇa-s)*. Later on, at the time of creation, Kṣetrajña presided over Pradhāna which brought about agitation. Equilibrium was disturbed and the great principle *(mahat)* was evolved. *Sattva guṇa* in the *mahat* predominated and brought about psychic subtle body *(liṅga śarīra)*. Kṣetrajña presided over it and created the universe.[36]

According to the theory of creation enunciated in the *Brahmāṇḍa Purāṇa*, Brahmā was Kṣetrajña and he awoke in the cosmic egg. He was the first embodied being called Puruṣa as he was lying in the abode of the cosmic egg. The first creator of beings is termed as Hiraṇyagarbha and this cosmic egg contains seven worlds, the Earth, Oceans, in fact everything including the sun, the moon, the stars, the planets and the Lokāloka mountain. The egg is covered with seven sheaths of the four elements, Mahat and Pradhāna wherein every succeeding one is ten times bigger than its preceding one.[37]

Before the origin of the world, the unmanifest was stationed in itself. The world, i.e. the effect was in a withdrawn

36. *Brahāṇḍa P.* I. 3.10-24.
37. *Ibid*, I.3. 26-31.

condition. The *guṇa*-s reached the state of disequlibrium and the world came into existence. Thereafter, when they reached the state of equilibrium, the world got dissolved. These three *guṇa-s*, i.e. *rajas*, *sattva* and *tamas* brought forth Brahmā and adopted the form of Rudra.[38] Thus, the trinity of gods, although characterised by distinct functions is in reality one divinty. The self born deity was characterised by three states. As Brahmā, he created the world, as Kāla, he destroyed it. As Puruṣa, he was *sāttvika*.[39]

It is needless to say that here when the first cause is imagined to be without a beginning and without an end and when at the same time it is identified with Hiraṇyagarbha, the monistic doctrine of the Vedānta philosophy is reconciled with the concept of unity in diversity reflected the the *RV*.[40] At the same time, monism is harmoniously blended with the dualism of the Sāṅkhyavādins who maintain that the disturbance in the state of *guṇa-s* which are the components of the Primordial matter (Prakṛti) is responsible for the creation of the world.[41]

The description of the process of dissolution of the universe presented in this *purāṇa* reveals the tendency of the authors of the *purāṇa*-s to incorporate the principles of *paramāṇukāraṇavāda* of the Vaiśeṣikas. Thus, they state

---

38. *Ibid*, I. 4. 2-8.
39. *Ibid*, I. 1.4. 17-19.
चतुर्मुखस्तु ब्रह्मत्वे कालत्वे चांतकृद्भवः।
सहस्रमूर्धा पुरुषस्तिस्रो ऽवस्थाः स्वयंभुवः।।
सर्व रजश्च ब्रह्मत्वे कालत्वे च रजस्तमः।
सात्त्विकः पुरुषत्वे च गुणवृत्तं स्वयंभुवः।।
ब्रह्मत्वे सृजते लोकान् कालत्वे संक्षयत्यपि।
पुरुषत्वे उदासीनास्तिस्रोऽवस्थाः स्वयंभुवः।।
40. *RV*. I. 164.46.
एकं सद्विप्रा बहुधा ददन्ति अग्निं यमं मातरिश्वानमाहुः।
41. *Sāṅkhya-pravacana-sūtram* I.61.
सत्त्वरजस्तमसां साम्यावस्थितिः प्रकृतेर्महान् महतोऽहंकारो
ऽहंकारात् पञ्च तन्मात्राणि उभयमिन्द्रियं तन्मात्रेभ्यः स्थूलभूतानि पुरुष इति पञ्चविंशतिर्गणः।
Also *Sāṅkhyakārikā* by Īśvarakṛṣṇa q. in *Tattvakaumudī*.

that during the process of dissolution *(pratyāhāra)*, the unmanifest *(avyakta)* swallows the manifest *(vyakta)*, i.e., the whole universe, entirely in the same way as Īśvara creates the manifest universe. Annihilation *(saṁhāra)* takes place at the end of Kalpa and Kaliyuga and the dissolution begins with the destruction of everything beginning with the molecule of the atoms *(dyaṇuka)*. In the course of dissolution, both gross and subtle elements *(bhūta-s* and *tanmātra-s)* are annihilated, when the evolutes of Prakṛti *(vikāra-s)*, beginning with *mahat* and ending with *viśeṣa* are destroyed, when reabsorption and dissolution *(pratisañcāra)* caused by its own characteristic nature have begun to take place; waters swallow smell *(gandha)*, the quality of the Earth. The Earth is transformed into the state of water. Water moves about here and there and then taste *(rasa)*, the quality of water gets merged into the fiery element *(jyoti)*. Then fire *(agni)* evaporates that water and the whole world is gradually filled with flames which spread everywhere. Then the wind element *(vāyu)* swallows up colour or form *(rūpa)*, the luminous quality of the essential quality of fire *(rūpatanmātra)*, the fiery element calms down Vāyu which blows off and destroys the fiery element (Tejas). The world is devoid of light. Tejas gets merged into Vāyu. Vāyu merges into its own cause. Ether (Ākāśa) swallows up the quality of touch (*sparśa*), the quality of Vāyu. Then Vāyu calms down and Ether which is devoid of form, colour, taste, touch and smell remains behind, after which everything is filled up with sounds and the great element shines. When that is dissolved, the ether having *śabdatanmātra* as its essence remains behind, after which the Cosmic Ego *(ahaṁkāra)* swallows the quality of *śabdatanmātra* as its essence remains behind, after which the Cosmic Ego *(ahaṁkāra)* swallows the quality of *śabda*. All the elements *(bhūta-s)* and sense-organ *(indriya-s)* are merged into *bhūta-s* simultaneously. Mahat characterised by cosmic intelleet (*budhi*) swallows *buta-s* and others. When the *bhuta-s* get merged into the equilibrium of *guṇa-s (guṇasāmya)*, the *mahat* is dissolved. The causes of the *bhūta-s* get dissolved in the cause of complete restraint *(prasaṁyama)*.[42] Obviously, the principles of Vaiśeṣika system have been harmoniously blended with those of the Sāṅkhyavādins when the author states that ignorance *(ajñāna)* is the cause of *tamas* and *rajas* which results into twofold activities *(karma-s)*, *i.e.* auspicious ones and inauspicious ones, and it is the root-cause of all calamities and misfortunes.[43] Prakṛti is reality. Evolute *(vikāra)* is unreal. The state if being existent *(sadbhāva)* is truth or reality. This reality, *i.e.* Brahman is without name and form, but Kṣetrajña has name and form.[44] All the objects beginning with *mahat* and ending in *viśeṣa* undergo midifications and hence they are distinct *(vilakṣaṇa)*.[45] The immutable or indestructible *(akṣara)* does not perish, nor does it diminish.[46] Subtle body *(pura)* is its resort and hence it is called *puruṣa*.[47] The universe continues to last till the end of primary and secondary creation period.[48] This Parkṛti is the cause of creation and destruction. It has neither a beginning nor an end.[49] The constituents of the Primordial Matter *(guṇa-s)* are responsible for the multiplicity and diversity in the great elements *(bhūta-s)*

---

42. *Brahmāṇḍa P.* III.IV. 4.2-24.
43. *Ibid*, III. IV. 4.41-42
    अज्ञानं तमसो मूलं कर्मद्वयफलं रजः।
    कर्मजस्तु पुनर्देहो महादुःखं प्रवर्तते।।
    श्रोत्रजा नेत्रजा चैव त्वग्जिह्वाघ्राणजा तथा।
    पुनर्भवकरी दुःखात्कर्मणा जायते तृषा।।
44. *Ibid*, 85.[cd]-86
    प्रकृतिं सत्यमित्याहुर्विकारो ऽनृतमुच्यते।।
    असद्भावोऽनृतं ज्ञेयं सद्भावः सत्यमुच्यते।
    अनामरूपं क्षेत्रज्ञनामरूपं प्रचक्षते।।
45. *Ibid*, 90.
46. *Ibid*, 94.
47. *Ibid*, 95.
48. *Ibid*, 110.
49. *Ibid*, 111.

in the sense objects and in the physical forms as well as the separation of living deings.[50]

**Creation-account from the Agni Purāṇa-**

Holuves E. has rightly pointed out that "for what is quintessential in Indian philosophy is its spiritual idealism and the quintessence of its idealism is in the Upaniṣads. The thinkers of idea in all ages have turned to the Upaniṣads as to the fountain head of India's speculative thought.[51] The Puranic speculative thought also reflects the same trait. That is why we notice that the nature of Brahman described in this Purāṇa is so much in consonance with the principles of the Vedānta doctrine that the Upaniṣadic *mahāvākya-s* such as 'This Self is Brahman' *(ayam ātmā brahma)* and 'Thou art that' *(tat tvam asi)* are quoted by the author of the *Agni Purāṇa* with slight variations.[52] The creation-order *(sṛṣṭyutpattikrama)* describes Brahman as the first cause which subsequently gave rise to Ether *(Ākāśa)*, Ether produces *(Vāyu)*, Wind created fire *(Agni)*. Fire produced water *(Āpaḥ)*, Water produced the Earth *(Pṛthivī)* and the Earth created this subtle body.[53] Again, exactly in consonance with the fundamental doctrine of the Upaniṣads, the composer of the *Agni Purāṇa* holds that the highest knowledge leads

---

50. *Ibid*, 34.
51. Holuves Edward, *Introduction to the Philosophy of the Upaniṣads*, London, 1924, p.2.
52. *Agni P.* 377. 1[cd]-
अयमात्मा परं ब्रह्म अहमस्मीत्युच्यते ।।
Also *Agni* P. 377. 23[ab]-
अयमात्मा परं ब्रह्म तद्ब्रह्म त्वमसीति च ।
53. *Ibid*, 377. 8[cd]. 9[ab]-
यतो ब्रह्मण आकाशं खाद्वायुर्वायुतोऽनलः ।।
अग्नेरापो जलात्पृथ्वी ततः सूक्ष्मं शरीरकम् ।
Also *Tait. UP.* 2/1
तस्याद्वा एतस्मादाकाशः सम्भूतः आकाशाद्वायुः
वायोरग्निरग्नेरापः अद्भ्यः पृथिवी ............ ।

to salvation *(mokṣa)*.[54] The description of the state existing prior to the creation of the world presented by this Purāṇa reflects the philosophical thought expressed in one of the creation-hymns of the *RV*.(X. 129) wherein he states that there was neither existence, nor non-existence prior to the creation of the universe.[55] Again, the Highest Principle is described as unborn *(aja)*, without a beginning *(anādi)*, without an end *(ananta)*, indestructible *(avināśin)*, eternal *(nitya)*, everlasting *(śāśvata)*, ancient *(purāṇa)*, omnipresent *(sarvagata)* in consonance with the philosophical thought expressed in the Upaniṣads.[56] At the same time, the Primordial Matter is described as made up of three constituents *(triguṇātmika)* and following the Sāṅkhya theory, the composer of this Purāṇa also states that three constituents play among themselves.[57]

The fact that three full separate chapters of the *Agni Purāṇa* contain an exposition on meditation *(dhyāna)*,[58] *dhāraṇā*[59] and concentration *(Samādhi)*,[60] indicates their importance in the eyes of the composer of this Purāṇa. These three are the three different stages of the Aṣṭāṅga-

---

54. *Agni P*. 377.24[cd]-
मुच्यतेऽसारसंसारात्ब्रह्मज्ञो ब्रह्म तद्भवेत्।।
55. *Ibid*, 377.168[ab]-
न सन्नासन्नसदसदेतत्सावयवं न तत्।
56. *Ibid*, 376-
अव्यक्त आत्मा क्षेत्रज्ञः क्षेत्रस्यास्य निगद्यते।
ईश्वरः सर्वभूतस्य सन्नसन्सदसच्च सः ।।
*Agni* P. 381. 2[cd]-
आत्माऽजरोऽमरो ऽभेद्यस्तस्माच्छोकादिकं त्यजेत्।
Also *Katha Up*. II. 18-19.
57. *Ibid*, 381.7, 8[ab]-
नैव तस्य कृतेनार्थो नाकृतेनेह कश्चन।
तत्त्ववित्तु महाबाहो गुणकर्मविभागयोः।।
गुणा गुणेषु वर्तन्त इति मत्वा न सज्जते।
Also *Bh. Gītā* III.28.
58. *Agni* P. 374.
59. *Ibid*, .375.
60. *Ibid*, . 376.

yoga of Patañjali, out of which each preceding stage is said to be culminating into the next one. The term *dhyāna* is appropriately defined as meditation with unswerving concentration of mind.[61] Haridhyāna or meditation of Hari even for a moment or a half of it is said to be leading to the highest destination which cannot be secured even by performing sacrifices.[62] Dhyānayoga is said to be extremely pure and deviod of all faults,[63] as also leading to liberation *(apavarga)*.[64] The term *dhāraṇā* is rightly explained as unswerving concentration of mind on the object to be meditated upon.[65] It is of two kinds, concrete *(mūrta)* and abstract *(amūrta)*.[66] The term *samādhi* is explained as firm concentration of mind on any desired deity and the Yogin is like a fire in a windless place where he can neither hear, nor smell, neither see nor eat, neither experience the feeling of touch nor can think.[67]

These three, however, are just different steps which ultimately are supposed to lead to the knowledge of the Self *(ātman)*, that is neither existence *(sat)*, nor non-existence *(asat)*, it is neither endowed with parts *(na sāvayavam)*,

---

61. *Ibid*, 374.1[ab], 2-
62. *Agni*, P. 374. 6,7 -
    एवं मुहूर्तमर्धं वा ध्यायेद्यः श्रध्दया हरिम्।
    सोऽपि यां गतिमाप्नोति न तां सर्वेर्महामखैः।।
63. *Ibid*, 13[cd]-
    ध्यानयज्ञः परः शुद्धः सर्वदोषविवर्जितः।।
64. *Ibid*, 15[ab]-
    ध्यानयज्ञः परस्तस्मादपवर्गफलप्रदः।
65. *Ibid*, 375.1[cd], 2-
    धारणा मनसो ध्येये संस्थितिर्ध्यानवद् द्विधा।
66. *Ibid*, 375.1[cd], 2-
67. *Ibid*, 376.2-3.
    ध्यायन्मनः संनिवेश्य यस्तिष्ठेदचलः स्थिरः।
    निर्वातानलवद्योगी समाधिस्थः प्रकीर्तितः।।
    न श्रुणोति न चाघ्राति न पश्यति न रस्यति।
    न च स्पर्शं विजानाति न च संकल्पयते मनः।।

nor is it impartite *(na nirgatāvayavam)*, it is neither distinct, nor indistinct, indescribable... but is just one *(ekam Brahma)*.[68]

The Yogin is advised to place his steady seat at a sacred place, the seat is neither too high nor too low and concentrate his mind and actions of sense-organs by bringing his body and neck in a balanced posture.[69] The composer of this Purāṇa, regards the principles of Pātañjalayoga as a helpful means to an end, viz. salvation.

The composer of the *Brahma Purāṇa* also has shown his inclination towards the principles of Yoga system of philosophy. He has stated that the Yogin should select a solitary, quiet place. Being self-controlled, he should keep his body, legs and head in a steady posture and should place both the hands on the navel. Seated in the lotus posture, he should fix his eyes on the tip of the nose and control his vital airs and speech. He should subdue his activities of ignorance *(tamas)* by means of good element *(sattva)*. Maintaining a pure, quiet posture, he should always be in union with the Highest Lord *(Puruṣottama)*.[70]

The *Vāyu Purāṇa* presents a detailed account of the control of the control *(prāṇāyāma)* and withdrawal of breaths *(pratyāhāra)* and stresses the importance of Oṁkāra, salutation to the sun and moon, Svastika posture *(svastikāsana)* half-lotus posture *(ardhapadmāsana)*, firm posture, fixation of one's own gaze on the tip of one's own nose and control over senses[71] and defines the terms *dhāranā*, *pratyāhāra* and *dhyāna* in accordance with the Yoga system. Thus, control over *prāṇa* and *apāna* is *prāṇāyāma*, concentration

---

68. *Ibid*, 377.16-17
    न सन्नासन्न सदसदेतत्सावयवं न तत्।
    निर्गतावयं नेति नाभिन्नं भिन्नमेव च।।
    भिन्नाभिन्नं ह्यनिर्वाच्यं बंधसंसारकारकम्।
    एकं स ब्रह्म विज्ञानान्प्राप्तं नैव च कर्मभिः।।
69. *Ibid*, 373.1-3.
70. *Brahma* P. 127.15-20.
71. *Vāy*. P. 11,13-14, 16, 18.

of mind is *dhāraṇā*, abstinence from the objects of sense-organs is *pratyāhāra*.[72]

**Creation-account from the Bhaviṣya Purāṇa-**

The creation-account of the *Bhaviṣya Purāṇa* throws light on the attempt to synthesize the principles of different systems of philosophy. Thus, according to the description of creation *(sṛṣṭivarṇana)* of this Purāṇa, the world was full of darkness in the past. That stage was devoid of any distinct feature and hence was incomprehensible. Then arose the Lord, unmanifest, beyond the reach of sense-organs, subtle, eternal. The same is the Highest Lord *(Puruṣottama)* who is designated as Brahman.[73] Īśa was desirous of creating various beings and after meditation, initially created waters. He, then, placed semen *(vīrya)* in them which was afterwards transformed into an egg, out of which the threefold creation in the form of deities, demons and human deings came into existence.[74] Brahmā, the grandfather *(pitāmaha)* of the world was born out of it and the same is also termed as Kṣetrajña, Puruṣa, Vedhāḥ, Śambhu and Nārāyaṇa.[75] After presenting this doctrine, it is stated that this mundane egg got divided into two parts which produced the heaven and the earth.[76] Later on, this account is combined with the principles of the Sāṅkhya theory and Mahat is said to have given rise to *ahaṅkāra*, *ahaṅkāra* to three constituents *i.e. sattva, rajas* and *tamas* and these three are said to have produced five sense-organs, six subtle organs and all beings.[77] The Primordial Matter *(pradhāna)* is agitated and modifications *(vikāra-s)* came into being.[78] The creation-account of the Mundane Egg (Brahmāṇḍotpattivarṇana) of the same Purāṇa shows

---

72. *Ibid.* P. 11.28[cd], 29-30
73. *Bh.* P. I.2.9-12.
74. *Ibid*, I.2.13-14[ab].
75. *Ibid*, 2.16-17.
76. *Ibid*, I.2.22.
77. *Ibid*, I. 2. 24-27
78. *Ibid*, I.2.34.

the impact of *māyāvāda* of Saṅkarācarya on the Puranic philosophy as herein it is stated that the cause of the world in fact is one but the same appears to be many.[79]

**Ceration-account from the Viṣṇu Purāṇa—**

According to the composer of the *Viṣṇu Purāṇa,* Vāsudeva is the cause of the world.[80] The nature of this Vāsudeva, however, is exactly like that of Brahman, which is imagined to be the Highest Cause by the Vedāntins. The cause is described here as devoid of form, colour and such other attributes or characteristics, the highest of all, the Supreme Self situated in every Self.[81] Its nature is so much in consonance with the principles of the Vedānta doctrine that in the immediately following verses it is designated as Brahma, eternal *(nitya),* unborn *(aja),* indestructible *(akṣaya),* without any modification *(avyaya),* pure *(nirmala),* of the same nature *(ekasvarūpa).*[82] Puruṣa is said to be its first form, unmanifest (Prakṛti) and other manifest principles such as Mahat and others are its other forms[83] and that which is beyond Pradhāna, Puruṣa, manifest *(vyakta)* form and time *(kāla)* is termed as the highest abode of Viṣṇu.[84] Again, in consonance with the fundamental Upaniṣadic doctrines this is described as without any support,

79. *Ibid,* I. 2. 8.
80. *Viṣ .P. I.2.12*
81. *Ibid,* I.2.10.
पर: पराणां परम: परमात्मात्मसंस्थित: ।
रूपवर्णादिनिर्देशविशेषेण विवर्जित: ।।
82. *Ibid,* I.2.13.
तद्ब्रह्म परमं नित्यमजमक्षयमव्ययम् ।
एकस्वरूपं तु सदा हेयाभावाच्च निर्मलम् ।।
83. *Ibid,* I.2.15.
परस्य ब्रह्मणो रूपं पुरुष: प्रथमं द्विज ।
व्यक्ताव्यक्ते तथैवान्ये रूपे कालस्तथा परम् ।।
84. *Ibid,* I.2.20.
अक्षय्यं नान्यदाधारममेयमजरं ध्रुवम् ।
शब्दस्पर्शविहीनं तद्रूपादिभिरसंहितम् ।।

immesurable, without decay or old age, steady, devoid of sound, touch, form etc. It is imagined to be without a beginning and without an end but all pervading in nature.[85] It is, however, interesting to know that here, the composer of this Purāṇa is synthesizing the Vedānta doctrine with the principles of the Sāṅkhya system of philosophy, as here this eternal unmanifest principle is designated as Prakṛti and at the same time looked upon as the highest cause that is identical with Viṣṇu who created Pradhāna and Puruṣa;[86] who is believed to be the Lord of all lords and situated everywhere by its subtle and gross forms.[87] While imagining Ahaṅkāra as the outcome of Mahat and the cause of elements such as Akāśa, Vāyu, Tejas, Water and the Earth, the narrator of the creation-account considers the five sense-organs of knowledge and the five sense-organs of activities also to have come into existence out of this Ahaṅkāra[88] which in the course of time lead to the creation of Egg in the form of Brahma[89] and which is imagined to be the support of Viṣṇu, the Lord of the world.[90] The three constituents *(guṇa-s) i.e. rajas, sattva, tamas* are said to be having an ability of creation, maintenance and destruction and the Lord of the world, *i.e.*, Viṣṇu is here imagined to be resorting to these elements in due order and assuming the forms of Brahmā, Viṣṇu and Śiva respectively[91] and performing this threefold function.[92] The

---

85. *Ibid*, I.2.19.
अव्यक्तं कारणं यत्तत्प्रधानमृषिसत्तमैः।
प्रोच्यते प्रकृतिः सूक्ष्मा नित्यं सदसदात्मकम्।।

86. *Ibid*, I.2.24[ab].
विष्णोः स्वरूपात्परतो हि ते द्वे रूपे प्रधानं पुरुषश्च विप्र।

87. *Ibid*, I.2.32.
विकासाणुस्वरूपैश्च ब्रह्मरूपादिभिस्तथा।
व्यक्तस्वरूपश्च तथा विष्णुः सर्वेश्वरेश्वरः।।

88. *Ibid* I.2.36-50.

89. *Ibid*, I.2.54-55.

90. *Ibid*, I.2.56.

91. *Ibid*, I.2.61, 64.

creation-accounts of the Viṣṇu Purāṇa, contain a unique blending of various accounts presented by the authors of earlier works.

We have here the personified as also abstract form of the Highest Reality; the two forms of Brahman *mūrta* as well as *amūrta*, destructible as well as indestructible situated among all the beings. The indestructible is Brahman and the destructible one is the entire world.[93] Elsewhere, the composer of the same Purāṇa speaks of two types of Brahman, one is known as *śabda brahma* and the other one is termes as *para brahma* and according to the composer of this *purāṇa*, one can reach *para brahma* only after having mastered *śabda brahma*.[94] It is further stated that those desirous of achieving salvation should meditate upon the highest Brahman which is all pervading, omnipresent, eternal, the cause of all beings.[95] Knowledge acquired through scriptures leads to *śabda brahma* and that arising out of the discriminating power leads to *para brahma*.[96] Hazra has rightly pointed out, "It is gratifying to note that this personification did not proceed from childish imagination but has a sound philosophical basis. The *Bhagavadgītā* (X. 4.7, 32-39) tells

92. *Ibid*, I.2.61, 66.
सृष्टिस्थित्यन्तकरणीं ब्रह्मविष्णुशिवात्मिकाम्।
स संज्ञां याति भगवानेक एवं जनार्दनः।।
93. *Ibid*, I.22.55.56.
द्वे रूपे ब्रह्मणस्तस्य मूर्तं चामूर्तमेव च।
क्षराक्षरस्वरूपे ते सर्वभूतेष्ववस्थिते।।
अक्षरं तत्परं ब्रह्म क्षरं सर्वमिदं जगत्।
एकदेशस्थितस्याग्ने ज्योत्स्ना विस्तारिणी यथा।।
94. *Ibid*, VI.5.64.
द्वे ब्रह्मणी वेदितव्ये शब्द ब्रह्म परं च यत्।
शब्दब्रह्मणि निष्णातः परं ब्रह्माधिगच्छति।।
95. *Ibid*, VI. 5.67.
96. *Ibid*, *VI. 5. 61*.
आगमोत्थं विवेकाच्च द्विधा ज्ञानं तदुच्यते।
शब्दब्रह्मागममयं परं ब्रह्म विवेकजम्।।

us that the Paramātman or Bhagavat is allcomprising and all powerful and that the entire creation, subjective or objective, abstract or concrete proceeds from Him... ."[97] Personified Viṣṇu of the *Viṣṇu Purāṇa* is identical with the abstract highest principle termed as Brahman hence he is glorified as the liberator of his worshippers.

**Creation-accounts from the Brahmavaivarta Purāṇa-**

The creation-accounts of the *Br. V. Purāṇa*, however, seem to be different from those of other *purāṇa-s*. Here Śrīkṛṣṇa residing in *goloka* is said to be the creator. Initially it is stated that from his right side, three constituents of Prakṛti came into existence, which in their turn gave rise to the principles such as great principle *(mahat)*, ego *(ahaṅkāra)*, five subtle essences *(tanmātra-s)* named *rūpa, rasa, gandha, sparśa* and *śabda*.[98] The account that uptill now tallies with the theory of evolution of the Sāṅkhya system is later on combined with the Vedānta system on the one hand and the teaching of Bhaktiyoga on the other. It is stated that the concrete *(mūrta)* form of the Lord Nārāyaṇa who is young, who has sable *(śyāma)* complexion, who wears yellow garment *(pītāmbara)* and a garland of forest flowers *(vanamālā)*, who is possessed of four arms has come into existence[99] and from the left side of Srīkṛṣṇa, pure, five-mouthed Digambara, *i.e.*, Śiva came into existence. This created being was the best *(vara vareṇya)* as also the cause of causes *(kāraṇānām kāraṇam)*.[100]

Thereafter, it is stated that out of different limbs of Śrīkṛṣṇa, the groups of gods and goddesses such as Mahālakṣmī, Durgā, Sāvitrī, Kāmadeva, Rati, Agni, Varuṇa, Vāyu were born and all of them started singing the praises of Śrīkṛṣṇa. Then from the left side of Śrīkṛṣṇa, a maiden was born.[101]

---

97. Hazra R.C., *Viṣṇu Purāṇa*, "Introduction", ed. by Wilson, Calcutta, 1961, p.i.
98. *Br. V.P.* I.3.3-5.
99. *IIbid*, I.3-6.
आविर्बभूव तत्पश्चात् स्वयं नारायणः प्रभुः ।
श्यामो युवा पीतवासा वनमाली चतुर्भुजः ।।
100. *Ibid*, I.7-10
101. *Ibid*, I.53-63.

In another creation-account of the same *purāṇa*, Brahmā is said to have practised austerities and created the Earth. Thereafter, he created eight mountains known as Sumeru, Kailāsa, Malaya, Himālaya, Udaya, Asta, Suvela, Gandhamādana, seven oceans named Lavaṇa, Ikṣu, Sūrya, Dadhi, Dugdha, Jala, seven islands, seven subislands, seven boundary mountains, seven heavenly worlds, seven nether worlds, together forming the mundane egg or the *brahmāṇḍa*. These worlds as also the inhabitants thereof are described as artificial and ephemeral and Vaikunṭhaloka, Śivaloka and Goloka are glorified as eternal.[102] In the same Purāṇa further, as per Nārada's request, the Lord throws light on the nature of the Highest Reality and states that whatever is qualified is visible.[103] It is patent to the senses*(pratyakṣa)*, whereas the Paramātman is eternal Parama Brahma which resides in the bodies of all beings and witnesses their activities and beings are totally dependent on it.[104] When the Highest Cause is described as formless, attributeless, independent, the cause of all causes, the highest joy and the cause of the Highest Bliss, which is beyond the Primordial Matter of Prakṛti, but which submerges in Prakṛti, the narrator had in his view the tenets of the Vedānta doctrine.

The same *purāṇa* also contains the etymological explanation of the word Prakṛti according to which Prakṛti is a combination of two words *pra* and *kṛti*. *Pra* stands for *prakṛṣṭa* i.e. excessiveness and *kṛti* is *sṛṣṭi* or creation. According to another explanation, the letters *'pra'*, *'kṛ'* and *'ti'* stand for the three constituents of the Primordial Matter of the Sāṅkhyavādins, i.e. the *sattva*, *rajas* and *tamas* respectively.[105]

---

102. *Ibid*, I.7.1-20
103. *Ibid*, I.14.9.
104. *Ibid*, I. 14.12-14.
105. *Ibid*, II. 1. 5-6.

प्रकृष्टवाचकः प्रश्च कृतिश्च सृष्टिवाचकः।
सृष्टौ प्रकृष्टाया देवी प्रकृतिः सा प्रकीर्तिता।।
गुणे प्रकृष्टसत्त्वे च प्रशब्दो वर्तते श्रुतौ।
मध्यमे रजसि कृत्वा तिशब्दस्तमसि कृतः।।

It is certain that following the exposition of the Kevalādvaitavāda or *māyāvāda* of Śaṅkarācārya according to which the creation is explained from two different points of view, *i.e. pāramārthikī* or of the highest level and *vyāvahārikī* or of worldly level, the composer of this Purāṇa also has explained the account of creation from two different points of view. Thus, from the worldly point of view, the universe consists of several parts such as various mountains, islands, heaven, nether world. All of them have come out of Brahmā. From the highest point of view, however, Brahmā is the Highest Cause *(paramakāraṇa)* and hence it is the cause of the highest delight *(paramānandakāraṇa)*.

The most striking feature of this *purāṇa* is the fact that it not only contains a synthesis of Sāṅkhya and Vedānta systems of philosophy, but here these two are combined with the half-man, half-woman doctrine *(ardhanārīnaṭeścvara siddhānta)*. The narrator states that the creator of the Highest Person got divided into two halves, his right half was turned into Pumān and the left one into Prakṛti which is imagined to be an everlasting, occult power in the form of Brahma. According to this account, these two forms, i.e. the male one and the female one have come out of the same creator and in reality, they are not different from each other. The author specifically states that the difference between a man and a woman is no difference at all.[106] The parellel to this half-man half-woman doctrine of the *Brahmavaivarta Purāṇa* is found in the creation-account of Egyptian mythology according to which Atum, who is the beginningless God and the first creator is imagined to be having both male as also female elements and termed as the great He-She.[107]

Thereafter, the principles of Sāṅkhya and Vedānta systems are combined with the concept of worship of personified deities in the statementas such as "This assumed an embodied

106. *Ibid*, I.24.22$^{ab}$.

107. Bedagkar G.S., "Egyptian, Hebrew and Greek Accounts", *Myths of Creation*, ed. by Dange Sindhu S., Bombay, 1987.

form of Durgā[108].... who destroys the sorrow of human beings and bestows good conduct or religion *(dharma)*, truth *(satya)* holiness *(puṇya)*, fame *(kīrti)*, glory *(yaśas)*, auspiciousness *(maṅgala)*, pleasure and salvation on them and protects the afflicted people and is worshipped by human beings and sages and the same is indetified with Śrīkṛṣṇa's power and the Highest Lord is strong because of this power in him.[109] In fact, it is just because of this power that he can create the world.[110] This power is *śakti* in the real sense of the term, as the word *śakti* is a combination of two words, *'śaka'* meaning prosperity *(aiśvarya)* and *'ti'* meaning valọur *(parākrama)*.'[111] It is interesting to know as to how even in this *purāṇa*, the Vedānta doctrine stating the Highest Cause to be without any shape or attribute is harmoniously blended with the doctrine of the worship of personified Being when the composer of this *purāṇa* states that the believers in one without shape *(nirākāravādins)* regard this as the subtle element and for the devotees of Viṣṇu (Vaiṣṇavas), the same is Śyāmasundara.[112]

The most noteworthy feature of the philosophy of the *Br. V. Purāṇa* is the account of the secret of Rādhā *(Rādhārahasya)*, according to which Rādhā was born of Kṛṣṇa himself. She constitutes the left half of Śrīkṛṣṇa and Rādhā and Kṛṣṇa together formed the two aspects of the controller of the world. The Lord Kṛṣṇa himself has thrown light on Rādhākṛṣṇa relationship. He has identified

---

108. *Br. V.P.* II.1.14.

गणेशमाता दुर्गा या शिवरूपा शिवप्रिया।
नारायणी विष्णुमाया पूर्णब्रह्मस्वरूपिणी।।

109. *Ibid*, II.1.16-18.

110. *Ibid*, II.2.9.

न हि क्षमस्तथा ब्रह्म सृष्टिं स्रष्टुं तया विना।
सर्वशक्तिस्वरूपा सा तया च शक्तिमान् सदा।।

111. *Ibid*, II.2.10.

ऐश्वर्यवचनः शक् च तिः पराक्रमवाचकः।
तत्स्वरूपा तयोर्दात्री या सा शक्तिः प्रकीर्तिता।।

112. *Ibid*, II.2. 13-15, 18[ab].

Rādhā with satisfaction, nourishment, bashfulness, hunger, thirst, extreme mercy, devotion incarnate, the body of the embodied ones, his own support, who is supported by himself.[113] Rādhā and Kṛṣṇa are like Prakṛti and Puruṣa who unitedly create the universe.[114] From worldly point of view, the portion explaining the secret of Rādhā of this Purāṇa represents the univeral truth of the mating of the male with the female *(maithunīsṛṣṭi)* leading to creation and from spiritual and philosophical point of view, Rādhā, is Kṛṣṇa's power and hence, the mere utterance of the word Rādhā is said to enable the aspirants to achieve salvation.[115]

It is equally noteworthy that the metaphysical principles stated in the *Br. V. Purāṇa* show an impact of the Vedānta doctrine when the composer of this Purāṇa states that the Highest Cause is only one and the entire world consisting of movable and immovable forms including human beings are its manifestations[116], which is beyond the Primordial Matter (Prakṛti). While explaining the metaphysical doctrine the author of the *Br. V. Purāṇa* also has followed the principles of *māyāvāda* of Śaṅkrācārya and stated that the twofold mundane existence consiting of sentient beings and insentient things is unreal like the bubble of water or

---

113. *Ibid*, II.67. 70-72.

114. *Ibid*, II.67.73.

त्वयाऽलं कव्यदाने च सदा नालं त्वया विना।
अहं पुमांस्त्वं प्रकृतिर्न स्रष्टाऽहं त्वया विना।।

115. *Ibid*, II.49.40, 42.

'रा' शब्दोच्चारणाद् भक्तो याति मुक्तिं सुदुर्लभम्।
'धा' शब्दोच्चारणात् दुर्गे धावत्येव हरेः पदम्।।
'रा' इत्यादानवचनो 'धा' च निर्वाणवाचकः।
ततोऽवाप्नोति मुक्तिं च तेन राधा प्रकीर्तिता।।

For more etymologies, Dange Sindhu S., *Etymolgies and Flexible Forms from the Purāṇa-ṣ— Some Glimpses*, Aligarh, 1989, pp. 87-89.

116. *Ibid*, I.24.17.

एकमेव परं ब्रह्म शेषे वत्स भवक्षये।
वयं प्रलीनास्तत्रैव जगदेतच्चराचरम्।।

dream and it is the cause of attraction or infatuation[117] and the thought that the Supreme Reality is indentical with the Individual Self [118] echoes the truth underlying many Upaniṣadic statements such as — Everything indeed is Brahman *(Sarvam khalu idam Brahma)* or thou art that *(Tat tvam asi).*

**Creation-accounts from the Varāha Purāṇa–**

The creation-account of the *Varāha Purāna* mentions the endless space *vyoma)* as the ultimate cause out of which the principle of atomic intellect was created. This intellect is threefold, viz., consisting of three elements, *sattva, rajas* and *tamas.*[119] Although this account seems to have incorporated a combination of some principles of the Vedānta and Sāṅkhya systems of philosophy, it is not in full agreement with them. Thus, instead of Brahman or Sat of the Vedāntins, space *(vyoma)* is stated as the first cause and instead of Prakṛti or Pradhāna of the Sāṅkhyavādins as the next created principle, the threefold intellect consisting of *sattva, rajas* and *tamas* as its constituents is said to have come out of the first principle. Thereafter, Pradhāna was created which further gave rise to Kṣetraña and from that the intellect came into being.[120] Thus, the threefold intellect is once stated as the first cause and in the following

---

117. *Ibid,* IV. 78.17

जलबुद्बुदवत्सर्वं संसारं सचराचरम्।
प्रभाते स्वप्नवन्मिथ्या मोहकारणमेव च।।

Also *Br. V.P.* II. 49.48.

आब्रह्मस्तम्बपर्यन्तं सर्वं मिथ्यैव पार्वति।
भज सत्यं परं ब्रह्म राधेशं त्रिगुणात्परम्।।

118. *Ibid,* IV.78.22[ab].

अहमात्मा च सर्वेशः सर्वज्ञानात्मकः स्मृतः।

119. *Var.* p. II.7.

आदावाहं व्योम महत्ततोऽणुरेकैव मत्तः प्रबभूव बुद्धिः।
त्रिधा तु सा सत्त्वरजस्तमोभिः पृथक्पृथक् स्वत्त्वरूपैरुपेता।।

120. *Ibid,* 2.8.

तस्मिंस्त्रिकेऽहं तमसो महान्स सदोच्यते सर्वविदां प्रधानः।
तस्मादपि क्षेत्रविदूर्जितो यो बभूव बुद्धिस्तु ततो बभूव।।

account is said to have arisen out of Kṣetrajña who is an outcome of Pradhāna. Pradhāna, however, is imagined to be the effect of the Intellect. These mutually contradictory details are, thus, characterised by the state of disorder.

In another account of the same *purāṇa*, void is said to have given rise to gross elements and an egg with generative fluid is said to have arisen in waters due to the combination of those elements.[121] And according to yet another account, all-pervading Nārāyaṇa who is atomic in nature *(paramāṇuḥ)*, pure *(vigatakalmaṣaḥ)* and who is beyond the qualities of *sattva, rajas* and *tamas (sattvarajastamodriktaḥ)*, who is neither long, nor short, neither big, nor small (*i.e.* attributeless) is said to have created water. Evidently, here, the basic principle behind these speculations has the Vedānta system as its foundation according to which the final cause is always attributeless (*nirguṇa)* and shapeless *(nirākāra)*. But with a view to simplify the philosophical doctrine and attact the masses, this is described as concrete *(mūrta)* form of Nārāyaṇa who is broadchested *(ūruvakṣaḥ)*, wearing yellow garment (*pītāmbaraḥ)* and supporting the earth *(kṣitidharaḥ)*.[122]

In fact, there are several such instances even elsewhere, where the composers of the *purāṇa-s* consciously and cleverly aim at harmonious blending of the Highest *(para)*, attributeless *(nirguṇa* and *nirviśesa)* abstract principle and 'attributepossessing' *(sanguṇa saviseṣa)* lower *(apara)* divinity. The former is the object of knowledge meant for a limited few and the latter is the object of worship meant for the vast majority of people. The former represents esotoric doctrine, the latter represents exotoric doctrine.[123] The *saguṇa* and *nirguṇa* aspects of the Highest Cause complementing each other form one of the fundamental principles of Hinduism.

---

121. *Ibid*, 2.10

    शून्यं त्वासीत्तत्र शब्दस्तु खं च तस्माद्वायुस्तत एवानु तेजः।
    तस्मादापस्तत एवानु देवि मया सृष्टा भवती भूतधात्री।।

122. *Ibid*, 74. 5ff.

123. For the terms and their explanation see Deussen Paul, *The System of Vedānta*, Chicago, 1912. pp.102-103.

The composers of the *Purāṇa-s* retained the same tradition and popularised their religion by introducing a unique fusion of knowledge *(jñāna)* and devotion *(bhakti)*.

**Creation-accounts from the Bhāgavata Purāṇa —**

The composer of the *Bhāg. Purāṇa* also aims at the synthesis of the Vedānta, Sāṅkhya and Yoga systems when he described concrete *(mūrta)* or abstract *(amūrta)* aspects of the Highest Reality. Thus, he states that Nārāyaṇa is the highest object of knowledge, the highest goal and the final beautitude is due to him. Although Nārāyaṇa is a name of a personified being, he is described here as attributeless *(nirguṇa)* and it is stated that through his occult power *(māyā)*, he has assumed three atrributes, *i.e. sattva, rajas and tamas* for the creation, maintenance and dissolution of the universe. The theory of monism, thus is harmoniously blended with the *Sāṅkhya* view and it is further elaborately developed in statements such as - These attributes are at the basis of five gross elements *(mahābhūta-s)*. The senses and organs always bind the Individucal Soul in effects, cause and agency and though the Self is really free, he is enveloped by occult power *(māyā)*.[124] Further, Nārāyaṇa is indentified with the glorious Lord Viṣṇu whose movements are incomprehensible through these attributes. He is said to be desirous of being many and assuming different forms, accepted as the cause, time and action. It is due to the presence or direction of this God that time became the cause of the imbalance in the three attributes *(guṇa-s)* and action became the cause of the great principle *(mahat)*. *Mahat* was magnified by *rajas* and *stattva;* it underwent modifications and gave rise to a thing in which *tamas* is dominant ... that evolute was *ahaṅkāra* which got transformed into three kinds — *vaikārika* or *sāttvika, tāijasa* or rājasa *and tāmasa. Tāmasa ahaṅkāra* produced Ether which had sound *(śabda)* as its special characteristic.

---

124. *Bhāg. P.* II.5.16-19.

Ether produced air *(vāyu)*, having touch as its distinguishing characteristic. Due to the pressure of time *(Kāla)*, action *(karma)*, unseen *(adṛṣṭa)* and innate disposition, *vāyu* underwent modifications and fire *(tejas)* possessing colour and form characteised by touch and sound was evolved. *Tejas* in its turn gave rise to water having taste as its characteristic. Through inheritance from the previous elements, water was endowed with form, colour, touch and sound. Water got transformed and the Earth with smell as its special abttribute came forth and again interiting other attributes from the previous causes, it had taste, touch, sound and colour as its special characteristics.[125] From the *vaikārika* or *sāttvika ahaṅkāra*, the mind, ten gods, fire presiding over five sense-organs, viz, *dis'*, *Vāyu*, *Sūrya*, *Varuṇa* and Aśvins as presiding over the sense-organs of knowledge and the other five, viz. fire-god, Indra, Upendra, Mitra, Ka and Prajāpati presiding over the organs of action were produced. From the *taijasa* or *rājasa ahaṅkāra* undergoing change were evolved five congnitive and five conative organs. Intelligence and Prāṇa were evolved out of the *taijasa ahaṅkāra*. As long as these elements *(bhūta-s)*, sense-organs *(indriya-s)* and the constituents *(guṇa-s)* were unamulgamated, they were unable to create body. Afterwards, they were directed by the will of God. They came together, created the main and subsidiary constituents and brought forth the body of gross and subtle constituents. At the end of thousands of years, during the deluge, the Supreme Self brought life into the Mundane Egg and having burst open the mundane egg *(brahmāṇḍa)* the Supreme Man possessing thousands of thighs, feet, arms, eyes and thousands of mouths and heads came out.[126] The details of this description can be traced back to those of the Huge Person *(Viraṭ Puruṣa)* of the creation-hymn (Puruṣasūkta) of the *RV*.[127] Again, like the composer of the Puruṣasūkta, the narrator of the creation-account of the *Bhāg.P.* states that the Brāhmaṇa class is

125. *Ibid*, II.5.20-29.
126. *Ibid*, II.5.18-35.
127. *RV*. X.90.

the mouth of this Man. Kṣatriyas are his arms. From the thighs of the Lord, Vaiśya came into existence and Śūdra came forth from his feet. The earth *(Bhūrloka)* was created from his feet, the intermediary regions *(bhuvarloka)* from his navel. The heavenly world (*svarloka*) was created from his heart and from his chest the *maharloka was produced.*[128] It is further stated that the greatness and power of the Cosmic Man are unlimited, the three worlds, viz., *bhūḥ, bhuvaḥ* and *svaḥ* are the feetlike parts of the Cosmic Man.[129] Obviously, this part of the account shows an impact of a similar account presented by the composer of the Puruṣasūkta who stated that this much is the greatness of this Huge Person, but this Person is greater than that greatness, an account which throws light on the omnipotence of the Supreme Being.[130] When the Supreme Man is said to be characterised by both knowledge *(vidyā)* and ignorance *(avidyā)*, the composer of the *Bhāg. Purāṇa* also is taking into consideration both the levels, the higher one *(para)* as also the lower one *(apara)* with which the Supreme Reality is looked upon by the persons who want to reach it. Furthermore, the God is described as transcendental to the Matter from which the Cosmic Egg. *(Brahmāṇḍa)* and the Huge (*Viraṭ)* consisting of gross elements *(bhūta-s)*, sense-organs *(indriya-s)* and objects of senses are produced[131] and the universe is said to be placed in or rested on the glorious Nārāyaṇa.[132] Like Brahman imagined as the first cause by the Vedāntins, Nārāyaṇa is regarded as the first

---

128. *Ibid,* II.5.37-38.

129. *Ibid,* II.17$^{cd}$-18.
महिमैष ततो ब्रह्मन् पुरुषस्य दुरत्ययः।
पादेषु सर्वभूतानि पुंसः स्थितिपदो विदुः।
अमृतं क्षेममभयं त्रिमूर्ध्नोऽधायि मूर्धसु।।

130. *RV* X. 90.3.
एतावानस्य महिमा अतो ज्यायांश्च पूरुषः।
पादोऽस्य विश्वा भूतानि त्रिपादस्य अमृतं दिवि।

131. *Bhāg.* p. 6.19-21.

132. *Ibid,* II.6.30$^{ab}$.
नारायणे भगवति तदिदं विश्वमाहितम्।

Puruṣa, whose real nature is absolute, whose real knowledge is pure, who is underlying the interior of all, who is accurate, changeless and beyond all who is attributes, perfect, full, beginningless, endless, eternal and alone (without a second)[133]. Similarly, the *catuḥślokī* of the Bhāg.P. containing the quintessence of the philosophy of this Purāṇa, states that it is only due to *māyā* that what remains after the creation of the universe is only the Supreme Reality and it exists even after the dissolution *(pralaya)*. It has entered everything and being, at the same time it can be stated that in a way it has not entered the worldly manifestations.[134]

In another cosmogonic account, the Lord is described as the supreme soul of all the souls and the master of all the souls, who alone existed in the beginning and the power of time causes commotion of *guṇa-s* into *māyā*.[135] Viṣṇu who is endowed with perfect intellectual power inseminates his own image into her through Puruṣa who is his own part *(aṁśa)*.[136] The rest of the account is in agreement with the theory of the Sāṅkhyavādins. The composer of the *Bhāg*. P. has presented the creation-account more than once. The names of the first cause or the creator appear to be different, as he is termed as Nārāyaṇa, Viṣṇu or the Lord or the narrator, but this difference being just in names cannot be regarded as real.

When the author of this *purāṇa* accepts the Sāṅkhya theory, the metaphysical truth is very well conveyed by him as he states that though the soul (Puruṣa) resides in the body

---

133. *Ibid*, II.6.38-39.

स एष आद्यः पुरुषः कल्पे कल्पे सृजत्यजः।
आत्माऽऽत्मन्यात्मनाऽऽत्मानं संयच्छति च पाति च।।
विशुद्धं केवलं ज्ञानं प्रत्यक्सम्यगवस्थितम्।
सत्यं पूर्णमनाद्यन्तं निर्गुणं नित्यमद्वयम्।।

134. *Ibid*, II.9.32-35

135. *Ibid*, III. 26. 3[ab].

अनादिरात्मा पुरुषो निर्गुणः प्रकृतेः परः।

136. *Ibid*, III.5.

which is a product of Prakṛti, he is not affected by the *guṇa-s* of Prakṛti such as pleaure, pain etc. For Puruṣa is destitute of *guṇa-s*. However, when the soul or the *jīva* is attached to the consitutents of Prakṛti, he is deluded by ego *(ahaṅkāra)* and through false attribution, he regards himself to be the doer. Due to the same ego, he loses his independnce and blessed state and due to his association with Prakṛti and the effects of actions, he gets entangled in mundane existence *(saṁsāra)*.[137] And as long as there is an attachment for the sensual objects, one cannot free oneself from this mundane existence and the best course to curb the senses is to follow the path of devotion *(bhaktiyoga)*.[138]

The author of the *Bhāg.P.* regards the eightfold path of *yoga (aṣṭāṅgayoga)* as a means which enables the aspirant to achieve final beatitude. This *purāṇa* contains a separate and through exposition on this *yoga* which is in full agreement with the Principles of Patañjali, wherein the importance of fixing a seat in a clean holy place, control of the bodily posture, practice of breath-control, systematic inhalation, retention and exhalation of breath and vice versa, fixed attention *(dhāraṇā)*, withdrawal of senses *(pratyāhāra)*, steadineses of mind, meditation on the complete form of God is stressed[139] and the principles of Pātañjalayoga are simplified by synthesizing them with the teaching of the path of devotion *(bhaktiyoga)* through statements such as, with perfect and intense devotion, one should contemplate Hari who dwells in the cave in the form of one's own heart.[140] Similarly, the *Yogin* is advised to meditate upon the incarnate God, having gracious face, reddish lotus-like eyes, wearing resplendent Kausthubha jewel and a *vanamālā* and who is adorned with various ornaments with wholehearted devotion even while standing, walking, sitting....[141] and the aspirant is assured that Viṣṇu manifests himself in

137. *Ibid*, III.27, 1-3.
138. *Ibid*, III.27.4-5.
139. *Ibid*, III. 28.8-12.
140. *Ibid*, III.28.31.
141. *Ibid*, III.28.18-19.

the cave of his own heart.[142] Thus, here also Pātañjalayoga is prescribed as a means that enables the aspirant to free himself from the flow of the constituents *(guṇa-s)* forming limitations and realise that there is no distinction between him and the object of meditation and he can unite with the Supreme Realtiy.[143]

**Creation — account from the Nārada Purāṇa**

According to the creation-account of the Nārada Purāṇa, the Lord Viṣṇu is the First Cause. Although Viṣṇu is the name of the personified God, his description is the same as that of Brahman of the Vedāntins. Thus, it is stated that the primival Lord Viṣṇu was without a beginning and without an end, unaging and immortal. He is unmanifest, eternal, unchanging, the creator, the supporter of beings and one in whom the beings ultimately merge. He created the great principle *(mahat)* and then Ether *(Ākāśa)*. From Ākaśa originated water, from water the earth and from the earth[144]....... which undoubtedly shows an impact of the Upaniṣadic theory of creation upon it.[145] These five elements *(dhātu-s)* are present in the bodies of mobile beings and the body can function through their activities. The skin, the flesh, the bones, the marrow and the sinews constitute the earth element in the body. The energy, the gastric fire, the eyes and the body temperature constitute the fire element in the body. The ears, the nostrils, the mouth, the heart and the belly are the five ether elements in the body. The phlegm, the bile, the sweat, the fat and the blood are the water elements in the body.[146] The *Nārada Purāṇa* is certainly unique as here the philosophical speculations are combined with the exposition of the organic structure of the body on

142. *Ibid*, III.28.33.

143. *Ibid*, III.28.35-36.

144. *Nār. P.* I.42.13-19.

145. *Tait.* Up. 2/1.

तस्माद्वा एतस्मादाकाशः सम्भूतः । आकाशाद्वायुः ।

वायोरग्निः । अग्नेरापः । अद्भ्यः पृथिवी ।

146. *Nār . P.* I. 42. 74-78.

the one hand and with the principles of Pāśupata philosophy on the other. *Tantra* here is said to be consisting of three categories *(padārtha-s)* and four sections *(pada-s)* known as enjoyment *(bhoga)*, liberation *(mokṣa)*, holy rites *(kriyā-s)* or ritualistic observances *(caryā)*. The *padārtha-s* are of three kinds : *(1) Paśupati*, (2) Paśu and (3) Pāśa. The individual souls are called *paśu-s* and the Lord Śiva is Paśupati.[147] The greatest Ātman with the properties of *sat, cit* and *ānanda* representing Being, Consciousness and Bliss respectively is eternal. He is all-pervading, the only seed, the Lord of all.[148] Śiva possesses Śakti and is able to bestow enjoyment and liberation upon the *paśu-s*.[149] There is only a single principle *(tattva)* named Śiva who is possessed of diverse *śakti-s*.[150] Śakti leads to liberation from the bondage of mundane existence whereby the Highest Bliss *(nirvāṇa)* known as pure principle of Self *(ātmatattva)* is achieved.[151]

**Creation-account from the Skanda Purāṇa—**

The philosophical speculations of the *Skanda Purāṇa* also reflect the inclination on the part of the composer of this *purāṇa* to follow the monistic doctrine. The Supreme Cause is termed as Viṣṇu or Hṛṣīkeśa. At the same time, in consonance with the Vedānta doctrine it is described as the Self of all *(sarvātmā)*, omnipresent *(sarvagaḥ)*, omniscient *(sarvajñaḥ)*, the source of all *(sarvasaṁbhavaḥ)*, all pervading *(sarvavyāpī)*, the support of the entire world *(jagaddhātā)*, omnipotent *(sarvaśaktidharaḥ)*, the Lord of the world *(jagadīśaḥ)*, the witness of all *(sarvasākṣī)* and unchanging *(avyayaḥ)*, unborn *(ajanmā)*, eternal *(śāśvataḥ)*, encompassing *(vibhuḥ)*. It is equally noteworthy that the composer of this *purāṇa* views the Supreme Cause from esoteric as also exoteric points of view and describes Viṣṇu as possessed

147. *Ibid*, I. 63, 13-14.

148. *Ibid*, I.63.25.

149. *Ibid*, I.63.27.

150. *Ibid*, I.63. 37[cd].

तत्त्वं वस्तुत एकं तु शिवाख्यं चित्रशक्तिकम्।

151. *Ibid*, I.63.108.

of attributes *(saguṇaḥ)* as also without any attribute *(viguṇaḥ)*.[152] When he looks upon the Highest Cause as possessed of attributes, he takes cognisance of his being full of attachment *(saṅgī)* and performer of activities *(karmī)*. At the same time, he emphatically describes his real nature and declares that he is without any attachment *(nissaṅga* or *saṅgavarjita)*, without any activity *(niṣkarmā)* without any greed *(nirlobhaḥ)*, free from ego (*nirahaṅkārī*) and without any love for anybody *(niṣkiñcanajanapriyaḥ)*.[153] While further throwing light on his omnipresence and ominpotence, rightly does the composer of this *purāṇa* point out that being inside, he moves about outside.[154] When imagined in his personified form, this Cause is described as wearing divine garlands and adorned with *vanamālā-s* and when viewed from the highest point of view, it is eternal *(sanātana)*, *pure (śuciprada)* first Brahma *(ādya Brahma)* which can bestow perfection *(siddhiprada)*.[155] Like many other composers of *purāṇa-s*, even this narrator considers the cause of the world as being endowed with divine nature which is superior to worldly nature and hence following the contents of the Puruṣasūkta of the *RV* he describes this one as being possessed of thousand eyes, thousand feet, thousand arms and thousand faces.[156]

Even here, the monistic doctrine is synthesized with the principles of Sāṅkhya system. Principles headed by Pradhāna are twenty-four in number and insentient in nature and Puruṣa who is sentient is spoken of as the

---

152. *Ska*. P. V.1.63.76-79, 117[ab].

153. *Ibid*, V.1.63.128-129

सगुणो विगुणश्छंदो निःसंगो विगुणो गुणी।।
निर्गुणो गुणवान्सङ्गी कर्मी धर्मी च कर्मदः।।
निष्कर्मा कामकामी च निःसंगः संगवर्जितः।
निर्लोभो निरहंकारी निष्किंचनजनप्रियः।।

154. *Ibid*, V.I.63. 152[ab].

अंतःस्थो बाह्यकारी च बहिःस्थो वै बहिश्चरः।

155. *Ibid*, V.I. 64.

156. *Ibid*, V.I. 63.232.

twently-fifth one.[157] Following the usual tendency of the composers of the *purāṇa-s*, this Sāṅkhya doctrine is further synthesized with the principles of *Yoga* and self-control, *prāṇāyāma*, meditation and concentration are said to be the means of metaphysical devotion *(ādhyātmikī bhakti)*.[158]

**Creation-accounts from the Liṅga Purāṇa —**

According to the creation-account of the *Liṅga Purāṇa*, Brahmā created the world and slept for thousand *yuga-s* and then with a desire to create living beings (*prajā*-s) practised severe austerities.[159] Thereafter, he assumed the form of half-man-half-woman, divided himslef into eleven parts and out of half of his form, he created Umā. Later on Umā created Lakṣmī, Durgā and Sarasvatī.[160]

In another metaphysical account, Śiva is imagined to be the Highest Cause and he is said to be having both the types of forms, *i.e.* the real *(sat)* and the unreal *(asat)*. It is specifically emphasized that both these are the forms of Śiva only. There is nothing else that is other than Śiva and hence Śiva is termed as the Lord of both of them.[161] Following the doctrine of Absolute Monism the composer of this *purāṇa* holds that Maheśvara is identical with everything, the past *(bhūta)*, the present *(vartamāna)* and future *(bhaviṣyat)*.[162] Śiva is said to be constituted of destructible and indestructible forms; at the same time he is imagined to be higher than those forms. Out of these two forms, destructible form is manifest and indestructible

---

157. *Ibid*, V.I.7.17-18.
158. *Ibid*, V.I.7.26-27.
159. *Liṅ. P.* I.41.37-38.
160. *Ibid*, I.41.43-44.
161. *Ibid*, II.15.5.
 उभे ते शिवरूपे हि शिवादन्यं न विद्यते।
 तयोः पतित्वाच्च शिवः सदसत्पतिरुच्यते।।
162. *Ibid*, II.18.3.

one is unmanifest and nothing is higher than Śiva himself.[163] According to the composer of this *purāṇa, Śiva is* definitely the Highest cause as he is said to be creating, maintaining and dissoving the world.[164]

The composer of this *purāṇa* speaks of three different forms of the Supreme Lord. According to him, he is without any attribute *(niṣkala)* for the *Yogin-s*, identical with the world for *jñānin-s* and possesssed of attributes *(sakala)* for those who exist in this mundane existence. This omnipresent Lord is also worshiped in the form of phallic image.[165]

This phallic *liṅga* is of two types- gross and subtle. The gross is external whereas the subtle is internal in nature.[167] The gross *liṅga* is a symbol made of clay, wood etc., which is within the direct reach of the aspirant's sense-organs and becomes a symbolical means to attain the Highest Reality.[167] But whether the Lord is with or without attributes does not make any difference at all, because in reality, everything or being is just the manifestation of Śiva.[168] Any type of splendid *liṅga* can be installed with wholehearted devotion and splendid indeed is the result.[169] *Liṅga* after all is a concrete symbol which when touched or seen leads to the gratification of the minds cf the

163. *Ibid*, II.6-7.
क्षराक्षरात्मकं प्राहुः क्षराक्षरपरं तथा।
शिवं महेश्वरं केचिन्मुनयस्तत्त्वचिंतकाः।।
उक्तमक्षरमव्यक्तं व्यक्तं क्षरमुदाहृतम्।
रूपे ते शंकरस्यैव तस्मान्न पर उच्यते।।
164. *Ibid*, II.16.19.
165. *Ibid*, I.75.30-32.
166. *Ibid*, I.75.19.
167. *Ibid*, I.75.22.
168. *Ibid*, I.75.23[cd].
निश्कलः सकलश्चेति सर्वं शिवमयं ततः।
169. *Ibid*, I.74.21-25.
170. *Ibid*, I.74.28.
नृणां तनुं समास्थाय स्थितो रुद्रो न संशयः।
दर्शनात्स्पर्शनात्तस्य लभंते निर्वृतिं नराः।।

aspirants.[170]

The composer of this *purāṇa* has presented the description of the Supreme Lord and stated that the heaven is the head of the Lord, the sky is his navel, the moon, the sun and the fire are his eyes, the quarters are his ears, the nether worlds constitute his feet. The ocean is his cloth, the gods are his arms. The constellations are his ornaments. Prakṛti is his wife and Puruṣa is his *liṅga*. From his mouth, all Brāhmaṇas came into being, from his arms the Kṣatriyas, from his thighs the Vaiśyas and from his feet the Śūdras.[171] Thus, the Ṛgvedic concept of the Transcendental Reality, having different things and beings as just the differents parts of his body, which in reality excells all of them and remains over and above them is further developed in this *purāṇa*.

**Creation-accounts from the Kūrma Purāṇa-**

The reference to the fourfold division of society as constituting parts of the Huge Person is also found in the *Kūrma Purāṇa*.[172] But some of these details are combined with an account which is partly fictitious and partly mythological in nature. Thus, it is stated that at the beginning of the Kalpa period, God Viṣṇu who was asleep on the coils of the serpent *Śeṣa*[173] on the vast ocean of the primeval cosmic waters, got up, desired to create the universe and the God Brahmā was born of him, who subsequently created nine mind-born sons and the entire world.[174]

The author of this *purāṇa-* has also followed the popular trend of the composers of other *purāṇa-s* and incorporated an account of the evolutionary theory of the Sāṅkhyavādins in this work. However, here unmanifest *(avyakta)* is imagined to be the First Cause and instead of describing it as insentient in keeping with the Sāṅkhya system, it is said to be having

---

171. *Ibid*, I.74.7-10
172. *Kūr. P.* I.25.
173. *Ibid*. I.2.3.
174. *Ibid*, I.2.25.
175. *Ibid*, I.4.6.
अव्यक्तं कारणं यत्तन्नित्यं सदसदात्मकम् ।
प्रधानं प्रकृतिश्चेति यमाहुस्तत्त्वचिंतकाः ।।

both existence and non-existence as its forms.[175] At the time of dissolution *(pralaya)*, the constituents of Prakṛti are in the state of equilibrium.[176] At the end of dissolution called the night of the God Brahmā, the Supreme Lord known as Śiva is said to have entered both Prakṛti and Puruṣa and agitated them and then *mahat, buddhi, ahaṅkāra, tanmātra-s, indriya-s* and *bhūta-s* came into being.[177] Since Śiva is regarded as the Supreme Lord whose entry into Prakṛti and Puruṣa and the act of agitation are responsible for the creation of the world, this theory is appropriately known as the Śaiva-Sāṅkhya theory of creation which clearly shows the influence of the principles laid down in the *Sāṅkhyakārikā* upon it, but regards Puruṣottama to be the presiding Supreme Deity whose presence is necessary for inducing indifferent *(udāsīna)* Puruṣa to activate insentient Prakṛti.[178] Śiva of the *Liṅga Purāṇa*, thus, plays the role of Puruṣottama of the Bh.Gītā.[179]

The Īśvaragītā section of the *Kūrma Purāṇa* is so much in consonance with the Upaniṣadic doctrines that it contains quotations from the Upaniṣads such as *Kaṭha, Śvetāśvatara* etc. Here, *ātman* conceived as the Highest Self is described pure *(śuddha)*, subtle *(sūkṣma)*, alone *(kevala)*, eternal *(sanātana)*, sentient *(cinmātra)*, the innermost of all *(sarvāntara, antaryāmī)*, *puruṣa, prāṇa*, Maheśvara, time *(kāla)* and unmanifest *(avyakta)*. This world originates from Him and it again merges into Him. He is a conjurer *(māyin)* who through his *māyā* assumes various forms.[180]

**Creation-account from the Mārkaṇḍeya Purāṇa-**

---

176. *Ibid*, I.4.10.

गुणसाम्ये तदा तस्मिन्पुरुषे चात्मनि स्थिते।
प्राकृतः प्रलयो ज्ञेयो यावद्विश्वसमुद्भवः।।

177. *Ibid*, I.4.11-20.

178. *Ibid*, II. 2.1-3.

179. *Bh. G.* IX. 10.

मयाध्यक्षेण प्रकृतिः सूयते सचराचरम्।
हेतुनानेन कौन्तेय जगद्विपरिवर्तते।।

180. *Kūr. P.* II.2.4-6.

In the *Mārkaṇḍeya Purāṇa*, Mārkaṇḍeya narrates the account of creation and Brahmā is mentioned as the first male cause that is responsible for the creation, maintenance and dissolution of the world. He is described as Hiraṇyagarbha. Immediately thereafter, however, Pradhāna or Prakṛti is stated as the cause. It is described as imperceptible, subtle and permanent along with Brahmā, who is described as imperishable, undecaying, immeasurable, self-dependent, devoid of odour, form, taste, sound, touch and who neither has a beginning nor an end.[181] Brahmā is said to be having three qualities, existing in equipoise and the first principle Pradhāna is said to have come into existence out of him. It enveloped *mahat*. *Mahat* was enveloped by the imperceptible one in the same manner in which the seed is enveloped by its rind. It was threefold, characterised by goodness, passion and ignorance. From it, *ahaṅkāra* came into existence, giving rise to *bhūta-s* and others. *Ahaṅkāra* which was enveloped by the imperceptible modified itself and created subtle elements *(tanmātra-s)*. *Tanmātra-s* gave rise to Ether, Air, Light, Water and Solid matter having sound, touch, and smell as their special elements. From *ahaṅkāra*, five organs of knowledge, five organs of action and mind were created.[182] Prakṛti is described as permanent and Puruṣa is delimited by it.[183] The earlier part of this account seems to be full of contradictions. Once Brahmā is stated as the first cause and then imperceptible Pradhāna or Permanent Prakṛti is mentioned as the cause of the world. Again, Brahmā is described as possessing three qualities out of which Pradhāna has arisen. But this account concludes with the statement-Brahmā is both Prakṛti and the Soul. Thus, it is clear that these contradictions are more apparent than real.

**Creation-account from the Garuḍa Purāṇa-**

According to the account of the Garuḍa Purāṇa, the

181. *Mārk P.* 42.27-34.
182. *Ibid*, 42.35 - 49.
183. *Ibid*, 42.70cd.

Lord Vāsudeva, also known as Nara-Nārāyaṇa is the great soul, Parabrahma. He is the Creator and the destroyer of the universe. Everything exists in him. He exists in the form of male being *(Puruṣa)* and Time *(Kāla)*. He is without a beginnning and without an end. Intellect, mind, the principles such as Ether, Air, Fire, Water and Earth originate out of him. He is the golden egg (Hiraṇyagarbha). The Lord assumes bodily form for the purpose of creation. Having assumed and body of Brahmā, he creates the world.[184] The world consisting of the celestials, demons and human beings lies inside the egg. At the end of Kalpa, Hari assumes the body of Brahmā and creates the world. As Viṣṇu, he protects it and as Rudra, he destroys it. When Brahmā is engrossed in performing the activity of creation, he assumes the form of a boar, holds up the earth with his tusks.[185]

The first creation was *mahat*, the second the *tanmātra-s*, the third was known as the creation of organs *(vaikārika)*. This creation is known as the material or elementary creation *(prakṛta)* which arises out of intellect. The fourth creation is primary *(mukhya)* and the fifth is that of lower animals (*tiryaksrotas* otherwise known as *tiryakyonya*). The sixth is the creation of celestials that tend upward *(ūrdhvasrotas)*. The seventh is the creation of human beings *(arvāksrotas)*. The eighth is the creation of *anugraha* and the creation of the *kaumāra-s* is the ninth one.[186]

It is clear from this account that even though the incarnate Lord Vāsudeva is here imagined to be the first cause, he is in no way different from Nara-Nārāyaṇa or Viṣṇu. The personified deities may have different names but in reality they are the same. The whole account, thus, is based on the theory of Absolute Monism which is combined with the concept of personification of gods on the one hand and the concept of the trinity of gods on the other. At the same time, it is linked with the mythoficticicus account of creation.

184. *Gar. P.* I.4.3-9.

185. *Ibid*, I.4.10-13.

186. *Ibid*, I.4.14-19.

## Findings from the Creation-accounts

Having taken into consideration the contents of the various creation-accounts, it will certainly be worthwhile to undertake an attempt at their in-depth study especially in the light of the remarks passed by Winternitz. He has stated that "the authority of the *purāṇa-s* certainly cannot be compared with that of the Vedas. *Itihāsa* and *purāṇa-s* were to a certain extent merely a supplement to the Veda, principally intended for the instruction of women and Śūdras who were not entitled to the study of the Veda...... Only the Veda, says Rāmānuja, serves the attainment of the Highest knowledge, the knowledge of Brahman, while Itihāsa and Purāṇa lead only to the cleansing from sins. The Purāṇas then are the sacred books of the second grade. This is easily explained, for originally, the Purāṇas were not priestly literature at all. The Sūta-s or bards were undoubtedly the creators and bearers of the oldest *purāṇa* poetry as well as of the epic."[187] If, thus, as Winternitz holds, the *purāṇa-s* are the sacred books of the second grade and narrations of bards meant only for women and Śūdras, it is necessary to investigate the facts which induced the composers of the *purāṇa-s* to incorporate these cosmogonic, cosmological and philosophical accounts in these works, the accounts which are usually meant for the elite, the so-called intelligentsia? The term cosmology stands for a family of related inquiries and hence it is a name for a branch of metaphysics.[188] Hence, it is better to suppose that such contents are not meant for the masses. While pondering over these points, initially one is likely to form an impression that these accounts are out of place and contrary to the purpose with which the *purāṇa-s* were composed, This purpose is reflected in a wellknown verse which states; "By Itihāsas and Purāṇas the Veda is to be

---

187. Winternitz M., "Purāṇas and their Position in Indian Literature", *History of Indian Literature*, Vol. I, Delhi, 1972, pp 577-578.

188. Milton K. Munitz, "Cosmology", *Encylopaedia of Philosophy*, ed. by Paul Edwards (ed. in chief), New York, 1967, p. 237.

strengthened for the Veda fears an unlearned man, thinking that the latter might injure it."[189] But on second thoughts, especially when one knows that the creation *(sarga)* portions of the *purāṇa-s* form an integral part of the *pañcalakṣaṇa purāṇa-s*, one can very well know the significance of these accounts. It is true that sometimes the composers of the Puraṇas have advocated as many welknown theories propounded by the exponents of different schools as were popular during that age consequently, their creation-accounts are characterised by a motely confusion. However, the purpose behind their effort is definitely laudable. Like bees gathering honey from different flowers, the compsosers of the *purāṇa-s* have put together the views of different schools of Indian philosophy and presented them in the creation *(sarga)* portions so as best to appeal to the people of varied interests, kinds and temparaments.

Finally, the philosophical and cosmogonic contents of the *purāṇa-s* can be reviewed keeping in mind some of the view-points explained in the earlier chapter.

From historical point of view, events in relation to the time factor throw light on the evolutionary process which shapes the present as also the future. Thus, historically speaking, the cosmogonic, cosmological and philosophical contents of the *Purāṇa-s* have their roots in the past. The Ṛgvedic Aryans were taken aback due to the amazing regularity of the course of nature. They knew very well that their life was totally dependent upon those natural forces. Looking upon them as various divinities, they started revering and adoring them and singing their praises through the hymns they composed. The Ṛgvedic religion, thus, was polytheistic in nature, which represented the belief in the multiplicity of gods. At the same time, it reflected the monistic trend representing the concept of unitary godhead especially after the realisation that these divinities were the manifestations

---

189. इतिहासपुराणाभ्यां वेदं समुपबृंहयेत्।
बिभेत्यल्पश्रुताद्वेदो मामयं प्रहरेदिति।।
The verse q. in *M.Bh. Ādi.* 1.263 and *Vāy P.* 1.201; *Pad. P.* V.2.51.

of the same Reality.[190] Besides these hymns, the Ṛgveda also contains a few others which though limited in number are cosmogonic, cosmological and philosophical in nature. These hymns reveal a conviction of the Ṛgvedic Aryans that the visible world must have its own cause. Naturally they were eager to know it and its nature. They tried to throw light on it in their own way. Curiously enough, during the days of the Brāhmaṇa-texts, religion revolved around the institution of sacrifice. Importance of gods was subordinated to the institution of sacrifice. Still, people continued indulging in cosmogonic, cosmological and philosophical speculations in their own way, sometimes regarding Prajāpati as torturing and mortifying himself and creating the universe[191] or at times considering water to be giving rise to a golden egg and propagating itself[192] or even considering *asat* or Puruṣa to be the cause of the world.[193] The fullfledged development of philosophical thoughts, however, is reflected only in the Upaniṣads. According to one view, they are the first recorded attempts at systematic philosophising,[194] whereas according to another opinion, the oldest Upaniṣadic philosophy can exist in a very restricted sense, as they do not contain the thoughts of one single philosopher or one uniform school of philosophers, but a teaching of various men and various periods. Yet the genuine Upaniṣads contain a few fundamental doctrines which give them an appearance of uniformity[195] and the most fundamental doctrine of monism, *i.e.* "The Universe is the Brahman and the Brahman is the Ātman",[196] the doctrine of complete identity between the Individual soul and the Supreme Self

---

190. *RV.* X. 164.46
    एकं सद्विप्रा बहुधा वदन्ति अग्निं यमं मातरिश्वानमाहुः।
191. *Śat. Br.* II.2.4.
192. *Ibid,* XI. 1, 6.1-11.
193. *Ibid,* VI.1.1.
194. Hume R.B. "The Place of the Upanishads in the History of Philosophy", *The Thirteen Principal Upaniṣads,* London, 1921, p.2.
195. Winternitz, *op.cit.,* pp. 244, 246.
196. Deussen, q. by Winternitz, *op.cit., p. 247.*

which leads to deliverance and Eternal Bliss.[197] All these philosophical speculations have definitely shaped the nature and contents of the philosophy and cosmogony of the *mahāpurāṇa-s* as they clearly reflect both polytheistic and monistic traits which are complementary to each other. But even though the monistic doctrine of the *purāṇa-s* is to be traced back to the Upaniṣadic philosophy in general, it is to be noted that the Upaniṣads fall within two categories — (1) The older ones or the Vedic which are fourteen in number and (2) the later ones or the non-Vedic, also known as the Upaniṣads of the Atharvaveda, which are more than one hundred in number and these non-Vedic Upaniṣads are further classified into six categories as follows —

i) The works presenting the Vedānta doctrines
ii) Those teaching Yoga
iii) Those extolling the ascetic life
iv) Those glorifying Viṣṇu
v) Those glorifying Śiva and
vi) Those glorifying Śākta or some other inferior sects[198]

and the Puranic cosmogonic, cosmological and philosophical contents show that they are more in agreement with the non-Vedic or later Upaniṣads than with those of the Vedic ones. This later phase, being more varied and comprehensive in nature seems to have suited their purpose.

From sociological point of view, every element of society in in 'the process of change. The Puranic contents having cosmogonic, cosmological and philosphical speculations forming an integral part of religion can be studied in the light of the concept of social change. 'When a society is in a stable condition, its members find their inherited religion satisfactory on the whole. But in period of rapid transition, the existing thoughts and values no longer serve its needs[199] and the phenomenon of religion undergoes changes. Thus, religion is

197. Winternitz, *op.cit.*, p.260.

198. Classification first proposed by Deussen, q. by Winternitz, *op.cti.*, pp. 239-240.

199. Shah A.B., *Religion and Society in India*, Bombay, 1981, p. 14.

marked by both, change and continuity. Puranic philosphical and cosmogonic speculations also show these trends. On the one hand, they continued the earlier monistic and polytheistic traits of the Vedic religion and at the same time by assimilating the views of various systems of philosphy readily available in the later Upaniṣads and synthesizing them all with the doctrine of absolute monism, they gave a new turn to the old principles in order to attract the masses, to preserve and protect their religion and to wean away large sections of society from the attractive features of Budhism and Jainism.

The Puranic philosophical speculations are more cohesive and comprehensive in nature. Knowing full well that the Highest Reality in its abstract form was beyond the reach of the masses, the composers of the *purāṇa-s* replaced it by concrete divinities, though the basic principle behind this multiplicity was stressed by them every now and then through statements such as- 'Those who do not respect Viṣṇu can never reach Śiva or those who distinguish between Viṣṇu and Śiva go to hell[200] or' Viṣṇu himself is Rudra and Rudra himself is Janārdana'[201] or 'I am the supporter, the cause of the world, I am unborn, the only Lord'.[202] Realising very well that the Puranic religion was the need of the time, the authors of the *purāṇa-s* played an important role in bringing the followers of the different religious cults into a composite Hindu society.[203] Thus, this part of Puranic religion was a product of changing social and historical circumstances which in their turn brought about a desirable social change by integrating Hindu society which might have disintegrated in the absence of this religions change.

---

200. *Kūr.* P. I.15.87.
मन्यन्ते ये जगद्योनिं विभिन्नं विष्णुमीश्वरात्।
मोहादवेदनिष्ठत्वात् ते यान्ति नरकं नराः।।

201. *Ibid,* I.15.89
यो विष्णुः स स्वयं रुद्रो यो रुद्रः स जनार्दनः।
इति मत्वा भजेदेवं स याति परमां गतिम्।।

202. *Ibid,* II.31[ab].
अहं धाता जगद्योनिः स्वयंभूरेक ईश्वरः।

203. Akhtar J.D., 'Introduction' to the ed. of *Viśṇupurāṇam* by M.N. Dutt, Delhi, 1978, p xviii.

CHAPTER — III

# VARṆA-SYSTEM IN THE PURĀṆAS

The philosophical and cosmogonic portions of the *purāṇa-s* formed an integral part of the Puranic religion. Hence an attempt was undertaken to explain the nature and contents of these portions in the earlier chapter. The authors of the *purāṇa-s* have also expressed their views regarding the *varṇa* and *āśrama* systems. They also formed the constituents of the Puranic religion. Hence, their nature will be discussed in the following chapters.

## VARṆA SYSTEM

The term religion is wide in its connotation. It not only stands for the belief in the suprernatural being, but it also refers to "various beliefs and practices."[1] *Varṇa* and *āśrama* systems that originated in India were the outcomes of beliefs and practices of ancient Indian religion. If religion, as stated by Max Müller, is a "faculty of faith in man",[2] *varṇa* and *āśrama* systems evolved out of the faith of ancient Indian people and shaped their behavioural patterns for several years.

The term *varṇa* is closely related to the term 'caste'. In fact, caste was a further development of the *varṇa* system existing in ancient India.

*Varṇa and āśrama* systems together formed the Vedic way of life *(trayīdharma)* and the social order was founded on them. Ancient Indians attached paramount importance to this order. Even the author of the *Arthaśā*stra stated that this order had the sanction of the Veda-s behind it and the disturbance in it would lead to a co-mixture of *varṇa-s* (*varṇasaṅkara*) which in its turn might bring about

1. See Stanely A. Cook, "Religion", *Encyclopaedia of Religion and Ethics*, Vol. X, ed by James Hastings, Edinburg, New York, Forth ed. 1956 (1918), p. 663.
2. Max Müller, *Introduction to the Science of Religion*, London, 1987, p. 13.

the destruction of society as well as the state[3] and hence the ruler was expected to preserve it.[4]

Chronological review of the details of *varṇa* and *āśrama* systems will throw light on how these sysetms existing in the days of the main *purāṇa-s* were shaped by those that existed in the past and at the same time how they were in the state of incessant flux.

The Ṛgveda, the oldest of all the Veda-s refers to the three classes of society named Brahma, Kṣatra and Viś.[5] The Puruṣa-sūkta of the Ṛgveda contains a reference to the four orders of society, *i.e. Brāhmaṇa,* Rājanya, Vaiśya and Śūdra as originating from the sacrifice of the First Being and arising out of his mouth, arms, things and feet respectively, but it is doubtful whether the order in which they are mentioned indicated their status in the society of that time. The reference to these classes is found also in later works. In the course of time, their functional importance went on increasing and Hindu religion itself was termed as *varṇāśramadharma.* Importance of sacrificial and ritualistic activities also increased over the years and with it increased the prestige of the priestly class. Brāhmaṇa *varṇa* was regarded as the best of all the *varṇa-s* and persons belonging to this *varṇa* could enjoy special privilege. Thus, according to Manu, the Brāhmaṇa was the Lord of all *varṇa-s* due to his preeminence, superiority of his origin, his observance of particular restrictive rules and his particualr sanctification.[6] Brāhmaṇa, Kṣatriya and Vaiśya only were the twice-born ones but the Śūdra had only one birth and there was no fifth *varṇa.*[7] Even an ignorant Brāhmaṇa was a great divinity.[8] Manu held that in the absence of heirs, the property of

---

3. Kautilya, *Arthaśāstra* 1.3.16-17.
4. *Ibid,* I. 3.14-15.
5. For more detils see Ghurye G.S., Caste, Class and Occupation, Bombay, 1961, pp. 42ff.
6. *Manu. S.* X. 3
7. *Ibid,* X.7.
8. *Ibid,* IX. 317[ab].

Kṣatriyas, Vaiśyas and Śūdras could be taken by the king but not that of the Brāhmaṇa-s.[9] Even Yājñavalkya held the persons belonging to Brāhmaṇa *varṇa* in high esteem and stated that the Brāhmaṇas expert in Vedic studies are superior to all other castes and those engaged in performing religious rites are superior to them and those endowed with the knowledge of Self are superior even to those who perform religious activities.[10]

In the Ṛgvedic age, the functions of the four *varṇa-s* were not precisely demarcated, but the post-Vedic period was characterised by such demarcation. Thus, according to Manu, the most resplendent one assigned separate duties and occupations to the persons of the four *varṇa-s* in order to protect the universe. He assigned to Brāhmaṇa-s teaching and studying the Veda, sacrificing for their own benefit and for that of others and giving and accepting alms. He commanded the Kṣatriya to protect people, to bestow gifts, to offer sacrifices, to study the Veda, to trade, to lend money, to cultivate the land and the occupation of serving other three *varṇa-s* was prescribed for the Śūdra.[11] Manu elaborated the Ṛgvedic idea of the fourfold division of society further and spoke about status-difference existing in stratified *varṇa* society. Thus, according to him, the Brāhmaṇa sprang from the mouth of the Primeval Being. As he was the first born and endowed with the Veda, he was by right the Lord of the entire creation.[12] Brāhmaṇa according to Manu, was an eternal incarnation of the Sacred Lord, for he was born in order to fulfil the sacred law.[13]

Yājñavalkya's views regarding the status of the Śūdras are undoubtedly more liberal as is clear from his statement One is respected according to one's endowment of learning, religious deeds, age, friends and wealth and even

---

9. *Ibid*, IX. 189.
10. *Yāj. S. I. 198.*
11. *Manu S.* I. 88-90.
12. *Ibid*, I.93.
13. *Ibid*, I.98.

a Śūdra who is endowed with them deserves respect.[14] The list of Yājñavalkya's well defined duties laid down for persons belonging to four *varṇa-s* is fully in agreement with that presented by Manu.

Hārīta's account of the origin of the four *varṇa-s* is exactly in consonance with those of the Puruṣa-sūkta and Yājñavalkyasmṛti wherein it is stated that Brahmā created sinless Brāhmaṇa-s from his mouth, Kṣatriya-s from his arm, Vaiśyas from his thigh and the Śūdras from his feet for the sake of the accomplishment of the performance of sacrifice.[15] Brahmin, according to Hārīta, was the son of a Brāhmaṇa born of a Brāhmaṇa wife and was expected to perform six functions, *i.e.* teaching, learning, sacrificing, officiating as priest, bestowing and accepting gifts.[16] Kṣatriya had to protect the subjects in a righteous manner, had to learn, perform sacrifice, bestow gifts upon Brāhmaṇa-s[17] and Vaiśya had to rear cattle, get himself engaged in agriculture and trade and bestow gifts upon the Brāhmaṇa-s. He could learn and perform sacrifice as well[18] and the Śūdra had to wait upon the members belonging to the remaining three *varṇa-s*[19] According to Hārīta, a Śūdra was supposed to wear old and tattered garment and eat the remnant part of the food left over the a Brāhmaṇa.[20]

According to Uśanas, a brahmin should study the Vedas after the thread ceremony which was to be performed in the eighth year of conception *(garbhāṣṭame varṣe)*.[21] He should always wear the sacred thread and have a tuft of hair on his head.[22] According to him, the status of Brāhmaṇas

14. *Yāj. S.* I.116.
15. *Hārīta*, I, 12, 13[ab].
16. *Ibid*, I.18.
17. *Ibid*. II.2-3.
18. *Ibid*, II.6-9.
19. *Ibid*, II. 11.
20. *Ibid*, II.13.
21. Uśanas S. I.4.
22. *Ibid*, 79.
सदोपवीती चैव स्यात् सदा बद्धशिखो द्विजः।

was the highest as is indicated by his statement : Kṣatriyas and other castes are never to be saluted by the Brāhmaṇas even if they are endowned with knowledge, good works and other accomplishments and be sufficienty proficient in the *śruti*.[23] While asking for alms, a Brāhmaṇa should utter the word '*bhavati*' initially, the Kṣatriya-s in the middle and the Vaiśya at the end.[24] The difference in the order of the words was an indication declaring the *varṇa* to which the person belonged. Uśanas makes a clear-cut distinction between castes and outcasts and considers outcasts as degraded castes which is revealed through his statement : One may receive alms from his own caste members or from all castes but he should shun the outcasts[25]. The advice of Uśanas for the twice-born ones to rinse their mouths after conversing with the outcasts *(antyaja-s)*,[26] Cāṇḍāla-s and Śūdras[27] is a clear indication not only of a stratified society but also of a degraded stauts of the Śūdras. The fact that purificatory notion differered from *varṇa* to *varṇa* also throws light on the *varṇa* hierarchy existing in those days which is revealed through Uśanas's statement : A Brāhmaṇa is purified by water, going to his heart, a Kṣatriya by a drop going to his throat, a Vaiśya by that entering into his mouth, while a Śūdra and a woman by merely touching (the water with lips)[28] It is noteworthy that according to Uśanas women were as impure and degraded as the Śudra-s. It is also remarkable that Uśanas regarded the Vedic study as the basic criterion of the state of being a Brāhmaṇa and hence stated that a Brāhmaṇa not studying the Veda will fall off from the dignity of a Brāhmaṇa.[29]

---

23. *Ibid*, I. 45.
24. *Ibid*, I.52

    a Brāhmaṇa should say "*Bhavati bhiksām delhi*", a Kṣatriya should say "*Bhikṣām bhavati delhi*". and a Vaiśya, "*Bhikṣām delhi bhavati*".
25. *Ibid*, I.54; also *Manu S. . 49.*
26. *Uśanas S.* II.2.
27. *Ibid*, II.4.
28. *Ibid*, II.15.
29. *Ibid*, III.42[ab].

Discussion on Vedānta was essential for the twice-born ones and Uśanas stated that a person who just studies duly the Veda *(saṁhitā)* but does not discuss the Vedānta becomes a Śudra along with his entire family.[30] The twice-born onces were expected to wear the sacred thread, but along with such outward symbols, Uśanas attached equal importance to the principles of good conduct such as truth and control over passion which is clear from his statement : such conduct leads to the attainment of emancipation.[31] Superiority of the Brāhmaṇa *varṇa* over others is hinted at in the chapter on purification *(śauca)* when Uśanas states that a Brāhmaṇa attains purity within ten days, a Kṣatriya within fifteen days and a Śūdra within a month,[32] but all the persons born in the families of the Kṣatriyas, Vaiśyas and Śūdras who serve good Brāhmaṇas pure within ten days like a Brāhmaṇa himself.[33] The touch of a Cāṇḍala was supposed to defile a person and a person coming into his contact had to purify himself by bathing.[34]

The details regarding the duties of four *varṇa-s* mentioned in the *Atrisaṁhitā* are in consonance with those expresed elsewhere[35] and persons belonging to different *varṇa-s* were expected to stick to their respective duties. *Varṇa* duty was regarded as one of the significant rigid norms that regulated the social life of Indian people existing at that time and the violation of this norm was seriously objected. Hence it is stated that a Śūdra who follows his duty enjoys the celestial region. The Śūdra engaged in recitation of the Gāyatrī and offering the oblations to the sacred fire should be killed by the king. If Kṣatriyas and Vaiśyas perform duties other than their own, they are to be outcasted. A Brāhmaṇa selling milk would become a Śūdra within three days and for selling meat,

30. *Ibid*, III.82[ab].
31. *Ibid*, III.89.
32. *Ibid*, VI.34.
33. *Ibid*, VI..35.
34. *Ibid*, VI.75.
35. *Atri.S.* I.13-15.

shell-lac and salt, he was to be outcasted.[36] All the twice-born ones were expected to perform morning and evening rites *(sandhyā)* through which they could reach the celestial region.[37]

When Atri states purity, desire for good unto others, absence of jealousy, absence of avarice, self-restraint, charity and mercy as the characteristics of a Brāhmaṇa,[38] it is clear that according to him, the state of being a Brāhmaṇa did not just depend upon the criterion of birth, it also depended upon other criteria such as virtues, the inner qualities of a person. At the same time, the statement that one half of the sin of Brāhmanicide visits a man for killing Kṣatriyas and six and twelve protions for killing Vaiśyas and Śūdras[39] respectively reveals that the *varṇa* distinctions were characterised by stratification. Similarly, the statement that a Brāhmaṇa touching the partakes of food even unknowingly touched by outcast should perform a Prājāpatya[40] throws light on the dispised status of the outcasts and the belief of the people in the theory of pollution. Again, the statement that for partaking of Cāṇḍala's food, a Brāhmaṇa should perform a Cāndrāyaṇa, a Kṣatriya, a Sāntapana, a Vaiśya should perform penance and live on the Pañcagavya for six nights and a Śūdra should perform the same for three nights[41] also indicates the existence of stratified society characterised by *varṇa* gradations and the despicable status of the Cāṇḍālas which was lower than even that of the Śūdra-s. *Atrisaṁhitā* also considers the learned Brāhmaṇas as respectable and hence advises people to make gifts unto a Brāhmaṇa well-read in the Vedas and well-versed in all scriptures.[42]

---

36. *Ibid*, I.19-21.
37. *Ibid*, I.26.
38. *Ibid*, I.33.
39. *Ibid*, I.26.
40. *Ibid*, I.171.
41. *Ibid*, I.172.
42. *Ibid*, I.334.

**Varṇa System in the Puranic Age -**

When we come down to the Puranic age, we realise that the authors of the *purāṇa-s* have retained some features of the rigid *varṇa* system existing in India, at the same time, posing themselves to be more liberal in their outlook, they tried to show that it was flexible as well.

**Creation-accounts in the Purāṇa-s.**

Thus, the creation account of the *Bhāg.P.* has retained the details of the Puruṣasūkta of *RV.* and the Brāhmaṇa, Kṣatriya, Vaiśya and Śūdra distinguished by their specific functions are said to have originated from the mouth, arms, thighs and the feet of the Viraṭ Puruṣa respectively,[43] at the same time, each *varṇa* is said to be having special characteristics of its own and the qualities such as tranquility, self-discipline, reflection, purity, contentment, forbearance, straightforwardness, devotion to the Lord, compassion and truthfulness are stated as the natural qualities of a Brāhmaṇa, qualities such as valour, strength, courage, devotion to Brāhmaṇas, qualities like leadership are termed as the inmate qualities of Kṣatriyas, qualities such as faith in god, a settled disposition to philosophy, sincerity, the service of the Brāhmaṇas and endless craving for acquisition are said to be the charscteristic marks of the Vaiśyas and devoted and sincere service to the twice-born, the cow and the gods, contentment with what is gained from it are described as the distinguishing features of the Śūdra-s.[44] Thus, *varṇa* differences, according to this *purāṇa* were inborn and had their correlation with a specific set of characteristics.

According to the creation-account of the *Viṣ. P.*, Brahmā is the creator of the world and the Brāhmaṇas, Kṣatriyas and Vaiśyas have come out of the mouth, the breast and

---

43. *Bhāg. P.* XI. 17.13.
विप्रक्षत्रियविट्शूद्रा मुखबाहूरुपादजाः।
वैराजात् पुरुषाज्जाता य आत्माचारलक्षणाः।।

44. *Ibid*, XI. 17.16-19

the thighs of Brahmā and are surcharged with the principle of goodness *(sattva)*, passion *(rajas)* and dullness *(tamas)* respectively.[45] It is wellknown that the propounders of the Sāṅkhya system of philosophy consider them to be having special characteristics of their own, *i.e. sattva* is looked upon as the best of all, and *tamas* causing ignorance is regarded as the worst of all and *rajas* occupies the middling place. This reference to the three *varṇa-s* as being surcharged with these three constituents of Primordial Matter *(prakṛti)* hints at the hierarchical gradation of the three *varṇa-s* which is certainly a later development and as pointed out earlier, it is doubtful whether it prevailed in the Ṛgvedic age.

The *Kūr.P.* gives just the paraphrase of the famous Puruṣasūkta and states that the Almighty Lord created Brāhmaṇas from his mouth, Kṣatriyas from his arms, Vaiśyas from his thighs and Śūdras from his feet, but futher adds that Brahmā created all castes excepting the Śūdras for the purpose of the performance of sacrifices.[46] Obviously, the correlation of the three *varṇa-s* with the sacred institution of sacrifice indicates the impurity with which the Śūdra *varṇa* was believed to be characterised.

### Different *Varṇa-s* and their Specific Duties-

According to the works on Dharmaśāstra, persons belonging of different *varṇa-s* had special previleges of their own, at the same time, they were supposed to carry out their specific duties. The authors of the *purāṇa-s* also stick to the rigid duties of *varṇa*-s *(varṇadharma*-s*)* as is clear from the account of the *Kūr.P.* which mentions performance of sacrifices, presiding over sacifices of others, giving charitable gifts, acceptance of charitable donations, Vedic studies and teaching of the Vedas as the duties of the Brāhmaṇas, giving away charitable gifts, self-study of the Vedas and performance of sacrifices as duties of Kṣatriyas and Vaiśyas, chastisement of the subjects, *i.e.* the main-

45. *Viṣ.P.* I.6.3-6.
46. *Kūr. P.* I.2. 25-26.

tenance of law and order and fighting with the enemies as the special *dharma* of a Kṣatriya, agriculture as the special occupation of a Vaiśya and rendering services to the twice-born castes as the means of acquiring *dharma* by Śūdras.[47]

Similarly the author of the *Bra.P.* lays down the same conventional rules for the members of the four *varṇa*-s and mentions merciful acts, giving away gifts, penance, performance of sacrifices, teaching, acceptance of gifts as the special duties of Brāhmaṇas,[48] protection of earth, punishment of the wicked, protection of the righteous and cultured people as the specific duties of the Kṣatriyas, cattle - rearing, trade, agriculture as the means of livelihood of the Vaiśyas[49] and allows the Śūdras to bestow gifts, perform sacrifices *(pākayajña-s)* and rites in honour of ancestors.[50]

The creation-account of the *Bhāg.P.* tallies with other similar accounts in so far as the performance of sacrifices, study of the Veda and giving away gifts are stated as obligatory for all the twice-born ones and Brāhmaṇa alone was allowed to receive gifts, teach the Veda and conduct sacrifices,[51] but at the same time, according to this account, if

---

47. *Ibid*, I.2.38-40.
यजनं याजनं दानं ब्राह्मणस्य प्रतिग्रहः।
अध्यापनञ्चाध्ययनं षट् कर्माणि द्विजोत्तमाः।।
दानमध्ययनं यज्ञो धर्मः क्षत्रियवैश्ययोः।
दण्डो युद्धं क्षत्रियस्य कृषिर्वैश्यस्य शास्यते।।
शश्रूषैव द्विजातीनां शूद्राणां धर्मसाधनम्।
कारुकर्म तथाजीवः पाकयज्ञादि धर्मतः।।
48. *Bra.P. 114.3-4.*
49. *Ibid*, 8-10.
50. *Ibid*, 14.
दानं दद्याच्च शूद्रोऽपि पाकयज्ञैर्यजेन च।
पित्र्यादिकं च वै सर्वं शूद्रः कुर्वीत तेन वै।।
51. *Bhāg*. P. XI.17.40.
इज्याध्यनदानानि सर्वेषां च द्विजन्मनाम्।
प्रतिग्रहोऽध्यापनं च ब्राह्मणस्यैव याजनम्।।

a Brāhmaṇa regards the acceptance of gifts as detrimental to his good name, he may maintain himself by other two means only; if he regards them too as not free from blemish, he may take out living ears of corn fallen in the fields.[52] The attitude of the author of the *Bhāg.P.* towards *varṇa* occupations is definitely liberal as it is stated that the Brāhmaṇa in distress may support himself by trading in things that are lawful. In an extremity, he may take to arms for earning his livelihood. The Kṣatriya may follow the occupation of the Vaiśyas or in extreme straits, may live by chase or take to some Brahmanical occupation. The Vaiśya may practise the occupation of the Śūdras and the Śūdras that of a mechanic or a weaver of mats. But a man who is not under a compelling necessity should not prefer to remain in any blameworthy occupation and the Brāhmaṇas and Kṣatriyas should never resort to menial service.[53] Thus, even though, the views of the author of this *purāṇa* regarding *varṇa* occupations were liberal, he definitely regarded the duty and the status of the Śūdras as despicable.

According to *Nār.P.*, the duties of *varṇa*-s *(varṇadharma-s)* had a divine sanction. The author of this *purāṇa* has stated that the *varṇa*-s are four in number and the thread ceremony marks the second birth of the three upper groups which for the same reason are known as the twice-born ones *(dvija-s)*; people are expected to stick to their duties strictly and persons giving up their respective duties are regarded as heretics *(pāṣaṇḍa-s)*.[55] The twice-born one *(dvija)* was expected to follow the activities laid down in the *gṛhyasūtra*-s and *smṛti*-s.[56] The author is in strict conso-

52. *Ibid*, XI.17.43.
53. *Ibid*, XI. 17.47-49.
54. *Nār. P.* I.14.8.
ब्राह्मणाः क्षत्रिया द्विजाः प्रोक्तास्त्रयस्तथा।
मातृतश्चोपनयनाद्विजत्वं प्राप्यते त्रिभिः।।
55. *Ibid*, I.14.9.
एतैर्वर्णैः सर्वधर्माः कार्या वर्णानुरूपतः।
56. *Ibid*, I.14.10-11.

nance with the contents of the most of the writers on Dharmaśāstra while laying down the duties of persons belonging to four *varṇa*-s. He states that making gifts *(dāna)*, performance of sacrifice *(yajana)*, officiating as priest *(vṛttyartha-yājana)*, Vedic study *(vedograhaṇa)*, activities pertaining to fire *(agniparigraha)* are the duties of Brāhmaṇas. Vedic study, bestowing gifts upon Brāhmaṇas *(viprebhyaḥ dāna)*, performance of sacrifices, earning livelihood by means of weapons *(sśāstrājīva)*, protection of the earth *(mahīpālana)*, punishing the wicked *(duṣṭaśāsana)* and protection of the righteous and cultured ones *(siṣṭapālana)* are the duties of Kṣatriyas. Vedic study, cattle-rearing *(pāsśupālya)*, trade *(vāṇijya)* agriculture *(kṛṣi)* are the duties of Vaiśyas[57] and bestowing gifts and service to the persons belonging to other three *varṇa*-s *(brahmakṣatriyaviśām śuśrūṣa)* are the duties of Śūdras.[58] The author of the *Vām.P.* also expects persons belonging to the four *varṇa*-s to carry out their activities in strict consonance with the *varṇa* duties and states that no man in this world should give up the conduct peculiar to his *varṇa* and stage of life and a person forsaking his duties incurs the wrath of the sun.[59]

The author of the *Mārk.P.* also follows the works on Dharmasśāstra and states that liberality, study and sacrifice are the duties of Brāhmaṇas, irreproachable sacrificial and educational occupations, acceptance of gifts from the purified form his threefold means of livelihood. Liberality, study, sacrifice is the threefold duty of a Kṣatriya and protection of the earth and subsistence of weapons are his means of livelihood. The duties of Vaiśyas are the same and merchandise, cattle-rearing and agriculture are their means of livelihood. His attitude towards the Śūdra *varṇa* is liberal, as besides obedience

57. *Nār. P.* I.24. 19, 20, 23, 24, 25.

58. *Ibid*, I.24.27.
दद्याद्यानानि शूद्रोऽपि पाकयज्ञैर्यजेन्न च।
ब्राह्मणक्षत्रियविशां शुश्रूषानिरतो भवेत्।।

59. *Vām. P.* I.15.64.
स्वानि वर्णाश्रमोक्तानि धर्माणीह न हापयेत्।
यो हापयति तस्यासौ परिकुप्यति भास्करः।।

to the twice-born ones, liberality and sacrifice also are mentioned as their duties and handicraft, nourishing the twice-born ones *(dvija-s)* buying and selling are mentioned as their means of livelihood.[60] At the same time he has stated that a person following the duty in consonance with the norms of *varṇa* system achieves perfection.[61]

*Varṇa* duties laid down by the author of the *Gar.P.* are in agreement with those mentioned in the *śruti*-s and *smṛti*-s. In fact this author considers the *śruti* and *smṛti* as the two eyes for proper understanding of the duties.[62] Hence, following these works he states that sacrifices, Vedic study, gifts in accordance with the instructions in the *śāstra*-s constitute the common virtue of the Brāhmaṇas, Kṣatriyas and Vaiśyas.[63] Presiding over others' sacrifices, teaching of the Vedas, acceptance of money, gifts etc. *(parigraha)* constitute the extra activities of the highest class. Living with weapons, protection of all living beings, cattle-rearing, trading and business are the ways of subsistenc for Vaiśyas and the service of all other twice-born people is the duty of the Śūdra-s.[64] The same *purāṇa* further states that the strict adherence to one's own duty enables one to attain the greatest goal[65] but at the same time, this *purāṇa* allows a Brāhmaṇa to pursue usury, agricultural and trading activities in times of calamity, i.e. when no other source of income is available. According to this author, a Brāhmaṇa is not tainted by any sin.[66]

---

60. *Mār. P.* 25. 3-6.
61. *Ibid. P.* 25.9.
62. *Gar. P.* I.213. 3[b].
   श्रुतिस्मृती ह विप्राणां लोचने कर्मदर्शने।
63. *Ibid*, I.213.10.
   इज्याध्ययनदानानि यथाशास्त्रं सनातनः।
   ब्रह्मक्षत्रियवैश्यानां सामान्यो धर्म उच्यते।।
64. *Ibid*, I. 231.11-13.
65. *Ibid*, I.213.23[ab].
   यथोक्तकारिणः सर्वे प्रयान्ति परमां गतिम्।
66. *Ibid*, .213.91.
   कुसीदकृषिवाणिज्यं प्रकुर्वीत स्वयं परम् (कृतम्)। आपत्काले स्वयं कुर्वन्नेनसा भुज्यते द्विजः।।

The list of duties to be performed by the persons belonging to four *varṇa*-s stated in the *Agni P.* is also not different from that of the works on Dharmasśāstra, except the fact that besides the usual ones, the protection of the good and suppression of the wicked are considered as the special duties of Kṣatriyas and practising handicrafts as that of the Śūdras.[67]

The details regarding the righteous duties of persons belonging to the four *varṇa*-s stated in the *Kūr.P.* also are more or less the same, but the author does not allow the Śudras to practise handicrafts.[68]

The author of the *Brahmāṇḍa P.* has depicted an unusual picture of the Kali Age and stated that in this age, the twice-born people neither study the Vedas nor perform sacrifices. The kings are mainly the Śudras. The Śudras and *antyayoni*-s have alliances and associations with the Brāhmaṇas.[69] The Śūdras take to the conduct of life of the Brāhmaṇas and the Brāhmaṇas behave and act like thieves.[70] They will no longer protect their share in the offerings (of taxes etc.). The Brāhmaṇas will be dependent on the Śūdras and the twice born ones will make obeisance to the Śūdras.[71] The Brāhmaṇas will sell out the benefit of their penance and performance of sacrifices.[72] When the Kali Age steps in, the enemies of the system and discipline of *varṇa*-s

---

67. *Agn. P.* 151. $8^{cd}$. $9^{cd}$.
क्षत्रियस्य विशेषेण पालनं दुष्टनिग्रहः ।।
शूद्रस्य द्विजशुश्रूषा सर्वशिल्पानि वाप्यथ ।।
68. *Kūr. P.* I.2-40.
शुश्रूषैव द्विजातीनां शूद्राणां धर्मसाधनम् ।
कारुकर्म तथाजीवः पाकयज्ञादि धर्मतः ।।
69. *Brahmāṇḍa* p. I.2.39-40.
70. *Ibid*, I. $2.42^{cd}$, $43^{ab}$.
शूद्राश्च ब्राह्मणाचाराः शूद्राचाराश्च ब्राह्मणाः ।।
राजवृत्ताः स्थिताश्चोराश्चोराचाराश्च पार्थिवाः ।।
71. *Ibid*, 48-49
72. *Ibid*, $51^{b}$.
तपोयज्ञफलानां च विक्रेतारो द्विजोत्तमाः ।

and stages of life are born.[73] The Śūdras become expert in interpreting affairs concerning religious activities and the study of the Vedas. The kings born of the wombs of the Śūdras begin to worship and perform horse-sacrifice.[74] When these are looked upon as the signs of Kali age, obviously it is implied that it is a topsy turvy type of situation which is far from being an ideal one and one can infer that strict consonance with one's own *varṇa* duties was regarded as the most desirable virtue.

Again, we are not surprised to know that following the conventions of the time, the author of the *Vāy.P.* also has stressed the importance of one's own duty *(svadharma)* and has looked upon a person giving up his duty as a fallen one *(patita)*.[76] Even according to the author of the *Nār. P.*, abandonment of one's own *dharma* and acceptance of the duty of somebody else is censureworthy and a person doing so is to be regarded as a heretic and is worthy of being discarded by righteous codes.[77]

Thus, the above contents show that the authors of the *purāṇa*-s stressed the importance of the concept of one's own duty *(svadharma)* in consonance with Manu's statement : 'It is better to discharge one's own assigned duty though full of demerits than to carry out that of

---

73. *Ibid*, 66[cd].
74. *Ibid*, 67.
    अधीयते तदा वेदाञ्छूद्रा धर्मार्थकोविदाः।
    यजन्ते चाश्वमेधेन राजानः शूद्रयोनयः।।
75. *Vāy. P.* I.8. 161-163.
76. *Vām. P.* I.15.33.
    स्वधर्मं यः समुत्सृज्य परधर्मं समाश्रयेत्।
    अनापदि स विद्वद्भिः पतितः परिकीर्त्यते।।
77. *Nār. P.* I. 25.2.
    यः स्वधर्मं परित्यज्य परधर्मं समाचरेत्।
    पाषंडः स हि विज्ञेयः सर्वधर्मबहिष्कृतः।।

another'.[78] Or similar thoughts expressed by the author of the *Bhagvadgītā* such as 'one's own duty though full of demerits is far better than the duty of somebody else even though it is performed in an excellent manner. It is better to die while carrying out one's own duty. Terrible indeed is the duty to others'.[79] Or 'A person engaged in carrying out one's own duty achieves perfection'.[80]

It is wellknown that the author of the *Bh.G.* held that the difference in nature of the activities of the members of the four *varṇa*-s was to be attributed to the difference in the proportion of the three constituents of Primordial Matter *(Prakṛti)*.[81] Even Manu considered the Vedic study, penance, purity, control over senses, performance of religious rites and meditation to be that characteristics of the *sattva* element, performance of activities with a desire to secure the fruit, absence of courage, resorting to bad activities, interest in the objects of senses as the special features of *rajoguṇa* and greed, dream, absence of faith in God, begging nature as the distinct characteristics of *tamoguṇa*. The authors of the *purāṇa*-s touch upon the same point. Thus, the author of the *Bh.P.* has stated in clear-cut terms that the activities of the Brāhmaṇas, Kṣatriyas, Vaiśyas and Śūdras were divided into three categories in keeping with the characterietics which were innate to their respective nature.[82] Thus, peace, penance, self-control, purity, forgiveness, straightforwardness, knowledge, special knowledge, belief in God (or Almighty) are declared to be the natural activities of the Brāhmaṇas. Valour, brilliance, courage, skilfulness, firmness on the battlefield, charity, Lordship

78. *Manu S.* X.97[ab].
वरं स्वधर्मो विगुणो न पारक्यः स्वनुष्ठितः।
79. *Bh. G.* III.35.
80. *Ibid*, XVIII. 45[ab].
81. *Bh.G.* 17.41-44.
82. *Bh. P.* I.44.24.
ब्राह्मणक्षत्रियविशां शूद्राणां च परस्परम्।
कर्माणि प्रविभक्तानि स्वभावप्रभवैर्गुणैः।।

are the innate deeds of the Kṣatriyas. Agriculture, cattle-rearing, trade are the activities befitting the Vaiśya and servitude is natural to the Śūdra.[83] The author of the *Bhāg.P.* also considers the Brāhmaṇas as possessing tranquility of mind, an ability to hold discussion on religious topics, purity, contentment, forgiveness, devotion to God, mercy and truthfulness as their unique qualities. Kṣatriyas according to him, have prowess, strength, forbearance, patience, liberality, energy, gravity...... as their exclusive characteristics and Vaiśyas have belief in god, desire to be charitable and absence of pride as their special attributes.[84]

**Supremacy of the Brāhmaṇa Varṇa-**

As is shown earlier,[85] almost all the authors on Dharmaśāstra regarded the Brāhmaṇa *varṇa* to be the best of all, the cream of the entire society. The authors of the *purāṇa*-s have retained the same traditional view regarding their supremacy.

The author of the *Bhāg.P.* held the *Brāhmaṇa varṇa* in high esteem and declared that the body of a Brāhmaṇa was not meant for performing insignificant deeds but it was specially for the sake of performing austerities and for the acquisition of the Highest Bliss.[86] The author of the *Pad. P.* also regarded him as the best of all the *varṇa*-s,

---

83. *Ibid*, I.44. 25-27.
शमस्तपो दमः शौचं क्षान्तिमार्जवमेव च ।
ज्ञानं विज्ञानमास्तिक्यं ब्रह्मकर्म स्वभावजम्।।
शौर्यं तेजो धृतिर्दाक्ष्यं युध्दे चाप्यपलायनम्।
दानमीश्वरभावश्च क्षात्रं कर्म स्वभावजम्।।
कृषिगोरक्षवाणिज्यं वैश्यकर्म स्वभावजम्।
परिचर्यात्मकं कर्म शूद्रस्यापि स्वभावजम्।।
84. *Bhāg. P.* XI. 17. 16-18
85. *Manu s.*X. 53.
86. *Bhāg. P.* XI. 17.
ब्राह्मणस्य हि देहोऽयं क्षुद्रकामाय नेष्यते।
कृच्छ्राय तपसे चेह प्रेत्यानन्तसुखाय च।

who was the Lord Nārāyaṇa himself and who was to be considered as the resort of all the gods.[87] While glorifying the Brāhmaṇa *varṇa* the author of this *purāṇa* has also stated that living beings are the best of all the existing beings; those who are endowed with intellect are the best of all living beings; human beings are the best of all those who are endowed with intellect and the *brahmaṇa-s* are the best of all human beings.[88] The author of the *Kūr.P.* in no way differed from others in regarding the *brāhmaṇa varṇa* as the supreme *varṇa* and hence stated that a person desirous of worshipping different goddesses as per his or her sweet will should worship the Brāhmaṇas.[89]

The author of the *Nār.P.* also has poured showers of encomium upon the *Brāhmaṇa varṇa* and has regarded the greatness of the Brāhmaṇas to be similar to that of the river Ganges or the moon.[90] *Bh.P.* also is all in praise for a Brāhmaṇa and considers him to be the Lord of all the *varṇa*-s right from birth,[91] the best of all by virtue of

---

87. *Pad. P.* IV. 14.1.
ब्राह्मणः सर्ववर्णानां गुरुदेव द्विजोत्तम।
सर्वामराश्रयो श्रेयः साक्षान्नारायणः प्रभुः।।

88. *Ibid*, I. 32.201.
भूतानां प्राणिनः श्रेष्ठाः प्राणिनां मतिजीविनः।
मतिमत्सु नराः श्रेष्ठा नरेषु ब्रह्मजातयः।।
Compare *Manu S.* I. 96
भूतानां प्राणिनः श्रेष्ठाः प्राणिनां बुद्धिजीविनः।
बुद्धिमत्सु नराः श्रेष्ठा नरेषु ब्राह्मणाः स्मृताः।।

89. *Kūr. P. II. 26.36.*
यो हि यां देवतामिच्छेत्समाराधयितुं नरः।
ब्राह्मणान् पूजयेद्विद्वान् स तस्यास्तोषहेतवः।।

90. *Nār. P.* I.6.59.
वर्णानां ब्राह्मणः श्रेष्ठस्तारकाणां यथा शशी।
यथा पयोधिः सिन्धूनां तथा गङ्गा परा स्मृता।।

91. *Bh. P.* II.5.1.
त्रयाणामेव वर्णानां जन्मतो ब्राह्मणः प्रभुः।
Manu S I 93 d.
धर्मतो ब्राह्मणः प्रभुः।

his birth and worthy of being worshipped,[92] the most sacred of all the sacred ones and the best of all the teachers, endowed with excellence and he has been thus created by the creator.[93] While glorifying Brāhmaṇa, the author further states that he is the sacred highest place of the world[94] and the depository of the principle of the Vedic lores, the support of all beings.[95] The author of the *Pad.P.* also considers Brāhmaṇa to be the greatest of all the *varṇa*-s. In his eyes, he is Lord Nārāyaṇa himself.[96] According to him, all the holy places existing in the Brahmāṇḍa, ocean and reservoir of water are at the feet of a Brāhmaṇa.[97]

**Customs and Varṇa-hierarchy-**

The Puranic contents reflecting the *varṇa* system prevalent in those days throw light on the fact that not only religious or cermonial customs but also the behavioural patterns differed from *varṇa* to *varṇa*. Thus, the age-limit prescibed for the thread-ceremony *(upanayana-saṁskāra)* indicates differentiation as well as hierarchical gradation of *smṛti*-writers like Manu,[98] the authors of the *purāṇa*-s

92. *Ibid*, II.5.3[cd].
जन्मना चोत्तमोऽयं च सर्वार्चा ब्राह्मणोऽर्हति।

93. *Ibid*, II. 5.9.
पूतानां परमः पूतो गुरूणां परमो गुरुः।
सर्वसत्त्वान्वितो विप्रो निर्मितो ब्रह्मणा पुरा।।

94. *Ibid*, II.6.14[ab].
ब्राह्मणो जगतां तीर्थं पावनं परमं यतः।

95. *Ibid*, II.6.13.
वेदवेदांगशास्त्राणां तत्त्वं यत्र प्रतिष्ठितम्।
आधारः सर्वभूतानामग्रजन्मन्नमोऽस्तु ते।।

96. *Pad.* p. IV. 14.2
ब्राह्मणः सर्ववर्णानां गुरुदेव द्विजोत्तम।
सर्वामराश्रयो ज्ञेयः साक्षान्नारायणः प्रभुः।।

97. *Ibid*, IV. 14.12.
ब्रह्मांडे यानि तीर्थानि यानि तीर्थानि सागरे।
उदधौ यानि तीर्थानि तिष्ठंति द्विजपादयोः।।

98. *Manu. S.* II.36.

also state that the thread ceremony should be performed at the age of eight in the case of Brāhmaṇa boys, at the age of eleven in the case of Kṣatriya boys and at the age of twelve in the case of Vaiśyas. Thus, the author of the *Nār.P.* states that the investiture with sacred thread for a (Brāhmaṇa) boy should be in the eighth year of conception or birth, in the eleventh year in the case of Kṣatriya after conception and *upanayana* rite of a Vaiśya should be performed in the twelfth year of conception.[99] The rules regarding these age-limits were rigid as is known from another statement from the same *purāṇa:* If the twice-born is not invested with the sacred thread within these limits of time, know him to be fallen from the sacred Gāyatrī *mantra (gāyatrīpatita or sāvitrīpatita).* No one should even converse with him.[100] The author regards this fall as a sin and in keeping with the usual *smārta* trend, lays down the expiatory ways to be free from it. Thus, according to him, Kṛcchra penance performed for twelve years followed by the performance of Cāndrāyaṇa and two Sāntapana expiations *(prāyaścitta-s)* before the *upanayana* rite, will enable the person who transgresses the time-limit to save himself from meeting his fall. Otherwise, he will be on par with a slayer of a Brāhmaṇa.[101]

Again, the customs to be observed in the case of initiates at the time of the performance of the thread-cermony also varied from *varṇa* to *varṇa.* Thus, the same author further states that the girdle of a Brāhmaṇa boy should be of the *munja* grass, that of a Kṣatriya, should be of a

99. *Nār. P.* I. 25.11[ab], 12[ab], 13[ab].
गर्भाष्टमेऽष्टमे वाब्दे बटुकस्योपनयनम् |/11[ab]
गर्भेऽकादशमेऽब्दे तु राजन्यस्योपनयनम्/12[ab]
वैश्यस्योपनयनं प्रोक्तं गर्भाद्वादशमे तथा |/13[ab]

100. *Ibid*, I.25.14.
एतत्कालावधेर्यस्य द्विजस्यातिक्रमो भवेत् ।
सावित्रीपतितं विद्यात्तं तु नैवालपेत्कदा ।।

101. *Ibid*, I.25.15.15.16[ab].

bowstring and that of a Vaiśya should be woolen.[102] Here, the objects to be chosen seem to be symbolically representing the professions that the persons belonging to these *varṇa*-s were expected to follow. These details could be compared with those presented by Manu, wherein the only difference is that the girdle of a Vaiśya was supposed to consist of hempen threads.[103] Similarly, the wooden material to be utilised while making the sticks that the initiates were expected to have with them also differed from *varṇa* to *varṇa*. A Brāhmaṇa boy was expected to have a *palāśa* stick, a Kṣatriya boy an *udumbara* stick and a Vaiśya boy a *bilva* stick. The size of that stick also differed from *varṇa* to *varṇa*. If placed horizontally on the ground, the stick of a Brāhmaṇa boy was expected to reach his hair on the head, that of a *kṣatriya* was expected to come upto his forehead and the staff of a Vaiśya was expected to come to the tip of his nose.[104] The colour of the clothes to be worn at the time of the thread-ceremony also had to differ from *varṇa* to *varṇa*. The Brāhmaṇa boys were expected to wear ochre-coloured garments, the Kṣatriya boys had to wear red garments and the Vaiśya boys were supposed to wear yellow garments.[105]

The author of the *Bh. P.* has enlisted the sacred rites (*saṁskāra*-s) such as *garbhādhāna*, *puṁsavana*, *sīmantonayana*, *jātakarma*, *nāmakaraṇa*, *annaprāśana*, *cūḍopanayana*, *vratādeśa*, *samāvartana*, *pāṇigrahaṇa* etc. that the Brāhmaṇas could undergo and has specifically noted that only those who undergo these *saṁskāra*-s are Brāhmaṇas.[106] The Śūdras were never entitled to undergo

102. *Ibid*, I.25.16[cd], 17[ab].
मौंजी विप्रस्य विज्ञेया धनुर्ज्या क्षत्रियस्य तु।।
आवी वैश्यस्य विज्ञेया श्रूयतामजिने तथा।

103. *Manu S.* II.42.

104. *Nār. P.* I.25. 18-19, 20[ab]. *also Manu s.* II. 46.

105. *Nār. P.* I.25.20[cd], 21[ab].
तथा वासांसि वक्ष्यामि विप्रादीनां यथाक्रमम्।।
कषायं चैव मांजिष्ठं हारिद्रं च प्रकीर्तितम्।

106. *Bh. P.* I.42.8-10.

these *saṁskāra*-s.[107] Even the author of the *Agn. P.* has stated that the *upanayana saṁskāra* was restricted only for the three upper classes.[108] Denial of *upanayana saṁskāra* thus resulted into the denial of the right of being educated. In fact, according to the general trend which was in consonance with the principles of *smārta* religion,[109] the Śūdras could never perform any rite or sacrifice with the accompaniment of sacred incantation.[110] The author of the *Pad.P. also expects the Śūdras* just to wait upon the Brāhmaṇas, to wash their feet and to clean the left over of the their meals.[111] Similar stiffer attitude towards the Śūdras is also revealed in the *Bh.P.* when the author states that the Śūdras should just listen to the persons belonging to the upper classes but they should never learn.[112] Once again, the same trend of retaining the traditional *smārta* concept of *varṇāśrama-dharma* is revealed through an account of the description of the state of being a twice-born one presented in the *Gar.P.* according to which only the twice-born *varṇa*-s are entitled to undergo *saṁskāra*-s with the accompaniment of recitation of incantations *(mantra*-s).[113]

---

107. *Ibid,* I.42.14[ab].
संस्कारः क्रियमाणश्च न शूद्रे च प्रवर्तते।

108. *Agn, P.* 166.2.
वर्णधर्मः स विज्ञेयो यथोपनयनं त्रिषु।

109. *Manu. S.* X. 126.

110. *Vis. P.* III.8.33[cd].
अमंत्रयज्ञो ह्यस्तेयं तत्संगो विप्ररक्षणम्।

111. *Pad. P.* I.16.108.
द्विजानां पादशुश्रूषा शूद्रैः कार्या सदा त्विह।
पादप्रक्षालनं भोज्यमुच्छिष्टस्य प्रमार्जनम्।।

112. *Bh. P.* I.1.72.
अध्येतव्यं न चान्येन ब्राह्मणं क्षत्रियं विना।
श्रोतव्यमेव शूद्रेण नाध्येतव्यं कदाचन।।

113. *Gar. P.* I. 93.10.
ब्रह्मक्षत्रियविट्शूद्रा वर्णास्त्वाद्यास्त्रयो द्विजाः।
निषेकाद्याः श्मशानान्तास्तेषां वै मन्त्रतो क्रियाः।।

The *Pad.P.* considers Brāhmaṇa as the best of all the *varṇa*-s.[114] Firmly believing in the *varṇa* hierarchy, the author of this *purāṇa* lays down *varṇa* norms regarding the point as to who should bow down before whom and states that the members of the same *varṇa* can bow down before each other,[115] but the Brāhmaṇas should not bow down before the Kṣatriyas.[116] The same *purāṇa* has also stated that while bowing down before a Brāhmaṇa, one should say, 'May you live long' and on meeting a Brāhmaṇa, one should immediately inquire about his well being saying 'kuśala'. On meeting a Kṣatriya, one should say '*anāmaya*' and having met a Vaiśya, one should utter the word '*kṣema*', and having come across a Śūdra, one should inquire about his health with a word '*ārogya*'.[117] This advice to use different modes of expression in the case of persons beloging to different *varṇa*-s throws light on the *varṇa*-consciousness that characterised the people existing in the days of the *purāṇa*-s which again is certainly in agreement with the dictums of the *smārta dharma*[118] or hierarchically graded *varṇa*-society reflected in the Āp.Dh.S.[119]

**Varṇabheda and Marriage Forms-**

*Gar. P.* states eight different forms of marriage out of which the earlier four were meant for the Brāhmaṇas. Gāndharva and Rākṣasa for the kings (*i.e.* for the Kṣatriyas).

---

114. *Pad. P.* III. 51.51[d].
वर्णानां ब्राह्मणो गुरुः।

115. *Ibid*, III.51.51[ab].
सवर्णेन सवर्णानां कार्यमेवाभिवादनम्।

116. *Ibid*, III.51. 49[cd].

117. *Ibid*, III.51.29, Also *Manu. S.* II. 127.
ब्राह्मणं कुशलं पृच्छेत्क्षत्रबन्धुमनामयम्।
वैश्यं क्षेमं समागम्य शूद्रमारोग्यमेव च।

118. *Manu.* S.I. 93.
उत्तमाङ्गोद्भवाज्ज्येष्ठयाद् ब्रह्मणश्चैव धारणात्।
सर्वस्यैवास्य सर्गस्य धर्मतो ब्राह्मणः प्रभुः।।

119. *Āp. Dh. S.* I.1.4.
चत्वारो वर्णा ब्राह्मणक्षत्रियवैश्यशूद्राः। तेषां पूर्वः पूर्वो जन्मतो श्रेयान्।

*Āsura* was meant for the Vaiśya and Śūdra and the last form was regarded as censurable.[120] *Varṇa*-hierarchy, thus, was correlated with the gradation of marriage forms. This correlation also throws light on the fact that social customs differed from *varṇa* to *varṇa*. It is noteworthy that Manu has given exactly the same details.[121]

## Dharma in Distress (Āpaddharma)

Following the dictums of the *smārta dharma*, the authors of the *purāṇa-s* also hold that the persons belonging to different *varṇa-s* should stick to their own respective duties. In fact, they glorify such persons saying that they become sages.[122] According to the author of the *Nār. P.* a person giving up his own duty is looked down upon and is criticised by wise people as a heretic.[123] This is obviously in consonance with the thoughts expressed in the *Manu S.*[124] or in the *Bh. G.*[125] accoding to which a person engaged in carrying out one's own respective duty attains perfection. At the same time, it is interesting to note that the authors of the *purāṇa-s* allowed the persons beloging to specific *varṇa*-s to resort to duties other than their own.

---

120. *Gar. P.* 95.11.
चत्वारो ब्राह्मणास्याद्यास्तथा गान्धर्वराक्षसौ।
राज्ञस्तथासुरो वैश्ये शूद्रे चान्त्यस्तु गर्हितः।।

121. *Manu S.* III.24.
चतुरो ब्राह्मणस्याद्यान्प्रशस्तान्कवयो विदुः।
राक्षसं क्षत्रियस्यैकमासुरं वैश्यशूद्रयोः।।

122. *Nār. P.* I. 24. 30[ab].
सर्वे च मुनितां यांति स्वाश्रमौचितकर्मणा।

123. *Ibid*, I.24.9[cd].
स्ववर्णत्यागेन पाषंडः प्रोच्यते बुधैः।
Also *Ibid*, I.25.2.
यः स्वधर्मं परित्यज्य परधर्मं समाचरेत्।
पाषंडः स हि विज्ञेयः सर्वधर्मबहिष्कृतः।।

124. *Manu. S.* X.97[ab].

125. *Bh. G.* XVIII. 45[ab].

The authors of the *purāṇa*-s allowed the persons belonging to the two upper *varṇa*-s to resort to duties of the *varṇa*-s lower than their own at the time of distress. This is revealed through the statements such as : A Vaiśya can have agriculture as a means of his livelihood, but under no circumstance should a Brāhmaṇa resort to cultivation of land[126] or even in distress, a Brāhmaṇa should never resort to the occupation of a Kṣatriya.[127] The author of the *Gar.P.* regards only that *dvija* as the doer of his duty who carries out his own *varṇa* duty, failing which he will be regarded as 'fallen one' *(patita)* and boycotted by all religious norms.[128] This *purāṇa* expects the members belonging to various *varṇa*-s to shape their behavioural patterns in full agreement with the *smārta* religion.[129] The author of the *Br.P.* also states that a person who abandons his duty as a Brāhmaṇa and resorts to the duty of a Kṣatriya falls down from his *brahminhood* and is born as a Kṣatriya.[130] Such views of the authors of the *purāṇa*-s are in agreement with those stated by *smṛti*-writers who state that a Brāhmaṇa unable to subsist by his peculiar occupations may live according to the law applicable to Kṣatriyas, for the latter is next to him in rank. And if he cannot maintain himself by either, he may adopt a Vaiśya's mode of life employing himself in agrculture and rearing cattle.[131] A Kṣatriya who has fallen into distress may subsist by the means resorted

---

126. *Kūr. P.* II. 25.6.
तेन चावाप्यजीवंस्तु वैश्यवृत्तिः कृषिं व्रजेत्।
न कथञ्चन कुर्वीत ब्राह्मणः कर्म कर्षणम्।।
127. *Ibid*, 25. 5[cd].
तस्मात्क्षात्रेण वर्तेत वर्तते नापदि द्विजः।
128. *Gar. P.* 24.10.
स्वगृह्यचोदितं कर्म द्विजः कुर्वन्कृती भवेत्।
अन्यथा पतितो भूयात्सर्वधर्मबहिष्कृतः।।
129. *Ibid*, 24, 11.
युगधर्मः परिग्राह्यो वर्णैरेतैर्यथोचितम्।
देशाचारास्तथा ग्राह्याः स्मृतिधर्माविरोधतः।।
130. *Br. P.* 115.12.15.
131. *Manu S.* X.81-82.

to by persons belogning to the *varṇa*-s lower than his own but he must never adopt the mode of life prescribed for his betters.[132] Similarly, a Vaiśya, unable to subsist himself by his duties may even maintain himself by a Śūdra's mode of life and a Śūdra, unable to find service with the twice-born may maintain himself by handicrafts.[133]

The Puranic contents throwing light on the *varṇa* differences indicate that there was a wide gulf between the *traivaṇika*-s on the one hand and the Śūdras on the other hand and the *traivarṇikas* were never allowed to carry out the duties of the Śūdras. Thus, the author of the *Nār. P.* has stated that a Brāhmaṇa may resort to the activity of a Kṣatriya or a Kṣatriya may resort to the duties of a Vaiśya but a twice-born one *(dvija)* should never resort to the duties of a Śūdra. If, however, this rule is violated, the *traivarṇika* was looked upon as a fool and was warned that by violating *varṇa* dictums, he will attain to the state of being a Cāṇḍala.[134]

The author of the *Bhāg.P.* states that if a Brāhmaṇa is about to be overpowered by poverty, he can save himself by resorting to the duty of a Vaiśya by selling goods and if he is not released from peril, he may save himself by resorting to the use of weapons but under no circumstance, he should serve a person belonging to a lower *varṇa.* Similarly, Kṣatriyas would maintain themselves by resorting to the practice of the Vaiśyas or by hunting or by the practices of the Brāhmaṇas but they were not allowed to serve the Śūdras. Vaiśyas, however, could do so.[135] Of course these permissions were strictly restricted for the period of calamity or distress, as it is precisely stated that once that period was over, none should desire to maintain oneself with a cursed mode of life.[136] The views

---

132. *Ibid*, X.95.
133. *Ibid*, X. 98-99.
134. *Nār. P.* I. 24. 31, 32[ab].
135. *Bhāg. P.* XI. 17.47-48, 49[ab].
136. *Ibid*, XI. 17.49[cd].
 कृच्छ्रान्मुक्तो न गर्ह्येण वृत्तिं लिप्सेत कर्मणा।।

of the author of the *Viṣ.P.* are are in no way different from others when he also states that in times of distress, a Brāhmaṇa may resort to the duty of a Kṣatriya or that of a Vaiśya, a Kṣatriya may resort to the duty of a Vaiśya, but a Brāhmaṇa and a Kṣatriya should never resort to the duty of a Śūdra.[137] The author of the *Gar.P.* also has allowed a *dvija* to resort to money-lending *(kusīda)*, agriculture *(kṛṣi)* or trade *(vāṇijya)*[138] *Pad. P.* also echoes the same thought, *i.e.* due to the absence of the means of livelihood, Brāhmaṇas may resort to the life-mode of Kṣatriyas[139] and during adverse circumstance, the best of the *dvija*-s, i.e. a Brāhmaṇa may resort to agriculture or trade through an intermediary, but should not give up his activity.[140] On the whole, however, the authors of the *purāṇa*-s expected people not to give-up the conduct that was peculiar to their own *varṇa*. That is why a note of warning is sounded that a person forsaking his duties incurs the wrath of the sun.[141]

## Varṇasaṅkara and Social Structure

Regarding the *varṇa* conventions, Manu specifically stated that the Brāhmaṇa, the Kṣatriya and the Vaiśya *varṇa*-s are the twice-born (*dvija*-s), but the Śūdras have one birth only. He held that only those children that are begotten in the direct order of wedded wives equal in *varṇa* and married as virgins could be considered to be belonging to the same *varṇa* as that of their fathers. However, the sons begotten by twice-born men on wives of the next lower

---

137. *Viṣ. P.* III.8.39.
    क्षात्रं कर्म द्विजस्योक्तं वैश्यं कर्म तथापदि।
    राजन्यस्य च वैश्योक्तं शूद्रकर्म न चैतयोः।।
138. *Gar. P.* I. 313.91.
139. *Pad. P.* I. 70$^{cd}$.
140. *Ibid*, I.16.92$^{cd}$, 93$^{ab}$.
141. *Vām. P.* I. 15.64.
    स्वानि वर्णाश्रमोक्तानि धर्माणीह न हापयेत्।
    यो हापयति तस्यासौ परिकुप्यति भास्करः।।

*varṇa*-s are similar to their fathers but blamed on account of the fault inherent in their mothers.[142] The works on Dharmaśāstra generally show that even though *anuloma* forms of marriage were preferred to those of *pratiloma*, the latter were prevalent in society. On the whole, however, it was believed that the Śūdras belonged to the lowest rung of the ladder. The authors of the *purāṇa*-s continued the same tradition and stated that if the Śūdra males were to have marital relations with the females belonging to the *varṇa*-s higher than their own, especially with the Brāhmaṇa woman, the stability of society will be endangered. Thus, the author of the *Mārk. P.* stated that a Śūdra approaching a Brāhmaṇa woman is born as a worm and one begetting an offspring of her is born as an insect living within wood and a Cāṇḍāla committing the same sin is born as a hog, a small worm or a diver.[143]

The author of the *Gar.P.* has dealt with the concept of mixed castes *(varṇasaṅkara)* at full length. Thus, he has stated that a son begotten by a Brāhmaṇa father on a Kṣatriya mother is called Mūrdhābhiṣikta, while a son by him on a Vaiśya woman is called Ambaṣṭha. A son by a Brāhmaṇa father on a Śūdra woman is called either Niṣāda or Parvata. A son begotten by a Kṣatriya father on a Vaiśya mother is called Māhiṣya and a son born of a Śūdra mother by a Vaiśya father is called Karaṇa. A son born of a Brāhmaṇa mother by a Kṣatriya father is called Sūta, and a son begotten by a Vaiśya father on a Brāhmaṇa woman is called Vaidehaka. A son born of a Brāhmaṇa mother by a Śūdra father is called Cāṇḍāla, the most despicable of all social orders. A son born of a Kṣatriya mother by a Vaiśya father is called Māgadha and a son begotten by a Śūdra father on a Kṣatriya mother is called Kṣetramba. A son begotten by a Śūdra father on a Vaiśya woman is called

142. *Manu S.* X. 5-6.

143. *Mārk P.* 15.16.

तस्यामपत्यमुत्पाद्य काष्ठान्तः कीटको भवेत्।
सूकरः कृमिको मद्गुश्चण्डालश्च प्रजायते ।।

Āyogava. A son born of a Karaṇa mother by a Māhiṣya father is called Rathakāra.[144] These details are more or less similar to those stated by Manu.[145] They indicate that the origin of caste system is an outcome of *varṇasaṅkara.*

The author of the *Agn. P.* also has dealt with the concept of mixed castes *(varṇasaṅkara)* in a more or less the same way and has stated that contrary to the natural order, the son of a Brāhmaṇa woman through a Śūdra is known as Cāṇḍāla, from a Kṣatriya Sūta, and from a Vaiśya Devala. A son born to a Kṣatriya woman and a Śūdra male contrary to the natural order would be known as Pukkasa. A son born to a Kṣatriya woman and a Vaiśya male would be Māgadha and from a Śūdra, Āyogava.[146] The contents of the *Agn. P.* also indicate that though a number of exogamous types of marriages were prevalent in those days, endogamy was considered to be an ideal form of marriage which is clear from the author's statement : There are thousands of *pratiloma* forms of marriage.... Marriage should only be between the members of the same class and should not be with the members of either higher or the lower class.[147] The authors of the *Purāṇa-s* considered *varṇasaṅkara* as a cause of fear[148] and held that improper marriage was to be avoided.[149]

---

144. *Gar. P.* I. 96.1-5.
145. *Manu S.* x. 8-19.
146. *Agn. P.* 151.11-12.
चण्डालो ब्राह्मणीपुत्रः शूद्राच्च प्रतिलोमतः।
सूतस्तु क्षत्रियाज्जातो वैश्याद्वै देवलस्तथा।।
पुष्कसः क्षत्रियापुत्रः शूद्रात्स्यात्प्रतिलोमजः।
मागधः स्यात्तथा वैश्याच्छूद्रादायोगवोऽभवत्।।
147. *Ibid,* 151.13.
वैश्यायां प्रतिलोमेभ्यः प्रतिलोमाः सहस्रशः।
विवाहः सदृशैस्तेषां नोत्तमैर्नाधमैस्तथा।।
148. *Vām. P.* 14.43ab.
संतत्या हानिरश्लाध्या वर्णसंकरतो भयम्।।
149. *Ibid,* 41[cd].
न कर्तव्यं गृहस्थेन वृथा दारपरिग्रहम्।

## The Concept of Pollution and Outcasts

In the course of time, the *varṇa* differences leading to hierarchical gradation of society were intensified, *varṇa*-s were ranked as superior or inferior, people started thinking in terms of purity and impurity and the concept of stratification gave rise to the concept of pollution. Manu regarded the Brāhmaṇa to be far above others and stated, 'Let him not stay with outcasts nor with Cāṇḍalas, nor with Pukkasa-s, nor with fools, nor with overbearing men, nor with low caste men, nor with *antyavasāyins*. Let him not give to a Śūdra an advice, nor the remnants of his meal, nor food offered to the gods. Let him explain the sacred law to such man, nor impose upon him a penance. For, he, who explains the sacred law to a Śūdra or dictates to him a penance will sink together with that man into the hell called *asaṁvṛta*.[150] The contents of the *purāṇa*-s throw light on the fact that even in the Puranic age, the *traivarnika*-s not only considered the Śūdras to be inferior to them, but they also regarded them to be impure.

Thus, author of the *Mārk. P.* states that a person who was in constant contact with them incurred sin and by receiving favours from that outcast, a man would become an insect that lives among stones and by accepting any valuable thing from an outcast, a *dvija* will be born as an ass and a person performing sacrifice for an outcast will become a worm.[151]

## Faults arising out of intermixture of *varṇa*-s (*saṅkaradoṣa*-s)

The author of the *Kūr. P.* has laid down strict rules regarding the avoidance of intermingling of castes. According

---

150. *Manu S.* IV. 79-81.

151. *Mār. P.* 14.83-84.

इमे कृमित्वमापन्ना भक्ष्यन्तेऽत्र पिपीलिकैः।
नीचप्रतिग्रहदानाद्याजनाद्यात्यसेवनात्।।
पाषाणमध्यकीटत्वं नरः सततमश्नुते।
पश्यतो भृत्यवर्गस्य मित्रस्याप्यतिथेस्तथा।।

to him, a Brāhmaṇa should reside in a land naturally frequented by black antelope or inundated by holy and welknown rivers. An excellent Brāhmaṇa should not stay anywhere else except within a *krośa* by holy river. He should not live in the same place with that of fallen castes, Cāṇḍalas, Pukkasa, *Śūdras* and the people of the lowest castes called *antyavasāyin*-s.[152] According to the traditional belief, the Brāhmaṇas due to their inherent holiness were superior to the remaining *varṇa*-s and hence were expected to keep themselves away from the members of the lowest castes and avoid contacts with them. In fact, mingling of castes was regarded as a sin of intermixture. The author of the *Kūr. P.* has enumerated a number of sins of intermixture (*saṅkaradoṣa*-s) such as sharing the same bed, sharing a common seat, sitting in the same row, sharing of the same vessel, partaking of the food in the company of the members of other *varṇa*-s, presiding over sacrifices, teaching, having marriage alliance.[153] In fact it was believed that close association with them would transmit a sin from one man to another and hence a sensible man was expected to avoid intermingling of castes.[154] But such intermingling defects could be avoided by separation of groups with a boundary-line of ashes, or by water, door, pillar or pathway or absence of direct thouch with the person.[155]

---

152. *Kūr. P.* II. 16. 26-27.
अर्धक्रोशान्नदीकूलं वर्जयित्वा द्विजोत्तमः।
नान्यत्र निवसेत्पुण्यां नान्त्यजग्रामसन्निधौ।।
न संवसेच्च पतितैर्न चण्डालेन पुक्कसैः।
न मूर्खैर्नावलिप्तैश्च नान्त्यैर्नान्त्यावसायिभिः।।

153. *Ibid*, II. 16. 28-29.
एकशय्यासनं पंक्तिर्भाण्डपक्कान्नमिश्रणम्।
याजनाध्यापने योनिस्तथैव सहभोजनम्।।
सहाध्यायस्तु दशमः सहयाजनमेव च।
एकादशैते निर्दिष्टा दोषा सङ्करसंज्ञिताः।।

154. *Ibid*, II.16.30.
समीपे वा व्यवस्थानात्पापं संक्रमते नृणाम्।
तस्मात्सर्वप्रयत्नेन संकरं वर्जयेद्बुधः।।

155. *Ibid*, II.16.31-32.

### Food to be accepted-at whose hands ?
### *(bhakṣyābhakṣyavicāraḥ)*

*Kūr. P.* lays down rules regarding at whose hands the food can be accepted and it is stated that a Brāhmaṇa should not eat food offered by a Śūdra... and he who eats it, except in an emergency is born as a Śūdra.[156] A Brāhmaṇa who partakes of the condemned food of a Śūdra for six months becomes Śūdra even when he is alive and after his death, he will become a dog. The *varṇa* of a person in his next birth depends upon the *varṇa* of a person who offered food to him in his previous birth at the time of his death.[157] The author has further stated that cooked food should not be accepted at the hands of actors, dancers, carpenters, smoths... mongers, washerman, the vendors of liquors, minstrels, blacksmiths, impure persons, potters, painters, usurers, outcasts, goldsmiths, hunters, a person who sells *soma* juice and especially a Cāṇḍala.[158] The reference to the persons following various occupations categorized with the outcasts and Cāṇḍalas, who according to the traditional belief contaminated the food and defiled persons belonging to higher *varṇa*-s probably suggests that their status was as low as that of outcasts and Cāṇḍalas.

### Period of Impurity and *Varṇa* - hierarcy

Manu laid down various rules regarding the period for which one was impure after the death of one's nearest

---

156. *Kūr. P.* II 17.1.
नाद्याच्छूद्रस्य विप्रोऽन्नं मोहाद्वा यदि कामतः।
स शूद्रयोनिं व्रजति यस्तु भुङ्क्ते ह्यनापदि।।

157. *Ibid,* II.17.1.2-3.
षण्मासान्यो द्विजो भुङ्क्ते शूद्रस्यान्नं विगर्हितम्।
जीवन्नेव भवेच्छूद्रो मृतः श्वा चाभिजायते।।
ब्राह्मणक्षत्रियविशां शूद्रस्य च मुनीश्वराः।
यस्यान्नेनोदरस्थेन मृतस्तद्योनिमाप्नुयात्।।

158. *Ibid,* II. 17.1.4-6.s

kinsman. He stated that a Brāhmaṇa shall be pure after ten days, a Kṣatriya after twelve, a Vaiśya after fifteen and a Śūdra after a month.[159] The difference in period for purification bespeaks about the difference in the status of those *varṇa*-s and it is wellknown that in this *varṇa*- hierarchy, the Brāhmaṇas were at the top and the Śūdras at the bottom. Following this *smārta* convention, the author of the *Gar. P.* has laid down the same rule.[160]

The fact that the *varṇa*-gradation had its correlation with the concepts of purity and impurity *(śaucāśauca)* is also reflected in the verses of the *Vām.P.* Thus, according to its author, for Brāhmaṇas, impurity lasts for one day and night, for Kṣatriyas three days, for Vaiśyas six nights and for Śūdras twelve days.[161] It is equally noteworthy that according to this author the *Śrāddha* day for persons belonging to these four *varṇa*-s, was not the same, as he has stated that men of all the *varṇa*-s should perform the *śrāddha* ceremony after ten, twelve and fifteen days in due order.[162]

### Varṇadharma in Social Flux

It is interesting to note that besides these details which are mostly in consonance with the traditional works on Dharmaśāstra, there are also other details which indicate that the authors of the *purāṇa*-s were throughly aware of the task that they had to carry out as per the need of the time, that of popularising Hinduism whose existence was threatened by the rise and popularity of Budhism and Jainism. That is why, some contents of the *purāṇa*-s re-

---

159. *Manu S.* V. 83.
160. *Gar. P.* II.39.12.
161. *Vām. P.* 15. 46.
    ब्राह्मणानामहोरात्रं क्षत्रियाणां दिनत्रयम्।
    षड्रात्रं चैव वैश्यानां शूद्राणां द्वादशाह्निकम्।।
162. *Ibid,* 15.47.
    दशद्वादशमासार्ध्दर्मासससंख्यैर्दिनैश्च तैः।
    स्वाः स्वाः कर्मक्रियाः कुर्युः सर्वे वर्णा यथाक्रमम्।।

veal liberal ideology adopted by the authors especially regarding the determining factor of the status of an individual. These contents show, that the status of a individual was not just to be ascribed, it could very well be achieved.

It is indeed remarkable that according to the author of the *Bh.P.* the Vedic study could enable any person to achieve the state of being a Brāhmaṇa. While stressing this point, the author has cited number of examples of demons such as Rāvaṇa and others, Cāṇḍalas, Dāsa-s, Lubdhakas, Ābhīras, Dhīvaras who studied the Vedas and achieved higher status.[163] He has further stated that the Śūdras could enhance their status by performing activities which are usually caried out by the Brāhmṇas, even by using the language which is generally used by the Brāhmaṇas and Kṣatriyas or by being in their company,[164] *i.e.* by 'sanskritizing' themselves, by taking to customs of the Higher *varṇa*-s, by adopting Brahmanic way of life.[165]

Again, it is interesing to know how in order to popularise Hinduism, the authors of the *purāṇa*-s stressed that purity or sanctity depended more on the behaviour *(ācāra)* than just the lores learnt. The state of being a Brāhmaṇa depended on good conduct, excellent activities performed by an individual.[166] As shown earlier, these details are similar to

---

163. *Bh. P.* I.41. 1-2.
वेदाध्ययनमप्येतद्ब्राह्मण्यं प्रतिपद्यते।
विप्रवद्वैश्यराजन्यौ राक्षसा रावणादयः।।
श्वादचांडालदासाश्च लुब्धकाभीरधीवराः।
येऽन्येऽपि वृषलाः केचित्तेऽपि वेदाननधीयते।।

164. *Ibid*, 3.
शूद्रा देशांतरं गत्वा ब्राह्मण्यं क्षत्रियं श्रिताः।
व्यापारकारभाषाद्यैर्विप्रतुल्यैः प्रकल्पितैः।।

165. For more details and explanation of the term 'Sanskritization', see Srinivas M.N., *Religion and Society among the Coorgs of South India*, Oxford, 1952, p. 32. Also, Srinivas M.N. *Caste in Modern India*, Bombay, 1970, p.42ff.

166. *Bh. P.* I.41.9.
अधीत्य चतुरो वेदान्यदि वृत्ते न तिष्ठति।
न तेन क्रियते कार्यं स्त्रीरत्नेनेव षंढकः।।

the contents of *Uśanas* and Hārīta. The overall outlook of this *purāṇa*-s towards the Śuras being liberal, it is specifically stated that the tuft of hair *(śikhā), the sacred syllable* 'om' (praṇava), *ceremonial rites* (*saṁskāra*-s), evening worship *(sandhyā)* girdle *(mekhalā)*, sacred wooden staff *(daṇḍa)*, the skin of a deer *(ajina)*, the sacred thread *(yajñopavīta)* and such other auspicious marks do not characteise Brāhmaṇas.[167] As a matter of fact, there is no difference at all between a Śūdra and a Brāhmaṇa.[168] Even the Śūdras, endowed with merits, with which they can carry out (excellent) deeds *(anuṣṭhānaguṇa*-s*)* are as good as Brāhmaṇas. The difference in the names of these *varṇas, i.e.* 'Brāhmaṇa' and 'Śūdra is neither spiritual nor caused by any external factor.[169] While assuming that excellence could be achieved just through *saṁskāra*-s, it must be borne in mind that persons achieving such excellence could not be as great as Vyāsa.[170] Hence, birth *(jāti)* cannot determine the status of an individual. Brāhmaṇas are in no way superior to persons belonging to any other *varṇa* either internally or externally in respect of experiencing pleasure, having prosperity, order, fearlessness, prowess..., form..., activity, weakness, steadiness, intelligence, the spirit of detachment, religion, valour, the group of three (i.e. *dharma, artha* and

---

167. *Ibid*, I.41.10.
शिखाप्रणवसंस्कारसंध्योपासनमेखलाः।
दंडाजिनपवित्राद्याः शूद्रेष्वपि निरंकुशाः।।

168. *Ibid*, I.41.15[cd].
शूद्रब्राह्मणयोस्तस्मान्नास्ति भेदः कथंचन।

169. *Ibid*, I. 41.29.
सामग्र्यनुष्ठानगुणैः समग्रा यतः संति समा द्विजानाम्।
तस्माद् विशेषो द्विजशूद्रनाम्नो नाध्यात्मिको बाह्यनिमित्तको वा।।

170. *Ibid*, I.41.30.
संस्कारतः सोऽतिशयो यदि स्यात्
सर्वस्य पुंसोस्त्यतिसंस्कृतस्य।
यः संस्कृतो विप्रगणप्रधानो
व्यासादिकैस्तेन न तस्य साम्यम्।।

*kāma*), proficiency etc.[171] According to the conventional belief, white, red, yellow and black colours are assigned to Brahmaṇas Kṣatriyas Vaiśyas and Śūdras respectively. The author of the *Bh.P.*, however, denied it unequivocally by his statement: "The Brāhmaṇas are not as bright as the rays of the moon, the warriors do not have the colour of Kiṁśuka flower, Vaiśyas do not have the colour of turmeric and the colour of Śūdras in not that of coals.[172] If the colour of body, that of hair, the way of walking, experiences of pleasure and pain, similarly blood, skin, flesh, bones and marrow of persons belonging to all the *varṇa*-s are alike, why should they be regarded as different from each other?[173] If the Lord (the Father, the Creator) of all these four *(varṇa-s)* is the same, there is no difference caused by births *(jāti-s)*.[174] The author of *Bh.P.* has cited a number of wellknown examples such as those of Vyāsa, Parāśara, Kaṇāda, Vasiṣṭha, Māṇḍavya, Ṛṣyaśṛṅga, Mandapāla etc. who were highly respectable in society in spite of their low birth and emphasized that likewise even a person born in bad family can be honourable due to knowledge, penance or *saṁskāra*-s.[175]

---

171. *Ibid*, I. 41. 35-37.
तस्मान्न च विभेदोस्ति न बहिर्नांतरात्मनि।
न सुखादौ न चैश्वर्ये नाज्ञायां नाभयेष्वपि।।
न वीर्ये नाकृतौ नाक्षे न व्यापारे न चायुषि।
नांगे पुष्टे न दौर्बल्ये न स्थैर्ये नापि चापले।।
न प्रज्ञायां न वैराग्ये न धर्मे न पराक्रमे।
न त्रिवर्गे न नैपुण्ये न रूपादौ न भेषजे।।

172. *Bh.* P. I.41-41.
न ब्राह्मणाश्चन्द्रमरीचिशुभ्रा शूद्रा न क्षत्रियाः किंशुकपुष्पवर्णाः।।
न चेह वैश्या हरितालतुल्याः शूद्रा न चाङ्गारसमानवर्णाः।।

173. *Ibid*, I.41.42.
पादप्रचारैस्तनुवर्णकेशैः सुखेन दुःखेन च शोणितेन।
त्वङ्मांसमेदोस्थिरसैः समानाश्चतुष्प्रभेदा हि कथं भवंति।।

174. *Ibid*, I.41.45[cd].
एवं प्रजानां हि पितैक एव पित्रैकभावान्न च जातिभेदः।

175. *Ibid*, I. 41.26-31.

### Brāhmaṇadharma and Morality

As seen earlier, by and large, following the traditional features of *smārta dharma,* the authors of the *purāṇa*-s, held the Brāhmaṇas in high esteem. At the same time they excpected them to cherish certain moral principles and to abide by the dictums of virtue, good conduct. In fact, in the eyes of the Puranic authors, these principles consituted the Brāhmaṇadharma. For the same reason, the author of the *Kur.P.* stressed that a Brāhmaṇa should never mentally conceive of that type of love or wealth which is devoid of *dharma.*[176] In the same *purāṇa* it is stated elsewhere that the Brāhmaṇas should not indulge in talk which is not wholesome and which will displease the listener.[177] The author of the *Bh.P.* also has stressed the importance of good conduct of the Brāhmaṇa *varṇa* and stated that the Vedas learnt along with six auxiliary limbs do not purify those who are devoid of virtuous conduct. Really speaking, excellent conduct is the distinguishing feature of the Brāhmaṇas.[178] The same author has elsewhere stated that the Brāhmaṇas that are overpowered by (faults) arising out of speech, mind and body are wretched and they can never purify themselves by performing even hundreds of sacrifies.[179] The author of the *Br.P.* also considers good conduct *(sadācāra)* as the basic determinant of *dvijatva* and states that a *vipra* who has swerved from his own

---

176. *Kūr. P.* II.15.39.
नित्यं धर्मार्थकामेषु युज्येत नियतो द्विजः।
न धर्मवर्जितं काममर्थं वा मनसा स्मरेत्।।

177. *Ibid,* II.16.1.
न हिंस्यात्सर्वभूतानि नानृतं वा वदेत्क्कचित्।
नाहितं नाप्रियं ब्रूयान्न स्तेनः स्यात्कथञ्चन।।

178. *Bh. P.* I. 41.8.
आचारहीनान्न पुनंति वेदा यद्यप्यधीताः सह षड्भिरङ्गैः।
शिल्पं हि वेदाध्ययनं द्विजानां वृत्तं स्मृतं ब्राह्मणलक्षणं तु।।

179. *Ibid,* I. 43.9.
वाङ्मनःकायजैर्दुष्टैर्हता ये ब्राह्मणाधमाः।
ते न शुद्धिं व्रजंतीह अपि यज्ञशतैरपि।।

duty will attain the state of being a Śūdra.[180] Again, in the same *purāṇa*, it is emphaticlly stated that behaviour, i.e. good behaviour is the determining factor of brahminhood *(dvijatva)* and a Brāhmaṇa is Brāhmaṇa worth the name in this world only because of his course of conduct.[181] The outlook of the *purāṇa* regarding the state if being a Brāhmaṇa is so liberal that he believes that even a Śūdra can attain this state by following the right course of conduct. According to this *purāṇa*, brahminhood, as a matter of fact, constitutes the nature of a person which can be common to all.[182] Thus, it is implicitly implied that birth is not the only determining factor of *dvījatva* or brahminhood. No wonder, therefore, if it is further stated that wherever there is attributeless, pure Brahma, Brāhmaṇa exists there.[183] Equally remarkable is the statement made by the author of the *Bh.P.* that there is nothing like *'brāhmaṇajāti'*[184] and the thought expressed in this *purāṇa* is definitely in agreement with the similar thoughts experssed in the *Br.P.* elsewhere, *i.e.* a Śūdra who is endowed with knowledge, general as well as special, who is pure and who is interested in carrying out his duty following the righteous course of conduct obtains the fruit of that activity[185] and a Śūdra, endowed

---

180. *Br. P.* 115.17[cd].
स्वधर्मात्प्रच्युतो विप्रस्ततः शूद्रत्वमाप्नुयात्।

181. *Ibid.* 115.12.57.
कारणानि द्विजत्वस्य वृत्तमेव तु कारणम्।
सर्वोऽयं ब्राह्मणो लोके वृत्तेन तु विधीयते।।

182. *Ibid*, 115. 12.58.
वृत्ते स्थितश्च शूद्रोऽपि ब्राह्मणत्वं च गच्छति।
ब्रह्मस्वभावः सुश्रोणि समः सर्वत्र मे मतः।।

183. *Ibid*, 115.12, 59[ab].
निर्गुणं निर्मलं ब्रह्म यत्र तिष्ठति स द्विजः।

184. *Bh. P.* I.40.31[a].
ब्राह्मण्यजातिर्नृषु नास्ति काचित्।

185. *Br. P.* 115.21.
यस्तु शूद्रः स्वधर्मेण ज्ञानविज्ञानवाञ्छुचिः।
धर्मज्ञो धर्मनिरतः स धर्मफलमश्नुते।।

with the knowledge of the sacred texts is in fact *dvija* himself and a Brāhmaṇa resorting to bad conduct is no longer endowed with the state of being a Brāhmaṇa, on the contrary, he becomes a Śūdra.[186]

The author of the *Bh.P.* has stated the characteristic features of the Brāhmaṇas. According to him, the Brāhmaṇas are those who can distinguish between that which is worthy of being discarded and that which is worth accepting *(heyopādeyatattvajnāḥ)*. They never tread unjust path *(tyaktānyāyapathāgamaḥ)*, they have control over their senses, mind and speech *(jitendriyamanovācaḥ)*, they are (ever) inclined to perform good activities *(sadācāraparāyanāḥ)*,[187] they are endowed with proper vision or outlook *(samyakdarśanasampannāḥ)*, they are possessed of balanced state *(samādhisthāḥ)*, they are free from anger *(hatakrodhāḥ)*, free from attachment *(tyaktasaṅgāḥ)*, devoid of jealousy *(vimatsarāḥ)*,[188] free from sorrow *(viśokāḥ)*, free from pride, calm *(s–āntāḥ)*, they are desirous of accomplishing welfare of all beings *(sarvaprāṇihitaiṣiṇaḥ)*,[189] they are the knowers of truth and the knowers of the Superme Reality *i.e.* Brahma *(satyabrahmavidaḥ)*, they have faith in all the *śāstra*-s.[190] In fact the Lord Brahmā has put restrictions on them. They remain within those limits and hence are called Brāhmaṇāḥ.[191] The author of this *purāṇa* undoubtedly expects the Brāhmaṇas to be endowed with these virtues and thus indicates that birth is not the only criterion determining *brāhmaṇya*.

A deliberate attempt to popularise Hinduism by enhancing the status of Śūdras is also noticed in the *Vār.P.*, where the author mentions a rite of initiation *(upanayana*

---

186. *Ibid*, 115.53[ab], 54[ab].

शूद्रोऽप्यागमसंपन्नः द्विजो भवति संस्कृतः।

स ब्राह्मण्यं समुत्सृज्य शूद्रो भवति तादृशः।

187. *Bh. P.* I.44.1
188. *Ibid*, I.44.3.
189. *Ibid*, I.44.4[ab].
190. *Ibid*, I.44.6[ab].
191. *Ibid*, I.4.7[cd].

*saṁskāra)* for the Śūdras.[192] When all other *purāṇa*-writers follow the footsteps of the authors of Dharmaśāstra, the mention of this rite which was a necessary prerequisite of the right to education is indeed unique. By giving the Śūdras an opportunity to get initiated and by enhancing their status thereby, the author has tried to bring them on par with the *traivarṇika*-s. According to this rite, the altar to be prepared at the time of the initiation rite was to be of eight cubits and the initiate was supposed to have the skin of blue goat, wooden staff and blue cloth.[193] Although other details of this rite differed from the same laid down for the three other *varṇa*-s, it is certainly remarkable that the rite prescribed for the Śūdras was characterised by an utterance of incantation *(mantra)* which was supposed to be a distinguishing privilege of the twice-born ones.

The above observations show that in the Puranic age, the traditional value and belief systems of *smārta dharma* were so deeply rooted in the structure of Indian society that it was rather difficult for the authors of the *purāṇa*-s to deviate from them. Hence most of the *purāṇa*-s have incorporated these principles in their works. Traditional *varṇa* duties did serve some functions in the past. Hereditary occupations provided the members of younger generation to be in close company with the members of old generation, to learn and imbibe the necessary skill which to some extent was inherited by them through their genes. Moreover, when a large number of people continued sticking to the same age-old framework of the fourfold division of society, social life was very well regulated and stabilised. Knowing this full well, the authors of the *purāṇa*-s tried

---

192. *Var. P.* 128.22.

शूद्रस्यापि प्रवक्ष्यामि मद्भक्तस्य वराङ्गने।
यस्तु दीक्षां समासाद्यं मुच्यते सर्वकिल्बिषैः।।

193. *Ibid.* 128.24.

Also Dange S.A., *Encyclopaedia of Puranic Beliefs and Practices*, Vol. III, Delhi, 1987, P. 912.

to continue the same old tradition. Thus, the author of the *Viṣ.P.* states that even by waiting upon dvija-s, a Śūdra conquers his own world and is blessed.[194] At the same time, as already pointed out, the authors of the *purāṇa*-s were fully cognisant of the need of modifications demanded by the passage of time and therefore also wrote against the rigidity of the *varṇa* system. Lawgivers such as Manu, Yājñavalkya, Gautama, Baudhāyana have thoroughly dealt with the principles of elevation and degradation of the caste *(jātyutkarṣa* and *jātyapakarṣa)* that led to the transition of one caste to another.[195] Dange S.S. has pointed out, 'It is quite obvious that the principle of *jātyutkarṣa* (elevation of caste) primarily worked in the context of intercaste marriages, though Yājñavalkya extended its application to the context of adopting other's way of livelihood.[196] The authors of the *purāṇa*-s who were liberal in their ideology talked about the concepts of *varṇotakarṣa* and *varṇāpakarṣa.* As shown earlier, they stressed the importance of the nature of internal qualities of man and the type of work performed by a person. Thus, in the days of the *purāṇa*-s, transitory *varṇa* system was characterised by enough scope to climb up the social ladder and to achieve the status of a higher *varṇa* or as shown earlier to become a member of that *varṇa*-group. Hence this transitory aspect of the Puranic *varṇa*-system was closer to Yājñavalkya's views regarding the *utkarṣa* and *apakarṣa* than to the views expressed by other law-givers.

### The Functional Aspect of the *Varṇa*-system

From sociological point of view, "function" includes

---

194. *Viṣ. P. V.2.23.*
द्विजशुश्रूषया वैष पाकयज्ञाधिकारवान्।
निजान् जयति वे लोकाञ् शूद्रो धन्यतरस्ततः।।

195. For more details see, Dange S.S., "The Principle of Jātyutkarṣa in the Social Evolution", Pub. in *AJYAYA-SRI* (Prof. Ajay Mitra Shastri Fel. Vol II), Delhi, 1989, p. 603.

196. *Ibid*, Dange S.S., p. 606.

use, utility, purpose, motive, intention, aim, consequences[197] and social function refers of observable objective consequences.[198] The standardized social activities of cultural items are functional for the entire social and cultural system.[199] If studied with this view point, the *varṇa*-system in the Puranic age also was a standardized social activity. But, change, being the law of nature, this activity also underwent changes over a period of time and as an objective consequence, it served an important function, viz. that of integrating Hindu society.

197. Merton R.K., "Manifest and Latent Functions", *Social Theory and Social Structure*, New Delhi, 1972, p. 77.

198. *Ibid*, p. 78.

199. *Ibid*, p. 79.

CHAPTER — IV

# ĀŚRAMA SYSTEM IN THE PURĀṆAS

Like *varṇa* system, *āśrama* system also had formed an integral part of ancient Indian religion. At the same time, it was a constituent of the social structure existing in ancient India. Like any other social phenomenon, it too had its roots in the past. Hence, a chronological review of the *āśrama* system existing in ancient India will throw light on its repurcussions on the same existing in the Puranic age.

P. Deussen has derived the term *āśrama* from the root ***śram*** which connotes to exert oneself and has stated that the term means —

(1) a place where austerities are performed, a hermitage and

(2) the action of performing austerities. He has further raised a question as to which of these two meanings is the original.[1]

Although, the original meaning of the term is doubtful, there cannot be even an iota of doubt regarding the fact that the word came to mean 'a stage of life', an order of life. All the works on Dharmaśāstra as also the *purāṇa*-s invariably use the term in this sense.

According to Deussen P., 'at the time when the Indians lived in the Punjab, there was no question either of a brahmanical order of life or of castes and 'āśrama-s. Over a passage of time, however, it became a custom and more and more a law that every young Aryan... belonging to the group of *dvija*-s or *traivarṇika*-s should spend a series of years as a *brahmacārin* in the house of a *guru* or brahmanical teacher. This was the period of learning and vigorous training, the period devoted to the practice of self-denial and mor-

1. P. Deussen, *Encyclopaedia of Religion and Ethics*, Vol. II (4th ed.), ed. by James Hastings, New York, 1958, p. 128.

tification. Later on, this *āśrama* system was extended over the whole life of the Aryans.[2]

While tracing the origin and development of the idea of *āśrama*-s, Kane has rightly pointed out that the word *āśrama* does not occur in the Saṁhitās or Brāhmaṇas. This, however, cannot be stretched to mean that the stages of life denoted by this word in the *sūtra*-s were unknown throughout the Vedic period. Kane has also stated that the word *brahmacārī* occurs in the *Ṛgveda* and the *Atharvaveda* and the term *brahmacarya* is mentioned in the *Tait.S.*, the *Śat.Br.* and other ancient works. Thus, the stage of *brahmacarya*, was wellknown in the past.[3] Kane has further pointed out that from the times of the most ancient *dharmasūtra*-s, the number of *āśrama*-s has been four, though there are slight differences in the nomenclature and in their sequence. Thus, according to his observation, *Āp. Dh. S.* gives the stage of a householder *(gārhasthya)*, the stage in preceptor's family *(ācaryakula)*, the stage of being a *muni (mauna)* and the stage of a forest-dweller *(vānaprasthya)*.[4] Kane has also stated that the *Gautama Dh. S.* enumerates the four *āśrama*-s as *brahmacārī, gṛhastha, bhikṣu* and *vaikhānasa*[5] and Vasiṣṭha names four *āśrama*-s as *brahmacārī, gṛhastha, vānaprastha* and *parivrājaka*.[6]

While disucssing the point of the number of *āśrama*-s referred to in the ancient texts, Kane has rightly quoted a passage from the *Ch.Up.* which refers to the three branches of *dharma*, the first constituted of sacrifice, study and charity which represents the stage of a householder, the second constituted of the performance of *tapas* representing *vānaprastha* and the third that of a *brahmacārī* studying in the house of his teacher[7] and has inferered that

2. *Ibid*, pp. 128-9.
3. Kane P.V., *History of Dharmaśāstra*. Vol. II Pt. I, Pune, 1941, p.
4. *Āp. Dh. S.* 9.21.1.
चत्वार आश्रमा गार्हस्थ्यमाचार्यकुलं मौनं वानप्रस्थ्यमिति।
5. *Gaut. Dh. S.* III.2.
6. *Vas. Dh. S.* VII. 1-2; also *Baudh. Dh. S.* II.6.17.
7. *Ch. Up.* II. 23.1.

probably at the time of the *Ch. Up.*, there was no clear line of demarcation between the *vānaprastha* and the *sannyāsa* and they rather coalesced into each other.[8] Kane has also stated that in the times of the earliest Upaniṣads at least three *āśrama*-s were known and all the four were known by their specific names to Jābālopaniṣad.[9] Deussen also has expressed the same view and stated that in the older Upaniṣads, the theory of *āśrama*-s was in the course of formation and until, the post-Vedic age, the separation between the third and the fourth was not strictly carried out, but the *Muṇḍaka Up.* and *Jābāla Up.* refer to the fourfold number of *āśrama*-s. The distinction between the *vānaprastha* and *sannyāsa* was gradually established.[10]

## Brahmacaryāśrama

### Works on Dharmaśāstra and the Contents of the *Purāṇa*-s —

According to Manu, the state of being a *dvija* was equivalent to the state of being learned and a non-learning *dvija* was as good as Śūdra.[11] He considered *upanayana* or *mauṇjībandhana* as the distinguishing mark of a *dvija* after which the initiate was expected to take an instruction of a vow *(vratādeśa)*.[12] The *purāṇa*-s continued the same tradition. Thus, the author of the *Bhāg.P.* states that on attaining the second birth known as *upanayana*, a man of the twice-born classes should study the Veda at the call of the preceptor.[13] Manu laid down various rules which a *brahmacārin* was supposed to follow, which include stay at the preceptor's residence, control over the sense-organs, daily bath, bestowing offerings to gods, bringing fuel.[14] Manu

8. Kane P. V., *op. cit.*, p. 420ff.
9. Kane P.V., *op.cit.*, p. 422.
10. Deuseen P., *op.cit.*, p. 129.
11. *Manu S.* II.168.
12. *Ibid*, II.170, 173.
13. *Bhāg.* P. X.17.22.
14. *Manu S.* II.170.

expected an initiate to wait upon his preceptor in every respect and laid down a rule that he should fetch a pot full of water, flowers, cowdung, earth and *kuśa* grass as much as required by his teacher and should daily go out to beg food. Manu also stated that an initiate should not beg from the relatives of his teacher or from those of his own or from his mother's blood relations and the houses of persons accused of mortal sin *(abhiśasta-s)*[15] were purely banned for an initiate. Manu considered *brahmacarya* to be a vow and expected *brahmacārin* to subsist on alms and eat the food brought from one person only. According to him the subsistence of a student on begged food was as good as fasting and it was the foremost duty of a student to exert himself on studying and serving his teacher,[16] to behave decently and sit down only when asked by his teacher to do so, eat less, wear less valuable dress than that of his teacher, to get up early and go the rest late. According to Manu, a student should not converse with his teacher while reclining on bed or sitting or eating or standing with an averted face. He should neither listen to the words censuring his teacher, just or false nor himself indulge in the same.[17] He should purify himself by sipping water, worship during both twilights with a concentrated mind at a pure place.[18] Thus, the norms laid down by Manu indicate that since the teacher was responsible for imparting knowledge, teaching lores and was the prime agent responsible for the socialization of the students, he was regarded as an extremely revered and respectable person. Manu considered the stage of *brahmacarya* as a period of rigorous training, hard work and hardships, characterised by simplicity. Hence control over sense-organs was regarded by him as a necessary prerequisite for this training.

Besides these norms that are common to the above-

---

15. *Ibid*, II.183-185.
16. *Ibid*, II.191.
17. *Ibid*, II. 193-195.
18. *Ibid*, II.200,201.

mentioned three works, there are other expectations also, stated in these works. E.g., Yājñavalkya insisted that a student should study when called upon by his preceptor to do so[19] and carry a staff, a deer-skin, sacred thread, girdle. He should secure alms from the house of a Brāhmaṇa of unimpeachable character, offer his adoration to the sacred fire and then having performed *āpoṣaṇa* rite and adored the edibles with permission of his preceptor, he should take meals silently.[20] Even according to Manu, a girdle, a black antelop skin and a staff were the distinguishing marks of a *brahmacārin*[21] and a person devoid of these marks is not a follower of an order and hence is required to perform a penitential rite.[22]

The authors of the *purāṇa*-s continued the same tradition and regarded these marks as symbols of *brahmacarya.* Thus, the *Bhāg.P.* states that on attaining the second birth, a *dvija* should wear deer-skin, sacred thread, carry a staff, a rosary of *rudrākṣa* beads, a water pot and *kuśa* grass and should have matted hair.[24] Following in the footsteps of Manu, and author of the *Bhāg.P.* also considered *brahmacarya* to be a vow and the foremost duty to be observed by *brahmacārin*[25] and therefore laid down expiatory ways for the purification of the Vedic student, stating that if a man observing *brahmacarya* dissipates the virility even involuntarily, he will have to bathe, perform *prāṇāyāma* and repeat the Gāyatrī-*mantra.* He should worship the fire, the sun, his *ācārya,* a cow, a *brāhmaṇa,* elders and gods.[26] Again, in strict consonance with the rules and norms

---

19. *Yāj. S.* I.27.
20. *Ibid,* . 31-33.
21. *Manu S.* .13[a].
22. *Ibid,* I.14[ab].
23. *Bhāg. P.* X.17.22.
24. *Ibid, X.17.23.*
25. *Ibid,* X. 17.25[b].
26. *Ibid,* X. 17.25-26.

laid down by the authors of Dharmaśāstra, the authors of *purāṇa*-s also expected a religious student to beg his food morning and evening and place it before his perceptor along with whatever else he might get and use only that which he is permitted to take.[27] Similarly, like all the authors of works on Dharmaśāstra, the *purāṇa*-s also expected a religious student to revere his teacher, to be either in his company or in his vicinity day and night and to ardently wait upon him and stay at his residence giving up all sorts of enjoyments and observing his vow till the completion of his studies.[28] The accounts of these expectations are so mush in consonance with each other that many a time even the verses presenting these accounts occuring in different *purāṇa*-s are just the same.[29] Again, following the conventions of the Dharmaśāstra tradition, the *purāṇa*-s also expected a religious student to maintain ritual purity, perform *ācamana*, bathe before morning and evening rites, have straightforward conduct, practise *japa*, go on pilgrimage, have restrained mind, body and speech.[30]

According to Vasiṣṭha, a religious student was expected to have controlled speech, eat at specific times, i.e. in the fourth, sixth or eight hour of the day and go out for begging.[31] He was supposed to have matted locks or a tuft of hair on his head. He was expected to follow his teacher while walking, stand while he was seated and remain seated

---

27. *Ibid*, X, 17.28, also. *Vām. P.* 14.5-7, *Mārk. P.* 25. 12-14, *Agn. P.* 153.14, *Nār. P.* I.25.28, *Viṣ.P.* III. 10.12-14, *Kūr. P.* 125.26[ab].
28. *Bhāg. P.* X.17.29-30.
    शुश्रूषमाण आचार्यं सदोपासीत नीचवत्
    यानशय्यासनस्थानैर्नातिदूरे कृताञ्जलिः।
    एवंवृत्तो गुरुकुले वसेद् भोगविवर्जितः।
    विद्या समाप्यते यावद् बिभ्रद् व्रतमखण्डितम्।।
29. *Vām.* P. 14.4-7, *Mārk. P.* 25.11-14.
30. *Bhāg.* P. X.17.34.
31. *Vas. Dh. S.* VII.7-9.
    संयतवाक्। चतुर्थषष्ठाष्टमकालभोजी। भैक्षमाचरेत्।

while he was sleepping.[32] He had to dedicate unto his preceptor all that he had received by begging and was allowed to eat with his permission. He was not supposed to sleep on a cot, brush his teeth. He was supposed to aviod the use of collyrium, oil and umbrella. He was expected to stand during day and sit during night and had to bathe thrice a day.[33] Thus, Vasiṣṭha also considered the first stage of life as an arduous and strenuous one.

The *Viṣṇu S.* also laid down more or less similar norms, some of which are so rigid according to the author that he lays down expiatory ways if one fails to observe them. Thus, the author has attached paramount importance to the order in which a student was expected to learn the texts at the feet of the preceptor and hence has stated that a student attempting to study any other work without studying the Vedas degrades himself and his progeny to the status of a Śūdra,[34] or if a student has failed to live on alms or to perform the *homa*-s for a week in succession in spite of having good health, he will have to practise the vow of *avākīrṇin*[35] or if a student does not get up before the sun-rise, he has to fast for the entire day and night and repeat the Gāyatrī-*mantra*.[36]

Ram Gopal has thrown light on the nature of life and the daily routine of the *brahmacārins* existing in the days

---

32. *Ibid*, VII. 11-12.
जटिलः शिखाजटो वा। गुरुं गच्छन्तमनुगच्छेदासीनश्चेत्तिष्ठेच्छयानश्चेदासीन उपासीत।

33. *Ibid*, VII. 14-16.
सर्वभैक्षं निवेद्य तदनुज्ञया भुञ्जीत। खट्वाशयनदन्तप्रक्षालनाभ्यञ्जनवर्जी तिष्ठेदहनि रात्रवासीत। त्रिःकृत्वोऽभ्युपेयादापः।

34. *Viṣṇu. S.* XXVIII. 36.
यस्त्वनधीतवेदोऽन्यत्र श्रमं कुर्यादसौ ससंतानः शूद्रत्वमेति।

35. *Ibid*, XXVIII. 52.
अकृत्वा भैक्षचरणमसमिध्य च पावकम्।
अनातुरः सप्तरात्रमवाकीर्णिव्रतं चरेत्।।

36. *Ibid*, XXVIII. 53.

of the *sūtra* literature.[37] The details presented by him[38] reveal that the authors of the *sūtra*-s have either laid down more or less the same or similar rules.

According to the deep-rooted norm laid down by the works on Dharmaśāstra, a *brahmacārī* was not supposed to beg from his preceptor or from his own relatives or from his own family members.[39] The same is preserved by the *Kūrma P.*[40] Similarly, Manu's view regarding the utmost reverence that the students were supposed to have for their perceptors is shared by more than one *purāṇa* and while stating it they quote Manu's verse[41] verbatim which states that a student should go away from the place where people indulge in the censure of his preceptor.[42] Likewise, sharing Manu's view regarding the things that a *brahmacārī* should bring to the hermitage for the sake of his preceptor, the *Kūr.* and *Pad. Purāṇas* quote his verse which states 'Let him fetch a pot full of water, flowers, cowdung, earth and *kuśa* grass, as much as may required by his teacher, and daily go to beg food.[43] The *Mat.P.* lays down ideal normative patterns for *brahmacārin*-s such as diligent study when called for the preceptor, getting ahead of the preceptor and going to bed after him, having mild nature, control over passion, steadfastness, absence of fickleness and

---

37. Ram Gopal, *India of Vedic Kalpasūtras*, 2nd end. Delhi, 1983, (1959), pp. 323ff.
38. *Baudh. Dh. S.* I.2.3.19-29; *Āp.Dh. S.* I.2.18-32; *Gaut. Dh. S.* I.2.11-36; *Āśv. Gr. S.I.* 19.9-13; I . 22. 3-6.
39. *Manu S.* II.184.
40. *Kūr. P.* II. 12.57.
ब्रह्मचारी हरेद्भैक्ष्यं गृहेभ्यः प्रयतोऽन्वहम्।
गुरोः कुले न भिक्षेत न ज्ञातिकुलबन्धुषु।।
41. *Manu S.* II. 208.
42. *Kūr. P.* II.146; also *Pad. P.* III.53.6.
गुरोर्यत्र परीवादो निन्दा चापि प्रवर्तते।
कर्णौ तत्र पिधातव्यौ गन्तव्यं वा ततोऽन्यतः।।
43. *Manu S.* II. 182; *Pad. P.* III. 53.19; *Kūr. P.* II. 14.19.
उदकुम्भं सुमनसो गोशकृत्मृत्तिकां कुशान्।
आहरेद्यावदर्थानि भैक्ष्यञ्चाहरहश्चरेत्।।

application to study and assures that a student imbibing them attains his end.[44]

**Taboos —**

Manu laid down various taboos for the initiates such as abstinence from honey, meat, garlands, perfumes, substances used for flavouring food, women, refraining from doing injury to living creatures, anointment of body, use of collyrium, shoes, umbrella, abstinence from sensual desire, anger, covetousness, dancing, singing, playing upon musical instruments, abstinence from gambling, idle disputes, backbiting, lying, abstaining from looking at women and touching them and from hurting others.[45] The fact that the taboos laid down by Yājñavalkya and Hātīta are the same as stated by Manu indicates that self-control was regarded as a means which enabled the *brahmācarin*-s to tread their strenuous path in those days. A comparative study of the norms laid down by different authors of the works on Dharmaśāstra points to the fact that the norms laid down by a certain author at a given period of time tend to be widespread and hence the same norms were laid down by more than one author. It is equally noteworthy that these norms soon formed an integral part of Indian culture and in the course of time got deeply rooted in the structure if Indian society, so much so that even in the Puranic age, the authors of the *purāṇa*-s continued cherishing the same.

For the same reason, even according to the *purāṇa*-s, the Vedic students were supposed to avoid honey, sleep during the day, use of umbrella, anointment, water-sports, entertainments such as dancing, music, musical instruments, use of collyrium, touch of women, contact with the heretics and Śūdras.[46]

---

44. *Mat. P.* XI. 2.

45. *Manu S.* II.183.185; also *Śāṅkh. Gr. S.* III. 9, *Gaut. Dh. S.* I.2.19, 22-23, 25; *Vaikh. Dh.* S. I. 2.6. Also *Baudh. Dh. S.* I. 2.24.
नृत्तगीतवादित्रगन्धमाल्योपानच्छत्रधारणभ्यञ्जनवर्जी ।

46. *Pad. p.* III. 53.8-9, 17-18, 21; also *Kūr. P.* 16[cd], 17, 20; *Nār. P.* I. 25, 30[cd]. 31-33; *Gar. P. I. 94. 19;* Agn. P. *153. 14cd. 15;* Vāy. P. 8.174; *Brah. P.* 14.22-27.

Dakṣa classified *brahmacārin*-s into two categories, *i.e.* a *brāhmaṇa* in a state of pupilage who wishes to pass on to the state of a householder *(upakurvāṇaka)* and one who leads a life of perpetual celibacy *(naiṣṭhika)*.[47] The *purāṇa*-s have retained the same traditional view.[48] Both Manu and Yājñavalkya are in praise for a person who wishes to pass the whole of his life at the residence of his teacher. Manu expects him to serve his teacher diligently till the end of his life and states that a Brāhmaṇa who serves his teacher till the dissolution of his body reaches the eternal mansion of Brahman[49] and according to Yājñavalkya he is not reborn.[50] The *purāṇa*-s, however, do not make any such comparison, nor do they show their inclination towards any one of these two.

Thus, it is clear that the authors of the works on Dharmaśāstra considered *brahmacaryāśrama* as the first preparatory stage which enabled the members of the three upper classes to learn at the feet of their preceptors, to earn their livelihood thereafter and to inculcate excellent values and moral principles during the process of socialisation. Initially, this stage of life was just a way of doing things. The same way was resorted to by the members of the three classes *(traivarṇika-s)* over a period of time and thus it got firmly rooted in the structure if Indian society.

It is, however, noteworthy that the *varṇa* system reflected in the *purāṇa*-s shows a liberal ideology adopted

---

47. *Dakṣa S.* I.8.
द्विविधो ब्रह्मचारी तु स्मृतः शास्त्रे मनीषिभिः।
उपकुर्वाणकस्त्वाद्यो द्वितीयो नैष्ठिकः स्मृतः।।

48. *Agn. P.* 153. 16[cd].
नैष्ठिकं ब्रह्मचारी वा देहान्तं निवसेद्गुरौ।
also *Gar.P.* I. 49[cd].
ब्रह्मचार्य्युपकुर्वाणो नैष्ठिको ब्रह्मतत्परः।

49. *Manu. S.* II. 245, 246.
Here the word used is *upakurvāṇa*, which is the same as *upakurvāṇaka*.

50. *Yāj. S.* I. 50[cd].
ब्रह्मलोकमवाप्नोति न चेह जायते पुनः।

by the authors of the *purāṇa*-s and an attempt on their part to popularise religion by throwing it open to the masses, by allowing the persons belonging to any *varṇa* other than the Brāhmaṇa to enhance their status with their deeds and even by allowing the Śūdras to get themselves initiated. The details regarding the *brahmacaryāśrama*, however, throw light on the same age-old rigid values and beliefs which shaped the behavioural patterns of people existing in those days. The close and mutual association between the *varṇa* and *āśrama* system in ancient India is wellknown. It has already been shown that the *Var.P.* lays down *upanayana saṁskāra* for the Śūdras. This *saṁskāra* marked the beginning of the *brahmacaryāśrama* and hence we expect the authors of the *purāṇa*-s to throw *brahmacaryāśrama* open for all the sections of society including even the Śūdra-s. Such references, however, are conspicuous by their absence in the *purāṇa*-s.

## Gṛhasthāśrama

The life of every *dvija* had to pass through four *āśrama*-s and a *gṛhastha* had to perform the duty of establishing a family and to beget a son.[51] Most of the works on Dharmaśāstra expect a *dvija* to get married and enter into the second stage of life. Manu has laid down four different options regarding the period for which the vow of studying the Vedas under the guidance of a teacher should last. They are — (1) the period of thirty-six years, (2) half that time, (3) a quarter of that time or (4) until the student has perfectly learned the Vedas, and according to Manu, a Vedic student should enter the order of householder threafter.[52] The views of Hārīta and Śaṅkha are in agreement with the fourth view stated by Manu.[53] Gautama's view regarding

51. P. Deussen, *op. cit.*, p. 130.
52. *Manu S.* III.1.
53. *Hārīta S.* IV. 1.
गृहीतवेदाध्ययनः श्रुतशास्त्रार्थतत्त्ववित् ।
असमानार्षगोत्रां हि कन्यां सभ्रातृकां शुभाम् ।।

this matter is liberal, as he allows a disciple to choose and adopt any one of the four orders, i.e. that of a *brahmacārin*, of a *gṛhastha*, *vaikhānasa* (forest-dwelling hermit) and a *bhikṣu* (mendicant).[54]

Yājñavalkya has placed three options before the Vedic students, viz., completion of the Vedic studies, completion of the vow of celibay or the completion of both, the Vedic studies as well as the vow of celibacy and has stated that a *dvija* who has been a celibate should enter the second stage of life.[55]

The *Bhāg.P.* has followed Gautama's view and stated that after having paid the fees to the preceptor and having had a bath *(samāvartana* rite*)*, a Vedic student can enter house or can dwell in a forest or renounce the world.[56] The *Vāmana P.* is in agreement with Manu's fourth view mentioned above and Yājñavalkya's first view on the one hand and the view expressed by Gautama on the other and states that having studied one or two or all the Vedas and having paid the fees to the preceptor, a Vedic student should enter the householder's life with the permission of the teacher, or the stage of a hermit or that of an ascetic.[57] The *Nār.P.*, however, expects the Vedic student to get married after the completion of the period of study.[58] Some other *purāṇa-s* expect him to complete the vow of celibacy and after having paid the fees to the preceptor and taken his permission enter the second stage of life.[59]

The *Kūr. P.* lays down an order in which the members of society should keep on entering the four stages of life

---

54. *Gaut. Dh. S.* I.51-52.
    ब्रह्मचारी गृहस्थो भिक्षुः वैखानसः।
55. *Yāj. S.* I.51-52.
56. *Bhāg.P.* XI. 17, 37[cd], 38[ab].
    गुरवे दक्षिणां दत्त्वा स्नायाद् गुर्वनुमोदितः।
    गृहं वनं वोपविशेत् प्रव्रजेद् वा द्विजोत्तमः।।
57. *Vām. P.* 14, 7-8; also *Mārk P.* 25.15-16.
58. *Nār. P.* I.26.1-2; *Vis. P.* III.9.7.
59. *Brah. P.* 114-29; also *Agn. P.* 153. 16; *Pad. P.* III. 54. 1-2.

one after the other, wherein the stage of celibacy, that of a householder, that of a hermit and that of an ascetic have been stated in succeeding order, but at the same time adopting liberal ideology allows the members of society not to be in strict consonance with the said order especially if it is difficult for them to follow the same.[60] However, it laid down certain restrictions in enjoining the strict rule that the reverse order is never to be followed and thus, a hermit should never become a householder and an ascetic should not resort to the forest.[61]

Regarding the suitable match to be selected by a person who intends to enter the second stage, the authors of works on Dharmaśāstra make distinction between the internal marks and external marks to be taken into consideration while selecting a suitable girl. According to Manu, a *dvija* should marry a girl of the same *varṇa* who is endowed with auspicious physical marks.[62] He regarded wife's beauty as an important factor and stated that if a wife is not radiant with beauty, she will not attract her husband, if she is beautiful, the whole house is bright, otherwise, everything will appear dismal.[63] *Hārīta* has an addition to make in this respect, i.e. a maiden to be selected as a match should come from different family, should have perfect limbs and good character.[64] *Vasiṣṭha* has some more additions to make, *i.e.* she should not belong to the same

---

60. *Kūr.P.* I.3.2[cd].
क्रमेणैवाश्रमाः प्रोक्ताः कारणादन्यथा भवेत्।।

61. *Ibid*, I.3-8.
वानप्रस्थाश्रमं गत्वा न गृहं प्राविशेत् पुनः।
स संन्यासी वनञ्चाथ ब्रह्मचर्यञ्च साधकः।।

62. *Manu S.* III. 4[cd].
उद्वहेत द्विजो भार्यां सवर्णां लक्षणान्विताम्।

63. *Ibid*, III.61[ab], 62.
यदि हि स्त्री न रोचेत पुमांसं न प्रमोदयेत्।
स्त्रियां तु रोचमानायां सर्वं तद्रोचते कुलम्।।
तस्यां त्वरोचमानयां सर्वमेव न रोचते।।

64. *Hārīta S.* IV. 1[ab],2.

family *(asamānārṣeyā)*, she should be a virgin *(aspṛṣṭamaithunā)*, younger than him *(yavīyasī)*[65] and she should not be related to him within five degrees on the mother's side and within seven degrees on the father's side.[66]

The authors of the *sūtra*-s have laid down more or less the same norms. *Mān.Gr. Sūtra* expected a wife to have a brother, to belong to the same *varṇa* but different *pravara*, to be younger than the bridegroom *(yavīyasī)* and *nagnikā* (a girl who has not yet attained womanhood and experienced the emotion of youth or who is about to step into youth).[67] Gobhila,[68] Āpastamba[69] and Gautama[70] expressed the same view regarding the *gotra* and *pravara* of a wife and expected her to be endowed with auspicious marks, to have proportionate limbs,[71] to be intelligent, beautiful, hale and hearty, to have relatives, to have good moral conduct and to be virgin.[72] The author of the *Mānava Gr.S.* has stated wealth and birth in good family as additional details and has indicated the order of preference with regard to these factors wherein consideration of intelligence ranks as the first one and therefore the most important, learning and knowledge as the second one, beauty as the third one

---

65. *Vas. Dh. S.* VIII. 1.
66. *Ibid, VIII.2.*
    पञ्चमीं मातृबन्धुभ्यः सप्तमीं पितृबन्धुभ्यः।
    Also *Var. Gr. S.*
67. For different explanations of the term *nagnikā* see Ram Gopal, *op. cit. p.* 212.
68. *Gobhila Gr. S.* III. 4.3.
    असगोत्रान् दारान् कुर्वीतेति।
69. *Ap. Dh. S.* II. 5.1.
    सगोत्राय दुहितरं न प्रयच्छेत्।
70. *Ghaut. Dh. S.* I.4.2; also *Vār. Gr. S.* X.2.
    असमानप्रवरैर्विवाहः।
71. *Sāṅkh. Fr. S.* I. 4-48, 50.
    या लक्षणसंपन्ना स्यात्। यस्या अभ्यात्मङ्गानि स्युः। आवर्तावपि यस्मै स्यातां प्रदक्षिणौ ग्रीवायाम्।
    also *Gobhila Gr. S. II. 1-2;* Kauṣ. Gr. S. *I. 1.9-10.*
72. *Āp. Gr. S.* I. 3. 8.

and wealth as the last and therefore the least important one.[73]

The authors of the *purāṇa*-s have retained the same views. The *Padma P.* expects a wife to be endowed with good conduct and purity *(sīlaśaucasamanvitā)*, possessed of beauty, devoid of the defects of womb and belonging to a different *gotra*.[74] The *Gar.P.* expects her to be of a different *piṇḍa (asapiṇḍā)*, younger (than the bridegroom — *yavīyasī)*, hale and hearty (free from disease — *arogiṇī*), having a brother *(bhrātṛmatī)*, belonging to different *gotra (asamānārṣagotrajā)*, not related within five degrees on the mother's side and seven degrees on the father's side and belonging to the same *varṇa*.[75] The *Kūr.P.* expects a wife to be befitting (her husband) *(sadṛśā)*, auspicious *(śubhā)*, endowed with beauty and distinguishing marks *(rūpalakṣaṇayūktā)*, devoid of the fault of womb *(yonidoṣavivarjaitā)*, belonging to a different *gotra (asamānārṣagotrajā)*, at the same time possessed of good and pure conduct *(sīlaśaucasamanvitā)*.[76] The *Agni P.* expects the bride and bridegroom to hail from the families of equal status.[77] The *Viṣṇu P.* has given a long list of defects such as having an extra limb, being devoid of one of the limbs, having hair on body, birth in an ignoble family, ...wickedness, ...having a male-like form, harsh voice, ...having her eyebrows close to each other *(saṁhatabhruvam)* having gaps between teeth and having awful face.[78] The above details indicate that even in the Puranic age, the conventional expectations of a wife remained almost the same. It is noteworthy that besides the expectations regarding the nature of *varṇa* and family background, age, *gotra*, *pravara*, the looks of the bride, the composers of the *sūtra*-s con-

73. *Mān. Gr. S.* I. 7.6-7.
74. *Pad. P.* III.54.10.
75. *Gar. P.* I. 95, 2-3, 12; also *Agn. P.* 151.8.
76. *Kūr. P.* II. 15.9-10.
77. *Agn. P.* 151. 13[cd].
    विवाहः सदृशैस्तेषां नोत्तमैर्नाधमैस्तथा ।
78. *Viṣ.P.* III. 10.17-22.

sidered learning and intelligence of the bride as important factors. These points, however, are conspicuous by their absence in the *purāṇa*-s.

While laying down internal marks *(lakṣaṇa*-s*)*, the *Āśvalāyana Gr.S.* also expects a bride to be endowed with (excellent) marks such as intelligence, beauty, good conduct and sound health.[79] At the same time it states that (excellent) marks cannot be easily known.[80] Hence eight different lumps of clay should be placed before the girl while testing her excellent qualities and the girl should be asked to select one of them. According to the author of this *sūtra*, the nature of the lump selected by the girl will throw light on the nature of that girl herself and accordingly the bride should be selected. Thus, e.g., if the girl selects a lump which is made of clay from a field of grass, that will indicate that her progeny will have (ample) food.[81] The *Varāhagṛhyasūtra* also lays down somewhat similar conventional rules for the selection of a bride *(kanyāvaraṇa)*. It states that four types of lumps of clay should be brought to the girl at the time of slecting her as a suitable match, one from a ploughed land, the other one from the land of the sacrificial altar, the third lump should consist of cowdung and the fourth one should be made of clay from the cemetary-ground. If the girl selects the lump made of clay from the cemetary-ground, one should not select her as the suitable match.[82] The authors of the *purāṇa*-s, however, have not laid down internal marks.

---

79. *Āśv. Gr. S.* I. 5.3.

80. *Ibid*, I.5-4.
दुर्विज्ञेयानि लक्षणानि।

81. *Ibid, I. 5.5.6.*
अष्टौ पिण्डान् कृत्वा..... पिण्डानभिमन्त्र्य कुमारीं ब्रूयादेषामेकं गृहाणेति। क्षेत्राच्चेदुभयतः सस्याद् गृह्णीयादन्नवत्यस्याः प्रजा भविष्यतीति विद्यात्।

82. *Varāha Gr. S.* X. 9-10
चतुरो लोष्टानाहरेत् – सीतालोष्टं वेदिलोष्टं गोमयलोष्टं श्मशानलोष्टं च।..... श्मशानलोष्टं चेद् गृह्णीयान्नोपयच्छेत।

## Pañcamahāyajñānuṣṭhāna

The earliest reference ot the *pancamahāyajña*-s is found in the *Śat.Br.*[83] Manu expected the householder to perform five great sacrifices with the sacred fire kindled at the time of wedding and cook his food with the same.[84] According to him, performance of five sacrifices was an essential duty of a householder. Teaching and studying combined together formed a sacrifice offered in honour of Brahman *(brahmayajña)*. The offerings of water and food *(tarpaṇa)* was a sacrifice in honour of manes *(pitṛyajña)*. Daily *homa* was a sacrifice offered to gods *(daivayajña)*, offering of oblations *(bali-s)* was a sacrifice in honour of *bhūta*-s *i.e.* various powers or spirits *(bhūtayajña)* and hospitable reception to guests was a sacrifice in honour of guests *(atithiyajña)*.[85] Even Gautama stated that a householder should study the Vedas and make offerings to gods, manes, guests, animal and the sages.[86] Even during the days of the *sūtra*-s, a householder was supposed to perform five great sacrifices regularly and the *sūtra*-s thoroughly explain the nature of these *mahāyajña*-s.[87] In this respect also, the *purāṇa*-s have continued the same tradition. The *Nār.P.* has named the same *yajña*-s as five great sacrifices[88] and has declared that a person not performing these sacrifices is termed by the wise ones as *brāhmaṇa.*[89] Even the *Vām.P.* has censured

83. *Śat. Br.* XI. 5.6.
84. *Manu S.* III. 67.
85. *Ibid.* III. 70-71.
86. *Gaut. Dh. S.* I.3.
87. *Āśv. Gr. S.* I. 1-4.
ॐ अथातः पञ्चयज्ञाः। देवयज्ञो भूतयज्ञः पितृयज्ञो ब्रह्मयज्ञो मनुष्ययज्ञ इति। तद्यदग्नौ जुहोति स देवयज्ञो यद्बलिं करोति स भूतयज्ञो यत्पितृभ्यो ददाति स नितृयज्ञो यस्त्वाध्यायमधीयते स ब्रह्मयज्ञो यन्मनुष्येभ्यो ददाति स मनुष्ययज्ञ इति। तानेतान्यज्ञानहरहः कुर्वीत।।
88. *Nār. P.* I.27.76; also *Agn. P.* 166. 12; *Kūr. P.* II. 18.100.
89. *Nār. P.* I. 27.75.
पञ्चयज्ञपरित्यागी ब्रह्महेत्युच्यते बुधैः।
कुर्यादहरहस्तस्मात्पञ्चयज्ञान्प्रयत्नतः।।

a person who does not perform *homa* at the proper time, and a person who does not offer oblations to the manes and who does not worship the gods, as a eunuch *(saṇḍha)*.[90] The *Viṣṇu P.* also expected a house-holder to please the maternal grandfather, great grandfather, great great grandfather and offer oblations[91] in honour of gods and sages.[92] The author of the *Sk. P.* also has advised householders to offer oblations in honour of fire, after doing the same in honour of gods, sages and forefathers, after purifying themselves with bath and worship with flowers and unguents.[93]

*Manuṣyayajña or Atithiyajña* — Welcome to and honour of guests were the significant principles of ancient Indian culture. No wonder, therefore, if the *Manu S.*, the pioneering work on Dharmaśāstra expresses the same view and states that he who does not feed his guests lives not, though he breathes.[94] The authors of the *sūtra*-s continue the same tradition.[95] The *purāṇa*-s also highly cherish the same tradition and vehemently criticise a person from whose house, a guest has to go away with shattered hopes[96] and

---

90. *Vām. P.* 15. 28.
न जुहोत्युचिते काले न स्नाति न ददाति च।
पितृदेवार्चनाध्दीनः स षण्ढः परिगीयते।।
91. *Viṣ. P.* III. 11.30.
92. *Ibid,* III. 11. 27.
93. *Sk. P.* III.16. 14-15.
तस्मात्स्नातः शुचिर्भूत्वा देवर्षिपितृतर्पणम्।
यज्ञस्यांते तथैवादभिः काले कुर्यात्समाहितः।।
सुमनोगन्धपुष्पैश्च देवानभ्यर्च्य मानवः।
ततोऽग्नेस्तर्पणं कुर्याददद्याच्चापि बलींस्तथा।।
also *Vām. P.* 14. 35; *Mārk. P.* 25.21[cd].
94. *Manu S.* III.72.
95. *Par. Gr. S.* II. 9.12
यथाऽर्हं भिक्षुकानतिथींश्च संभजेरन्।
*Sāṅkh, Gr. S.* IV. 11. 803.
पितृदेवतातिथिभृत्यानां शेष भुंजीत।
96. *Brah. P.* 114. 36; *Viṣ. P.* III.11.70; *Mār. P.* 26.27.
अतिथिर्यस्य भग्नाशो गृहात्प्रतिनिवर्तते।
स दत्त्वा दुष्कृतं तस्मै पुण्यमादाय गच्छति।।

advise the householders to welcome the guest with *arghya*, *pādodaka* etc.,[97] by offering seat, by washing his feet.[98] The *Kūr.P.* assures that a worshipper of a god and guest attains the highest place.[99] It is needless to say that the thought expressed by the *Mārk.P.* that a person who does not give away anything to guests but eats himself is the devourer of sin *(kilbiṣa)*[100] is exactly in consonance with the same thought expressed by Manu.[101] This thought viz. *kevalāgho bhavati kevalādī* goes back to the Bhikṣusūkta of *RV* (X. 117.6[d]), and has become a proverbial expression. Likewise, in order to stress the importance of *atithipūjana*, the *Viṣṇu P.* has declared that a householder should worship the guest with his entire strength; by doing so, he worships all the deities and Viṣṇu considers the worship of a guest who has come at the evening time to be equivalent to worship of gods.[102] Such a guest is regarded as a person sent or brought by the sun himself.

**Offering of *Gṛhabali* and *Agniparicaraṇa* and *Sandhyāvidhi*-**

Following the dictums laid down by Manu and other authors on Dharmaśāstra, even the *purāṇa*-s expect householders to offer oblations to beings[103] and gods[104] and wait

97. *Sk.P.* III. 26.20.

98. *Viṣ. P.* III.11.59.
अतिथिं तत्र संप्राप्तं पूजयेत्स्वागतादिना।
तथासनप्रदानेन पादप्रक्षालनेन च।।

99. *Kūr. P.* 26.75.
एवं गृहस्थो युक्तात्मा देवतातिथिपूजकः।
वर्तमानः संयंतात्मा याति तत्परमं पदम्।।

100. *Mār. P.* 26. 32.
तस्यादत्त्वा तु यो भुङ्क्ते स्वयं किल्बिषभुङ् नरः।

101. *Manu. S.* III. 118[ab].
अघं स केवलं भुङ्क्ते यः पचत्यात्मकारणात्।

102. *Viṣ. P.* III.11.109.
तस्मात्स्वशक्त्या राजेन्द्र सूर्योढमतिथिं नरः।
पूजयेत्पूजिते तस्मिन्पूजितास्सर्वदेवताः।।

103. *Mār. P.* 26.24.
एवं गृहबलिं कृत्वा गृहे गृहपतिः शुचिः।
अप्यायनाय भूतानां कुर्यादुत्सर्गमादरात्।।

104. *Vis.P.* III. 11.41.

upon fire.[105] The *Kūr.P.* considers the *agnihotra* as the highest *dharma*.[106] Hārīta advised *gṛhastha*-s not to neglect morning and evening adorations and recite the Gāyatrī-*mantra* till the stars make their appearance in the sky.[107] The *purāṇa*-s follow the same conventions and expect a householder to get himself engaged in morning and evening rites.

**Gṛhasthāśrama and Good Behaviour**

The works on Dharmaśāstra do not lay down any norm regarding good behaviour of householders in general. Manu, however, has laid down norms regarding good behaviour unto women. He held women on respect and expected all the male members to treat them with honour, which is clear from the statements — 'Women must be honoured and adorned by their fathers, brothers, husbands and brothers-in-law who desire their own welfare. The families in which female relations live in grief perish.[108]

During the *sūtra* period, the Aryans attached paramount importance to certain fundamental principles of moral and ethical values. Vasiṣṭha regarded good conduct as a great duty binding on all. In Vasiṣṭha's opinion, a householder should suppress his anger and joy.[109] The *purāṇa*-s also have stressed the same point. The *Vām.P.* considers good conduct *(ācāra)* as an important value of a *gṛhastha* and states that a householder should always have good conduct, otherwise, he can neither gain any good in this world, nor

---

105. *Ibid*, III. 12[cd].
 द्विकालं च नमेत्संध्यामग्निमुपचरेत्तथा।
 Also *Bhāg.P.* X. 18.8.
106. *Kūr. P.* II. 24.1.9.
107. *Hārīta S.* IV. 16. 41.
108. *Manu. S.* III.55.
109. *Vas. Dh. S.* VI. 1.

in the yonder world.[110] The *Pad.P.* also declares that a householder is not a *gṛhī* merely because of a house he dwells in, he is so due to the principles of forgiveness, mercy, knowledge of the eternity of the spiritual knowledge.[111] The *Kūr.P.* also expects a householder to be always engaged in his portion of study *(svādhyāyaśīla)*, to speak truth, conquer anger, to be free from the pairs of opposites such as attachment, fear, anger, greed, attraction and to be devoid of jealousy, to be soft-natured, characterised by self-control, engaged in doing work which is beneficial to his parents, ...resorting to the group of three *(trivarga, i.e. dharma, artha* and *kāma)*, ...ever given to forgiving (others) and being merciful.[112]

### *Gṛhasthāśrama*- the Best of all the *Āśrama*-s

Manu held *gṛhastha* in high esteem and considered the *gṛhasthāśrama* to be the best of all the stages of life. Hence, he stated that just as all living beings subsist by the support from air, similarly, all orders subsist due to the support from the householder.[113] The works on Dharmaśāstra regarded the stage of a householder as a social duty as also a sacred bond. This stage was never regarded as just a means of attaining and enjoying sensual pleasures. On the contrary, an entry into this stage was a means with which members of society could free themselves from the three kinds of debts, i.e. the debt unto gods, the debt towards the sages and the debt unto forefathers. The works on Dharmaśāstra attached great importance to the concept of sacrifice. According to them,

---

110. *Vām. P.* 14.15.
गृहस्थेन सदा कार्यमाचारपरिपालनम् ।
न ह्याचारविहीनस्य भद्रमत्र परत्र च ।।
111. *Pad. P.* III. 54.24$^{cd}$. 25.
112. *Kūr. P.* II. 15.21-26; also *Pad. P.* III. 54. 22, 24, 26.
113. *Manu S.* III. 77.

the family life was very will regulated and disciplined through this stage. This was the only stage which enabled the members of society to resort to the three goals of human life, to earn, to enjoy sensual as well as sexual pleasures, to carry out duties leading to monetary gain; without which society could not just survive. It was through this stage that one could lead to the continuity of one's own race and to the perpetuity of human race thereby. Knowing full well that human race will simply die out in the absence of this stage, the authors of the *purāṇa*-s expressed the same ideas through their works. Thus, the *Mārk.P.* states that the *gṛhasthāśrama* is the support of everything, the whole universe is placed in it and hence, it is the best of all.[114] This *purāṇa* is all in praise for this *āśrama* and states that the forefathers, the sages, the beings, the human beings, insects, worms, ,moths, birds and even demons depend on a householder for their livelihood. In fact, one nourishes the entire world by resorting to the state of a householder.[115] The *Mārk.P.* further asserts that a householder nourishes the entire earth and conquers the world he longs for.[116] According to the *Vāyu* and *Brah. purāṇa*-

114. *Mārk. P.* 26.6.
सर्वस्याधारभूतेयं वत्स धेनुस्त्रयीमयी।
यस्यां प्रतिष्ठितं विश्वं विश्वहेतुश्च या मता।।

115. *Ibid*, 26.4, 5.[ab]
पितरो मुनयो देवा भूतानि मनुजास्तथा।
कृमिकीटपतंगाश्च वयांसि पितरोऽसुराः।।
गृहस्थमुपजीवंति ततस्तृप्तिं प्रयांति च।।

116. *Ibid. P.* 26.3.

s, the stage of a householder is stability itself and the source (womb) of the three stages.[117] Even the *Bra.P.* considers this stage as the best of all, as the Vedic students, ascetics and in fact all living beings depend on it.[118] The *Vām.P.* also considers this to be the best of all the stages *(uttama āśrama)*.[119]

These observations indicate that the conventional belief regarding the superiority of the *gṛhasthāśrama* got so firmly rooted in the structure of Indian society that the authors of the *purāṇa*-s could not think in any other way. The same belief shaped their behavioural patterns even in the Puranic age and hence the *purāṇa*-s also considered the *gṛhasthāśrama* as the best of all the *āśrama*-s. At the same time, it is noteworthy that the *varṇa* system in the Puranic age had undergone some amount of change because of the liberal ideology adopted by the authors of the *purāṇa*-s. Such changes were not discernible in the structure of the *āśrama* system. As shown earlier, it was only after the completion of the first stage, *i.e. brahmacaryāśrama*, that people could enter the stage of a householder. If according to the Puranic contents, the commencement of the *brahmacaryāśrama* was marked by the initiation *(upanayana)* ceremony and if only the *traivarṇika*-s could get themselves initiated, does it not imply that the *gṛhasthāśrama* was meant only for the twice-born ones and not for the non-*dvija*-s ? The works on Dharmaśāstra, however, throw light on the fact that the *gṛhasthāśrama* could be pursued by all the sections of society, including the *śūdra*-s. However, the Puranic contents indicate the rigidity of the *āśrama* system.

---

117. *Vāy. P.* 8.172[cd]

   त्रयाणामाश्रमाणां च प्रतिष्ठा योनिरेव च।

   Also *Br. P.* 144.34[cd]

   तेषां गृहस्थः सततं प्रतिष्ठा योनिरुच्यते।

118. *Bra. P.* 114.34[cd]

   भिक्षाभुजश्च येकेचित्परिवाड् ब्रह्मचारिणः।

   तेऽप्यत्र प्रतितिष्ठन्ति गार्हस्थ्यं ते वै परम्।।

119. *Vām. P.* 1. 15.63.

**Vānaprasthāśrama**

(Works on Dharmaśāstra and the Contents of the *Purāṇa*-s)

Regarding the right time for a person to be a forest dweller Manu stated that when a householder has wrinkles on his body, when his hair turns grey and when his sons beget sons, one may resort to a forest, either committing his wife with his sons or accompanied with his wife.[120] According to the *Bhāg.P.* and *Agni Purāṇa* the third part of life *(tṛtiya bhāga)* is the proper time for a person to enter into this *āśrama*[121] and the *Kūr.P.* regards the second part of life as the right time.[122] Though the *Mārk. P.* does not mention any specific part of life as a suitable time, it states that when one sees the decayed state of one's own body, one should resort to the forest for the sake of the purification of one's own self.[123] According to the *Viṣ.P.*, when a householder becomes aged *(vayaḥpariṇataḥ)* and has done whatever is worthy of being done *(kṛtakṛtya)*, he may resort ot the forest.[124]

Following the social norms existing in the days of the works on Dharmaśāstra, the *Bhāg.P.*, and the *Kūr.P.* left the same option for a householder who is desirous of becoming a recluse, *i.e.* either he alone can resort to the forest or he can be accompanied with his wife while doing so.[125]

Manu expected a recluse to wear a skin or a tattered garment, bathe evening and morning, always have his hair in braids and have his nails unclipped. These, according to Manu, are the external signs indicative of renounce-

---

120. *Manu S.* V. 2, 3; also *Hārīta S.* V.2; *Yāj. S.* III.45.

121. *Bhāg. P.* X. 181[d]; *Agn. P.* 160.40.

122. *Kūr. P.* II.21.1[b]; also *Pad. P.* III. 58.1.

123. *Mārk. P.* 25.24; *also* Vām. P. I.15.56.

124. *Viṣ. P.* III. 9.18.
वयः परिणतो राजन्कृतकृत्यो गृहाश्रमी।
पुत्रेषु भार्यां निक्षिप्य वने गच्छेत्सहैव वा।।

125. *Bhāg. P.* XI. 18. 1[ab]; *Viṣ. P.* III. 9. 18[d]; *Gar. P.* I. 102. 1[b]; *Agn. P.* 160. 4[b]; *Nār. P.* I. 27. 85[d]; *Bra. P.* 114.39.

ment of worldly pleasures and simple way of living[126] and even in this respect the *purāṇa*-s followed the same conventions and continued the old tradition. Thus, e.g., the *Bra., Viṣṇu, Bhāg., Nār. purāṇa*-s expect a recluse to have his hair, beard and nails unclipped and have matted hair *(keśaśmaśrujaṭādharaḥ* or *nakhaśmaśrujaṭādharaḥ)*.[127] The *Bhāg.P.* expects him to wear bark garment, grass, leaves and the hide of animals.[128] According to the *Viṣ.P.*, he should have a skin of a black antelope *(kṛṣṇājina)* and an upper garment[130] and the *Pad.P.* expects him to have tattered garment *(cīravāsāḥ)*.[131]

Manu expected a recluse to be always busy in reciting the Vedas, be patient in hardships, ever liberal but never a receiver of gifts and compassionate towards all living creatures and offer *agnihotra* with three sacred fires.[132] According to Manu's expectation, a recluse has to be engaged in performing severe austerities, such as rolling on the ground or standing during day on tip toe, stand or sit down alternately, going at the *savana*-s, at the time of sunrise, at midday and at the time of sunset[133] and increase the rigour of his austerities gradually in the course of the three seasons, in summer, exposing himself to the heat of five fires, during rainy season, live under open sky and in winter be dressed in wet clothes.[134] Hārīta also laid down more or less the same or similar norms for a recluse. According to him, a recluse should remain in the midst of five fires in summer, live without shelter in rainy

126. *Manu S.* VI. 6
127. *Bra. P.* 114.40.
पर्णमूलफलाहारः केशश्मश्रुजटाधरः।
भूमिशायी भवेत्तत्र मुनिः सर्वातिथिद्विजः।।
also *Viṣ. P.* III. 9; *Bhāg. P.* XI. 18. 3; *Nār. P.* I. 27. 86b; *Pad. P.* III 56.6[ab].
128. *Bhāg. P.* XI. 18.2[cd].
129. *Viṣ. P.* III.9.20.
130. *Kūr. P.* II.27.
131. *Pad. P.* III. 58.8.
132. *Manu S.* VI. 8.9.
133. *Ibid*, VI.22.
134. *Ibid*, VI.23.

season, remain in water in the dewy season and stand practising penance[135] and by doing so, he is freed from sins and is purified.[136] Yājñavalkya also expected a recluse to be tolerant and characterised by self-control and stated that he should sleep on an open ground at night and spend the day standing on the forepart of the foot or just standing, sitting, travelling of practising Yoga.[137]

The *purāṇa*-s undoubtedly have cotinued the same tradition. Following the norms laid down by the *Yāj.S.*, the *purāṇa*-s expect a recluse ot stabilise his intellect. The continuity of the earlier tradition is also revealed through the statements such as, a recluse should be free from hatred, the pairs of opposites and fear. Fasting at night, he should simply be intent on meditation upon the Highest Reality. He should have control over his senses and the feeling of anger. He should always observe the vow of celibacy and should never approach his wife.[138] The *Kūr.P.* expects a recluse to avoid censure, falsehood, sleep, laziness, have one fire and no house.[139] These are obviously different signs of self-control. According to this *purāṇa*, the vow of a recluse who enjoys sexual pleasures in the company of his wife is no longer effective.[140] The same *purāṇa* also states that a Brāhmaṇa who having once resorted to the forest indulges in sexual intercourse with his wife, violates his holy vow and has to perform expiatory rite

---

135. *Hārita* S. V.7.
136. *Ibid*, V.10.
137. *Yāj.S.* III. 51.
138. *Pad. P.* II. 58. 15-16.

न द्रुह्येत्सर्वभूतानि निर्द्वंद्वो निर्भयो भवेत्।
न नक्तं किञ्चिदश्नीयाद्रात्रौ ध्यानपरो भवेत्।।
जितेंद्रियो जितक्रोधस्तत्त्वज्ञानविचिंतकः।
ब्रह्मचारी भवेन्नित्यं न पत्नीमपि संश्रयेत्।।

also *Kūr. P.* II. 26.16.

139. *Kūr.p.* II.27.20
140. *Ibid*, II. 23. 17.

यस्तु पत्न्या वनं गत्वा मैथुनं कामतश्चरेत्।
तद्व्रतं तस्य लुप्येत् प्रायश्चित्तीक्रियते प्रस्तुतः।।

and a child born out of such intercorse is untouchable from the point of view of Brāhmaṇas. Neither that child nor his successor has the right to study the Vedas.[141] The *Viṣ.P.* is all in praise for the attitude of tolerance on the part of a recluse and it equates tolerance with penance.[142] The norm of self-control is obviously in consonance with that laid down by Manu, according to whom a person attains to immoratality by control over senses and pairs of opposites.[143] The *Kūr.P.* quotes a verse from the *Manu S.* sharing its view regarding bath to be had at three different times, oblations to be offered to gods and manes and rigorous austerities to be performed by a recluse by standing on one foot and drinking nothing else, but just the rays.[144]

The *Agn.P.* quotes verses from the *Manu S.* while expressing its view regarding the nature of penance to be performed by a recluse.[145] Sharing Manu's view regarding the penances such as Cāndrāyaṇa[146] etc., the *Nār.P.* also lays down the same norm for a recluse.[147] The *Vām.*, *Mārk.* and *Bra. purāṇa*-s expect a recluse to live hard life and state that he should sleep on the ground.[148] Similarly, the *purāṇa*-s have incorporated in them the popular and widespread dictums of the works on Dharmaśāstra such as enkindlement of fire *(agnihotra)*, revising one's own portion of study *(svādhyāya)*, performance of sacrifices *(yajana)*, worship of guests *(atithipūjā)* and worship of gods *(devapūjā)*.[149]

---

141. *Ibid*, II. 27. 17-18.
142. *Viṣ. P.* III. 9. 22[cd].
143. *Manu S. VI. 60.*
144. *Kūr. P.* II. 27.30[ab]; also *Manu. S.* VI. 60.
145. *Agn. P.* 160. 4[cd]. 5[ab].
ग्रीष्मे पञ्चतपा नित्यं वर्षास्वभ्रावकाशिकः।
आर्द्रवासाश्च हेमन्ते तपश्चोग्रं चरेद्वली।।
also *Kūr. P.* II. 27. 29. and *Manu. S.* V. 23.
146. *Manu S.* VI. 9.
147. *Nār. P.* I. 27. 90[cd].
वानप्रस्थः प्रकुर्वीत तपश्चान्द्रायणादिकम्।
148. *Vām. P.* I. 15. 57[c], *Mārk. P.* 25.25[c]. *Bra. P.* 114. 40[c].
149. *Kūr. P.* II. 27. 6[cd], 7[ab].
स्वाध्यायं सर्वदा कुर्यान्नियच्छेद्वाचमन्यतः।
अग्निहोत्रञ्च जुहुयात्पञ्च यज्ञान्समाचरेन्।

Manu has laid down certain norms regarding the eatables to be consumed by a recluse. According to him, a recluse should eat vegetables that grow on dry land or in water, flowers, roots and fruits, products of pure trees and oils extracted from the forest-fruits.[150] He can either eat food cooked on fire or eatable ripened by time or may constantly subsist just on flowers and fruits that have fallen down,[151] but should avoid honey, flesh, mushrooms grown on the ground and vegetables called *bhūstṛṇa*, *śigruka* and *śleṣmātaka*.[152] Likewise, Yājñavalkya also has laid down certain rules regarding the type of food that a recluse can have. According to him, a recluse should have a restricted diet. He should not beg from the retreats of other *vānaprastha*-s. He should eat eight handfuls or he can live on air and proceed towards the north-east quarter till the destruction of his body. Or he can eat fruits ripened at proper time.[153] According to Hārīta, a recluse can take his meals, at the fourth, sixth or eighth period, cooking the food himself or he can sustain himself with air.[154] Thus, the works on Dharmaśāstra regard the food or eatables as the means with which a recluse has to somehow sustain himself. Even in this matter, the *puraṇa*-s expressed similar views. Thus, the *Bhāg.P.* expects a recluse to subsist himself on roots and wild fruits.[155] The *Nār.*[156] and the *Pad.*[157] *purāṇa*-s expect a forestdweller to eat eight morsels of food but abstain from eating anything at night. The *Kūr.P.* expects him to have a limited food or to eat that food at

---

150. *Manu S.* VI. 13.
151. *Ibid*, VI. 17[ab], 21.
152. *Ibid*, VI. 14.
153. *Yāj. S.* III.54-55.
154. *Hārīta* S. V. 6.
155. *Bhāg. P.* X. 18[ab]; also *Nār. P.* I.27.87[a].
156. *Nār. P.* I. 27.88[cd].
अष्टौ ग्रासांश्च भुञ्जीत न कुर्याद्रात्रिभोजनम्।
157. *Pad. P.* III. 58.34[cd]
ग्रामादाहृत्य चाश्नीयादष्टौ ग्रासान् वने वसन्।

night which has been brought during day as per one's own capacity.[158] Regarding the eatables to he avoided, the *purāṇa*-s also expect a forest-dweller to abstain from eating honey, meat of mushrooms grown on earth *(bhauma kavaca)*.[159]

The comparison between the Puranic contents laying down the norms for forest-dwellers and those laid down by the works on Dharmaśāstra indicates that in the days of the works on Dharmaśāstra, the *vānaprathāśrama* was a preparatory stage during which the members of society prepared themselves for the final stage of renouncing all sorts of enjoyments and pleasures and aspired for achieving salvation. These norms got so deeply rooted in the structure of Indian society that they formed a part and parcel of the accepted way of life resorted by the forest-dwellers and the authors of the *purāṇa*-s did not deviate from them.

## Sannyāsāśrama

While dealing with the concepts of *sannyāsa* and *sannyāsāśrama* with historical perspective, one knows that the *sūtra*-s and the *smṛti*-s use the term *yati* to represent the fourth *āśrama* and the meaning of this term when it occurs in the oldest of Vedic texts appears to be different. The *Ṛgveda* does contain this term, but its meaning is doubtful.[160] In ancient India, the goals of existence that people had in their view were four, viz. *dharma, artha, kāma* and *mokṣa*. Salvation (*mokṣa*) was the highest or supreme goal which fascinated people of different spheres of life, the *summum bonum* consisting in non-return *(anāvṛtti)* to the world of pleasures and sorrows.[161]

---

158. *Kūr. P.* II. 27.12[acd].
यताहारो भवेत्तेन
नक्तं चान्यं समाश्नीयाद्दिवा चाहृत्य शक्तितः।
159. *Ibid*, II. 27. 12[cd]; also *Pad. P.* III. 58. 12.
160. Kane P.V., *History of Dharmaśāstra*, Vol. II, Pt. I, Pune, 1941, p. 418.
161. Kane P. V.A., *op.cit.*, p. 422.

According to Kane, as a person grows older, he is convinced of the futility of enjoyments and worldly pleasures and he starts pondering over the problem of the life beyond, prepares himself for the performance of penance and self-abnegation and finally aspires to achieve the supreme goal of *mokṣa*.[162] *Sannyāsāśrama*, thus, was a stage which could lead to the spiritual goal.

On the basis of a comparative study of the Upaniṣadic texts,[163] P. Deussen has inferred that until the post-Vedic age, the separation between the third and the fourth *āśrama*-s was not strictly carried out, but it was gradually established.[164] With the knowledge of the futility of worldly existence, the authors of the law-book held the same view.

Manu, Yājñvalkya, Hārīta and others considered the attainment of liberation as the final goal of human life and accordingly laid down specific norms for the ascetics. By and large, the *purāṇa*-s continued the same tradition.

Manu held that one may direct one's own mind to the attainment of final liberation after having studied the Veda-s, having begotten sons and having offered sacrifices, according to one's own ability and having performed the *iṣṭi* in honour of the Lord of creatures during which the entire property is given away as sacrificial fee.[165] Here, Manu is indirectly hinting at the order of the *āśrama*-s, wherein the stage of the Vedic study in the first stage known as the *brahmacaryāśrama* and the stage of begetting the sons is the second stage known as *gṛhasthāśrama*. As per Yājñavalkya's norms, the stage of a forest-dweller is optional.[166] Though Hārīta does not refer to the time-limit for entering the fourth *āśrama*, he states that a person can enter this

---

162. Kane, P.V., *op.cit.*, p. 423.
163. Comparison of the passages form the *Ch. Up.* 8.15, Ch. Up. 2. 23. 1 with those from the *Śv. Up.* 6. 211, *Kaiv. Up. 24; Muṇḍ. Up.* 2.17.
164. *Comparative analysis presented by* Deussen P., op. cit., *p. 129.*
165. *Manu S.* VI. 36.
166. *Yāj. S.* III. 56.

stage having made gifts unto the departed manes, celestials and human beings and having performed *śrāddha* for the departed manes, after the completion of the *gṛhasthāśrama.*[167] Following Manu's idea that the entire span of life can be divided into four parts and the *sannyāsāśrama* is the fourth one, the *Agn.P.* has stated that one should renounce in the fourth part of one's own life.[168] *Br. P.* also lays down the same norm but adds that a person desirous of entering this stage should be free from jealousy and should give up his affection for his wife, sons and wealth.[169] At the same time, following the advice of the *Jābālopaniṣad,*[170] it states that a person should renounce the world on the day on which he is detached from worldly pleasures.[171]

Manu expected an ascetic to stabilize his intellect, to control his Self[172] and to give up all sorts of attachments and be free all the pairs of opposites and repose in Brahman alone,[173] to be possessed of the true insight into the nature of the world and stated that by the restraint of his senses, ...an ascetic becomes fit for attaining immortal-

---

167. *Hārīta S.* VI. 3-4.
168. *Agn. P.* 161. 1[cd].
    चतुर्थमायुषो भागं प्राप्य सङ्गात्परिव्रजेत् ।।
    also *Kūr. P.* II. 29. 1.
169. *Bra. P.* 114. 46.
    पुत्रद्रव्यकलत्रेषु त्यजेत्स्नेहं द्विजोत्तमाः ।
    चतुर्थमाश्रमस्थानं गच्छेन्निर्धूतमत्सरः ।।
170. *Jābāl.* 4.
    यदहरेव विरजेत् तदहरेव प्रव्रजेत् ।
171. *Agn. P.* 161. 2[ab].
    यदह्नि विरजेध्दीरस्तदह्नि च परिव्रजेत् ।
    also *Bhāg. P.* XI. 18.12; *Nār. P.* I. 27, 91[cd], 92[ab]; *Kūr. P.* II. 29.3; *Pad. P.* III. 59.3.
    यदा मनसि वैराग्यं ज्ञातं सर्वेषु वस्तुषु ।
    तदैव संन्यसेद्विप्रः पतितस्त्त्वन्यथा भवेत् ।।
172. *Manu S.* VI. 59.
173. *Ibid,* VI. 81.

ity.[175] Yājñavalkya's expectation is the same and hence he states that withdrawal of senses, relinquishing attachment and envy are the means with which one can attain immortality.[176] The authors of the *purāṇas* have expressed the same view.

Thus, the *Viṣ.P.* states that an ascetic should be free from all sorts of attachments, should be devoid of all sorts of vices such as desire, anger, pride, attraction.[177] According to the *Bhāg.P.* he should take delight in his own self *(ātmarata)*, He should be the knower of his self *(ātmavān)* and of equal sight *(samadarśanaḥ)* and he should brood over his own Self.[178] The *purāṇa*-s expect an ascetic not to be dejected; even when no eatable is secured, nor to be delighted having gained something.[179] In this respect, 'Let him not feel sorry when he obtains nothing, nor rejoice when he obtains something'.[180] According to Hārīta, an ascetic should meditate on the eternal Brahman.[181] Concentration on Brahman, which being abstract was beyond the reach of the sense-organs of the masses, was definitely not an easy task. Generally, the *purāṇa*-s are seen to be keen on simplifying almost every aspect of religion with a view to attract the masses. In this respect, however, there is no

---

174. *Ibid*, VI. 74.
175. *Ibid*, VI. 60.
176. *Yāj. S.* III. 61; also *Hārīta S.* VI. 22.
177. *Viṣ.P.* III. 9.27
    also *Nār. P.* I. 27. 92$^{cd}$, 93.
    वेदांताभ्यासनिरतः शांतो दांतो जितेंद्रियः ।।
    निर्द्वंद्वो निरहंकारो निर्ममः सर्वदा भवेत् ।
    शमादिगुणसंयुक्तः कामक्रोधविवर्जितः ।।
    also *Bhāg. P.* XI. 18.20; *Mār. P.* 25. 29.
178. *Bhāg. P.* XI. 18. 21$^{cd}$.
179. *Ibid*, XI. 18.33.
    अलब्ध्वा न विषीदेत काले कालेऽशनं क्वचित् ।
    लब्ध्वा न हृष्येद् धृतिमानुभयं दैवतन्त्रितम् ।।
180. *Manu S.* VI. 57.
181. *Hārita S.* VI. 26.

conscious effort on the part of the *purāṇa*-s to change the institutionalized norms of *sannyāsāśrama*. Thus, the *Kūr.P.* expects an ascetic to meditate upon the Highest Reality, which is unchangeable *(avyaya)*, perfect *(paripūrṇa)*, pure *(amala)*, the highest lustre *(param jyotiḥ)*, eternal *(sanātana)*, without any modification *(avikāra)*, without a beginning *(anādi)*, without an end *(ananta)*, the cause of the sentient element in the world *(jagat caitanyakāraṇa)*, attributeless *(nirguṇa)*.[182] It is needless to say that this description is exactly in consonance with that presented by the Upaniṣadic authors. Equally important is the point stated in the *Nār.P.* that an ascetic should get himself engaged in meditating over the sentences from the Upaniṣads *(upaniṣadvākyacintana)*.[183] Similarly, following the fundamental thought expressed in the Upaniṣads *i.e.* 'The knower of Brahman becomes 'Brahman' *'(Brahmavid brahmaiva bhavati)* the author states that through meditation an ascetic can attain the Highest abode *(parmasthānaprāpti)* and the Highest Bliss *(paramānandaprāpti)*.[184] It is equally important to note that elsewhere the *purāṇa*-s simplify religion by replacing the abstract attributeless Highest Principle by concrete god or goddess, thus providing scope for the masses to reach the Ultimate Reality through his or her worship. The authors of the *purāṇa*-s however, have retained the Upaniṣadic nature of the Highest Principle. At the same time, along with the reference to the *paramasthānaprāpti* or *paramānandaprāpti*, there is also a mention of the Highest Abode of Viṣṇu *(Viṣṇuparamapadaprāpti)*.[185]

---

182. *Kūr. P.* I. 27.103.

183. *Nār. P. I. 27. 103.*
पठेदुपनिषद्वाक्यं वेदार्थांश्च चिंतयेत्।
सहस्रशीर्षं देवं च सदा ध्यायेज्जितेंद्रियः।।

184. *Ibid.* I. 27.104.
एवं ध्यानपरो यस्तु यातिर्विगतमत्सरः।
स याति परमानंदं परं ज्योति : सनातनम्।।

185. *Ibid*, I.27. 106.
वर्णाश्रमाचाररताः सर्वपापविवर्जिताः।
नारायणपरा यांति तद्विष्णोः परमं पदम्।।

The *purāṇa*-s have laid down number of behavioural norms for ascetics. E.g. according ot the *Kūr.P.*, an ascetic should always get himself engaged in celibacy *(brahmacarya)* and should stay in forest, should be interested in the lores that enable a person to achieve salvation. He should be free from pride, censure and wickedness, and pairs of opposites such as love and hatred. He should consider a log of wood, stone and gold alike. He should not indulge in killing animals. He should be free from desire.[186] He should neither rejoice in life nor in death and thus should drink water which is purified with a piece of cloth. He should utter words which are purified by truth and should perform activities which are purified with his mind.[188] An ascetic's *dharma* is characterised by ten principles such as courage, forgiveness, control, absence of stealing, purity, control over senses, shame, knowledge, truth and absence of anger.[189] The *Kūr.P.* mentions the same as the vows of an ascetic.[190]

Works on Dharmaśāstra expected an ascetic to maintain himself by begging. They laid down elaborate rules regarding this activity. As per Manu's advice he should go to beg once a day. He should not be eager to obtain a large quantity of alms, as Manu believed that an ascetic who seeks alms eagerly is attached to sensual enjoyments. The *Mārk.P.* lays down the same rule.[191] Regarding the begging time, Manu stated that an ascetic should beg when no smoke ascends the kitchen, when pestle lies motionless, when embers have been extinguished, when people have finished their meal and when the remnants in the dishes have been removed.[192] Yājñavalkya expected him to

186. *Kūr. P.* II. 29.22-23; also *Pad. P.* III. 59. 18.

187. *Agn. P.* 161. 5.

188. *Ibid*, 61. 6$^{cd}$, 7$^{ab}$.

189. *Ibid*, 161. 17.

190. *Kūr. P.* II. 29.27.

191. *Mārk. P.* 25. 30$^{b}$.
भिक्षान्नं चैककालिकम् ।

192. *Manu. S.* VI. 56.

beg alms in the last part of the day in a village where no mendicant had gone before and according to Yājñavlkya the quantity of his food should be just sufficient to keep his body and soul together.[193] The *Viṣ.P.* lays down the same rule and states that an ascetic should visit that house in which fire is extinguished and the member of the family have already eaten their food.[194] The *Nār.P.* goes a step further and states that if an ascetic is interested in nourishing his body out of greed, he should be regarded as a *cāṇḍala*.[195] Even according to the *Kūr.P.*, an ascetic should beg only once and he who is attached to begging clings himself to sensual objects.[196]

The authors of the works on Dharmasśāstra have laid down strict rules to be observed by an ascetic regarding the vessels to be utilised by him while begging. Manu stated that such vessels should not be metalic. A gourd, a wooden bowl, an earthen dish or one made of split, cane are suitable for him.[197] According to Yājñavalkya, such vessels should be made of earth, bamboo or battle-gourd and they should be purified with water.[198] The *purāṇa*-s do not lay down any such rule, but state the places that should be visited by an ascetic while seeking alms. Thus, the *Bhāg.P.* states that he should enter and move about in towns and villages. He should wander on the entire earth endowed with holy regions, rivers, mountains, forests and hermitages[199] and the *Nār.P.* states that he should stay in a village for one night and in a town for three nights.[200]

---

193. *Yāj. S.* III. 59.
194. *Viṣ.P.* III. 9.29.
195. *Nār. P.* I. 27.99
196. *Kūr. P.* II. 30.2.
एककालं चरेद्भैक्षं न प्रसज्येत विस्तरे।
भैक्ष्यप्रसक्तो हि यतिर्विषयेष्वपि सज्जति।।
also *Nār. P.* I. 27. 97.
197. *Manu S.* VI. 53. 54.
198. *Yāj. S.* III. 60.
199. *Bhāg. P.* XI. 18.24.
200. *Nār. P.* I. 27. 95[ab].

According to Yājñavalkya, an ascetic should carry three staffs and water-pitcher *(kamaṇḍalu)*. He should live alone and wander about and resort to a village for begging alms.[201] According to Hārīta, this triple staff should be made of bamboo. It should be of equal knots and should measure four fingers. It should be covered with the down of a black calf and it is meant for physical and mental purification of an ascetic. According to Hārīta, an ascetic can wear a pair of sandals, but should not collect anything else.[202] These according to him, are the marks of his renunciation. Likewise, the *purāṇa*-s also expect an ascetic to be clad in scanty dress or be naked[203] and to have a single staff [204] or wear a single garment or two garments, have a sacred thread and a tuft of hair[205] or should have his head shaved and should wear a saffron-coloured garment.[206]

The *purāṇa*-s have divided ascetics into three categories, *i.e. jñānasannyāsin-s, vedasannyāsins* and *karmasannyāsins*. *Ajñānasannyāsin* was free from all sorts of attachments *(sarvasaṅganirmukta)*, free from the pairs of opposites *(nirdvandva)* and free from fear *(nirbhaya)*. *Avedasannyāsin* was without any possession *(niṣparigṛaha)*, having control over his senses *(vijitendriya)* and an aspirant of salvation *(mumukṣu)* and a *karmasannyāsin* was intent on performong great sacrifice *(mahāyajñaparāyaṇa)* and interested in

201. *Yāj.S.* III. 58.

202. *Hārīta S.* VI. 7.8.

203. *Nār. P.* I. 27. 94[ab].
नग्नो वा जीर्णकौपीनो भवेन्मुंडो यतिर्द्विजः।
also *Kūr. P. II. 29.10.*
जीर्णकौपीनवासाः स्यान्नग्नो वा ध्यानतत्परः।

204. *Agn. P.* 161. 19[ab].
एकदण्डी त्रिदण्डी वा योगी मुच्येत बन्धनात्।
also *Gar. P.* I 103[cd]. *Bhāg, P.* XI. 18.15.

205. *Pad. P.* III. 59. 31[cd].
एकवासा द्विवासा वा शिखी यज्ञोपवीतवान्।

206. *Ibid*, III. 59. 15.
मुण्डी शिखी वाथ भवेत् त्रिदण्डी निष्परिग्रहः।
काषायवासाः सततं ध्यानययोगपरायणः।।

dedicating everything to Brahman *(Brahmārpaṇapara)*. According to the fundamental doctrine of the Upaniṣads, the knowledge of the Highest Reality leads to salvation. Following the same thought, the authors of the *purāṇa*-s considered *jñānasannyāsin* as the best of all the kinds.[207]

As pointed out by Radhakrishnan S., an ascetic practice was a means for disciplining one's own nature and strengthening one's will.[208] The above observations show that it remained so even in the Puranic age. Achievement of salvation *(mokṣa)* was a goal aspired for in ancient India and it remained a frame of aspirational reference "worth striving for" which was a design for group living.[209] Such cultural goals usually shape the standardized practices and turn into institutionalized norms. Even in the Puranic age, the aspiration of people to strive for the achievement of *mokṣa* shaped the behavioural patterns of Indian people and made them stick to the same traditional institutionalized norm.

Recent development in the field of sociology shows that the emphasis has changed from studying how religion affects social behaviour to the analysis of how religious behaviour is socially determined.[210] The *āśrama* system existing in ancient India shows that religious behaviour in pursuit of the achievement of salvation was socially determined.

## Functional Aspect

It is pertinent to note that an attempt on the part of ancient Indians to pursue a common goal served a spe-

---

207. *Kūr. P.* 29.5. 9[ab].
त्रयाणामपि चैतेषां ज्ञानी त्वभ्यधिको मतः।

208. Radhakrishnan S., *Eastern Religions and Western Thought*, Oxford, 1939, p. 48.

209. For more details regarding cultural goals and institutionalized norms, see Merton R.K., *op. cit., pp. 186.-7.*

210. Gablentz's view, q. by Brothers John, *Redings in the Sociology of Religion*, Intrn., Oxford, 1967, P. vii.

cific function. As stated by Gablentz, "Society in striving for salvation becomes integrated in the pursuit of the meaning of salvation. Intergration is the function of salvation."[211] Even O'Dea Thomas and O'Dea Janet Avid have stated, 'Religion in the view of functional theory identifies the individual with his group, supports him in disappointment, attaches him to society's goals... and provides him with elements of identity. It acts to reinforce the unity and stability of society by supporting social control.[212] Interestingly, this view, is corroborated by Merton's statement "...Human society achieves its unity primarily through the possession by its members of certain ultimate values and ends in common."[213]

Thus, a comparative analysis based on the contents of the works on Dharmaśāstra and those of the *purāṇa*-s indicates that over the years there was hardly any change in the structure of Indian society due to the change in the nature of the *āśrama* system. Although the *varṇa* and *āśrama* systems are usually seen to be going hand in hand and both these together forming a unit were the component parts of Indian social structure; changes in the *varṇa* system resulting into its flexible nature did not have any impact on the *āśrama* system existing in the same age. As long as social life of Indian people was stable there was no need to bring about any change. Besides *gṛhasthāśrama*, no other *āśrama* could be entered into and aspired for by the Śūdra-s. Still an attempt to pursue the common goal and the sense of identification with the group with which the members of Indian society were characterised brought about social and cultural unity and integrity among Indian people.

---

211. Ibid, p. 47.

212. O'Dea Thomas and O'Dea Janet Aviad, The Socialogy of Religion, 2nd ed., Inc., 1983, p. 16.

213. Merton R., op. cit., p. 83.

## CHAPTER — V

# PURANIC DEITIES — TRINITY IN THE PURĀṆA-S

Having taken into consideration the nature of the creation-accounts narrated in the main *purāṇa*-s and the *varṇa* and *āśrama* systems reflected therein, it will be worthwhile to focus attention on another aspect of the Puranic religion. It is interesting to note that besides the descriptions of the Highest Cause or the causes in consonance with the various philosophical doctrines or systems such as Vedānta, Sāṅkhya, Vaiśeṣika etc., the *purāṇa*-s also present glorificatory accounts of personified deities in their manifest *(vyakta)* forms and describe the various ways of revering and adoring them. These accounts are historically traceable and when they are thus traced, they also throw light on the fact that Hinduism was in the state of incessant flux.

In fact, as is rightly pointed out by Monier-Williams, Indian religion underwent three stages — (i) Vedism, (ii) Brahmanism which grew out of Vedism and (iii) Hinduism which grew out of Brahmanism and these three principal phases really run into each other.[1]

The choronlogical review of ancient Indian religion indicates that the Ṛgvedic religion was polytheistic in nature. At the same time, it was characterised by monistic trait. Being amazed at the regularity of the course of nature and knowing full well that the ups and downs of their daily life were dependent on various natural phenomena the Ṛgvedic Aryans thought that each natural phenomenon was presided over by some deity or the other. The Ṛgvedic religion was the religion of prayers addressed to these deities. An attempt at adoration of these deities was meant for pleasing them, at the same time for getting their

1. Monier-Williams, Monier, *Brahmanism and Hinduism*, London, 1887, p.2

desire to have happiness, prosperity and good progeny fulfilled. Vying with each other, the Ṛgvedic Aryans showered praises on these deities. Each deity that was the object of adoration was regarded by them as the best and this tendency gave rise to the henotheistic trait of the Ṛgvedic religion. While glorifying them, the Ṛgvedic Aryans visualised them and as per their imagination, the forms of these deities were comparable to human forms. This resulted into the anthropomorphic aspect of the Ṛgvedic religion. The Brāhmaṇa-texts glorified the institutions of sacrifice. Everything else, including even the gods was subordinated to this institution. Complicated ritualistic activities were performed in honour of these gods. As pointed out by Monier Williams, the first aim of sacrifice was to present a simple thank-offering, the second to nourish the gods with the essence of the offered food and strengthen them for their daily duty of maintaining the continuity of the universe with a view to invigorate and gratify them and accomplish the specific desired objects or to attain superhuman powers and thereby the heavenly bliss. In the course of time, people became wearied with sacrifices and sacrificers and the minds of thinking men started taking refuge in speculative and metaphysical investigations.[2] Ritualism was, thus, replaced by spiritualism. In the words of Hopkins, 'In the Vedic hymns man fears the gods and imagines God. In the Brāhmaṇas man subdues the gods and fears God. In the Upaniṣads man ignores the God and becomes the God'[3]. The thinkers of the earlier Upaniṣads aimed at the escape from transmigration and the fear of continued metempsychosis. In later Upaniṣads, however, deities such as Viṣṇu or Śiva are glorified. Following the contents of these later Upaniṣads, the *purāṇa*-s also glorified personified deities such as Brahmā, Viṣṇu or Śiva or the Sun, the Mother Goddess and such other deities.

2. *Ibid*, pp.22-25
3. Hopkins E.W., *Handbook on hte History of Religions*. Vol. I, Boston, 1885 p. 216.

## The Concept of Personification —

Human mind has its own limitations. It is always bound by form and hence can reach embodied beings having forms. It is unable to reach the formless, perceive it and concentrate on it. Forms and symbols are the creations of human mind, still they play an important role of acting as inevitable intermediaries when an attempt to concentrate on the Transcendental Reality is undertaken. It is an initial attempt with which man tries to establish contact with the Supreme Reality. Knowing full well that the concentration on formless is difficult if not painful, man resorts to personified aspect through which he can reach the final goal.[4] The *Bh. Gītā* also has expressed the thought of the need to worship the personified being for the same reason.[5] The order laid down by the *Br. Up.* regarding the process of the creation of the world also corroborates the same. According to this order, this universe was then undifferentiated. It manifested itself only as name and form — It got such and such name and form. So even now the universe is manifested only as name and form-It gets such and such name and form.[6]

## Monier Williams' Theory of Personified and Human Gods —

Monier Williams tried to trace the origin of personified human gods and believed that the origin of such gods was influenced by the preaching of Buddha. According to him, Buddha's religion emphasizing the importance of charity, liberty. equality and fraternity attracted the masses and after his death Buddha was deified by his followers. This marked the beginning of new phase of religion. From that time onwards Indian people felt the need to revere personal and human gods.[7] This tendency further gave rise to deification

4. For more details, see Danielou Alain, *Hindu* polytheism, London, 1946, p. 331.
5. *Bh.Gītā* XII.5[ab].
   क्लेशोऽधिकतरस्तेषामव्यक्तासक्तचेतसाम् ।
6. *Br. Up.* I. 4.7.
7. *Monier William's Monier, op cit, pp.* 41-42

of the heroes of the two epics, the Rāmāyaṇa nad the Mahābhārata. According to Monier Williams, the origin of the concept of Trinity of Gods is to be traced back to this theory.

**The Origin of the Concept of the Trinity of Gods —**

Monier Williams further remarked that the cosmogonic, cosmological and mythological accounts of the Hindu scriptural texts dealing with the topic of the creation of the world throw light on the point that the act of creation necessarily involves two other acts of preservation and dissolution. This threefold activity gave rise to the concept of Trinity according to which Brahmā, Viṣṇu and Śiva are imagined to be the personified gods. Brahmā was the Creator, Viṣṇu the Preserver and Rudra-Śiva was the Dissolver and Reproducer and these gods have connection with the three *guṇa*-s of the Sāṅkhya system of philosophy. When the universal spirit is dominated by *rajoguṇa* (activity), he is Brahmā. When the same is dominated by *sattavaguṇa (goodness)*, he is Viṣṇu and when dominated by *tamoguṇa (indifference)*, he is Śiva. According to the true theory, however, no one of these three can dominate the other two. All are alike and their functions are interchangeable.[8] Monier Williams has further pointed out that one indestructible spirit can only become an object of meditation *(jñeyam)*..... and Brahmā, Viṣṇu and Śiva have only secondary existences in the sense the Supreme Being is to be worshipped through these manifestations.[9]

**Tiele's Views Regarding the Personification of Deities -**

While throwing light on the concept of personification of deities Tiele C.P. has remarked that religion is a mental condition, it is rooted in faith and it begins with emotion. The conceptions of faith, according to him, are the product of imaginations. Religious man, he believed, longs for something more than the vague feelings and abstract philosphical ideas. He desired to see his god either per-

8. *Ibid*, pp.44-45.
9. *Ibid*, pp.45-49

sonally or at least through his mental vision. His faith also rests on experience and it is awakened by what we see, hear and perceive.[10] The concept of religion is in close association with the concept of God and according to Tiele, the more abstract the conception of human imagery becomes, the more difficult it is found by man to seek and maintain communion with an exalted Being. Such communion, Tiele believed, is essential because religious man desires to feel his nearness to God. The worshipper is interested in loving the God with his soul, but as long as the God is above the worshipper, he is not satisfied. Concrete image beheld in his front enables him to strengthen his sentiment of relationship with the deity and this strong bond further leads to the union of the divine and the human.[11] This concrete manifestation represents the finite aspect of religion and according to Caird Edward's psychological discovery, the idea of the Infinite precedes that of the Finite.[12] Finiteness, however, leads to a sense of bond. These are bonds of sins committed knowingly or unknowingly, or of guilt or of limitations of our powers to control death. This awareness of our limitations leads to a sense of littleness or nothingness and man feels an utter need of some solid support for his weakness-support in the form of superhuman, mighty beings through whose help he can aspire to cut off the bonds of finiteness and achieve salvation. Man desires to develop a sentiment of kinship with these personified superhuman beings and this sentiment induces him to practise religious observances such as worship, prayers, offerings made to them which form the consitutents of the physiological aspect of religion. As is rightly pointed out by Tiele, worship has twofold character. Man approaches God and God approaches man, the worshipper invokes superhuman powers and they answer him[13] and prayer is the most general and constant

10. Tiele C.P., *Elements of Science of Religion*, Edinburg, 1889, pp. 14-35
11. *Ibid*, pp. 101-121.
12. Caird Edward, q. by Tiele C.P., *op.cit.*, p. 121.
13. Tiele, *op.cit.*, p. 131

means which enables a pious worshipper to aproach the divinity.[14] Similarly, religious worship in its origin and essence is an attempt to strive after union with God and the escape of the worshipper from the turmoil of everyday life, with its petty cares and great sorrows...[15] Thus, the philosophical aspect of religion aims at the obtainment of the knowledge of the abstract, formless, unmanifest Supreme Reality, whereas the physiological aspect of religion is in pursuit of both, the material as well as non-material objectives and is thus concerned with the pleasure belonging to the world as well as the yonder world. In an attempt to popularise and simplify religion, philosophical aspect was replaced by more simple physiological aspect. Puranic religion is a unique and harmonious blending of both these aspects. As is justly remarked by Baaren, the various elements which make up a religion are not static, not unchangeable and not separated by water-tight compartments, but are contained in dynamic system of relations, influencing each other mutually and at the same time influenced by religion as a whole.[16] While taking a general review of the various theories and approaches regarding religion and relating them with the concept of social change, Baaren has further observed that all such theories and approaches start from the assumption that social and cultural systems strive to maintain an equilibrium and social change is the result of the disturbance of this equilibrium either by external or internal factors. The course of the change according to him is then towards the establishment of a new equilibrium.[17] Puranic religion caused by the changes in society reveals the same trend. As pointed out earlier, both the ritualistic *(karmakāṇḍātmaka)* as well as metaphysical *(jñānakāṇḍātmaka)* aspects of the Vedic religion

14. *Ibid*, pp. 131-133.
15. *Ibid*, p. 152.
16. Baaren Th. P. Van., "Science of Religion as a Systematic Discipline", *Religion, Culture and Methodology*, ed. by Baaren Th. P. Van and Drijvers H.J.W., Edinburg, 1973, p. 47.
17. *Ibid*, p.69.

were beyond the reach of the common people and they were groping in darkness in the absence of some concrete aim in the form of religion *(dharma)*. When the new off-shoots of Hinduism viz. Buddhism and Jainism characterised by simplicity attracted them, social structure was disturbed and the authors of the *Purāṇa*-s advovated simple forms of worship of deities in their manifest and personified *(vyakta)* forms which appealed to the masses. As Chowdhari N.C. points out, ......Hinduism was a pure monotheistic religion whose true doctrines were to be found in the Upaniṣads, but after being swamped by Buddhism, it reappeared in the 7th or 8th c. A.D. in a grossly polytheistic form.[18] Polytheistic Puranic religion replaces the worship of the formless, attributeless *(nirguṇopāsanā)* by simple worship of the manifest personified divinity *(saguṇopāsanā)* without, however, ignoring the importance of the former one. As a matter of fact, Puranic religion is an outcome of the blending of both these types of worship according to which the immeasurable, formless Highest Lord makes his appearance (in this world) for the sake of the spiritual wellbeing of the people.[19] The *Purāṇa*-s laid down simplest means such as faith *(śraddhā)* or devotion (bhakti) and state that the activities faithfully performed lead to the fulfilment of longings. Faith leads to every accomplishment and the God (Hari) is pleased with faith.[20] Similarly, devotion is regarded as the easiest but the highest means of pleasing Hari who is not pleased even by gifts, penances or sacrifices which involve enormous amount of expenditure on sacrificial fees.[21]

---

18. Choudhari N.C., *Hinduism*, New Delhi, 1979, p. 27
19. *Bhāg.P.* X. 26.14.
    नृणां निःश्रेयसार्थाय व्यक्तिर्भगवतो नृप।
    अव्ययस्याप्रमेयस्य निर्गुणस्य गुणात्मनः।।
20. *Nār, P.* I.1.
    श्रद्धापूर्वाः सर्वधर्मा मनोरथफलप्रदाः।
    श्रद्धया साध्यते सर्वं श्रद्धया तुष्यते हरिः।।
21. *Ibid*, I.7.
    न दानैर्न तपोभिः यज्ञैर्वाबहुदक्षिणैः।
    भक्तिहीनैर्मुनिश्रेष्ठ तुष्यते भगवान् हरिः।

**The Doctrine of Trinity in the *Purāṇa*-s**

Although Ṛgvedic religion was polytheistic in nature, the Ṛgvedic Aryans were aware of the concept of unity in diversity which is reflected in the verse — In reality the existence is only one, but the wise men call it as many.[22] The fundamental doctrine of the early Upaniṣads was definitely monistic in nature, according to which the existence only was there in the beginning, one without a second[23] or where there is duality one sees another, smells another... hears another, thinks another, touches another.[24] However, this Sat being abstract in nature was beyond the reach of the vast majority of people and hence the authors of the *Purāṇa*-s imagined the existence of number of gods and allowed the devotees to choose any one of them. The threefold activity of the creation, maintenance and dissolution of the world was still important in the eyes of the authors of the *Purāṇa*-s, but instead of regarding Brahman as responsible for this threefold activity, they considered Brahmā, Viṣṇu and Śiva as responsible for this activity, which gave rise to the origin and development of the concept of the trinity of Gods. Out of these three gods the origin of Viṣṇu and Śiva can be traced back to the Vedic deities. It is interesting to know the change in their nature over the years. Scholars like Bhandarkar R.G., Monier-Williams M., Baneielou Alain tried to trace the origin and development of these deities which gave rise to Śaivism and Vaiṣṇavism. According to Monier Williams, Śaivism is setting aside of the truine equality of Brahmā, Viṣṇu and Śiva, the merging of the former two gods in the god Śiva and at the same time exaltation of Śiva..... to the position of a Supreme Being, infinite, eternal and indestructible. Śaivism means exclusive devotion to the personal god Śiva, who possesses bodily form. Rudra was Śiva's coresponding deity in the Ṛgvedic

---

22. *RV.* I. 164.46[c].
23. *Ch. Up.* VI. 2.
    सदेव सोम्य इदमग्र आसीदेकमेवाद्वितीयम्।
24. *Br. Up.* IV. 5.15.

age. Rudra of the Ṛgveda did have a wellmarked personality, but in the Ṛgvedic period he was known for his dreadful form and was propitiated for his favour. In the course of time, however, his terrific, ungodlike character was kept in the background and his epithet 'auspicious one', (Śiva) became significant.[25] Bhandarkar R.G. also has traced the origin of the god Śiva and observed that in *RV.* VII. 46.3 Rudra is said to be discharging shafts which run about the heaven and the earth. The fact that Rudra is prayed not to afflict children with disease[26] and to keep everybody in the village free form illness[27] indicated that Rudra was believed to cause diseases. But besides these references, the *Ṛgveda* also contains a few others where Rudra is spoken of as possessing healing power or remedies[28] or the best physician of physicians[29]or the protector of cattle.[30] The Atharvaveda reflects still more later phase of the development of the concept of Rudra where he is elevated to a higher rank and imagined to be the controller of the stars and the moon.[31] The *gṛhyasūtra*-s once again describe him as a terrible god who is to be appeased but who had sway over regions away from home, over fields, cemetaries, mountains and rivers and according to Bhandarkar, Śiva's omnipresent supreme nature is to be traced back to such references. Bhandarkar holds that in Rudra-Śaivism the sentiment of fear is at the bottom.[32] Thus, Śiva of later times is to be traced back to Rudra of the Vedic times. In the Ṛgveda he is praised as the lord of songs, the lord of sacrifices, the best and most bountiful of gods who grants

---

25. For more details see Monier Williams M., *Brahmanism and Hinduism*, London, 1887, pp.73-77.
26. *RV.* VII. 46.2.
27. *Ibid*, I. 114.1.
28. *Ibid*, I. 43.4.
29. *Ibid*, II. 33.4.
30. *Ibid*, I. 114.9.
31. *AV.* XIII. 4.28
32. Bhandarkar R.G., *Vaiṣṇavism, Śaivism and Minor Religions Systems*, Bombay, 1913, pp. 102-106.

prosperity and welfare to quadrupeds and biped. He is the lord of nourishment who drives away sin, but is terrible as a wild beast, is destructive and fierce.[33] Destruction is always fearful and hence the *Atharvaveda* describes him as "the god that kills"[34] or "He is death, the demon... the cause of fears."[35] The *Muṇḍaka Up.* describes him as the inner Self of all beings and fire, the sun, the moon, the directions, the earth are imagined to be his limbs.[36] The *Mahābhārata* describes him as the beginning of the worlds or people, the destroyer and identifies him with time.[37]

## Śiva in the *Purāṇa*-s —

Keeping in mind this historical background, it will now be worthwhile to focus attention on Śiva in the *Purāṇa*-s. According to the *Liṅga P.*, Kṣetrajña is Puruṣa, Pradhāna is Prakṛti and the entire collection of modifications *(Vikārajāta)* is the manifest *(vyakta)* form of Prakṛti. Kāla is one more manifestation *(pariṇāma)* of the Manifest Prakṛti.[38] The author further states that some preceptors call Hiraṇyagarbha Puruṣa (and) manifest Pradhāna together as the Lord Śiva[39]. Whereas some others call that (Puruṣa) as the unmanifest form of Śiva and Pradhāna is imagined by them as the form of that Highest Lord.[40] The author further glorifies Śiva as the innermost soul of all beings and states that

---

33. *RV.* I.114.1, II.33.11.
34. *AV*. I.19.3-
35. *Ibid*, I.XVI. 6.26.
36. *Munnḍaka Up.* II.1.4.
37. *Mbh. Anu.* 45.313.
    आदिस्त्वमसि लोकानां संहर्ता काल एव च।
38. *LIn.P.* II.16.3-5.
39. *Ibid*, II.16.6.
    हिरण्यगर्भं पुरुषं प्रधानं व्यक्तरूपिणम्।
    कथयंति शिवं केचिदाचार्याः परमेश्वरम्।।
40. *Ibid*, II. 16.12
    सूत्राव्याकृतरूपं तं शिवं शंसंति केचन।
    अव्याकृतं प्रधानं हि तद्रूपं परमेष्ठिनः।।

being superior to all the beings he is termed as the highest.[41] He is the Highest Self, auspicious one, the Highest Lord who brings about the welfare.[42] The same author considers Śiva to have arisen out of unmanifest and still according to him, he is the ultimate cause of the world.[43] Again, in the same *Purāṇa*, Viṣṇu is described as bowing down before Śiva and as singing the praises of the latter by utilising various epithets such as pervading *(vyāpin)*, wind *(vāyu)*, having wind's speed *(vāyuvega)*, the support of lustre *(tejasām bhartā)*, water *(jala)* having speech, touch, taste and odour as his forms *(śabdasparśarasagandhasvarūpa)*, indestructible *(ananta)*, eternal *(śāśvata)*, the best *(variṣṭha)*, the embroyo of water (vārigarbha) and a *Yogin*,[44] insentient *(acetana)*, formless *(arūpa)* at the same time endowed with excellent form *(surūpa)* and the cause of mundane existence.[46] He is said to be having salvation as his nature *(mokṣarūpa)* at the same time salvation itself *(mokṣa)*[47], having two contradictory qualities—unmanifest *(avyakta)* at the same time manifest in the form of half man-half woman *(ardhanārīśarīra)*. Though named as Śiva, the author considers him to be on par with the Supreme principle (Brahma) of the Vedānta system. Again, in consonance with the Vedānta philosophy, he is described as beginningless, middleless and endless *(anādimadhyāntahīna)* or endowed with pure lustre, great lustre,[49] the intelligent Lord of both Pradhāna and Puruṣa having the nature of

41. *Ibid*, II. 16.15.
सर्वेषामपि भूतानामन्तर्यामी शिवः स्मृतः।
सर्वेषामपि भूतानां परत्वात्पर उच्यते।।
42. *Ibid*, II.17.3[cd].
43. *Ibid*, II.17.3[ab].
अव्यक्तादभवत्स्थाणुः शिवः परमकारणम्।
44. *Ibid*, II.18.3-10.
45. *Ibid*, II.18.12
46. *Ibid*, II.18.22
47. *Ibid*, II.18.23
48. *Ibid*, II.26.83[a].
49. *Ibid*, II.26.84[a].

the all-pervading sky[50], devoid of modification, having the essence of Vedānta as his nature *(vedāntasārasvrūpa)* and having time as his nature *(Kālarūpa)*.[51] It is indeed remarkable that this unmanifest aspect is beautifully synthesised with the manifest and personified one to simplify worship and appeal to the masses. For the same reason, in the succeeding verses of the same portion, he is described as having thousand hands and feet, having the sun and the moon as his eyes, wielding *pinäka*, wearing *kṛtti* garment, holding trident, wearing snake as his sacred thread and having voice which is comparable to the rumbling of clouds.[52]

The *Kūrma P.* also describes the personified form of the Lord Śiva and states that he is possessed of thousand beads *(sahasraśiras)*, having thousand feet*(sahasracaraṇākṛtiḥ)*, thousand arms *(sahasrabāhuḥ)*, having matted hair *(jatilaḥ)* having crescent of moon (half of the moon) on his head,[53] wearing tiger's skin, having three eyes,[54] having big eyes,[55] having an ugly form due to the third eye on his forehead *(virūpākṣaḥ)*.[56] Synthesising once again this manifest aspect with the unmanifest one, the author further describes him to be the support of all powers, the lord of the lord of *yoga*, enveloped with *yogic māyā* and remaining in the hearts of the *yogins*[57]. The *Liṅga P.* describes his attributeless *(nirguṇa)* nature and states that Śiva is signless *(sexless)*, without colour, taste

50. *Ibid*, I.26.85.
51. *Ibid*, I.26.87.
52. *Ibid*, I.26.89[cd], 90.
    सहस्रहस्तचरणः सूर्यसोमाग्निलोचनः ।।
    पिनाकपाणिर्भगवान् कृत्तिवासास्त्रिशूलधृक् ।
    व्यालयज्ञोपवीतश्च मेघदुन्दुभिनिःस्वनः ।
53. *Ibid*, II.5.8.
54. *Ibid*, II.5.9.
55. *Ibid*, II.5.13.
56. *Ibid*, II. 5.14.
57. *Ibid*, II.5.16.
    आधारं सर्वशक्तीनां महायोगेश्वरेश्वरम् ।
    योगिनां हृदि तिष्ठन्तं योगमायासमावृतम् ।।

or smell, beyond word and touch, devoid of quality, changeless, motionless[58] but in the same *purāṇa* elsewhere, Śiva's *linga* is identified with the Pradhāna as it is envisaged by the Sāṅkhyavādins and Puruṣa is said to be the possesser of that *liṅga*[59].

**Liṅga-worship —**

Śiva-liṅga worship is one of the distinct features of the Puranic religion. The word *linga* means "sign", the distinctive feature which symbolically represents Śiva. From the metaphysical point of view, Śiva is the same as the Supreme Reality (Brahman), which is said to be without any form as also distinguishing mark. For the same reason, even Śiva's characteristic mark is described as signless, without colour, taste or smell, beyond word and touch, without quality, changeless, motionless[60]. Just as popularisation of the worship of the personified deity was an atempt to simplify religion which can be pursued by the masses, simiarly an attempt to place before the masses a symbolical sign of that personified god was also meant for enabling the vast majority of people to approach the god. The *Liṇga* P. aptly throws light on the nature and significance of the *liṇga* when it states that from the signless comes forth the sign of the universe. This sign is the object of word and touch, of smell, colour and taste. It is the universal womb of the elements, subtle as well as gross[61]. The *Liṅga P.* elsewhere states that at the root is

---

58. *Ibid*, I.3.2[cd], 3[ab].
गन्धवर्णरसैर्हीनं शब्दस्पर्शादिवर्जितम् ।।
अगुणं ध्रुवमक्षय्यमलिङ्गं शिवलक्षणम् ।

59. *Ibid*, I.17.5[cd].
प्रधानं लिङ्गमारव्यातं लिंगी च परमेश्वरः ।

60. *Lin, P.* I.3.2[cd].3[ab].

61. *Ibid*, I. 3.3.4[cd].
विग्रहो जगतां लिङ्गमलिङ्गादभवत्स्वयम् ।
गन्धवर्णरसैर्युक्तं शब्दस्पर्शादिलक्षणम् ।।
जगद्योनिमहाभूतं स्थूलं सूक्ष्मं द्विजोत्तमाः ।

Brahmā, in the middle Viṣṇu, the Lord of the three worlds, above is the fierce Rudra, the great god, the eternal giver of peace, whose name is the sacred syllable AUM. The alter of the *liṅga* is the great goddess, the *liṅga* is the true divinity.[62] The author of the *Skanda P.* throws light on the symbolic nature of the *liṅga* stating that the Lord *Śiva* has pervaded all the three worlds through his *liṅga* form,[63] is the lord of the world, the creator of the creators of the world, the maker and the annihilator of the world.[64] The Lord Śiva is the great lord in the form of *liṅga*.[65] *The Liṅga* is said to be arising, getting sustained and getting dissolved. It is *liṅga* worth the name as it gets merged.[66] The significance of the term *liṅga* is also explained on the basis of the fanciful mythological account wherein it is stated that the male organ, *(liṅga)* of the Lord Śiva fell on the ground due to the curse of the sages. When it reached the earth, it started growing with tremendous speed, encompassed seven nether worlds, the entire earth and thereafter covered the intermediary region, the heavens after which there was no wind *(vāyu)*, no sky *(ākāśa)*, *ahaṁkāra*, *mahat*, unmanifest *(avyakta)*, time *(Kāla)*, great primordial matter *(mahāprakṛti)* none of these had separate existence of its own. Everything got dissolved in it from that very moment.[67] Due to that act of dissolving *(layanāt)*, the wise

---

62. *Ibid*, I.73.19-20.
63. *Ska.P.* I.1.7.4[ab].
त्वया लिंगस्वरूपेण व्याप्तमेतज्जगत्त्रयम्।
64. *Ibid*, I.1.7.6.
त्वं हि विश्वसृजां स्रष्टा त्वं हि देवो जगत्पतिः।
कर्ता त्वं भुवनस्यास्य त्वं हर्ता पुरुषः परः।।
65. *Ibid*, I.1.7.7[d].
लिङ्गरूपी महेश्वरः।
66. *Ibid*, I. 1.7.24.
उद्भाति स्थितिमाप्नोति तथा विलयमेति च।
तल्लिङ्गं लिङ्गमित्याहुर्लयनात्तत्त्ववित्तमाः।।
67. *Ibid*, I.1.6.25-29[ab].

men call it 'linga'[68], Mahādeva (Śiva) in the form of *Liṅga* sustains the world.[69] *Liṅga*, thus, is a symbol of Śiva and the worship of *liṅga*, therefore, amounts to the worship of Śiva through which the devotee is benefitted. *The* Padma P. stresses the importance *of* Liṅgapūjā and states that it has been resorted to by Brahmā etc. It removes all sins, destroys all troubles[70] and leads to the enjoyment of pleasures as also salvation.[71]

It is certainly interesting to undertake a attempt to trace the origin and development of the worship of phallus or *Liṅga*. In this connection, Bhandarkar R.G. has indicated the possibility of tracing it back to the *Śvet. Up.* which describes the god Īśāna as presiding over every *yoni*,[72] or all forms and *yoni*-s and points to an allusion to the physical fact of the *liṅga* and *yoni* connected together which is responsible for the typification of the philosophical doctrine of gods.[74] Bhandarkar has drawn one more inference regarding the origin of the *liṅga* worship. He believed that the original inhabitants of this country worshipped the phallus and just as the Rudra-Śiva cult borrowed several elements from the forest-dwellers, so it may have borrowed the element of phallic worship from the barbarian tribes at the time of their contact with the Aryans. Bhandarkar has pointed out that the *liṅga* worship was not in vogue

---

68. *Ibid*, I.1.6.29[cd], 30[ab].
 यस्माल्लीनं जगत्सर्वं तस्मिाल्लिगे महात्मनः।।
 लयनाल्लिंगमित्येवं प्रवदंति मनीषिणः।
69. *Ibid*, I.1.6.52[ab].
 लिंगरूपी महादेवो येनेदं धार्यते जगत्।
70. *Pad. P.* V.109.72.
 शिवलिंगार्चनं नाम ब्रह्मादिभिरनुष्ठितम्।
 समस्तपापशमनं सर्वोपद्रवनाशनम्।।
71. *Ibid*, V. 109. 73[a].
72. *Śvet. Up.*, IV.2
73. *Ibid*, V.2
74. Bhandarkar R.G., *op.cit.*, p. 114.

at the time of Patañjali, nor was it known in the time of Wema Kadphises, although his coins have the figure of the trident-holder Śiva and Nandin, the phallic emblem is cospicuous by its absence. According to Bhandarkar, this element might have crept in early enough among ordinary people who were in close contact with the uncivilized tribes and gradually it was spread among the higher classess as well.[75]

Even though Bhandarkar's inference regarding the origin of the *linga*-worship is significant in its own way, it is just a surmise, as he himself is careful in using the words- "...may have borrowed this elment of phallic worship...' suggesting thereby that even though inferences are based on logical reasoning, they may not always lead to precise conclusions. Moreover, his inference being a non-instantial type, *i.e.*, based on unseen or unnoticed phenomena may not be cent percent valid. Here, on the basis of the absence of the reference to the phallic image in Patañjali's works, it is inferred that *liṅga*-worship did not exist at that time, The fact that there could have been some other reasons for the non-mention or the absence of the phallic image in Patañjali's work or Wama's coin cannot be totally gainsaid. Under these circumstances, it is better to hold that it is rather difficult to state something positively with regard to the origin of the *liṅga*-worship. However, it is certain that once the custom of the *liṅga*-worship was in vogue, it was found to be adoptable. It was simpler and easier way of worshippping the divinity and the authors of the *purāṇa-s* very shrewdly incorporated it among their works in order to appeal to that section of society which resorted to the *liṅga*-worship and to attract the masses. As already pointed out, according to the authors of the *purāṇa*-s, the practice of *liṅga*-worship was capable of destroying all sorts of sins and removing troubles. It could confer both material as well as non-material types of gains in the form of enjoyment of pleasures *(bhukti)* and salva-

75. *Ibid.* pp. 114-115.

tion *(mukti)* upon the devotees.[76]

Even though, the *liṅga*-worship as such was a simpler means to approach the deity, the installation of *liṅga* was an elaborate and somewhat complicated process in the Puranic age. The *Matsya P.* contains a whole chapter which describes the marks of *liṅga*[77] and states that it should consist of gold and be attractive. The size of the *liṅga* should suit the size of the mansion in which it is to be placed or vice versa. On an even square one should place the sacred thread. The centres as also the upper parts of the *liṅga* should be of octagonal shape and the head should be of round shape. The navel of the phallus should be a circular knot.[78] Māgha, Phālguna, Caitra, Vaiśākha and Jyeṣṭha are the most auspicious months for the consecration of the images. Similarly, the second, third, fifth, seventh and tenth days of the bright fortnight, the full-moon day, especially the thirteenth day of a bright fortnight are the most auspicious for the consecration of idols. Pūrvāṣāḍhā, Uttarāṣādhā, Mūla, Pūrvābhādrapadā, Uttarābhādrapadā, Hasta, Aśvinī, Revatī, Puṣya, Mṛgasirṣa, Anurādhā and Svāti are the best asterisms for the consecration of idols. Budha, Bṛhaspati and Śukra are the auspicious planets for the consecration of an image[79]. The image should be installed on the Brāhma *muhūrta* in keeping with the prescribed rules on an auspicious day, at an auspicous place and under auspicious star when the rising asterism *(lagna)* is free from malific planets after worshipping the planets (when *grahapūjā* is over)[80]. Preliminary ceremonies *(adhivāsanam)* were to be performed for one night, three nights, five nights or seven nights as the case may be.[81] Installation of *liṅga*

76. *Pad. P.* V.109.73.
77. *Mat. P.* 263.
78. *Ibid*, 263.13-14
79. *Ibid*, 264.3-8.
80. *Ibid*, 264.9-12.
81. *Ibid*, 264.26.

was not only a complicated, laborious and time-consuming task, it also involved lot of expenditure as at the time of installation, a sculptor was to be worshipped with cloth, jewels and ornaments[82] and the officiating priest at the consecration of the image was to be honoured with cows, land, gold etc. and the image was to be named after the recitation of incantation (*mantra*) that glorified both the deities Śiva as well as *Viṣṇu*[83] with the accompaniment of pleasant tunes of music and chanting of Vedic hymns, as this was supposed to lead to prosperity and removal of ill-luck.[84] *Homa*-s were to be performed in keeping with one's own ability and the recitation of the prescribed Vedic incantation *(mantra)* and the *yajamāna* was expected to pay the fees again and again with a repeated performance of *homa*-s[85]. The above details indicate that on the one hand, the authors of the *purāṇa*-s were trying to simplify religion by replacing the institution of sacrifice by simple modes of worshipping the deities in their concrete or manifest forms and popularise religion. However, their attempt was only partially successful, as, on the other hand the ideas of the superiority of the priestly class and the fear of the means of livelihood of this class getting endangered still had sway over their minds which induced them to make earnest appeals to people to pay fees *(dakṣiṇā)* to the officiating priest.

### Worship—as a Simpler Means of Approaching the Divinity —

The *purāṇa*-s lay down extremely simple modes of worshipping Śiva according to which application of sandal wood paste *(gandha)* with the right hand, making the image

82. *Ibid*, 624.27.
83. *Ibid*, 264.31
ॐ नमो भगवते तुभ्यं शिवाय परमात्मने।
हिरण्यरेतसे विष्णो विश्वरूपाय ते नमः।।
84. *Ibid*, 264, 34
85. *Ibid*, 264.47
पुनः पुनः प्रकुर्वीत होमः कार्यः पुनः पुनः।
पुनः पुनश्च दातव्या यजमानेन दक्षिणा।।

of Śiva wear garment with the left hand, adorning the idol with ornaments, placing *naivedya* in front of the divinity, offering flowers are some of the easiest ways[86] that can be resorted to by any common man. Thus, according to the *Gar.P.* Śivārcana is a religious activity. The devotee is expected to sip water with three *mantra-s* beginning with *praṇava* etc. and ending with *svāhā (om ha, om hum, om svāhā)*.[87] The *Lin.P.* states that one should meditate on the three-eyed God *(Śiva)*[88] The place of worship should be sprinkled with sandal-paste and water mixed with the same.[89] According to this *purāṇa* offering of various flowers, sandal wood paste, camphor, tips of *Kuśa* barley grains *(yava)*, rice-grains, sesamum, incense, worship of Śiva, could lead to the accomplishment of various objectives. Mere circumambulation around Śiva's idol could bestow the fruit of the performance of hundred Aśvameda sacrifices upon the devotees[90]. Śivapūjā, according to this belief system could fulfil all sorts of desires entertained by various people. Thus, e.g., a person desirous of enjoying pleasures could enjoy them, a person desirous of attaining the kingdom could have it, one desirous of having a son could obtain the same and one suffering from disease could recover and be hale and hearty.[91] In fact, Śiva could fulfil all the concerned desires of the devotees.

86. *Lin. P.* II.24.15
87. *Gar. P.* I. 23.2-3.
88. *Lin. P.* I.27.2.
89. *Ibid,* I.27.8.
90. *Ibid,* II.24,39.
    प्रदक्षिणक्रमपादेन अश्वमेधफलं शतम्।
    तस्मात्संपूजयेन्नित्यं सर्वकामार्थसिद्धये।।
91. *Ibid,* II.24. 40, 41[cd].
    भोगार्थी भोगमाप्नोति राज्यार्थी राज्यमाप्नुयात्।
    पुत्रार्थी तनयं श्रेष्ठं रोगी रोगात्प्रमुच्यते।।
    यान्यांश्चिन्तयते कामांस्तांस्तान्प्राप्नोति मानवः।।

Thus, the worship of either personified Śiva or that of the phallic emblem was a very simple task which neither involved any complication nor required great expenditure and no wonder, therefore, if very soon it became a popularly accepted way of approaching the divinity. At the same time, it is interesting to note that even though the authors of the *purāṇa*-s tried to popularise Hinduism, their views as to who were the persons entitled to perform Śivapūjā point to their narrow outlook and indicate that the concept of social gradation still continued to have a strong hold over their minds which made them believe that the Brāhmaṇa-s and Kṣatriya-s only could worship Mahādeva themselves but the Vaiśya-s, Śūdra-s and women, however, could get the *pūja* performed by excellent *dvija*-s.[92]

## Viṣṇu

In the cosmological Trinity, Viṣṇu represents cohesive, centripetal tendency known as the quality of *sattva* element. Viṣṇu is behind existence, behind duration, behind whatever tends toward light, while Śiva is a centrifugal principle which represents dispersion, annihilation, non-existence, darkness. The name Viṣṇu can be derived from the root *viṣlṛ (viṣ)* which means to spread in all directions, to pervade. Viṣṇu thus, is one who holds the universe together, which in his absence might have fallen apart. The Bṛhaddevatā[93] derives the word Viṣṇu from different roots such as *viś* — to spread, or *viś* — to enter, or *visli* to surround, all of which can in the ultimate analysis be taken in the sense of pervasion. Viṣṇu exists in everything, brings everything under his control and triumphs over the power of destruction. For the same reason, the *Mahābhārata* states,[94] "He is Viṣṇu because he overcomes all." Viṣṇu, thus, is the inner power through which every-

92. *Ibid,* II.20.1.1,2,3$^{ab}$.
93. *Bṛhad.* II.69.
94. *Mbh., Udyoga* 70.73.
विष्णुः विक्रमणात् ।

thing is sustained and retained. He is a symbol of eternal life and is closely related to Śiva who is the lord of destruction. That which is destroyed is created or born once again and that which is created lasts for some time. This occurs and recurs. Viṣṇu and Śiva, thus, are not only interrelated, they are interdependent as well.[95]

Gonda J. has thrown light on the characteristic features of Viṣṇu reflected in various ancient works that indicate his growing importance over the years. He has pointed out, that Viṣṇu as one of the Ṛgvedic deities occupies just a subordinate position. The *RV.* I. 155.6 contains a reference to his three strides, the *RV.* I. 154.2 mentions him as one in whose three strides all beings dwell and his highest place is a well of honey which is the meeting and rejoicing place of gods. *RV.* I 114 refers to his dreadful nature. *RV., I.* ii.4, his pervading nature is described and in *RV.* I. 156.5 Viṣṇu is said to be helping the sacrificer to reach the powers of heaven. *RV.* VI. 69.1 and *RV.* VIII.25.12 show him as conferring wealth and other valuables upon the sacrificer and in *RV. 77.10,* he is said to be taking him to a safe state. The *Śat. Br.* (I.1.2,13) glorifies Viṣṇu as the god who helps the sacrificer in acquiring that pervading power which is characteristic of his own nature. The sacrificer imitates the God in taking three strides and gaining the earth, the intermediary region and the heaven and ultimately attains the same foundation *(pratiṣṭhā)*[96]. The *Mbh.* depicts Viṣṇu as the primeval Puruṣa and as eternal and omnipresent, Sat and Asat and the same time above Sat and Asat.[97]

### Viṣṇu in the *Purāṇa*-s —

According to the *Gar.P., Viṣṇu* is the ocean of all virtues *(sadguṇārṇavaḥ)* which is the seed *(bījabhūtaḥ)*[98] He became the source *(mūlarūpaḥ)* of the world, created the

95. Danielou Alain, *Hindu Polythesism*, pp. 149-50
96. Gonda J., *Vaiṣṇavism and Śaivism* - A comparison, New Delhi, 1976, pp. 1-32
97. *Mbh. Ādi.* 1.22.
98. *Gar. P.* II.15.1.

principle of *mahat* from which activity, five organs of perception and mind came into existence. With his gross body, he created all the gods.[99] Thus, Viṣṇu here is performing the task of creating the world. The description of Viṣṇu in the *Kūrma P.* is similar to that of Brahman of the Vedāntins and as such he is said to be performing the threefold task, that of creation, maintenance and destruction of the world.[100] Thus, creation is not the only activity that is performed by Viṣṇu. The functions of the gods of Trinity are interchangeable and hence Viṣṇu is identified with the supreme self, the highest sky, the highest abode and Brahmā and Rudra (Śiva) are just the outcomes of this part.[101]

The author of the *Nār.P.* describes him as indestructible *(akṣara)*, endless *(ananta)*, all pervading *(sarvavyāpī)*, unsoiled (*nirañjanaḥ*). Narāyaṇa who encompassed the world consists of mobile and immobile things, who having presided over the different constituents of Prakṛti created the three forms.[102] From the right part of this body, he created Prajāpati, from the middling portion, he created the lord Rudra who destroys the world and from the left part of his body, he created indestructible Viṣṇu and the same is designated by some as Śiva, by some others as Viṣṇu and by still others as Brahmā.[103]

According to the *Gar.P.*, Viṣṇu is the lord of all *(sarveśvaraḥ)*, endless*(anantaḥ)*, Brahman and Ātman residing in the bodies of all, eternal, devoid of body *(sarvadehavivarjitaḥ)*[104] and beyond the reach of the senses

---

99. *Ibid*, II.15.5-7.

100. *Kūr. P.* I. 17.35.

यस्मादभवन्ति भूतानि यत्र संयाति संक्षयम्।
सोऽवतीर्णो महायोगी पुराणपुरुषो हरिः।।

also *Ibid*, I.22.71.

यतः प्रवृत्तिर्भूतानां यस्मिन् सर्वं यतो जगत्।
स विष्णुः सर्वभूतात्मा तमाश्रित्य विमुच्यते।।

101. *Ibid*, I.22.74-75

102. *Nār. P.* I.3.2-3.

103. *Ibid*, 4-5

104. *Gar. P.* I.14.2-4.

*(atīndriyaḥ)*, the life-breath of life-breaths *(prāṇaprāṇaḥ)*, the witness *(tatsākṣī)*, the controller *(tanniyantā)*, having the nature of the Highest Joy *(paramānandarūpakaḥ)*.[105] the highest supporter *(paramaḥ dhātā)*, free *(muktaḥ)*, enlightened *(buddhaḥ)*, free from old age *(ajaraḥ)*, pervading *(vyāpī)*, true *(satyaḥ)*, the self *(ātmā)*, Śiva himself.[106] According to the author of this *purāṇa*, Viṣṇu is the ultimate cause of the world which can be indentified with Brahman of the Vedāntins. Similar description of Viṣṇu is also found in the *Vām. P.*, where Pralhada eulogises him as the god of gods, the best Hari, who is the head of all, the resort of the higher ones as also the lower ones, the lord of lords, without a middle and without an end.[107] Though he is described here as Nārāyaṇa, he is really identifiable with Brahman of the Vedantins as he is described as the merging place of those who have washed off their sins with knowledge and who are not reborn thereafter, wherefrom these beings are created and wherein they ultimately get dissolved.[108] Similarly in exact consonance with the Vedānta doctrine, he is described as self-luminous *(svayamprakāśaḥ)*. the lord of all lords *(sarveśvaraḥ)*.[109]

**Personification and Simplification —**

Like the personified form of Śiva, Viṣṇu's personified form also was visualised by the authors of the *purāṇa*-s and described accordingly. Thus, the *Nārada P.* describes Viṣṇu as the soul of the entire world and the only cause. At the same time, he is described as having eyes similar to blooming petals of lotuses, adorned with beautiful ear-

105. *Ibid*, I.14.8-9.

106. *Ibid*, 14.10.

107. *Vām. P.*, Saromāhātmya 8. 17-18.

108. *Ibid*, Saromāhātmya 8.21[abc], 22[abd].

यमक्षरं वेदाविदो वदन्ति विशन्ति यं ज्ञानविधूतपापाः ।
यस्मिन्प्रविष्टा न पुनर्भवन्ति
भूतान्यशेषाणि यतो भवन्ति यथोर्मयस्तोयनिधेरजस्रम् ।
लयं च यस्मिन् प्रलये प्रयान्ति ।

109. *Ibid*, Saromāhātmya 8.25[ab].

ornaments, having long arms, huge body, adorned with all ornaments, wearing gold sacred thread and the garland of *tulasī* leaves, appearing to advantage because of Kaustubha gem.[110] The worship of Viṣṇu is imagined to be exactly similar to that of Śiva, *i.e.* auspicious and yielding to worldly pleasures and salvation. Bathing *(snāna)*, morning and evening rites *(sandhyā)*, washing hands and feet *(pāṇipādaprakṣālana)*, sipping of water *(ācamana)*,[111] offering of flowers, application of sandal-wood paste,[112] praise and meditation of Viṣṇu *(stavana* and *dhyāna)*[113] are parts of Viṣṇu's worship. Utterance of incantations *(mantra-s)* such as *Om, Srīm, Śrīdharāya Viṣṇave namaḥ, Om hām hṛdayāya namaḥ*,[114] or *Om, ham, śirase namaḥ, Om hūm, śikhāyai vaṣat, Om hūm, kavacāya hum, Om haum netratrayāya vauṣat*[115] was supposed to enable one get rid of all diseases or afflicction caused by constellations *(graha-s)*.[116] Praise in honour of Viṣṇu *(stava)* or his worship *(pūjā)*, thus could serve practical purpose as also the highest purpose of obtaining Viṣṇuloka.[117] In the same *purāṇa*, elsewhere, Viṣṇu's meditation is regarded as a means to destroy all sins. This *purāṇa* considers Hari to be the same as Viṣṇu and appeals to the masses stating that one who has a pair of letters *'Ha'* and *'ri'* on the tip of his tongue crosses the ocean in the form of mundane

---

110. *Nār. P.* I.33.34-36[ab].

सर्वविश्वात्मकं विष्णुं सर्वलोकैककारणम्।
विकसत्पद्मपत्राक्ष चारुकुण्डलभूषितम्।।
दीर्घबाहुरुदाराङ्गं सर्वालङ्कारभूषितम्।
बिभ्रतं तुलसीमालां कौस्तुभेन विराजितम्।।

111. *Gar. P.* I.31.3.
112. *Ibid*, I.31.16; 33.2,6.
113. *Ibid*, I.31.30.
114. *Ibid*, I.31.5.
115. *Ibid*, I. 31.7.
116. *Ibid*, I.316,9,
117. *Ibid*, I. 33. 7[cd].

सर्वरोगविनिर्मुक्तो विष्णुलोकं समाप्नुयात्।

existence and reaches Viṣṇu's abode.[119] *Dhyāna* is regarded as the highest religion, the highest penance, extreme purity.[120] An attempt to simplify religion which appeals to the masses and fulfils their cherished desire is also revealed when it is stated in the same *purāṇa* that Viṣṇu's (here called Deva Nārāyṇa) meditation, even for a moment leads the devotee to the heavenly world[121] or of what use are gifts, pilgrimages, penances or sacrifices for one who perpetually meditates upon Viṣṇu (Nārāyaṇa)[122]? The author of the *Viṣṇu P.* lays down a number of fruits acquirable due to the worship of *Viṣṇu P.* such as fulfilment of one's longing obtainment of the heavenly world, beautiful abode in heaven and excellent beautitude *(nirvāṇa).*[123] The author of this *purāṇa* has uniquely synthesised the concrete and abstract aspects of this divinity through Viṣṇu's description presented by Pralhāda, who states that Viṣṇu is the highest goal *(paramārtha)*, gross *(sthūla)* as well as subtle *(sūkṣma)*, destructible *(kṣara)* as well as indestructible *(akṣara)*, concrete *(vyakta)* as well as abstract *(avyakta)*,

---

118. *Ibid*, I. 229. 19.
प्राणायामसहस्रैस्तु यत्पापं नश्यति ध्रुवम्।
क्षणमात्रेण तत्पापं हरेर्ध्यानात्प्रणश्यति।।

119. *Ibdi*, I. 228.19.
जिह्वाग्रे वर्तते यस्य हरिरित्यक्षरद्वयम्।
संसारसागरं तीर्त्वा स गच्छेद्वैष्णवं पदम्।।

120. *Ibid*, I. 230. 10.
ध्यानमेव परो धर्मो ध्यानमेव परंतपः।
ध्यानमेव परं शौचं तस्मात् ध्यानपरो भवेत्।।

121. *Ibid*, I. 230. 6.
मुहूर्तमपि यो ध्यायेन्नारायणमतन्द्रितः।
सोऽपि स्वर्गतिमाप्नोति किं पुनस्तत्परायणः।।

122. *Ibid*, I.230.1.
किं तस्य दानैः किं तीर्थैः किं तपोभिः किमध्वरैः।
यो नित्यं ध्यायते देवं नारायणमनन्यधीः।।

123. *Viṣ. P.* III. 8.6.
भौमं मनोरथं स्वर्गं स्वर्गे रम्यं च यत्पदम्।
प्राप्नोत्याराधिते विष्णौ निर्वाणमपि चोत्तमम्।।

beyond all digits *(kalātīta)*, the lord of all *(sakaleśa)*, unsullied *(nirañjana)* as also colouring the constituents *(guṇādhāra)*, but himself having soul devoid of quality *(nirguṇātman)*, situated among the constituents *(guṇasthita)* personified *(mūrta)* as also abstract *(amūrta)*, distinct *(sphuṭa)* as also indistinct *(asphuṭa)*, having terrible form as also gentle form *(karālasaumyarūpātman)*, endowed with nescience *(avidyā)* as also knowledge *(vidyāvidyāmaya)* having existence as well as non-existence as his forms *(sadasadrūpasadbhāva)*.[124] Outwardly these appear to be contradictory adjectives. However, this contradition is more apparent than real, as Viṣṇu here is the Supreme deity that is the cause of the creation, maintenance and destruction of the world[125] and hence in fact is identical with the highest, eternal, unborn, indestructible, unmodifiable Brahman of the Vedāntins.[126] If, from the highest point of view, Brahman is the cause of every manifestation, Brahmā, Viṣṇu and Śiva are just different names of the same reality, given to their different forms due to different funtions of creation, maintenance and dissolution of the world.[127] The author of the *Kūr. P.* also has presented details from esoteric and exoteric points of view. As mentioned by him in the Īśvaragītā section of this *purāṇa*, the Self is clean, pure, subtle, eternal, the innermost self

---

124. *Ibid*, I.20.9-11.

125. *Ibid*, I.2.4.
स्वर्गस्थितिविनाशानां जगतो यो जगन्मयः।
मूलभूतो नमस्तस्मै विष्णवे परमात्मने।।

126. *Ibid*, I. 2.13[ab].
तद् ब्रह्म परमं नित्यमजमक्षयमव्ययम्।

127. *Ibid*, I.2.66.
सृष्टिस्थित्यन्तकरणीं ब्रह्मविष्णुशिवात्मिकाम्।
स संज्ञां याति भगवानेक एव जनार्दनः।।
also *Ibid*, I.2.67.
स्रष्टा सृजति चात्मानं विष्णुः पाल्यं च पाति च।
उपसंह्रियते चान्ते संहर्ता च स्वयं प्रभुः।।

of all, sentiency incarnate and is beyond the *tamas* element.[128] In fact, he is devoid of any attribute, but is divided in three different ways because of these attributes leading to the activities of the creation, protection and dissolution of the world and hence assuming three different names, *i.e.* Brahmā, *Viṣṇu* and Hara.[129] In reality, however, all these activities are to be traced back to the highest abstract principle Brahman.[130] The *Kūrma P.* also identifies Viṣṇu and Rudra (Śiva) with each other and states that those who differentiate between them due to ignorance reach the hell, but those who regard them as identical achieve salvation and those who regard Viṣṇu and Rudra (Śiva) as the same or worship them go to the highest abode.[131] Again, the synthetic approach of the authors of the *Purāṇa*-s is rendered when it is stated that although Viṣṇu is held responsible for the sustenance or the protection of the world, in reality, the three gods are just three different forms of the same reality. Their functions are interchangeable and hence the *Kūr. P.* considers Viṣṇu as the cause of the world.[132] However, it is significant to note that since, the author of the *Br. V.P.* considers Kṛṣṇa as the Highest divinity identical with the Self of all, the Highest person,[133] Viṣṇu is said to be undertaking the task of protecting the world because of fear. The author of the *Nār. P.* considers Viṣṇu as the place of dissolution of the world.[134] The devotion for Viṣṇu is considered to be so

128. *Kūr. P.* II. 2.3.
आत्माऽयं केवलः स्वच्छः शुद्धः सूक्ष्मः सनातनः।
अस्ति सर्वान्तरः साक्षाच्चिन्मात्रस्तमसः परः।।

129. *Ibid*, I. 26.99.
त्रिधा भिन्नोऽस्म्यहं विष्णो ब्रह्मविष्णुहराख्यया।
सर्गरक्षालयगुणैर्निर्गुणोऽपि निरञ्जनः।

130. *Ibid*, I. 17.26.
कर्ता नेता च हर्ता च न मयास्ति समो विभुः।
अहमेव परं ब्रह्म परं तत्त्वं पितामह।।

131. *Ibid*, I. 15.87-89.

132. *Ibid*, I.22.71.

133. *Br. V. P.* IV. 55.9[cd].
विष्णुः पाति च संसारं यद्भयेन कृपानिधिः।

134. *Nār. P.* I.34.43.

important that even a Cāṇḍāla is regarded as superior to a Brāhmaṇa by virtue of his devotion for Viṣṇu.[135]

**The Mode of Worshipping Viṣṇu and Simplification of Religious aspect —**

Offering of flowers to Viṣṇu is the easiest means to collect meritorious deeds and such other fruits. The *Padma P.* expects the devotees to offer specific flowers in the specific months of the year. Thus, e.g. offering of Campaka, Damanaka, Bilva flowers and Śatapatra to Viṣṇu in the month of Caitra, that of Ketakīpatra-s in the month of Vaiśākha, that of Nānāpuṣpa-s in the month of Āṣādha helps them to acquire merits.[136] Similarly, offering of Atasīpuṣpa-s and Dūrvādala and Nānāpuṣpa-s in the month of Śrāvana helps one to fulfil one's own desire,[137] offering of Campaka flowers, Śvetapuṣpa-s, Raktasindūra-s, Kalhāra-s in the month of Bhādrapada, offering of Yūthikā, Navajāti-s, lotuses and such other flowers in the month of Aśvina leads to the obtainment of three goals of human life, *i.e. dharma, artha* and *Kāma*, offering of all *ṛtupuṣpa*-s, sesamum *(tila-s)*, sesamum-flowers *(tilapuṣpa-s)* leads to the acquisition of endless fruit *(anantaprāpti)*[138] and Viṣṇu's favour enables the worshipper to reach the abode of Vaikuṇtha.[139]

## Brahmā

The concepts of existence and annihilation are to be traced back to the concept of creation, their source which is the result of an equilibrium between two opposites, between centripetal and centrifugal principles. It is a balance between a tendency toward existence and a tendency toward annihilation, between light and darkness, between Viṣṇu and Śiva.[140] The source of the manifest world is the

135. *Ibid*, I.34.41$^{ab}$.
चंडालोऽपि मुनिश्रेष्ठ विष्णुभक्तो द्विजाधिकः।
136. *Pad. P.* VI.87.1-10.
137. *Ibid*, VI.87.13
138. *Ibid*, VI. 87. 15-19
139. *Ibid*, VI. 87.27.
140. Danielou Alain, *op.cit.*, p. 232.

result of the opposition of these two Beings representing two different concepts. For Brahmā, the masculine and personified form of the all pervading, everlasting principle, Brahman is this source. The origin of this Being can be traced back to the Veda-s, Brāhmaṇa-s and Āraṇyaka-s wherein he is sometimes termed as Hiraṇyagarbha[141] or one Principle, born out of "heat," moving by desire and duplicating himself.[142] *Br. Up.* identified Prajāpati with heart, Brahman and everything.[143] The *Muṇḍaka Up.* glorifies Brahmā as the source of all knowledge and describes him as "born before all the gods.[144] The *purāṇa*-s are replete with the mythological descriptions of the creation of the universe from the individual limbs of god Brahmā.[145] However, these descriptions are not taken into account since his personality as a Creator-god is very obvious.

The *purāṇa*-s describing the trinity of gods describe Brahmā as the first divinity (Ādyo Brahmā). However, from the highest point of view, Brahmā is not in any way different from Viṣṇu. As stated in the *Gar. P.*, Puruṣa only assumed three forms and turned into Brahmā, Viṣṇu and Bhava. Viṣṇu himself assumed the nature of Brahmā through *rajas* in order to create the world, that of Rudra through the element of *tamas* in order to destory the world and that of Viṣṇu through the element of *sattva* in order to expand the world. In fact, there is no difference at all among these three. Those who know this reality achieve salvation[146] and those who are unable to know the unity of

---

141. *Rv.* X.121. 1[ab].
हिरण्यगर्भः समवर्तताग्रे भूतस्य जातः पतिरेक आसीत्।

142. *Ibid*, X. 129.3-5.

143. *Br. Up.* V.3.1.
एष प्रजापतिर्यत् हृदयमेतत् ब्रह्म एतत्सर्वम्।

144. *Muṇḍ. Up.* I.1.2.
ब्रह्मा देवानां प्रथमः बभूव।
विश्वस्य कर्ता भुवनस्य गोप्ता।।

145. *Bhāg. P.* III. 12.3.47; *Ibid*, III. 20.18; *Kūr. P.* I. 7. 34ff; *Vām. P.* Saromāhātmya 22. 17-32,etc.

146. *Gar. P.* III. 4[cd], 5-6,8.

these gods go to the dreadful hell never to come back again from the same.[147] The author of the *Padma P.* also indicates the equality of both the gods when he states that a person worshipping Śiva and censuring Viṣṇu, stays in terrible hell.[148] The lord himself is Viṣṇu, Rudra and Brahmā residing in the (hearts of) all beings.[149] Again, a very wider perspective of the ideology adopted by the authors of the *Purāṇa*-s is reflected in the *Padma P.* when the author states purity *(śauca)*, truth *(satya)*, forgiveness *(kṣānti)*, absence of love and hatred, knowledge of Vedic lore and thoughtfulness *(vedavidyavicārajñatva)*, interest in the enkindlement of fire *(agnihotraratatva)*, interest in the worship of guests, devotion towards the father and the mother *(pitṛbhaktatva* and *mātṛbhaktatva)* as the characteristic marks of Vaiṣṇava (worshipper of Viṣṇu)[150]

While comparing Hinduism with Brahmanism, Monier Williams M. has stated that in Hinduism Brahmā, Viṣṇu, and Śiva have only secondary existences but the Supreme Being may be worshipped through the worship of these three manifestations or any one of these three manifestations, considered to be superior to others. Hinduism subordinates spiritual Brahman belonging to the period of Brahmanism with its first manifestation Brahmā to the personal deities Śiva and Viṣṇu or to some other form of these deities.[151] As already pointed out, the authors of the *purāṇa*-s have synthesised both esoteric as well as exoteric doctrines with each other. Hence they regard both attributeless, immeasurable, pure 'Brahman' as also per-

---

147. *Ibid*, III. 4.9.
विष्णुब्रह्मादिरूपाणामैक्यं न जानन्ति ये द्विजाः।
ते यान्ति नरकं घोरं पुनरावृत्तिवर्जितम्।

148. *Pad. P.* VI. 82.29.

149. *Ibid*, VI. 82.30.
अहं विष्णुरहं रुद्रो ह्यहं ब्रह्मा पितामहः।
सर्वभूतेषु सततं वसामि पुनः पुनः।।

150. *Ibid*, VI. 82.5.

151. Monier-Williams M., *op. cit.*, p. 49.

sonified Brahmā sometimes termed as Nārāyaṇa *(Nārāyaṇākhyaḥ)* and who is considered to be the grand-father of the world *(lokapitāmahaḥ)*[152] as the cause of the world, but consider Brahmā as just a manifestation of 'Brahman, and at the same time identical with 'Brahman'. For the same reson, the author of the *Viṣṇu P.* states that the highest incomprehensible Nārāyaṇa is the Lord of lords. The Lord who is the source of all, who does not have a beginning has Brahman as its nature.[153] Obiviously, Brahmā was the same as Brahman as it is stated that those desirous of achieving salvation worship personified God known as Vāsudeva (Brahmā) and reach Brahman. Without worshipping Vāsudeva who can achieve salvation ?[154] The Lord is 'personified' as also abstract, visible as also invisible[155] and although Brahmā, Viṣṇu and Śiva are the Lords of creation, sustenance and annihilation respectively, from the highest point of view, the Supreme Lord who in fact is the same as the abstract Supreme Reality termed as 'Brahman' is responsible for all the three activities *i.e.* creation, sustenance and annihilation.[156] This universe having both mobile as well as immoblile forms is pervaded by the greatness of the Supreme Lord. Whatever is seen in manifest form is in fact the outcome of that Jñānātman. Ignorant persons are deluded and hence they are unable to know the reality.[157]

The simplistic aspect of the worship of the three di-

---

152. *Viṣ.P.* I. 3.3[cd].
153. *Ibid,* I. 4.4.
    नारायणः परोऽचिन्त्यः परेषामपि स प्रभुः।
    ब्रह्मस्वरूपी भगवाननादिः सर्वसम्भवः।।
154. *Ibid,* I. 4.18.
155. *Ibid,* I. 4.24ab, ef.
    मूर्तामूर्तमदृश्यं च दृश्यं च पुरुषोत्तम।
    तत्सर्वं त्वं नमस्तुभ्यं भूयो भूयो नमो नमः।।
156. *Ibid,* I.4.31[cd].
    प्रसूतिनाशस्थितिहेतुरीश्वरस्त्वमेव नान्यत्परमं च यत्पदम्।।
157. *Ibid,* I.4.39-40

vinities is their worship through the sacred syllable 'Om' ('Aum'). The author of the *Nārada P.* has pointed out that the syllables 'a', 'u' and 'm' represent the form of Brahmā, Viṣṇu and Rudra respectively, these three together represent Parabrahman[158] and persons muttering this *praṇava mantra* of these three deities free themselves from all sorts of sins.[159] In this connection, the *Vāyu P.* states that the *praṇava mantra* is a bow, the Self is an arrow and Brahman is the target.[160] Similarly, the *praṇava* is said to be symbolically representing the three worlds,[161] the letters '*a*', '*u*' and '*m*' are regarded as symbols of *bhūloka, bhuvarloka* and *svarloka* respectively[162] and meditation is said to be the easiest means to attain the *praṇavapada,*[163] which bestows a fruit that cannot even be secured by the performance of Aśvamedha sacrifice in every month, for hundreds of years.[164]

Monier Williams M. has thrown light on the various possibilities of the symbolic significance of the sacred syllable 'Om ('Aum) and stated that the three letters originally were typical of the earlier Vedic trinity... the deities that were

---

158. *Nār. P.* I. 33.55-56
अकारं ब्रह्मणो रूपमुकारं विष्णुरूपवत्।
मकारं रुद्ररूपं स्यादर्धमात्रं परात्मकम्।।
मायास्तिस्त्रः समाख्याता ब्रह्मविष्णुशिवाधिपाः।
तेषां समुच्चयं विप्र परब्रह्मप्रबोधकम्।

159. *Ibid*, I.33.58[ab]. 59[ab].
जपन्तः प्रणवं नित्यं मुच्यन्ते सर्वपातकैः।
जपंश्च प्रणवं मन्त्रं ब्रह्मविष्णुशिवात्मकम्।।

160. *Vāy.P.* 20. 5[ab].
प्रणवो धनुः शरो ह्यात्मा ब्रह्म तल्लक्ष्यमुच्यते।

161. *Ibid*, 20,10[a].
ॐ कारस्तु त्रयो लोकाः।

162. *Ibid*, 20.9.

163. *Ibid*, 20.11[cd].
एवं ध्यानविशेषेण तत्पदं समुपासते।

164. *Ibid*, 20.16.
मासे मासे ऽश्वमेधेन यो यजेत शतं समाः।
न स तत् प्राप्नुयात् पुण्यं मात्रया यदवाप्नुयात्।।

not only the personifications of the three earlier forces of integration, disintegration and reintegration, but also of three principal objects in nature, Earth, Water or Sun and Fire or of the three worlds, Earth, Air and Sky or of the three forms of matter, solid, liquid and gaseous. They constitute the wellknown Trimūrti or triad of forms which characterised mythological Brahmanism and their bodies like those of human beings are composed of gross material particles were regarded as having divine and eteral character. These three gods differ from and are superior to all other divine and human organisms in that they are not subject to transmigration.[165] Although it is difficult to state positively whether the origin of the *praṇava* can be traced back to the Vedic trinity or not, even in ancient days, *praṇava* was certainly characterised by symbolic significance. The *Māṇḍūkya Up.* considers it as the one eternal syllable in which not only the past, the present and the future, but even that which exists beyond the three forms of time are included.[166] It is wellknown that the *Bh. G.* considers this syllable as a means which when memorised enables the devotee to reach the Highest Resort.[167] The *purāṇa*-s have continued the same tradition.

The above observations indicate the that main interest of the authors of the *purāṇa*-s was to simplify and popularise Hinduism. They, therefore replaced that abstract principle with the descriptions of personified gods and laid down very simple modes of worship which could easily followed by the masses. Among these personified gods, Brahmā, Viṣṇu and Śiva forming the Trinity were the major ones. The needs of society, thus, induced the authors of the *purāṇa-s* to bring about change in religion.

---

165. For more details, see Monier-William M., *op. Cit.*, pp.44-47.

166. *Māṇḍ. Up.* I.1.
ओमित्येतदक्षरमिदं सर्वं तस्योपरव्यानं भूतं भवद्भविष्यदिति।
सर्वमोङ्कार एव। यच्चान्यत् त्रिकालातीतं तदप्योङ्कार एव।

167. *Bh. G.* VIII.13.
ओमित्येकाक्षरं ब्रह्म व्याहरन्मामनुस्मरन्।
यः प्रयाति त्यजन्देहं स याति परमां गतिम्।।

CHAPTER — VI

# SOME OTHER DIVINITIES IN THE PURĀṆA-S

Besides Brahmā, Viṣṇu and Śiva, that occupy prominent poosition among the Puranic deities, the *purāṇa*-s contain glorification of several other divinities such as the female divinity (Goddess), the Sun, Kṛṣṇa, Rāma etc. The nature of these deities reflected in the *purāṇa*-s and the modes of worshipping them laid down by the authors of the *purāṇa*-s also throw light on the changing nature of religion.

## The Goddess-worship in the *Purāṇa-s* —

Monier-William M. has tried to trace the origin and development of Śāktism or Goddess worship.[1] According to him the earliest conceptions of this worship are reflected in the Veda. In his opinion, probably the Heaven and Earth are the most ancient of all Vedic gods and the union of these two have given rise to the world as is clear from the Ṛgvedic references which describe them as Janitrī (*RV.* X. 110.9), Pitarā (*RV.* III.3.11) or Mātarā (I.155.3). Williams M. also holds that the glorification of Uṣas who is imagined by the Ṛgvedic seers as the daughter of the sky throws light on the tendency of the Ṛgvedic Aryans to adore the female divinity. Danielou Alain, however, is inclined to trace the origin and development of the Goddess worship to the concept of Trinity. According to him, the universal substratum was called the Immensity (Brahman) which was characterised by the potentiality to manifest itself and exist for sometime and to get disintegrated or annihilated. The tendencey to exist and the tendency to disintegrate oppose each other and the tension generated between them leads to the first appearance of energy *(Śakti)* which can be represented as the power of Brahmā, Viṣṇu or Śiva. The combined form of these three is Īśvara and as his power, it becomes the Supreme Goddess (Bhagavatī),

1. For more details see Monier-Williams M., *op. cit.*, pp. 180-183.

the Resplendent one (Devī). It can even be perceived as the power appearing in the neutral Immensity from which the existence and the three basic tendencies *(guṇa*-s) themselves appear to arise, it is then called Illusion *(māyā)*. From the point of view of cosmology, the manifested form of this power is called Nature (Prakṛti). According to Danielou, this power represents the creative aspect of divinity which creates the world including the gods and through which the gods procreate. The Devīsūkta (Vāgambhruṇī-sūkta) of the *RV (X.* 125-4) throws light on the importance of the Goddess wherein speech *(vāk)* imagined to be the Goddess describes her own greatness saying "I am the giver of the fruit of action to the performer of the ritual sacrifice which nourishes the gods with offerings. I am the kingdom, the giver of wealth, the knower (or the essence of things). I come first in all rituals. The gods have established me in various abodes. My sphere is wide. I dwell in all things. From me comes the food one eats, all that one sees, .... all that has breath *(prāṇa)*, all the words one hears. Those who do not acknowledge me are destroyed. The *Devī Bhāgavata P.* also glorifies the female divinity, describes her as both with or without attributes and states that this divinity having attributes is to be resorted to by those who do not have any attachment.[2]

In this connection, the views expressed by Monier-Williams M. regarding the two systems, *i.e.* Śaivism and Vaiṣṇavism also are worth taking into consideration. He has pointed out that these systems separated into two great classes-(i) the followers of the right hand path *(dakṣiṇa-mārgī*-s) who consider the *purāṇa*-s their real Veda *(nigama)* and are either devoted to Śiva or Viṣṇu in their double nature as male and female without, however, showing their undue preference for the female or left hand side of the

2. *Devī Bhāg.P* I. 8. 40.
निर्गुणा सगुणा चेति द्विधा प्रोवत्ता मनीषिभिः।
सगुणा रागिभिः सेव्या निर्गुणा तु निरागिभिः।।
Danielou Alain, *op. cit*, 253-257.

deity or their fascination for mystic or sacred rites and (ii) the followers of the left-hand path (*vāmamargī*-s) who consider Tantra-s their Veda or *āgama* and devote themselves to the exclusive worship of the female side of Śiva and Viṣṇu termed as Durgā or Kālī, to Rādhā rather than Kṛṣṇa, but above all to Ambā or Devī, the mother goddess, identified with Śiva's consort and regarded in most comprehensive character as the great power (Śakti) of Nature, just one Mother of the universe (Jaganmātā, Jagadambā). She is the mighty force who carries out an important function of directing and controlling two different divinities-that of maintaining and fulfilling the natural appetites and passions and that of the acquisition of supernatural faculties *(siddhi)* and she represented in her person all other female manifestations of Brahmā, Viṣṇu and Śiva and was imagined to be assuming opposite characters. Her white and mild nature gave rise to the goddess such as Umā, Gaurī, Lakṣmī, Sarasavatī etc., the black or fierce nature was culminated into Kālī, Durgā, Caṇdī, Cāmuṇḍā etc. Śiva's consort represented the female energy of Śiva and led to the development of innumerable personifications[3] and the Puranic religion being assimilating in nature glorified many of them.

It is necessary to take into consideration the different forms of the Mother Goddess right from the day of the Ṛgveda. As pointed out by Kumar Pushpendra, the Mother Goddesses in the Ṛgveda are of three distinguishable types - (i) The gentle mother represented by Aditi, (ii) Virgin mother, the goddess of martial spirit and beauty represented by Uṣas and (iii) Sarasvatī, the special guardian deity of people. The mother goddess conception may be said to reach its culmination when the abstract idea of the Cosmic Principle as the source of all creation is conceived as female. In the *Ṛgveda* (X.125.6) wherein speech or Vāk is identified with the goddess, she appears .... as a champion of people, the Queen, the gatherer of treasures, most thoughtful, first of those who merit worship (RV X. 125.3), the first

3. Monier-Williams M., *op. cit.*, pp. 184.187.

creation as the word, the means of communication between gods and men (*RV*. X. 125.5). In a *Khila Rātri-sūkta* (*RV*. X.127), Śakti is called the mother, the resort of all human beings-she blazes forth with penance *(tapas)* and is worshipped by the devotees for obtaining the fruits of their actions Rātri, here, is imagined to be the sister of Uṣas and the substratum of creation (*RV*. 127.3.1). The *Śrīsūkta* which forms an appendix of the *Khilasūkta* of the *RV*. praises the goddess Śrī as the goddess of wealth, approached through the sacrificial fire with the intention that she should bestow on her devotees gold and domestic animals like cows and horses, health, good harvest, beauty, name and fame (appended to the fifth book of the RV 8-10). Though the *RV*. does not contain any mention of the names Ambikā, Umā, Durgā, Kālī, the Śakti worship of the latter was indebted to the goddess concept of the Vedic age. When we come down to the period of the later Vedic literature, the *Vāj. Sam*. (III.53) addresses Ambikā as Rudra's sister who is invoked to partake of her share in the sacrifice along with Rudra. The *Tait. Brā*. (I.6.10) and the *Śat. Brā*. (II.6.2.9), describe Ambikā as an autumn goddess related to Rudra. The *Tait. Ā*. (V.18) describes Umā. Rudra, here, is invoked as Umāpati and in the *Kena Up*. (III.25) she is termed as Umā Haimavatī. Kumar Pushpendra believes that in the *Śvt. Up*. (I.3), the Upaniṣadic conception of Śakti is fully developed and the absolute Brahman of the earlier Upaniṣads is replaced by the 'personal God' who is associated with his Śakti who is not an altogether separate principle, but belongs to him as his own. She is called Māyā and Śiva is Māyin *(Śvet. Up*. IV.10). *Sāṅkhāyana Śraut. S*. (IV.20) and *Sāṅkhāyana Gr. S*. (II.14.1) mention Bhadra Kālī. *Baudhāyana Dh. S*. (II.5.6), *Baudhāyana Gr. S*. (I.2.7.1, III. 3.2,9) and the *Manu S*. (III.89) refer to the offerings in honour of Durgā and Jyeṣṭhā. The *Muṇḍakopaniṣad* (I.2.4) uses the terms Kālī Karalī, Manojavā, Sulohitā, Viśvarūpā but they appear as the names of Agni's seven flames. Kumar Pushpendra believes that the concept of Śakti or Durgā was gradually developed in the later Vedic literature. He has further pointed out that the Śākta Upaniṣads belonging to the later epochs of

Indian history contain references and glorification of the goddess as well as Śakti cult. *Tripurā Tāpinī Up.* (I.6., V. 13-14), for example regards Śakti as the mother of the universe, the creative power of Śiva. The *Devī Up.* (II) describes her as the creator of Prakṛti and Puruṣa or of the individual souls, or of the world. The Sītopaniṣad indentifies Śakti with Prakṛti or creative power of the God Rāma called Mūlaprakṛti and Māyā. When we come down to the Rāmāyaṇa, we know that this epic does not reflect the existence of any independent cult of Śakti, but the Goddess (Devī) is glorified in a very high esteem. The *Mbh.* contains two complete hymns addressed to her (*Mbh.* IV. 6 and *Mbh.* VI. 23). The contents of these hymns indicate a fusion of the Vaiṣṇava and Śaiva goddesses and throw light on the point that the Śākta cult had attained great importance during the time of the epic.[4]

### The Mother Goddess in the *Purāṇa*-s —

Thus, the author of the *Brahma Vaivarta Purāṇa* describes the Goddess Prakṛti as having the nature of Brahma (Brahmasvarūpā), through which the Eternal Being creates the world and everything in this world is said to be deluded by it.[5] She is the highest, eternal power of the male Supreme Being because of which the Lord of the Self is powerful and without whom he is unable to create.[6] The author further states that the fundamental Prakṛti is only one and it is in the form of perfect Brahman but it manifests itself in five different ways in the universe in the form of : (i) eternal Māyā of Viṣṇu, (ii) the deity presiding over the life breaths of the Highest Lord Kṛṣṇa known as Rādhā, [iii) Lakṣmī, the beloved of Nārāyanā in the form of

4. For more details : Kumar Pushpendra, *Śakti cult in Ancient India*, Varanasi, 1974, pp. 14 -30
5. *Br. V.P.* I.30.12
6. *Ibid*, I.30.13
नारायणा सा परमा सनातनी शक्तिश्च पुंसः परमात्मनश्च।
आत्मेश्वरश्चापि यया च शक्तिमांस्तया विना स्रष्टुमशक्त एव।।

prosperity, (iv) the revered goddess Sarasvatī and Durgā and (v) the beloved of Śaṅkara, the mother of Gaṇeśa.[7]

In the Durgopākhyāna of the same *purāṇa*, Durgā is described as the mistress of the world (Īśānā), auspicious (Śivā), Māyā of Viṣṇu, eternal *(nityā)* true *(satyā)*, the auspicious Goddess Śarvāṇī, Ambikā, Vaiṣṇavī, Gaurī, eternal Pārvatī.[8] The author further explaines the etymological meanings of her various designations such as Śarvāṇī, Vaiṣṇavī, Gaurī, Pārvatī by the reason of her ablity to free the movable and immovable residing in the universe from the birth, death, old age[9] etc. She is the devotee of Viṣṇu, the strength of Viṣṇu, created by Viṣṇu in the world and hence designated as Vaiṣṇavī. Being Śiva's strength, she is described as Gaurī.[10] Being the presiding deity of the special festival known as Parvan, she is wellknown as Pārvatī.[11] The author of the *Varāha Purāṇa* describes the mother goddess as Mahāmāyā, having great lustre (Mahāprabhā), having her body besmeared with divine sandal wood paste, adorned with divine garland, residing in the three worlds *(trilokasthā)*, staying in three fires *(tryagnisthā)*, having three tridents *(triśūlinī)*, *having terrible eyes* (bhīmanetrā), awful *(bhayānakā)*, possessed of terrible face *(bhīmavaktrā)*.[12] Thus, the divine nature of the goddess Durgā is synthesised with a terrrible form of the same goodess in another form and the authors of the *purāṇa*-s consider them to be two different forms of the same reality. It is equally remarkable that in the same *purāṇa*, the author addresses the mother goddess as Sarvavatī, the omnipresent mistress of all beings *(sarvagā, sarvabhūteśī)*,

---

7. *Ibid*, I.30.18-21.
8. *Br. V.P.* IV. 57.2,3[ab].
9. *Ibid*, II.57.17.
   सर्वान्मोक्षं प्रापयति जन्ममृत्युजरादिकम्।
   चराचरांश्च विश्वस्थाञ्छर्वाणी तेन कीर्तिता।।
10. *Ibid*, II.57.21-22.
11. *Ibid*, II.57.25.
   महोत्सवविशेषे च पर्वन्निति सुकीर्तिता।
   तस्याधिदेवी या सा च पार्वती परिकीर्तिता।।
12. *Var. P.* 28.31

Ambikā, making nectar ooze forth, perfect having resemblance with full moon, having lustrous body, the source of the world great lore and destroyer of great demon[13] and states that a woman fasting on Navamī, taking only some flour gets all her desires fulfilled. More significant than this is the fact that more simple form of the worship of the Goddess in the form of the recitation of the *stotra* every morning which as per the assurance of the *purāṇa* enables the reciter to get all the boons and surmount all the calamities.[14]

The author of the *Kūr P.* describes the Mother Goddeess as Māheśvarī, power *(śaki)*, omnipresent *(sarvagatā)*, endless *(anantā)* beyond all attributes *(guṇātītā)*, situated at one place as also many places *(ekānekavibhāgasthā)*, having intense desire to achieve knowledge *(jñānarūpātitālasā)*.[15] The author further throws light on the nature of this Goddess stating that she in fact is just one power belonging to Maheśvara but appearing as many due to difference in attributes and plays in his vicinity in both higher and lower forms. She only produces the world. Neither the cause nor the effect is that of the Lord himself.[16] Thereafter the author throws light on the identity between power and one possessed of power and states that the Yogins who meditate on the Reality are aware of their identity.[17]

Describing the greatness of Śrīlakṣmī, the author of the *Brahmāṇḍa P.* states that although she is stationed here (on the earth), she abides in the heart of everyone and bestows the fruit of acts on all embodied beings in accordance with the nature of their activities.... she herself is Mahālakṣmī. She created three eggs in the form of three different abodes and three Śakti-s. From one egg

---

13. *Ibid*, 28.30
14. *Ibid*, 28.40-42
15. *Kūr. P.* I. 12. 6-7
16. *Ibid*, I.12.9-10
17. *Ibid*, I.12.28.
    शक्तिशक्तिमतोर्भेदं वदन्ति परमार्थतः।
    अभेदञ्चानुपश्यन्ति योगिनस्तत्त्वचिन्तकाः।।

Puruṣottama and Ambikā were born. From the other one were born Virica (Brahmā) and Śrī (the goddess of wealth) and from the third one were born Śiva and the Goddess of speech. She employed Brahmā in the task of creating the worlds, Vāsudeva in the task of sustaining and the three-eyed lord (Śiva) in the task of annihilation who stay in Brahmaloka, Vaikunṭhaloka and Kailāsa (respectively) and meditate on Mahālakṣmī who is the bestower of welfare.[18] The same *purāṇa* elsewhere describes the personified aspect of Kāmākṣī and describes her as wearing all the ornaments, holding lotuses in ten hands, who has placed her hand on her left thigh and who has the crescent of moon as her ornament, who later became four armed one and whose hands are looking attracitve due to noose, hoof, staff and five arrows. Lalitā herself is Kāmākṣī, who manifested herself in Kāñcī, Sarasvatī, Ramā and Gaurī. All (people) worship that first one only.[19] Thus, according to this *purāṇa*, these goddesses are different in name only.

**Personification of Kāmākṣī —**

The attempt aimed at simplification of religion is noticed when Kāmākṣī is personified and said to be clad in white garment, residing in white abode, worthy of being worshipped by a man observing the vow of calibacy, offering white flowers, white *naivedya*-s such as curd, milk, rice or pure thoughts *(saṅkalpa*-s)[20]

**Simplification :**

Kāmākṣī's *japa* is laid down as the simplest means to free oneself from the great sins. More the number of times the *japa* is undertaken, more the number of births whose sins are destroyed. Thus, the *japa* undertaken one lac times frees oneself from great sins, that undertaken two lac times destroys the sins committed in seven births and

---

18. *Brahmāṇḍa* P. III.4.40.3-9.
19. *Ibid*, III,4.39.12-14.
20. *Ibid*, III.4.41.21-22.

that undertaken three lack times frees oneself from sins committed in thousand births.[21]

The Devīmāhātmya section of the *Mārk. P.* describes Vaiṣṇavī as the support of the entire world situated in the form of the earth, having endless power, the seed of the world, the highest Māyā, enabling the deluded world to achieve salvation, destroying all kinds of diseases and fulfilling all desires.[22] Elsewhere, the author describes her to be having awful nature and terms her as Mahākālī, who has pervaded the entire world. When she is praised and worshipped with flowers, sandal-wood paste, incense etc., who bestows wealth, sons, intellignece and auspicious resort in the sphere of *'dharma'*. That very (terrible) goddess bestows enjoyments, heavenly abode and salvation upon people when she is worshippped.[23]

The author of the *Kūr. P.* throws light on the relation between the Supreme Lord and Śakti. The Supreme Lord, according to him, is the self of all situated in every thing and being. He assumed the body of all the gods[24] and the Lord himself, declares that the Highest Śakti belonged to him only. This Śakti itself is knowledge *(Vidyā)* with which he, situated as he is in the hearts of the *Yogins* will destroy illusion *(māyā)*. The lord himself is the impeller and the withdrawer of all powers. He is the support of all, the repository of nectar, approached by meditation, knowledge, devotion or the performance of activities with the spirit of dedication *(karmayoga)* by different groups of people.[25]

---

21. *Ibid*, III.4.41.27[cd].28[ab],29[ab].
    एकलक्षजपेनैव महापापैः प्रमुच्यते ।
    लक्षद्वयेन देवर्षे सप्तजन्मकृतान्यपि ।
    लक्षत्रितयजापेन सहस्रजनिपातकैः ।
22. *Mārk. P.* 88.3[ab], 4, 29[ab].
23. *Ibid.* 89.35, 38, *Ibid*, 90. 3[cd].
24. *Kūr. P.* II.4.8[cd].
    सर्वदेवतनुर्भूत्वा सर्वात्मा सर्वसंस्थितः ।
25. *Ibid*, II.4.19,20,24.

The author of the *Gar. P.* also lays down a mode of worshipping Durgā with the incantation *'Rhīm, Durge, Rakṣinī*, and with the words, 'O excellent mother Goddess Durgā, the giver of all implements of love and health. Grant unto me all desires accepting this offering'. From the third day of the month of Mārgaśīrṣa, the devotee is asked to worship the goddesses Gaurī, Kālī, Umā, Durgā, Bhadrā, Kānti, Sarasvatī, Mangalā, Vijayā, Lakṣmī, Śivā and Nārāyaṇī in the stated order. The author also presents a description of the Goddess Cāmuṇḍā who is looked upon as a form of Durgā who having terrible form due to the act of killing the demons Caṇḍa ad Muṇḍa, living in the cremation-ground, having a skull in her hand, riding on a great spirit, having a cluster of *mahāvimāna*-s (aerial chariots), around Kālarātri, surrounded by a number of attendants, having huge mouth, many arms, bearing bell, drum and *kiṇkiṇī*.[26]

The author of the *Nārada P.* also has described Śakti or the Mother Goddess. According to him Śakti is Viṣṇu's Supreme Energy which stimulated the process of the Universe. It is both positive and negative in nature and is described as Vidyā-avidyā (spiritual knowledge and Ignorance or Nescience). The effect of nescience is the cause of misery due to which the universe appears as distinct and separate from Great Viṣṇu and comprehension of the unity of everything is called spiritual lore *(vidyā)*. If Viṣṇu's Māyā is seen distinct from him it leads to the involvement in worldly existence. If, however, it is realised as the part of Viṣṇu, it frees one from metempsychosis. The world is the outcome of Viṣṇu's potency (Śakti) called Umā, Lakśmī, Girijā, Ambikā, Durgā, Bhadrakālī, Caṇdī, Māheśvarī, Kaumarī Vaiṣṇavī, Vārāhī, Aindrī, Śāmbhavī, Brāhmī.[27]

The later Vedic period shows some traces of the development of the worship of Śakti which culminated into its further development during the time of the Śākta Upaniṣads.

26. *Gar. P.* I. 38. 1-7

27. *Nār. P.* I.3. 6-15.

In the course of time, Śakti or the Mother Goddess represented the extraordinary supernatural power of any one of the Trinity of gods or of the Trinity of gods or of Īśvara who was "three together in one." As power, it was purely abstract in nature but as the tendency to approach the divine being through concrete or manifest form became more and more popular, this Śakti or divine power also was conceived by people in its concrete or manifest form. Human attributes were superimposed upon it and the same was deified by people in various forms such as Pārvatī, Gaurī, Lakṣmī, Kālī, Caṇḍikā, Kāmākṣī etc. Even though Śakti was conceived and named differently, basically it represented the same concept. Being interested in sailing along with the social current the authors of the *purāṇa-s* tried to assimilate every new phase, new phenomenon that made its apperance in society. They took cognisance of the growing popularity of the worship of female divinity in the form of Śakti and shrewdly absorbed it as a part of Puranic religion which was the religion of the masses.

**The Sun-God (Sūrya) —**

The concept of the adoration of the sun-god (Sūrya) is as old as the Ṛgveda. Srivastava V.C., Denielou Alain and others have thrown light on the nature of this deity as envisaged by the ancient Aryans. The name 'Sūrya' designates the orb of the sun, Sūrya is the most concrete solar deity, but his connection with the luminary is not lost sight.[28] The Ṛgvedic seers refer to Sūrya's form,[29] his lustre.[30] In Ṛgveda, he is the source of light, favouring the world by illuminating it.[31] The Ṛgvedic seers also praise

28. *Macdonell*, Vedic Mythology, Varansasi, 1963, p. 30.

29. *RV.* I.115.5.
सूर्यो रूपं कृणुते द्योरुपस्थे।

30. *Ibid*, VIII.56.5.
दिवि सूर्यो अरोचत।
also *Ibid*, VII . 63.4
दिवो रुक्म उरुचक्षसा उदेति।

31. *Ibid*, I.50.4-8.

him for his far-seeing and all-seeing nature.[32] The *Atharvaveda*[33] and the *Tait. S.*[34] also eulogise him for the same trait. No wonder, therefore, if elsewhere, he is glorified as the Highest light or the light of gods.[35] It is probably because of his far-seeing nature for which the organ of eye is generally responsible that, he is said to be the presiding deity of the eyes and is invoked to protect them.[36] In the *Ṛgveda,* he is said to be possessing healing power (X.37.4) and is invoked for eye-sight (X.37.7). The Ṛgvedic seers also praised him for his ability to bestow long span of life upon human beings (X.37.7; VII. 66.16). Elsewhere, he is described as having an ability of bestowing peace and prosperity. Knowing full well that the gait of Sūrya is related with the time factor, the Ṛgvedic seers also praised him as the maker of the year consisting of three hundred and sixty days. (*RV.* I. 164. 11. 14. 18). Similarly knowing the importance of light and heat bestowed by the sun without which human beings just cannot survive the *RV.* (IV. 54.2) also praises him for being the source of life and elevates him to the position of being the soul of the world (*RV.* I. 115.1) where the word soul is figuratively used in the sense of the cause. The idea of his being the soul or the original basis of the entire universe got so firmly rooted in the minds of ancient Aryans that the same was cherished by the sacrificial texts (*Śat. Br* VII. 5.2.27, *Āśva. Śr. S.* VI.5). The Upaniṣads also praise the sun as the giver of light *(Br. Up.)* but being essentially philosophical and spiritual in nature, they look upon the sun's quality from spiritual point of view.[37]

In the epic, the personality of the sun-god appears to be different. He is freed from anthropomorphic traits of the Vedic period and appears in human form. The epics refer to many solar deities such as Sūrya, Savitṛ, Mitra.

32. *Ibid,* II.35.8.
33. *AV.* II.16.2, *Ibid,* 10.3.
34. *Tait. Sam.* I.2.9.
35. *Ibid,* I.7.
36. *Śat. Br.* II.4.2.1.
37. Srivastava V.C. *Sun-worship in Ancient India,* Allahabad, 1972, pp. 50-126.

However, the basic reality behind all these names is the same as is clear from 'only one sun illumines everything'.[38] Even in the Rāmāyaṇa, he appears as the lord of the lustrous one[39] or one who illumines the earth[40] and even here, his primary function is that of dispelling the darkness. Many a time, he is termed as the maker of the day *(dinakara, divākara)* or the maker of lustre (Prabhākara, Bhāskara) in both the epics. But more significant than this is the fact that knowing very well that the phenomenon of rainfall totally depends upon the phenomennon of light, the sun is appropriately praised for this reason.[41] Similarly, rainfall is responsible for the production of food and nourishment of the animate world, for which, in the ultimate analysis, the sun-god only is to be praised. This god only in responsible for the concept of time and hence he is rightly glorified as Kāla, Kālacakrapravartaka, Kālādhyakṣa Kṛṣṇa.[42] The awareness of the fact that the sun has influenced the totality of human life and without him it is impossible for the animate world to survive induced people to elevate the sun to the highest position and praise him as the *bhūtādi*, the father, the mother, the Puruṣa, *sarvasya ādi*, Ananta etc.[43]

Having chronologically taken complete review of the references to the sun-god right from the Ṛgveda to the epics, Srivastav V.C. has shown as to how the *purāṇa*-s reflect the efforts of their authors to symbolise divergent traditions of religions and social customs in their works

---

38. *Mbh* Van. 137.7
    एकः सूर्यः सर्वमिदं विभाति।
    or *Mbh*. Śānti. 352.10.
    एकः सूर्यः सर्वमिदं प्रभासते।
39. *Rām*. VI. 6.105
    "......... ज्योतिषां पतिः"
40. *Ibid*, III.3.52.
41. *Mbh*. Śānti *264.11*.
    आदित्याज्जायते वृष्टिः।
42. *Mbh*. Van. 3-16.20-23.
43. *Ibid*, Van. 3. 16.24.

and as to how even the sun-worship in the Puranic world displays the same trends.[44] According to him, the *purāṇa*-s can be divided into two categories : (1) The early *purāṇa*-s such as the Viṣṇu, Vāyu, Mārkaṇḍeya, Brahmāṇḍa, Matsya etc. which belonged to the period ranging between the third and the fifth century A.D. and (2) The late *purāṇa*-s such as Bhaviṣya, Skanda etc. that belonged to the period ranging from the fifth century onwards. The earlier Puranic texts continue the older Vedic and Smārta traditions of sun-worships with minor changes and additions to suit the changed conditions. The earliest concept of the sun-god is the atmospheric Vedic concept. The *Viṣṇu P.* retains this atmospheric concept.[45] The *Mār. P.* invokes the sun-god in a sectarian fashion, wherein he is Brahmā, Śiva, Viṣṇu, Prajāpati and the supreme gate to final emancipation, even the cause of the universe, the creator, protector and annihilator of everything.[46] The early *purāṇa*-s glorify the benevolent aspect of this god describing his beneficial qualities such as release from the sin, the acquisition of long life, prosperity, freedom from diseases.[47] In the course of time, the authors of the *purāṇa*-s developed a tendency to humanise the sun-god. The sun-images also were constructed.[48] The sun-god in the early *purāṇa-s* was not in any way to be regarded as inferior to any one belonging to the Trinity of Gods. The *Mat. P.* indidates the equality of all these four gods.[49]

The later Puranic world witnessed the development of a fulfledged sun-sect. Moreover, later *purāṇa*-s glorify the Sun-god in highly metaphysical tone and consider the Sun as the highest deity, the Supreme Brahman, having both

---

44. For more details, see Srivastava V.C., *op. cit.*, pp. 204-271
45. *Viṣ.P.* II.8.1ff.
46. *Mār. P.* 103-8
47. *Ibid*, 27.23
48. *Mat. P.* 261.1-7.
49. *Mat . P.* 52.33.
    ब्रह्मणा चाथ सूर्येण विष्णुनाथ शिवेन वा।
    अभेदात् पूजितेन स्यात्पूजितं सचराचरम्।।

concrete *(sakala)* and subtle *(niṣkala)* forms. At the same time, at times they retain the atmospheric concept of the same god. The later *purāṇa*-s lay down the mode of worship which is influenced by the Vedic tradition, inginous system, Iranian system, Tantric practices and Śiva theology. The worship of the Sun in symbolic iorm is replaced by the image and temple worship in later *purāṇa*-s. From the 8th century onwards, Tantric cult had its sway over the minds of the worshippers. The worshippers of the sun were bound to be influenced by the changing circumstances. They were tempted to adopt and incorporate the Tantric practices.

In general it can be said that the tendency to attach importance to the natural phenomenon of the Sun is as old as the Vedic period. The happiness, prosperity, in fact the very survival of human species were dependent upon the Sun and hence the natural phenomenon in the form of the Sun was deified by people. The authors of the *purāṇa*-s continued praising this god. They regarded him as the lustrous divine being adorable by the gods, demons, semi-divine beings such as Yakṣa-s, planets and luminaries, the god that pervades the earth as well as the intermediary region with his rays. He is the same one as Āditya, Bhāskara, Bhānu, Savitṛ, Divākara, Pūṣan, Aryamā, Svarbhanu and Dīptadīdhita.[50] The author of this *purāṇa* considers this as the same as Brahmā, Mahādeva, Viṣṇu and Prajāpati.[51] The fact that he is said to be having Brahmā, Māheśvarī and Vaiṣṇavī body and threefold[52] nature indicates that in the eyes of this author the sun was the Supreme Being. He is said to be possessing both, ferocious appearance due to the moon and looked upon as the creator who has produced this world with both those forms.[53] The *Brahma P.* glorifies the Sun as possessed of great lustre *(Sumahātejāḥ)*

---

50. *Mār. P.* 016.62-64.
51. *Ibid*, 106.69[ab].
    यो ब्रह्मा यो महादेवो येा विष्णुर्यः प्रजापतिः।
52. *Ibid*, 106.71.
53. *Ibid*, 106.73,74[ab].

and dispeller of darkness *(tamonudaḥ)* as the first god *(ādidevaḥ)* of gods who is the lord (Īsvara) due to his overlorsdship *(aiśvarya)*. He is the first creator of beings *(bhūtānām ādikartā)*, the god of gods *(devadevaḥ)* and the maker of the day.[54] Rightly again in keeping with the Vedic concept, he is said to be the life *(jīvanaḥ)* of all beings. This Vedic concept is synthesised with the sectarian one and he is identified with Brahmā, the great God. Viṣṇu, Prajāpati, Vāyu, Indra, Soma, Vivasvān and Varuṇa.[55] Having taken into consideration the Vedic concept of the sun and his close association with the time, he is identified with Time *(kāla)* and said to be the Creator, sustainer and dissolver of the world and is considered to be superior to Śiva and hence looked upon as the Highest Lord (Parameśvara).[57]

The author of the *Bh.P.* rightly explains as to why Āditya should be regarded as superior to all, as the downpour of water *(vṛṣṭi)* is through him which further creates food and progeny and as everything originates out of him and ultimately merges into him.[58] The author of the *Bh.P.* knows the importance of the Sun-god as the generator of heat and his relation with the concept of time and hence pays tribute to him stating that the moments, *muhūrta*-s, days, nights, months, years, seasons and *yuga*-s are al-

---

54. *Br.P.* 31.7-10.
55. *Ibid*, 31.11.
    त्वं ब्रह्मा त्वं महादेवस्त्वं विष्णुस्त्वं प्रजापतिः।
    वायुरिन्द्रश्च सोमश्च विवस्वान्वरुणस्तथा।।
56. *Ibid*, 31.12[ab].
    त्वं कालः सृष्टिकर्ता च हर्ता भर्ता तथा प्रभुः।
57. *Bh. P.* 31.14[ab].
    शिवात्परतरो देवस्त्वमेव परमेश्वरः।
58. *Ibid*, I.54.5[cd], 6.
59. *Ibid*, I.54.8,9[ab].

ways due to Āditya[59] and the beings survive due to his heat.[60] According to the author of this *purāṇa,* the Sun is so important that the Trinity of Gods is said to be worshipping him.[61] With Puranic style, the author sings the praises of the sun saying, 'There is no God comparable to the Sun, there is no resort similar to the Sun, there is no religion like the sun, there is no wealth like the sun.'[62] Elsewhere, the author considers the sun to be identical with the Highest Reality and hence describes him as indestructible *(akṣaya)*, immeasurable *(aprameya)*, omnipresent *(sarvaga)* and the Primordial Matter consisting of three constitutents which is known as the cause of everything arising out of it.[63] Āditya is considered to be the Highest Deity *(parama daivata)* the source of the three worlds[64] the Highest Cause, from which everything arises into which everything merges.[65]

**The Worship of the Sun-god —**

*Simplification* — The attempt to simplify religion is noticed even in respect of the worship of the sun. The simplest modes of worshipping Āditya are laid down by the authors of the *purāṇa*-s and the worship of the Sun with the spirit of utmost devotion is said to be leading to strength *(bala)*,

---

60. *Ibid,* I, 54.11.
अभावो व्यवहाराणां जंतूनां दिवि चेह च।
जगन्प्रतपनमृते भास्करं वारितभास्करम्।।
61. *Ibid,* I.027. 1[cd].
पूजयंति सदा ह्येनं ब्रह्मविष्णुशिवादयः।
62. *Ibid,* .207.2[cd].3[cd].
63. *Ibid,* I.67.26.
अक्षयश्चाप्रमेयश्च सर्वगश्च स उच्यते।
तस्मादव्यक्तमुत्पन्नं त्रिगुणं सर्वकारणम्।।
64. *Ibid,* I. 161.2[ab].
65. *Ibid,* I.161.5[cd].
ततः संजायते सर्वं तत्रैव प्रविलीयते।
66. *Ibid,* I.120.64.

renown *(kīrti)* and the fulfilment of all longings.[66] The simplest way to adore the Sun is to pay obeisance to him by addressing him with glorificatory terms such as 'unborn' *(aja)*, maker of the three worlds *(lokatrayabhāvana)*, the self of all beings *(bhūtātman)*, extremely merciful *(mahākāruṇika)*, the stability of the world *(jagatpratiṣṭhā)*, desirous of leading to the welfare of the world *(jagadthitaiṣin)*, self-born *(svayambhū)*, the eye of the entire world *(lokasamastacakṣuḥ)*.[67]

The *Bh.P.* describes the mode of daily worship of the sun according to which the worshipper has to light the lamp, purify water, take bath, recite purifying incantation, resort to *pūraka, kumbhaka* and *recaka* varieties of *prāṇāyāma* and 'Oṁkāra' offer red, fragrant flowers, auspicious garments and resort to muttering of the sun's name *(japa)* and meditation.[68] The *Agn. P.* recommends the worship of the orb of the sun, eulogises him as Mārtaṇḍa, who favourably affects skin, blood, breath and vital energy; and is supposed to be the cause of virtue, material prosperity, fulfilment of desires and emancipation and is to be worshipped with a garland of flowers, lighted lamp, yellow pigment from the cow *(rocanā)*, saffron, water unbroken rice-grains, sprouts of paddy, barley, sesamum....[69] etc. According to the *Gar. P.* mere recitation of incantatins such as, 'Bow to Sūryāsana, bow to Sūryamūrti etc. enables the reciter to acquire merit and fulfil his desires.[70]

The *Liṅga P.* consideres the *Gāyatrī-mantra* to be the basic *mantra (mūlamantra)* to be recited in hounour of the sun[71] when the worshipper is supposed to imagine

---

67. *Ibid*, I.120.5.
68. *Bh.P.* I.49.3$^{cd}$, 4, 7, 17.
69. *Agn. P.* 301.14-19.
70. *Gar. P.* I.7.2.
71. *Liṅ.P.* II.22.9-10.
ॐभूर्भुवः सुवः तत्सवितुर्वरेण्यं भर्गो देवस्य धीमहि धियो यो नः प्रचोदयात्। ॐनमः सूर्याय खखोल्खाय नमः।

himself to be the sun,[72] worship the sun with sandal paste, red sandal, red flowers, sesamum... etc. He thereby achieves the merit obtained through the performance of sacrifice[73] and be in the close vicinity of the sun.[74] But the simplest way to worship the sun is just bowing down before him only once which enables the devotee to transgress the ocean of metampscychosis.[75]

The *purāṇa*-s also advise the worship of the image of Sūrya. Image-worship is certainly a later phase of religion. Knowing its popularity, the authors of the *purāṇa*-s also advised the devotees to place an idol of the sun and assured them that Bhānusthāpanā will enable them to attain lustre similar to that of the sun and achieve immortality, as also the fruit which is crore times more than that which is secured through performance of sacrifices, practice of severe asusterities, giving away gifts, visits to holy palces and worship of gods.[76]

**Influence of the Tantric Cult on the Method of Sun-worship —**

As pointed out by Srivastav V.C., the Tantric cult was becoming popular particularly in Eastern India from the 7th-8th centurey onwards and the sun-cult was influenced by the increasing popularity of this cult in later *purāṇa*-s. The worship of the sun was based upon the physical phenonmenon of Nature. Hence there was no necessity for the development of the concept of a female principle in

72. *Ibid*, II.22.18.
73. *Ibid*, II. 22. 25, 27. 28.
74. *Ibid*, II. 22. 35
    सूर्यमेव समभ्यर्च्य सूर्यसायुज्यमाप्नुयात् ।
75. *Bh. P.* I.60.18[cd].
    एको भानुनमस्कारः संसारार्णवतारकः ।
76. *Ibid*, I.162, 1,4.
    भानुं प्रतिष्ठाप्य नरः सर्वदेवमयं विभुम् ।
    प्राप्नोत्यमरतां वीर तेजसा रविसन्निभः ।।
    सर्वयज्ञतपोदानतीर्थदेवेषु यत्फलम् ।
    तत्फलं कोटिगुणितं स्थाप्य भानुं लभेन्नरः ।।

the Tantric sense.[77] In the course of time, popularity of the Tantric cult increased the importanace of symbolical mystical letters *(bīja*-s) or syllables invented for the sake of brevity to denote the root *(mūla)* or the essential part of such *mantra-s* or the name of the deity to whom it may be addressed or some part of the body over which it presides[78] and such incantations formed the part of the worship of the sun-god in the *purāṇa*-s. It seems that the authors of the *purāṇa*-s could not resist the temptation of including such incantations in prayers to be invoked in honour of the Sun-God.

**Adoration of other Divinities —**

Besides the trinity of Gods, the Mother Goddess and the Sun-God, the *purāṇa*-s also glorify other gods such as Kṛṣṇa or Gaṇeṣa in order to appeal to those sections of society which revered them and to popularise religion. Thus the *Br. V.P.* glorifies the Lord Kṛṣṇa as the the Self of all, the Highest Person to be adored by all and the bestower of delight upon all. When the author of this *purāṇa* describes Kṛṣṇa as being responsible for fastening every body or fascinating every one through his *mayā*[80] or when Śeṣa, is said to be supporting the world through Kṛṣṇa's fear or when Viṣṇu is said to be protecting the world through his fear[81] or when Indra is said to be downpouring water on the earth or when Death is said to be moving among the living beings or when Yama is described as the controller of sinners,[82] one knows that Kṛṣṇa is the Highest Lord

77. Srivastav. V.C. *op. cit.*, pp. 264.265.
78. Monier Williams M., *op. cit.*, London, p. 197.
79. *Gar. P.* I.23.7

ॐ हां हीं हूं हैं हौं हः शिवसूर्याय नमः।

ॐ हं स्वखोल्काय सूर्यमूर्तये नमः।।

also *Ibid*, 7.3.

ॐ हां हीं सः सूर्याय नमः।

80. *Br. V.P.* IV. 55.1.
81. *Ibid*, IV. 55. 9[cd].
82. *Ibid*, IV. 55. 12.

himself. Just as Brahmā, Viṣṇu or Śiva are different names of the same Reality, similarly even Kṛṣṇa is yet another name of the same Supreme Reality.

The *Nār. P.* eulogises Rāma as a revered divinity and states that incantations in honour of Rāma lead one to perfection. They help the devotees to transgress the ocean of mundane existence.[83] The recitation of these incantations was beliveved to be destroying even crores or thousand crores of sins, such as killing a brahmin, theft of god, consumption of liquor etc. committed knowingly or unknowingly.[84]

The *Pad. P.* lays down a mode of worshipping Gaṇeśa according to which Gaṇeśa is to be invoked through a very simple incantation to be recited in his honour - viz. 'Om, salutation unto Gaṇapati' and is to be worshipped with fragrant flowers, *modaka*-s, fruits, roots and other such things, curds, milk, incense and with the accompaniment of music.[85] The worshipper is assured that he can accomplish any work undertaken by him, nor will he have to face any obstacle. On the contrary he can bring the three worlds under this control[86]. The worship of Gaṇeśa enables a student to master the lore; a person desirous of acquiring wealth gets it in plenty; one desirous of becoming prosperous achieves prosperity through meritorious means and one desirous of having a son gets one through whom the entire family achieves salvation. Similarly, a person worshipping Gaṇeśa will never suffer from any disease nor will he be ever tormented by the (adverse effects) of planets or afflications caused by the departed souls *(pretayoni*-s).[87]

**Idol-worship —**

When abstract Supreme Reality was replaced by con-

---

83. *Nār. P.* I. 73.1.
84. *Ibid*, I. 73.5[cd], 6, 7[ab].
85. *Pad P.* I. 65.11-12.
86. *Ibid*, I.65.5.
87. *Ibid*, I.65.6-8[ab].

crete divinities and when symbolic form of worship was adopted as an easier means with which one can reach those divinities, idol-worship became more and more popular and was adopted by the author of the *purāṇa*-s as well. The *Var. P.* lays down instructions regarding the preparation of such idols and states that the act of bringing the necessary material to be used in preparing the idol should be followed by those of moulding, carving, purification, consecration and assures that idol-worship will deliver the devotees from the mundane existence.[88] The worship of idol with sandal-wood paste, camphor, saffron-powder, aloe *(aguru)*, *kuṁkuma*, with the offering of *pāyasa* in *naivedya* is recommended.[89] Idols of various materials such as stone, clay, copper, bronze, silver and gold[90] have been recommended by the author. The same *purāṇa* also praises the worship of Śālagrāma and states that the merit acquired by the worship of a hundred Śālagrāma-s cannot be recounted even for hundred years.[91] If twelve Śālagrāma-s are worshipped for a single day, the benefit acquired is the same which is secured by the worship of twelve crores of *liṅga*-s.[92] Even though a symbol is a means, with which the divinity was to be worshipped, all symbols were not considered to be alike. The author of this *purāṇa* considers Śālagrāma to be superior to all other idols and states that all deities and even the crystal-*liṅga-s* can be worshipped by people belonging to all the *varṇa* or by women or by Śūdra-s[93] and a note of warning is sounded that if a Śūdra or a woman touches it out of fascination, he or

---

88. *Var. P.* 181. 8-10.
89. *Ibid*, 181. 11-12.
90. *Ibid*, 182, 183, 184, 185, 186.
91. *Ibid*, 186.41.
92. *Ibid*, 186.40.
93. *Ibid*, 186. 42-44.
सर्ववर्णैस्तु संपूज्याः प्रतिमाः सर्वदेवताः।
लिङ्गान्यपि तु पूज्यानि मणिभिः कल्पितास्तथा।।
शालग्रामो न स्प्रष्टव्यो हीनवर्णैर्वसुन्धरे।
स्त्रीशूद्रकरसंस्पर्शो वज्रस्पर्शाधिको मतः।।

she will have to be in hell till the time of deluge.[94] However, without touching the idol, they could get it worshipped by others.[95]

Equally noteworthy are the norms laid down by the authors of the *purāṇa*-s to be observed at the time of the installation of an idol. For preparing stone-idol, beautiful flawless stone was to be selected after careful examination and the idol was to be carved out by a clever artisan.[96] One was supposed to provide a substratum for the idol,[97] offer *pañcagavya*, celebrate festival with the accompaniment of vocal and instrumental music and the recitation of the *sāmaveda* by Brahmins,[98] recitation of the Vedic prayers[99] with the offering of 108 oblations to be thrown into fire.[100] The fact that the presence of a brahmin was a must at the time of the installation of an image indicates that the class of brahmins was trying to retain its supremacy and keep its own means of livelihood in tact, and at the same time it was trying to attract the masses. As per the norms laid down by this *purāṇa* clay-idol should be installed when wood or stone is not available.[101] Moreover, the more the metal was precious out of which the idol was prepared, the more was the quantity of fruits secured by the worshipper. Thus, gold being more valuable than wood, stone, or bronze, the author says that the benefit of erecting idols becomes crore times more with

---

94. *Ibid*, 186. 44.
मोहाद्यः संस्पृशेच्छूद्रो योषिद्वापि कदाचन।
शयते नरके घोरे यावदाभूतसंप्लवम्।।
95. *Ibid*, 186, 45.
96. *Ibid*, 182.2.
97. *Ibid*, 182.9.
98. *Ibid*, 182.13.
99. *Ibid*, 182.14.
100. *Ibid*, 182.17.
101. *Ibid*, 183.4.
काष्ठानामप्यलाभे तु मृण्मयां तत्र कारयेत्।
शैलजां वा ततो भूमे मम कर्मपरायणः।।

gold-images.[102] Installation of gold-idols leads to the liberation of twenty-one generations of the worshipper who is finally merged into the Supreme Lord not to be born again.[103]

It is quite surprising that when the author of the *Var. P.* is liberal in his ideology in conferring even the initiation-rite upon the Śūdra-s which traditionally was the monopoly of the three higher classes *(traivarṇika-s)*, he is very narrow in his outlook in prohibiting them from worshipping Śālagrāma. Thus, though symbol-worship was a means to simplify religion, these symbols were not always thrown open for all the classes of society. The authors of the *purāṇa-s* could not put aside the thought of hierarchical gradation caused by *varṇa*-ranking in terms of superiority and inferiority. That is why it continues to upsurge time and again.

**Unity in Diversity -**

At the end, it must be stressed once again that even though the *purāṇa-s* abound in the glorification of various gods and goddesses, the difference in their nature is just superficial and not real. All these divinities happen to be the manifestations of the same Supreme Reality. As stated by the author of the *Brahmāṇḍa P.*, it is the Lord Śiva himself who has assumed the skin of a human being by which he is tied up. He wanders about on the earth in a concealed form.[104] Once the nature of the Highest Lord is known and the egoistic feeling (of mineness) regarding one's own body vanishes,[105] when one secures the knowledge of the omnipresent, quiet Self in the form of Bliss, there

---

102. *Ibid*, 186.30.
यत्फलं दारुशैलादिनाम्ना कांस्यादि राजते।
तत्फलं कोटिगुणितं सौवर्णस्य प्रपूजने।।

103. *Ibid*, 186.31.

104. *Brahmāṇḍa P.* III. 4. 43. 68
मनुष्यचर्मणा बद्धः साक्षात्परशिवः स्वयम्।
सच्छिष्यानुग्रहार्थाय गूढं पर्यटति क्षितौ।।

105. *Ibid*, III.4.50[ab].
देहाभिमाने गलिते विज्ञाते परमात्मनि।

is nothing that is yet to be achieved and yet to be known.[106] One's own body is just a temple and the Self is the Great Lord situated therein. Knowing this one should discard the faded, withered cast off flowers and such other offerings *(nirmālya)* in the form of ignorance and associate oneself with the thought of identity between the Individual Self and the Supreme Self.[107] The roots of the fundamental philosophical truth of the unity in diversity are as old as the Ṛgveda. The fullfledged development of this thought is reflected in the Upaniṣadic period in the famous *mahāvākya*-s such as *'sarvam khalu idam Brahma'*, *'ayam ātmā Brahma'*, *'tat tvam asi'* etc. According to the theory of Absolute Monism, attributeless abstract Brahman is the Supreme Realtiy. When it is associated with atrributes such as body, senses, mind etc., the same Reality assumes the forms of Individual Self *(jīva)*. Thus, *jīva* is not in any way different from Brahman *(jīvo Brahmaiva nāparaḥ)*. The *purāṇa*-s expressed the same thought and states, 'when bound by the noose (in the form of body, mind, senses etc.), he is the Individual Self *(jīva)*, when freed from this noose, he is the Supreme Lord (Maheśvara).[108] Knowing full well that this philosophical thought was beyond the comprehending ability of the masses, it is lucidly explained by the author with an appropriate illustration stating, "When covered with husk, the grain is known as paddy *(vrīhi)*, in a threshed out form, the same is a rice-grain *(taṇḍula)*.[109] From the highest point of view,

---

106. *Ibid*, III.5.51.
    यः पश्येत्सर्वगं शांतमानंदात्मानमद्वयम्।
    न तस्य किंचिदाप्तव्यं ज्ञातव्यं वावशिष्यते।।
107. *Ibid*, II.4.43.53.
    देहो देवालयः प्रोक्तो जीव एव महेश्वरः।
    त्यजेदज्ञाननिर्माल्यं सोहंभावेन योजयेत्।।
108. *Ibid*, II. 4.54[cd].
    पाशबद्धः स्मृतो जीवः पाशमुक्तः महेश्वरः।
109. *Ibid*, III.4.43.54[ab].
    तुषेण बद्धो व्रीहिः स्यात्तुषाभावे तु तण्डुलः।

the Superme Reality is only one, but for the sake of simplification, one can have the manifest form of any divinity before oneself, offer fruits, flowers, garments etc. in keeping with one's own capacity.[110] If that is not possible, even remembrance of the foot-wears *(śrīpādukādmṛtiḥ)* is enough. It far excels crores and crores of great gifts, great vows and great sacrifices.[111] But the manifest form placed before oneself is not the Supreme Self. Just as several holes of the flute are responsible for the different notes known as *ṣadja* etc., similarly many states of being arise out of the undifferentiated Supreme Self. They appear to be different, but in fact are not different at all.[112]

From anthropological point of view, religion is one of the most important aspects of culture found in every society significantly interacting with other cultural institutions. Religion as an integral part of culture consists of systematic patterns of beliefs acquired by man as a member of society. Furanic religion was a part of Hindu culture. Culture being dynamic in nature changes from time to time due to various reasons. Changes in society bring out changes in culture and cultural change leads to social change. When belief system underwent changes, monism was replaced by polytheism. Members of Hindu community started adoring personified deiteis and resorted to various new modes of worshipping the divinities.

---

110. *Ibid*, III.4.43.67[cd].
फलपुष्पांबरादीनि यथाशक्ति समर्पयेत्।

111. *Ibid*, III. 4. 43. 57.
कोटिकोटिमहादानात्कोटिकोटिमहाव्रतात्।
कोटिकोटिमहायज्ञात्परा श्रीपादुकास्मृतिः।।

112. *Viṣ. P.* II. 14.34
वेणुरन्ध्रप्रभेदेन भेदः षड्जादिसंज्ञितः।
अभेदव्यापिनो वायोस्तथास्य परमात्मनः।।

## CHAPTER-VII

# VOWS (VRATA-S), GIVING AWAY GIFTS (DĀNA) AND PILGRIMAGE (TĪRTHAYATRĀ-S)

Having dealt with the nature of Puranic deities and their worship, it will now be proper to concetrate attention on three other unique features of the Puranic religion viz., vows (*vrata-s)* giving away gifts *(dāna)* and pilgrimage (*tīrthayātrā*-s). The fact that a voluminous bulk of the *purāṇa*-s abounds in these three indicates the importance attached to them by the authors of the *purāṇa*-s. In fact, these authors are seen to be vying with each other in extolling them. Scholars like Kane P.V., Dange S.A. etc. have discussed these topics at full length and with a fairly thorugh treatment.[1] The objective of the present work is just to study the component parts of the Puranic religion from the point of view of its changing nature. That is why now the focus is on studying the relationship between religious change and social change. When studied with the angle, the Puranic religion throws light on the fact that the Puranic portions dealing with *vrata*-s, *dāna* and *tīrthayātrā* have some common features. Hence while studying the interrelationship between religious change and social change, they can be regarded as forming one unit with three subdivisions.

As already pointed out, from historical point of view, every change has its roots in the past and it is shaped and influenced by the changing circumtances. Religion is one of the component parts of culture. From sociolgical point of view, everything that is learned by man as a member of society forms and integral part of culture. For the same reason, the belief and value systems developed and cherished by human beings also form the constituents of culture as also of religion. Puranic religion was a constituent of Hindu culture existing in those days. It, too, was influ-

---

1. Kane P.V., "Vrata-s (Religious Vows) and Utsvas (Religious Festivals)" H. of Dh. Sh., Vol. V, Pt. I, Pune, 1958, pp. 1-462; "Tīrthayātra", *H. of Dh.S.*, Vol. IV, Pune, 1953, pp. 552-727; Dange S. A., *Encyclopaedia of Puranic Beliefs and Customs*, New Delhi, 1990, pp. 1524-1578.

enced by various factors and it will be intereresting to trace the mode of change and the factors responsible for bringing about this change.

While tracing the development of Puranic religion, once again it needs to be stated that during the days of the early Vedic period, especially in the Ṛgvedic period, sacrifice was one of the means utilised by ancient Aryans to appease the gods in order to have some material gains like worldly pleasures from them. In the days of the sacrificial texts, however, sacrifice which was all in all, was "represented to be the only door to prosperity on earth and to future bliss...."[2] During the Upaniṣadic period, the ritualistic activities were no longer considered to be essential. The futility of the worldly pleasures was known and for the same reason the knowledge of the Highest Reality was aspired for.

During the days of the works on Dharmaśāstra, the nature of religion once again underwent changes. The fourfold society was characterised by hierarchical gradation. But, the authors of the *purāṇa*-s tried to enhance the status of the Śūdra-s and attract the masses. The *āśrama* system which was firmly rooted in the structure of society remained as rigid as it was before. The Vedic religion was replaced by the *smārta* practices. Monism was replaced by polytheism. The esoteric Upaniṣadic religion could no longer appeal to people. Buddhism and Jainism arose as the offshoots of Hinduism whose popularity threatened the very survival of Hinduism. Sacrifice which required its every detail to be complete and perfect in all its parts could no longer attract the masses. 'When rituals were overdone, as an inevitable reaction, people were wearied with sacrifices and sacrificers[3] and the authors of the *purāṇa*-s tried to remodel and assimilate various beliefs and religious practices and incorporated them into Hinduism and transformed Hinduism

2. Hopkins E.W., *Handbook on the History of Religions*, Vol. I, Boston, 1895, p. 180.
3. Monier-William M., *op.cit.*, p. 27.

into a mass religion. This new religion 'forgets nothing, but absorbs everything'.[4] The *smārta* religion emphasised the importance of certain *vrata*-s such as Prājāpatya, Cāndrāyaṇa, Kṛcchra etc. and the concept of *dāna*. The authors of the *purāṇa*-s incorporated them as a part of their religion at the same time included many more which could replace the institution of sacrifice with its rigid and complex nature and could simplify and popularise their religion.

## Vows *(vrata-s)*

Kane has explained the meaning and the significance of the term *vrata* and stated that the derivation and semantic development of the word *vrata* have been the subject of great controversies. The word is to be derived from the root ***vṛ*** to choose and could mean (i) will, command, law, prescribed order, (ii) subservience, obedience, service, (iii) domain, (iv) order, regulated succession, realm, (v) calling, office, customary activity, carrying on, custom, (vi) religious duty, worship, obligation, (vii) any undertaking, religious or ascetic performance or observance, vow, sacred work, (viii) vow in general, fixed purpose and (ix) other specialised senses.[5] Kane has pointed out that the idea of *vrata* was very significant in the Vedic period and the Vedic gods and demons had to observe the immutably fixed ordinances laid down by themselves and the violation of the *vrata*-s was leading to the punishment. In the *Ṛgveda, vrata*-s were the laws or ordinances supposed to be laid down by all gods or by individual gods. In the Saṁhitā-s other than the *Ṛgveda*, in the Brāhmaṇa-s and Upaniṣads, the word *vrata* is used in the sense of (i) religious observance or vow or restrictions as to food and behaviour undertaken as a religious vow and (2) the special food prescribed for the sustenance when a person is engaged in a religious rite or undertaking. Yāska in the *Nirukta* has given both

4. For more details, Hopins, *op. cit.*, pp. 348-376.
5. Kane P.V., "*Vrata*-s.......'", op. cit., p. 1.

these meanings.[6] The *Tait.S.* (II.5.5.6) uses it in the first sense and the *Tait.S.* (V. 7.61) in the second sense. In the times of the Brāhmaṇa-s, the word '*vrata*' was also used in secondary senses derived from the sense of 'religious observance and obligation' viz. (i) a proper course or patttern of conduct for a person *(Ait. Br.* VIII.28) and (ii) an *upavāsa* i.e. act of the staying at night near Gārhapatya fire or fasting on the part of a sacrificer *(Ait. Br.* VII.2). The *sūtra-s* also use them in both the senses. The *vrata-s* may be obligatory (such as the *vrata*-s of a *brahmacārin* or of a householder or expiatory rites *(prāyaścita-s*). Śabara (on *Jai.* VI.2) takes the word to mean a mental activity, a resolve in the form "I shall not do this". Medhātithi on *Manu S.* (IV. 13) seems to have accepted this, while Kullūkabhaṭṭa on the same verse explains the word *vrata* as a specific mental resolve in the form of a rule 'this is not to be done by me.[7] According to Manu himself, *vrata* is a desire originating out of mental resolve *(saṅkalpamūlaḥ kāmaḥ).* According to the *Agn. P. 175.2-3), vrata* is a restrictive rule declared by the *śāstra*-s which is also called *tapas* as it causes hardship to the person who performs *vrata.* It is also called *niyama* because of the restraint of several sense-organs. Mitākṣarā on *Yāj.s.* also seems to be taking the word *vrata* in the sense of mental resolve to do something or to refrain from doing something, both being enjoined as duties.[8] Thus, the word *vrata* assumed various shades of meaning in the course of time. Kane P.V. has pointed out that *vrata* comprehends several items such as bath *(snāna),* the morning prayer *(prātaḥsandhyā),* mental resolve *(saṅkalpa),* enkindlement of fire *(homa),* worship *(pūjā)* of the deity or deities in whose honour the *vrata* is undertaken, fasting *(upavāsa),* feeding of Brāhmaṇa-s, maidens or unmarried

---

6. *Nirukta,* II.14.
7. Kullūkabhaṭṭa on *Manu S.* IV. 13.
इदं मया कर्तव्यमिदं न कर्तव्यमित्येवं विधिसंकल्पविशेषाद् व्रतम्।
8. Kane P.V., "*Vrata-s.....*", op. cit., pp. 1-29.

women or the poor or helpless, gifts *(dāna)*, and the observance of certain rules of conduct during the period of *vrata*.[9] As per the details stated by the author of the *Agn. P.* (175.12), a person undertaking a *vrata* has to take bath everyday. He should have a limited quantity of food. He should worship and honour his preceptor *(guru)*, gods and Brāhmaṇa and should eschew *kṣāra, kṣaudra, lavaṇa*, honey and meat.

Apart form these references stated by Kane P.V. a few others are also noteworthy. In the *Ṛgveda*, the seer addresses the invokers saying, "May you behold the valorous deeds of Viṣṇu who is a bosom companion of Indra and who observes all your *vrata*-s, where the word *vrata* is used in the sense of deeds or activities.[10] Elsewhere, Agni is glorified as the protector of the vow *(vratapā)* where the word *vratapā* is used in the sense of protector of the sacrificial activity.[11] The *Atharvaveda* used the word *vrata* in the sense of a religious activity or a religious ordinance.[12] The *Aṅgirasmṛti* presents the details of expiatory rites *(prāyaścitta*-s) such as Sāntapana and Prājāpatya according to which if a *dvija* drinks water from well or vessel of a Cāṇḍāla, a Brāhmaṇa has to perform expiatory rite known as Sāntapana and a Kṣatriya has to perform the rite known as Prājāpatya.[13] Uśanas seems to be using the word *vrata* in the sense of the work that is done regularly over a period of time as those who are given to the drinking of *soma*-juice, who know the true form of religion, who are truthful, who follow

---

9. *Ibid*, p. 31.
10. *RV.* I.22-19.
    विष्णोः कर्माणि पश्यत यतो व्रतानि पस्पशे इन्द्रस्य युज्यः सखा।
11. *Ibid*, VIII.11.
    त्वमग्ने व्रतपा असि देव आ मर्त्येष्वा।
12. *AV.* VI. 64.2.
    समानो मन्त्रः समितिः समानी।
    समानं व्रतं सह चित्तमेषाम्।।
13. *Angira S.* 5[ab].

regulations... are termed as *vratin*-s.[14] The same *smṛti* lays down many other purificatory or expiatory rites for persons who have committed offences, e.g. one who is guilty of Brahmanicide should valuntarily undertake fasting, jump down from a high place, enter into a burning fire or into water,[15] and states that by offering food to a learned (Brāhmaṇa) one is freed from Brahmanicide.[16] The killer of a Brāhmaṇa, who gives all his possessions to a Brāhmaṇa conversant with the Veda-s .... is freed from sins.[17] Parāśara also held that the atonement of sin will enable a person to get rid of it.[18] Gautama uses the term *vrata* in a much wider and elevated sense in as much as he considers the lives of a Brāhmaṇa and a king to be the perpetual vows.[19] Elsewhere he uses the term *vrata* in the sense of the observance of the rules of conduct such as bathing duly every day, nourishing a clean soul in a clean body, taking ablution every day.. etc.[20] Śaṅkhasmṛti lays down various *vrata*-s such as Aghamarṣaṇa, Prājāpatya, Taptakṛcchra, Parāka, Kṛcchra, Atikṛcchra, Sāntapana, Mahāsāntapana, Tuḷāpuruṣa, Cāndrāyaṇa etc. Thus, observance of Aghamarṣaṇa *vrata* consists of bathing thrice and taking an ablution in a river at night and for bear eating three meals, sitting in the *vīrāsana* posture and making gifts of milk cows and this vow was supposed to expiate all the sins. On the first three days of observacne of the Prājāpatya *vrata*, a vowist was expected to have meal in the morning, during the second three days, he was supposed to have meal only in the evening and eat only that food which is obtained by begging during the next three days, and fast for the last three days of the penance. At the time of the observance

14. *Uśanaḥ s.* IV. 3.
15. *Ibid*, VIII. 8.
16. *Ibid*, VIII. 9$^{ab}$.
17. *Ibid*, VIII. 11.
18. *Parāśsara S.* VIII. 8.
19. *Gautama Dh. S.* VIII.1.
    द्वौ लोके धृतव्रतो राजा ब्राह्मणश्च बहुश्रुतस्तयोः।
20. *Ibid*, IX.2.

of a Taptakṛcchra *vrata*, a vowist was supposed to take nothing but warm water, during the next three days, warm water with clarified butter, during the next three days warm water and was supposed to fast for the last three days. A Parāka *vrata* consisted in fasting for twelve successive days, Vāraṇa-kṛcchra *vrata* consisted in cautiously living upon fried barely powder for a month according to regulation. Atikṛcchra *vrata* consisted in continuous subsistence on Viva, Āmalaka and Kapittha fruits for a month. A Kṛcchra-Sāntapana *vrata* consisted in living on a compound of cowdung, cowurine, cow-milk, cow-butter, curdled cow milk and the washing of Kuśa blades on the first day of its observance and in fasting on the following day. When these activities were practised thrice, they constituted Mahāsāntapana *vrata*. A Tulāpuruṣa *vrata* consisted in eating fried barely powder and fasting on alternate days, for a month and a Vārdhika *vrata* which was supposed to destroy all sins, consisted in living on cow-dung, each day, for a month. A Cāndrāyaṇa *vrata* consisted in increasing and decreasing the number of morsels of food with successive increase or waning of the lunar phases[21] and declares that Kṛcchra-s enablė even the great sinners to free themselves from sins.[22] The Baudhāyanasmṛti presents similar details with some variations.[23] On the whole it appears that although all the authors of the treatises on Dharmaśāstra do not use the term *vrata* in the same sense, in the course of time, observance of a *vrata* involved the idea of foregoing or sacrificing something and at times undergoing physical affliction in order either to destroy sins or to attain some

---

21. *Śaṅkha S.* XVIII. 1-11; also *Vasiṣṭha Dh. S.* 24. 2, 3, 6; 23.44.45; 24.108; *Atrismṛti* III.14.
22. Śaṅkha. S. XVIII. 14[cd].
    पापात्मानस्तु पापेभ्यः कृच्छैः संतारिता नराः ।।
23. *Baudh. Smṛti* IV. 5. 5-12, 16, 17.

concrete benefit.

**Puranic *Vrata*-s —**

The *purāṇa*-s abound in elaborate descriptions of multifarious *vrata*-s. They are not only characterised by a variety of their nature, but also by the variety of objectives and reflect religion in the state of flux.

Kane P. V. has rightly drawn the attention towards the universal nature of *vrata*-s.[24] The Jainism lays down five great vows *(mahāvrata*-s) and five small vows *(aṇuvrata*-s). The Buddhists have the *pañcaśīla*-s. The contents of both the Testaments, Old and New reveal the sacredness of vows.[22] As is rightly stated by Kane P.V., Buddhism and Jainism were influential rivals of the ancient sacrificial system. It was in order to wean away common people from those two schisms that probably learned followers of the Vedic system glorified *vrata*-s and promised heaven and other worldly and spiritual rewards.[26]

The sacrificial-texts eulogise the learned priests and consider them to be on par with gods through statements such as "There are two kinds of gods, for the gods are gods, and priests that learned the Veda and teach it are human gods.[27] Elsewhere in the same Brāhmaṇa the sacrificial fee paid to the priests is identified with sacrifice itself.[28] The priests used to receive sacrificial fee also in kind, say in the form of a white horse or a white bull for an oblation to the sun[29] or twelve oxen and a plough.[30] A giver of a thousand kine was supposed to obtain all things of the heaven.[31] These sacrificial texts justify the act of charging sacrificial fee on the part of the Brāhmaṇa-s stating

24. Kane P.V., "*Vrata*-s....", *op. cit.*, p. 28.
25. *Ibid*, p. 43.
26. *Ibid*, p. 43
27. *Śat. Br.* II.2.2.6; 4.3.14.
28. *Ibid*, II. 4.4.5.
29. *Ibid*, II. 6.3.9.
30. *Tait. S.* I. 8.7.
31. Śat. Br. *IV. 5. 1. 11.*

that even gods seek rewards and hence the priests do the same (*Śat. Br.* III. 4.2.1) or the gods, manes and men all exist by what is sacrificed (*Śat. Br.* III.6.2.25). These texts extol the institution of sacrifice, the sacrificer and the sacrificial fee.[32] Hopkins believes that the sacrificial fee was a kind of a substitute for the sacrificial animal utilised because of the difficulty in meeting out the expenses on sacrificial animals to be killed at the time of the performance of sacrifice.[33] Man was expected to pay off three debts-debt unto gods, unto manes and unto seers[34] out of which debt unto gods was paid off by performing sacrifices. Naturally, therefore, performance of sacrifice was regarded as the foremost duty of man.

The authors of the *purāṇa*-s have replaced the instutition of sacrifice by simpler modes of pleasing the divinities and observance of *vrata* is one of them.

**The Constituents of a *Vrata* —**

The Puranic *vrata-s* were to be performed on pure days and on days when the constellations were auspicious. A *vrata* consisted of a beginning of a vow (*vratārambha*), determination (*saṅkalpa*), worship (*pūjā*), at times enkindlement of fire (*homa*), fasting (*upāvasa*), giving away gifts (*dāna*) and/or *viprabhojana* as its constitutent elements.

**Classification of *Vrata*-s —**

Puranic *Vrata*-s could be classified according to the specific time when they were to be performed and the duration for which the observance of these vows was to last e.g. there were *vrata*-s to be performed for a week or a fortnight, for a month, for three months (*traimāsika vrata*-s), for six months (*ṣaṇmāsika-vrata-s*) or even for the period of one year (*vārṣika* or *saṁvatsaravrata*-s). Such *vrata*-s were known as *sāmayikavrata*-s and the longer the period

---

32. References from the sacrificial texts from Hopkins E.W., *Handbook on the History of Religions*, Boston, 1895, pp. 179-193.
33. Hopkins, *op. cit.*, p. 200.
34. Śat. Br. I.7.2ff, *Tait. Br.* VI.2.10.5.

for which they were performed, greater was the fruit secured thereby. Similarly, there were *vrata*-s known as *grahavrata*-s and *nakṣatravrata*-s. Likewise there were *vāravrata*-s to be performed on certain days of a week and *tithivrata*-s to be performed on certain days of a month. Many such *vrata*-s were named after the *tithi* on which they were to be performed.

**The *Tithivrata*-s —**

The *Agni P.* gives a list of *tithivrata*-s to be performed right from the first day of the month with all elaborate details.[35] Among the *tithivrata*-s, Ekādaśīvrata was supposed to be the best of all. The author of the *Agni P.* considers it to be capable of leading to enjoyment and salvation just through a simple mode of fasting for the whole day and the worship of Viṣṇu. The *vrata* was also supposed to bestow wealth and lead to the acquisition of son and the obtainment of success in Viśṇuloka.[36] A person fasting on the third day of the bright half of the month of Vaiśākha was supposed to be getting inexhaustible fruit of all the good deeds performed by him when Viṣṇu was to be worshipped with unhusked *(akṣata)* rice and hence the vow was termed as Akṣatavrata and it was supposed to enable the *vratin* to get the fruit of the performance of the Rājasūya sacrifice.[37] According to the *Vāmana P.*, the second day of the dark half of the month of Śravaṇa is auspicious as Viśvakarmā Prajāpati sleeps on that day and its known as Aśūnyaśayanodita and hence suitable for the observance of this vow.[38] The author of the *Bhaviṣya P.* considers the seventh day of the bright half of the month Māgha as holy and capable of destroying sins.[39] On the two earlier days, *i.e.* on Pañcamī and Ṣaṣṭhī, the vowist was expected to have meal once a day. On the seventh

35. *Agn. P.* 176-180
36. *Ibid*, 187.9.
37. *Mat. P.* 65.2,4,6.
38. *Vām P.* 17.19.
39. *Bh. P.* I.97.1.

day, he was supposed to observe fast, on *aṣṭamī*, he was supposed to feed the brahmins whereby he could secure the fruit of the performance of the Rājasūya or Aśvamedha sacrifice[40]

**The *Māsavrata*-s —**

The author of the *Vāmana P.* presents the details of Kṛṣṇāṣṭamīvrata acording to which one has to observe fast on Aṣṭamī, have bath on Navamī and follow different procedures in different months e.g. in the month of Kārtika one should take bath in milk, worship with Karavīra flowers, incense with the exhuditation of Śrīvāsa, offer *naivedya* of honey and rice cooked in milk, give silver coins as priestly fee. In the month of Mārgaśīrṣa, one should bathe in curd and worship with Bhadra flowers..., in the month of Pauṣa, one should bathe in clarified butter, worship with auspicious Tagara flowers, and incense with the extract of Madhūka tree, offer *naivedya* of honey and cake, give *mudga* beans as the prescribed priestly fee for the propitiation of the Lord of the Universe. In the month of Māgha, one should bathe in water sprinkled with Kuśa grass, worship with musk, and Kadamba tree-incense, offer *naivedya* of sesamum and rice cooked together and give away gold as a sacrificial fee to a brahmin. On the eighth day of the month of Phālguna, one should observe fast and have self-control. One should bathe the divinity in *pañcagāvya* (milk, curd, clarified butter, cowdung and urine of a cow); worship the god with Kunda flower, sandal wood incense, offer jaggery and clarified butter in a copper plate and should give away two pieces of cloth as priestly fee to a brahmin and also offer *naivedya* to him. In the month of Caitra, one should have bath in water containing Udumbara, worship the divinity with Mandāra followers, incense, Mahiṣya guggula mixed with ghee and offering *naivedya* of sweets and ghee, prescribed *dakṣiṇā* of a deer-skin together with the *naivedya*. Likewise, the vow is to be completed resorting to various modes in the remaining months till the

40. *Ibid*, I. 97. 3,6,10.

41. *Vām. P.* 17.35-51

month of Śrāvaṇa.[41] The *Agni P.* also describes various *māsavrata*-s which are said to be enabling the *vratin*-s to enjoy pleasures and achieve salvation e.g. abstention from the use of flowers and salt in the month of Vaiśākha is said to be enabling a person to become a king.[42]

**Other *Sāmayikavrata*-s —**

The *Vāmana P.* lays down Akhaṇḍavrata to be begun on the eleventh day of the bright half of the month, when Viṣṇu is to be worshipped with flowers, leaves, fruits, herbs and plants till autumnal season when the vowist was to observe fast and remain self-controlled for the whole year.[43] The Dhanyavrata to be performed on the first day of the bright half of the month of Mārgaśīrṣa when Viṣṇu in the form of fire was to be worshipped with the preparation of alter for the sake of the performance of *homa* and the vow was to be performed for four months.[44] According to the *Nārada P.*, an unmarried virgin desirous of a bridegroom and matrimonial bliss, good fortune for her sons and husband should perform Gaurīvrata according to which the worship of the image of Gaurī made of gold, silver, copper of clay along with that of her lord (Śiva) on the third day in the bright half of the month of Caitra and the propitiation of the Brāhmaṇa women whose husbands and sons are alive enables the performer to attain wealth, good husband, learning, ability to command and happiness. The vow is to be performed for twelve years.[45] The same *purāṇa* also lays down Caturthīvrata to be performed for four years which was to begin on Mārgaśīrṣaśuddhacaturthī. During the first year of this vow, the *vratin* was supposed to have a single meal every day. During the second year one could have meal only at night. During the third and fourth years, one could have food without soliciting it. And in case, no food was offered, one should observe fast. One should

42. *Agn. P.* 198. 1[b], 2[ab], 3[ab], 4[cd].
43. *Vām. P.* 18.11-12, 23.
44. *Var. P.* 56. 2-5, 7.
45. *Nār. P.* 112. 2-5, 9,7.

then have a replica of the mouse of Vighneśvara made of gold or the mystic diagram of a lotus with good petals. A jar is to be placed over it along with a copper vessel filled with rice-grains and on it an image of Gaṇeśa was to be placed.[46] The *vrata* lays down the worship of this deity whereby one achieves excellent worldly pleasures and the absorption in the deity of Viṣṇu.[47]

**The Grahavrata-s and the Nakṣatravrata-s —**

The *vrata*-s in honour of planets and asterisms (the *grahavrata*-s and the *nakṣatravrata*-s) were supposed to enable the performer to have excellent wealth and the freedom from the trouble caused by afflicating *graha*-s.[48] The *Agni P.* presents the details of the *nakṣatravrata*-s and lays down the worship of Hari to be performed in the month of Caitra. On Mūla-*nakṣatra*, the feet of this Puruṣa are to be worshipped, on Rohiṇī, the lower parts of the legs, on Aśvinī the knees and on Āṣādha the thighs... On Citrā and Ārdrā, the hair was to be worshipped[49] and it is further stated that this Nakṣatrapuruṣa was Viṣṇu himself in the form of Śiva.[50]

**Vrata-s in Honour of the Sun —**

The *purāṇa*-s lay down *vrata*-s to be observed in honour of the sun of the sun-god. Thus, the *Varāha P.* lays down worship in honour of the sun-god known as Ārogyavrata whereby due to the worship of the sun for one year, the vowist is said to be getting health, wealth and grain in this life and a place in the yonder world from where there is no return.[51] The same *purāṇa* also lays down Sauryavrata whereby a timid man becomes valiant by fasting on

46. *Ibid*, I.113. 55-59.
47. *Ibid*, I.113. 67.69[a].
48. *Bh. P.* IV. 113.8, 38-39.
49. *Agn. P.* 196. 1,2.
50. *Ibid*, 196, 9[ab].
    नक्षत्रपुरुषो विष्णुः पूजनीयः शिवात्मकः।
51. *Var. P.* 62.2, 4.

Āśvayujanavamī and a deposed king gets back his kingdom, the ignorant man his knowledge and the fear-stricken man valour.[52]

**Pūjāvidhi-s** —

Most of the *vrata*-s were to be observed with the accompaniment of worship-rites *(pūjāvidhi-s)* to be performed with fragrant flowers, sandal wood paste *(candana)*, aloe *(aguru)*, camphor *(karpūra)*, incense *(dhūpa)*, lighting of a lamp, waving it before the idol of the god. Thus, the author of the *Bhaviṣya P.* states that while observing *vrata* in honour of the sun, one should have meals only at night, worship the sun, offer red lotuses and red sandal-wood paste, fragrance, incense and the *naivedya* of *pāyasa*.[53] The *Agni P.* lays down bathing with *pañcagavya* and *pañcāmṛta*, anointment with sandal wood paste etc., *dīpadāna*, offering of *naivedya* as constituents of Bhīṣmapañcakavrata.[54]

**Obtainment of Fruit *(Phalaprāpti)*** —

Most of the *vrata*-s were to be performed with a pure objective of some material gain such as prosperity, birth of a son acquisition of good husband, fulfilment of one's desires of longings, enjoyment of good fortune, good health, destruction of all sins, acquisition of merits or the fruits that can be secured through the performance of sacrifices such as Rājasūya, Aśvmedha or even thousand Aśvamedha sacrifices, obtainment of Sūryaloka, lordship over seven worlds, obtainment of Vaikuṇṭha or even the Highest abode *(paramapadaprāpti)*, Highest path *(paramāgatiprāpti)* or even salvation. To illustrate some of these objectives, Bhadrākhyasaptamīvrata of the *Bhaviṣya P.* is performed for the sake of the obtainment of auspicious things as also Brahmaloka.[55] Kāmadāsaptamīvrata of the same *purāṇa*

52. *Ibid*, 64, 1,2,6.
53. *Bh. P.* I.84. 3-4; also *Ibid*, I.98.5; also *Ibid I.* 100.4
54. *Agn. P.* 205. 3-4.
55. *Bh. P.* I.101.18.
56. *Ibid*, I.105-26,

was to lead to the fufilment of all desires.[56] Pāpanāśinīvrata of the same *purāṇa* was meant for the destruction of all sins.[57] Kalyāṇasaptamīvrata to be performed on the seventh day of the bright half of the month on Ādityadina was supposed to bestow wellbeing on the performer.[58] Śarkārasaptamīvrata performed on the seventh day of the bright half of the month of Caitra was supposed to enable the performer to reach Brahma.[59] Somoṣṭamīvrata to be performed on the eighth day of the bright half of the month falling on Monday when Soma was to be worshipped with white and red flowers, twenty-five lamps and auspicious *naivedya*-s along with the worship of a Brāhmaṇa couple of offering garments and ornaments, was supposed to enable the performer to enjoy pleasures in the world of the sun and other such worlds, to become valorous, wealthy and to have a son.[60] The Dvijanavamīvrata to be performed on the ninth day of the bright half of the month of Pauṣa,[61] when the goddess Bhagavatī was to be worshipped with banners was supposed to be bestowing protection.[62] The Madanadvādaśīvrata to be performed on the twelfth day of the bright half of the month of caitra when Hari or Madhusūdana was to be worshipped was supposed to enable the performer to enjoy good fortune and excellent son.[63] The Anaṅgatrayodaśīvrata to be performed on the thirteenth day of the month of Mārgaśirṣa when one was supposed to fast and control his senses was believed to be enabling the vowist to get the fruit of the performance of ten Aśvamedha

---

57. *Ibid*, I. 106. 11, also Rasakalyāṇinitṛtīyāvrata of *Mat.P.* 63.1, Śuklatṛtīyavrata of *Pad. P.* 64.1.
58. *Bh. P.* IV.48.1, 16.
59. *Ibid*, IV 49.2,16.
60. *Ibid*, IV. 59.2, 5, 7, 21, 22.
61. *Ibid*, IV. 61.46.
62. *Ibid*, IV. 53$^{ab}$, 54$^{cd}$.
    एवं ये पूजयिष्यंति ध्वजैर्भगवतीं नराः।
    रक्षां करोति सततं भवानी सर्वमंगला।।
63. *Ibid*, IV. 86.3, 8.20.

sacrifices. If it was performed in the month Puṣya, the same was supposed to bestow the fruit of the performance of Rājasūya sacrifice. If performed in the month of Māgha by worshipping Naṭeśvara with lotus, it was supposed to enable the performer to have many sons, excellent wealth, good fortune and the fruit of the performance of thousand Gomedha sacrifices. If performed in the month of Phālguna by worshipping Hareśvara with Karṇikāra flowers it was supposed to enable the *vratin* to have exquisite physical charm and when performed in the month of Caitra, it was supposed to bestow good fortune and the fruit of Naramedhayajña.[64] The Sampūrṇavrata to be performed on the bright half of the month of Phālguna during the time of the appearance of the asterism Hasta was supposed to enable the vowist never to suffer from the grief of separation from brothers and sons.[65]

**Recitation of Incantations —**

Many *vrata*-s were to be observed along with recitation of incantations. The *Mat. P.* states that as a part of Saptamīsnapanavrata, the Brāhmaṇa-s should recite the Vedic *mantra*-s which indicates that the traditional importance of the Vedic *mantra*-s did not diminish. But the *purāṇa*-s abound in number of *mantra*-s which are characterised by the simplicity of expression and clarity of meaning and express a desire on the part of the *vratin* to bow down before the deity and get his desire fulfilled. Thus, the author of the *Bhaviṣya P.* mentioning the details of the Āgneyīcaturdaśīvrata states : 'Bow to the trinity of gods in the form of the sun and fire. Bestow sons, pleasure and salvation (upon us)',[66] and invokes Vāsudeva having innumerable forms to uplift people who have plunged

64. *Ibid*, IV. 90, 7.01,12-13, 16, 18-22.

65. *Ibid*, IV. 109.5, 33.

66. *Bh. P.* IV.93 69.
नमस्त्रिमूर्तये तुभ्यं नमः सूर्याग्निरूपिणे ।
पुत्रान्यच्छ सुखं यच्छ मोक्षं यच्छ नमोऽस्तु ते ।।

67. *Ibid*, IV. 94,33.

into an endless great ocean in the form of mundane existence.[67] *Mantra* as a means of propitiating the deity was so simple in nature that mere listening to its recitation was supposed to enable the listner to free himself from sins.[68] To illustrate a few *mantra*-s of this type- The *mantra* which is a part of Śivacaturdaśīvrata, enjoins the worship of Maheśvara with the *mantra* 'Bow to the feet, bow to Śiva, the Self of all, bow to his head, the forehead, eyes, Bow to Hari, the three-eyed one.[69] Besides the *mantra*-s which are characterised by simplicity of nature and clarity of meaning, the *purāṇa*-s also lay down *mantra*-s such as *gham, dham, bham, ham*[70] which seem to be symbolic in nature and show Tantric influence. There are *mantra*-s in honour of the female divinities as well. Thus, the author of the *Bhaviṣya P.* propitiates Cāmuṇḍā with a praise in her honour wherein she is described as the killer of Mahiṣa, Mahāmāya, one who is wearing a garland of *muṇḍa*-s and inokes her for bestowing wealth and health upon the *vratin*.[71]

**Replacement of the Vedic Sacrifices and the Principle of Equality —**

The Vedic sacrifices could be performed only by the persons belonging to the three higher *varṇa*-s. *Vrata*-s could be performed by any member of society, even by the Śūdra-s and women, maidens and widows.[72] The author of the

---

68. *Ibid*, IV.94.72
ये च श्रुण्वन्ति सततं वाच्यमानं नरोत्तम।
ते सर्वे पापनिर्मुक्ता यास्यंति परमां गतिम्।।

69. *Ibid*, IV. 97.5.
पादौ नमः शिवायेति शिरः सर्वात्मने नमः।
ललाटं तु त्रिनेत्राय नेत्राणि हरये नमः।।

70. *Agn. P.* 177. 11a.

71. *Bh. P.* IV. 63.5
महिषघ्नि महामाये चामुण्डे मुण्डमालिनि।
द्रव्यमारोग्यविजयौ देहि देवि नमोऽस्तु ते।

72. *Ibid*, IV. 69, 82[ab].

73. *Ibid*, IV.206.6[ab].

*Bhaviṣya P.* specifically states that even a Śūdra could observe a vow provided he was endowed with the sense of extreme devotion[73] and suggests that the *varṇa*-distinctions never came in the way of observance of vows. It is wellknown that the authors of the works on Dharmaśāstra considered *mantra*-s to be holy and auspicious and monopolised the members of the three upper classes to recite the same. It is not surprising if this tradition still had sway over the minds of the authors of the *purāṇa*-s. For the same reason, even though the *vrata*-s were thrown open by them for persons belonging to all the *varṇa*-s, the author of the *Matsya P.* states that the Aṅgāravrata to be performed on the fourth day of the month falling on Tuesday should be performed with the recitation of the *mantra 'agnimūrdhādiva'*, but adds that in case a devotee is a Śūdra, he should just meditate over Bhauma (Mars) without uttering anything.[74] It is equally interesting to note that the same *purāṇa* elsewhere lays down Rohiṇīcandraśayanavrata to be performed on the fifteenth day of the bright half of the month falling on Monday or during the appearance of the asterism Brahma and states that the gods especially the god Viṣṇu, the moon are to be worshipped with the *mantra* 'Somāya Vardhāya Viṣṇave ca *namo namaḥ* and further adds that a Śūdra also may observe it.[75] This throws light on the attempt on the part of the authors of the *purāṇa*-s to adopt liberal outlook regarding the religious norms to be followed by the Śūdra-s. By and large, the attitude of the authors of the *purāṇa*-s towards Śūdra-s seems to be liberal which is clear from the state-

74. *Mat.P.* 92.28-
अग्निमूर्धादिवो मन्त्रं जपन्नास्ते उदङ्मुखः।
शूद्रस्तूष्णीं स्मरन् भौममास्ते भोगविवर्जितः।।

75. *Ibid*, 57.6.

76. *Nār. P.* I. 23.2.
ब्राह्मणक्षत्रियविशां शूद्राणां चैव योषिताम्।
मोक्षदं कुर्वतां भक्त्या विष्णोः प्रियतरं द्विज।।

ments such as 'Ekādaśīvrata can enable all the sections of the fourfold division of society to achieve salvation.[76]

***Dāna* as a part of *Vrata*—**

Compared to the expenses incurred on the performance of sacrifices with elaborate procedures, utmost precision and rigidity, observance of *vrata*-s was a much more simpler task and the importance of *vratācaraṇa* was stressed primarily with a view to simplify the nature of religious activities, to popularise the old religion and to transform it into a mass religion. At the same time, it is obvious that with the replacement of the institution of sacrifice by *vratācaraṇa*, the means of sustenance of the priestly class was adversely affected and this class had to strive hard in order to safeguard their interests. For the same reason the act of giving away gifts to priestly class in cash or kind is one of the important constituents of *vratācaraṇa*. The concept of *dāna* will be the theme of discussion of the very next section of this chapter and hence suffice it to say at this juncture that the authors of the *purāṇa*-s have laid down a number of *vrata*-s which stress the importance of making gifts of various kinds ranging from simple gifts of water, garments, bed, a pair of sandles, umbrellas, *cāmara*, mattresses, white sheet pillows, fruits, food to silver-images, gold-images, gold, priestly fee, a gift of a cow or a cow with an ox etc. to be given to Brāhmaṇa-s or to a Vipra and his wife or to a preceptor and enabled the class of Brāhmaṇa-s not only to survive but also to prosper. It is equally remarkable that apart from these so-called precious gifts of silver, gold, gold-images, cows etc. involving a considerable amount of expenditure, the *purāṇa*-s also contain a list of offerings to be presented to the Brāhmaṇa-s which were cheap and within the reach of the masses. Thus, while observing Kalyāṇasaptamīvrata, the *vratin* was expected to offer white cloth, fruits, incense, flowers, sandal paste, eatables, raw sugar and salt to the Brāhmaṇa-s.[77] More significant than this is another point and that is the *purāṇa*-s also lay

77. *Mat. P.* 74.11.

down *vrata*-s like Śivarātrisaptamīvrata, when the *vratin* had to just worship Śiva, keep himself awake for the whole night, observe fast and recite the *mantra*, 'Bow to Śiva' *(namaḥ Śivāya)*.[78] A deliberate attempt to simplify religion is clearly noticed when the details regarding these *vrata*-s are at times seen to be interspersed with statements of assurance such as 'Even a person devoid of wealth will get the same fruit by observing fast by using flowers and reciting *mantra*-s.[79] Similarly, it is equally important that though the authors of the *purāṇa*-s mostly present a long list of aricles to be presented to Brāhmaṇa-s there are rare mentions of *annadāna* and *dakṣiṇādāna* in honour of poor, blind and even misers such as that at the time of the observance of Sūryavrata which ennoble the concept of *vrata*.[80] Similarly, there are references which throw light on the fact that *dāna* of aricles enlisted was not always compulsory. The authors of the *purāṇa*-s also state that the devotee can give away *dakṣinā* to Brāhmaṇas in keeping with his ability.[81]

**Underlying Principles behind the Observance of a *Vrata* —**

Even though most of the authors presenting the details of the *vrata*-s lay down *pūjāvidhi*-s, fast, recitation of *mantra*-s, *dāna* etc. as essential parts of *vratācaraṇa*, at times they throw light on the basic underlying principles behind the observance of *vrata*-s which though mentioned at a limited number of times certainly ennoble and elevate the concept of *vrata*. Even these principles indicate that popularisation of *vratācaraṇa* was not just an outcome of faddish attitude on the part of the authors of the *purāṇa*-s. They believed that a *vratin* was supposed to cherish certain moral principles and was expected to have control

78. *Agn. P.* 193.2-4.
79. *Mat. P.* 62.37.
वित्तहीनोऽपि कुरुते वर्षत्रयमुपोषणैः।
पुष्पमन्त्रविधानेन सोऽपि तत् फलमाप्नुयात्।।
80. *Bh.P.* I.169.8[cd].
81. *Mat.P.* 60. 43; also *Bh. P.* I.169.8[d].

over his senses and was supposed to be prepared to sacrifise something or the other. For the same reason, the author of the *Agni P.* considers *vrata* to be identical with penance *(tapas)* as the physical sufferings of the observer of a vow are comparable to those who practise penance.[82] The principle of control over his senses was the most important principle which characterised *vrata*. This is reflected in statements such as- 'Fast indeed is that which is devoid of enjoyments'[83] or 'The act of drinking water frequently or that of eating betel or day-dreaming or enjoyment of sexual pleasure will spoil fast (which many a time was a constituent of a *vrata*).[84] It is equally noteworthy that according to the authors of the *purāṇa*-s all the *vrata*-s have common *(sāmānya)* tenfold *dharma* comprising of principles of forbearance, truth, mercy, charity, purity, control over senses, worship of god.... etc.[85]

**Other Noteworthy Points —**

The authors of the works on Dharmaśāstra lay down *vrata*-s such as Cāndrāyaṇa, Kṛcchra, Sāntapana, Prājāpatya etc.[86] Some texts use the word *vrata* in the sense of expiatory rites with which sins are to be expiated e.g. *govrata* laid down in *Viṣṇusmṛti* was to be practised for expiating

---

82. *Agn. P.* 175.3[ab].
व्रतं हि कर्तृसन्तापात्तप इत्यभिधीयते।

83. *Ibid*, 175.6[ab].
उपवासः स विज्ञेयः सर्वभोगविवर्जितः।

84. *Ibid*, 175.10.
असकृज्जलपानाच्च ताम्बूलस्य च भक्षणात्।
उपवासः प्रदूष्येत दिवास्वप्नाच्च मैथुनात्।।

85. *Ibid*, 175.10,11[ab].
क्षमा सत्यं दया दानं शौचमिन्द्रियनिग्रहः।
देवपूजाग्निहरणं सन्तोषोऽस्तेयमेव च।।
सर्वव्रतेष्वयं धर्मः सामान्यो दशधा स्मृतः।

86. *Śaṅkhasmṛti* XVIII. 1.8, *Viṣṇusmṛti* 46; *Vasiṣṭhasmṛti* 24.2,3,6; *Vasiṣṭha Dh. S.* 23.4,45. *Ibid*, 24.1-5; *Baudhāyanasmṛti* 4.5.6-11, 16-17.

the sin of cow-killing[87] or for having some concrete benefit. E.g. the same text lays down fasts and worship to be undertaken on the eleventh day of the bright forthight in the month of Āgrahāyaṇa and worship of Vāsudeva and feeding the Brāhmaṇa-s on the twelfth day was supposed to enable the vowist to be born in white island.[88] Āpastamba held that the practice of a Cāndrāyaṇa could lead to the atonement of the sin.[89] *Vasiṣṭhadharmasūtra* clearly states that a person performing Aśvamedha sacrifice is able to free himself from the sin of killing a Brahmin and *japa*, *tapa*, *homa* and *upavāsa* could replace such sacrifices.[90] The authors of the *purāṇa*-s continued the same tradition with thorough elaboration and multifarious additions. Another point worth noting in this connection is the fact that usually the authors of the *purāṇa*-s expect a *vratin* to offer vegetarian type of *naivedya* but there are also a few cases when even though the *vratin* himself was supposed to observe fast, he had to worship the goddess with the offerings of sacrificial beasts, wine, flesh[91] etc.

Lastly it is also worth noting that though the *purāṇa*-s lay down a number of *vrata*-s which are mostly in honour of various gods and goddesses, they also contain *vrata*-s like Yamadvitīyāvrata which are purely secular in character while performing which no god or goddess is to be worshipped. Thus, e.g. according to Yamadvitīyāvrata to be performed on the second day of the bright half of the month of Kārttika called Yamadvitīyā, a person taking food in the house of one's own sister, giving her clothes and ornaments and taking food from her hand attains excellent jewels, wealth and food-grains.[92]

---

87. *Viṣṇusmṛti* 40.24.
88. *Ibid*, 39. 1-4.
89. *Āpastamba S.* X. 12.14.
90. *Vasiṣṭha Dh. S.* 22. 6, 8.
91. *Bh. P.* IV. 61. 47-48,52; also *Ibid*, IV. 63.3.
92. *Nār. P.* I.111.20-21

Thus, it is clear from the above observations that the term *vrata* is as old as the *Ṛgveda*. Since it is to be derived from the root **vṛ** which conveys a number of meanings, it could be used in various senses. The references to the occurrence of the term indicate that the meaning of this term could not remain constant. It changed from time ot time. The authors of the *purāṇa*-s were influenced by the usage of the term by the authors of the works on Dharmaśāstra and use it in the sense of a vow which is characterised by certain regulations regarding its time, duration and other details as to in whose honour the *vrata* was to be observed or what was the procedure to be followed while observing the *vrata*. The Puranic *vrata*-s were mostly in honour of gods or goddesses, who were supposed to be pleased through worship and in return were believed to be favouring the vowist by bestowing some concrete benefit or material gain. The authors of the *purāṇa*-s considered these *vrata*-s to be as important and noble as sacrifices which enabled the *vratin*-s to secure the same fruits as those which were secured through the performance of sacrifices. Thus, replacing the institution of sacrifice by comparatively less expensive and less complicted procedures, the *vrata*-s characterised by a variety could appeal to the masses of varied interests and desires.

## *Dāna* (Gifts)

Dāna was another important component part of the Puranic religion. Kane P. V. has thoroughly dealt with concept of *dāna* from historical point of view.[93] Dange S. A. has thrown light on the concept of *dāna* as one of the Puranic beliefs and practices[94] and Acharya Kala has discussed the Puranic records of gifts.[95] In this section, the same concept will be dealt with in the light of the impact of

93. Kane P. V., '*Dāna* (Gifts),' *H. of Dh. S.*, Vol. II, Part-II, Pune, 1941, pp. 837-888.

94. Dange S.A., *Ency. of Puranic Beliefs and Practices*, Vol. II, Delhi, 1987, pp. 632.658.

95. Acharya Kala, *Puranic Records of Gifts*, Thesis, Univestity of Bomby, 1985.

changing social circumstances on this component part of religion.

The analysis of the various details of *dāna* mentioned in the *purāṇa*-s throws light on the fact that the authors of he *purāṇa*-s have presented the accounts of *dāna* in four different ways. Sometimes *dāna* is eulogised by them as a pure concept. At times *dāna* is mentioned as one of the essential parts of *vrata*, sometimes as a part of *śrāddhakarma* and at times as a part of pilgrimage. The accounts of *dāna* falling under any one of these four categories hinge on the superstitious belief that charity or the act of making gift is a meritorious deed which enables the donor to obtain number of material and non-material benefits ranging from simple matters such as the fulfilment of one's own desires to the obtainment of the region of Viṣṇu or the heavently world or even freedom from the cycle of births and deaths. Charity or generosity was one of the noble virtues cherished by Indian people right from the Ṛgvedic age which had formed one of the constituent elements of ancient Hindu culture.

**The Concept of *Dāna* during the Vedic Period —**

The *Ṛgveda* is replete with the praises of various kinds of gifts (*RV.* I. 125, V. 61, VII. 18.22-25) as also various donors (*RV.* VIII. 6.46-48; VIII. 21-24, X. 62). The Ṛgvedic seers have praised a gift of cows (*RV.* VIII. 5.37), of horses (*RV.* V. 18.5), of camels and mares (*RV.* VII. 16.10, VIII. 46.22) and even the gift of food (*RV.* X. 117). The *Ṛgveda* also refers to persons making various gifts and obtaining various fruits thereby. Here we come across references such as ¼th of those giving cows or fee *(dakṣiṇā)* get an opportunity of being in heaven, those giving gold become immortal, those giving garments live longer (*RV.* X. 107, 2, 7, 8). The sacrificial texts throw light on the fact that gift of horses, cows and even of gold, clothes were accepted as *dakṣiṇā*. (*Tait. Br.* II. 2-5). The author of the *Tait.S.* (V. 1.6.3) has glorified *dāna* and has considered it to be penance. The *Br. Up.* (V. 2.3) mentions charity *(dāna)* as one of the three virtues (the other two being self-restraint and compassion). The *Tait.Up.* has laid down faith *(śraddhā)*, grace *(śrī)*, modesty *(hrī)* and fear (in one's own heart — *bhī*) as the norms regarding the act of *dāna*.

**Dāna during the Days of the Works on Dharmaśāstra —**

Manu expects a householder to give alms to an ascetic as also to a student and considers giving away alms to be as meritorious as giving away cows and holds that the fruit acquired by both these acts is the same.[96] He emphasizes the importance of making gifts to a Brāhmaṇa and Brāhmaṇa-s rich in sacred learning and austerities are figuratively looked upon by him as the mouth-fire. He believes that an offering made in the mouth-fire of such Brāhmaṇa-s saves one from great sin.[97] He is all in praise for gifts and lays down various fruits obtained by donors by making various types of gifts. Thus, he holds that a giver of water can quench his thirst, a giver of food gets imperishable happiness, a giver of sesamum desirable offspring, a giver of a lamp the most excellent eyesight. A giver of land obtains land, a giver of gold long life, a giver of a house excellent mansions, a giver of silver exquisite beauty. A giver of a horse a place in the world of Aśvins, a giver of an ox good fortune, a giver of a cow the world of the sun. A giver of a carriage or a bed a wife, a giver of protection supreme dominion, a giver of grain eternal bliss, a giver of Veda, *(Brahman)* union with Brahman.[98] Manu has praised both the donor and the receiver and stated that if the gift is given and received respectfully, both the donor and the receiver go to the heaven.[99] Although Manu expects people to make gifts to Brāhmaṇa-s, according to him, such Brāhmaṇa-s should be learned and the gifts can be made

96. *Manu S.* III. 95.
यत्पुण्यफलमाप्नोति गां दत्त्वा विधिवद् गुरोः।
तत्पुण्यफलमाप्नोति भिक्षां दत्त्वा द्विजो गृही।।
97. *Ibid*, III. 96, 98.
98. *Ibid*, IV. 229-232.
99. *Ibid*, IV. 235.

in consonance with one's own ability.[100] Yājñavalkya has presented a list of various articles such as earth, lamp, horses, food, cloth, water, sesame seed, gold, sandals, umbrellas etc. to be given away and states that a person giving them becomes immensely happy.[101] According to him, good-tempered kine giving milk, having golden horns and silvery hoofs covered with cloth should be given away with vessels made of bell metal and with *dakṣiṇā* and a giver of a cow delivering a calf *(ubhayatomukhī dhenu)* enjoys the celestial region for years equalling the number of the hair existing on her body as well as that of her calf.[102] Kātyāyana also regards a Brāhmaṇa delivering instruction as honourable and states that a person superseding such a Brāhmaṇa and making gift is visited with the sin of theft.[103] Even Bṛhaspati holds that by making gift unto a Vipra endowed with accomplishments, asceticism and self-control, one enjoys unending fruits.[104] According to him, by making gifts of gold, cow and lands one is freed from all sins. The gift of land is the best as one who gives away land gives away gold, silver, raiment, diamonds and precious stones[105] and gifts of kine, land and learning are supreme gifts that rescue the giver from all sins.[106] The author of the *Viṣṇu Dh. S.* also has praised *dāna* and considered protection to be the best of all gifts and stated that by giving protecion and land one attains the region which one wishes to obtain.[107] It has also eulogised the

---

100. *Ibid*, XI.6.

धनानि तु यथाशक्ति विप्रेषु प्रतिपादयेत्।
वेदवित्सु विविक्तेषु विविक्तेषु प्रेत्य स्वर्गं समश्नुते।।

101. *Yāj.S.* I. 210-211.
102. *Ibid*, I.204, 206.
103. *Kāt.S.* XV.7.
104. *Br. S.* 10.
105. *Ibid*, 4-5.
106. *Ibid*, 18.

त्रीण्याहुरतिदानानि गावः पृथ्वी सरस्वती।
तारयन्ति हिं दातारं सर्वान् पापदसंशयम्।।

107. *Viṣṇu Dh. S.* 92.2-3.

gift of cows and stated that a giver of ten kine attains the region *goloka*, a giver of a hundred cows the region of Brahmā and if a cow to be gifted is adorned, *i.e.* if its horns are adorned with gold, hoofs with silver and tail with strings of pearls, the donor can stay in heaven for as many years as there are hairs on the body of a cow and more so especially when the cow is brown.[108] The list of fruits secured by persons giving away various objects is more or less similar to that presented by Manu with some variations and additions.[109] According to the traditional view, a gift to a Brāhmaṇa, especially to a learned one, wellversed in the Veda-s is more meritorious. The same view is expressed by the author of the *Viṣ. Dh. S.* through the statements, 'whatever a man has given to a non-Brāhmaṇa, he shall get its equilvalent in the next world. If it is given to a well-read Brāhmaṇa, he will get thousand times of what he has given and if it is given to a Brāhmaṇa, well-versed in the Veda-s, he will get infinite times of what he has given.[110]

The above details indicate that concept of *dāna* is as old as the *Ṛgveda*. Charity was an important value, a cherished ideal which was a component part of Indian culture. Moreover, the contents of the works on Dharmaśāstra throw light on the tendency of their authors to link the nature of the fruit with the type of gift with a general assumption that the nature of the fruit is in consonance with the nature of the gift. Although *dāna* or *dakṣiṇā* was highly eulogised in the light of the benefits obtained thereby, and gifts were given away when sacrifices were performed, '*dāna*' did not replace the institution of sacrifice. As pointed out by Kane, according to the Śāstric concept of *dāna*, it is to be differentiated from *yāga* and *homa*. As stated by Śabara, Yāga consisted of abandoning something that belonged to one for the sake of a deity with the accompaniment of Vedic

108. *Ibid*, 92.6-9.

109. *Ibid*, 92. 11-31

110. *Ibid*, 93. 1-4.

*mantra*-s and *homa* consisted of throwing into fire something belonging to oneself, over which one abandons one's ownership, which is also intended for a deity, but *dāna* consists in the cessation of one's ownership of another over that thing occuring when the other one accepts that thing, even though the acceptance may be mental or vocal.[111]

**Puranic Concept of *Dāna*—**

The *purāṇa*-s extol the act of making gift to the skies and regard it as an excellent religious norm. As stated earlier, the *purāṇa*-s glorify *dāna* in four different ways and according to all the four types, a gift made to a Brāhmaṇa, especially wellversed in the Veda is regarded as more praiseworthy and more meritorious.[112] In this respect, the *purāṇa*-s continue the age-old Indian tradition especially that of the works on Dharmaśāstra. That the knowledge of a Brāhmaṇa was more valued is clear from the statement made by the author of the *Kūrma P.* that one should feed a Brāhmaṇa who is learned and religious-minded even though he is already well-fed, but not one who is foolish, even though he is starving for ten nights.[113]

**Various Types of *Dāna*-s and their Fruits—**

Following the traditional widespread belief, the authors

---

111. Śabara on *Jaim.* IV. 2.27.28
यजति ददाति जुहोतिषु सर्वेषूत्सर्गः समानः। तत्र यजतिर्देवतामुद्दिश्य उत्सर्गमात्रं जुहोतिरासेचनाधिकः ददातिरुत्सर्गपूर्वकः परस्त्वेन संबन्धः इत्येष एषां विशेष इति।
q. by Kane P. V., *op. cit.*, p. 841.

112. *Kūr. P.* II. 26.56.
दानधर्मात् परो धर्मो भूतानां नेह विद्यते।
तस्माद्विप्राय दातव्यं श्रेत्रियाय द्विजातिभिः।।
also *Ibid,* II.26.48.
धान्यान्यपि यथाशक्ति विप्रेषु प्रतिपादयेत्।
वेदवित्सु विशिष्टेषु प्रेत्य स्वर्गं समश्नुते।।

113. *Ibid,* II.26.64.
सुभुक्तमपि त्रिद्वांसं धार्मिकं भोजयेद् द्विजम्।
न तु मूर्खमवृत्तस्थं दशरात्रमुपोषितम्।।

of the *purāṇa*-s also emphasise the importance of various types of *dāna*-s such as the gift of a land, that of an umbrella, of food, lamp, seats, water, horse, buffalo, clothes, cows, sesamum, bed, vehicles, gold, silver etc. The author of the *Garuḍa P.* eulogises the concept of charity stating that it yields enjoyment in this world and salvation after death.[114] Gingelly seeds, iron, gold, cotton, salt, seven grains, plot of land and cow all these are holy gifts. The gift of gold yields happiness in heaven, that of a plot of land enables one to become a king.[115] A gift of a cow fulfilling wishes frees one from all sins.[116] The gift of an umbrella will help one to traverse after death the paths oppressed by the heat of the sun.[117] One engaged in the gift of lamps will brighten his path and his family and will be honoured among the luminaries of the sky.[118] A giver of seats, vessels or food-stuffs to Brāhmaṇa-s is in a position to have all sorts of enjoyments.[119] Following the tradition of the works on Dharmaśāstra,[120] the author of the *Kūrma P.* also states that a giver of land obtains everything, a giver of gold gets a long span of life, a giver of houses acquires excellent mansions, a giver of silver exquisite physical charm. A giver of garments reaches the region of the moon, a giver of horses gets excellent vehicle; a giver of ox prosperity. A giver of cow gets the region of the moon, a giver of vehicle and bed a wife, a giver of protection prosperity, a giver of grains eternal happiness, a giver of Brahman (knowledge) eternal Brahman. A giver of medicines health, happiness and long life, a giver of an umbrella gets protection from the scorching heat of the sun.[121]

The author of the *Agni P.* also is in praise for various

114. *Gar. P.* I. 51. 2[ab].
115. *Ibid*, II.32.13, 16[ab].
116. *Ibid*, II. 30.49.
117. *Ibid*, II.31.3.
118. *Ibid*, II.31.8.
119. *Ibid*, II.31.11.
120. *Br. S.* 5-8
121. *Kūr. P.* II. 26. 45-47, 51, 52[cd].

types of *dāna*-s and mentions various fruits secured through them. Thus, according to him, a gift of a cow leads to health, long life, good fortune and place in heaven, a gift of a buffalo good fortune, a gift of an ox the heavenly world, a gift of a cow along with a bull made to *dvija* will lead to enjoyments and salvation.[122] Along with the praise of gift of gold and land, the *Agn. P.* also eulogises the gift of an eight year old girl and states that the benefits of this gift would follow the giver in his seven births, he will elevate twenty-one generations of his family and even attain the world of Brahmā.[123] Even according to this *purāṇa*, various *dāna*-s are conducive to both enjoyment and emancipation and enable the donor to reach the heaven. Thus, according to him gifts of seat, metallic vessel, salt, fragrant sandal, incense, lamp, betel, iron, silver, gem and other rare materials lead to enjoyment and emancipation and a gift of sesamum and a vessel for keeping it will lead the giver to the heavenly world.[124] The author of the *Bhaviṣya P.* eulogises a gift of a maiden and states that a person making a gift of a maiden bedecked with ornaments protects the earlier seven and next seven generations and reaches the region of Prajāpati.[125] Like the nature of the *dānaphala*-s stated by the authors of the works on Dharmaśāstra, the nature of the most of the *dānaphala*-s mentioned in the *purāṇa*-s also is befitting the nature of the *dāna*-s.

**The Best *Dāna* —**

The *Saṁvarta S.* has praised the gift of food as the best of all *dāna*-s and stated that there is no other *dāna* which can excell this *dāna*.[126] The authors of the *purāṇa*-s have continued the same tradition, but besides the gift of food, have considered many more *dāna*-s as excellent.

122. *Agn. P.* 211. 4$^{ab}$, 6$^{cd}$, 28$^{ab}$.
123. *Ibid*, 211.37.
124. *Ibid*, 221. 42-43.
125. *Bh. P.* IV. 148. 1-2.
126. *Saṁvarta S.* 81$^{ab}$, 83.

Thus, the author of the *Brahmāṇḍa P.* has considered a gift of food to be the best, as beings are created from food, are sustained because of food and are reborn out of food. *Annadāna,* thus, is equivalent to *jīvadāna* and nothing else can excell *jīvadāna.*[127] The author of the *Garuḍa P.*, however, considers a gift of land as the best of all[128] and the author of the *Vāyu P.* considers a gift of life or life-breaths to be the best gift.[129] The author of the *Padma P.* regards water as the best *dāna.*[130] The author of the *Skanda P.* considers both, a gift of water together with a gift of food to be the most excellent in nature.[131] The *Agni P.* regards a gift of a lamp as the best *dāna,*[132] but the author of the *Padma P.* elsewhere considers a gift of a maiden as the most praiseworthy.[133] The author of the *Bhaviṣya P.* considers symbolic *dāna* of a salt-cow to be excelling all other *dāna*-s[134] and the *Linga P.* considers the gift of an image of Viṣṇu as the best gift.[135] While invoking a specific god at a specific time, the Ṛgvedic seers are seen to be praising him as the most honourable one. While praising a specific gift at a specific time, the authors of the *purāṇa*-s have a tendency to regard it as the best.

---

127. *Brahmāṇḍa P.* I. 16. 52[cd], 53.
अन्नदानात्परं दानं नान्यत्किंचित्तु विद्यते।
अन्नाद्भूतानि जायन्ते जीवंति प्रभवंति च।
जीवदानात्परं दानं नान्यत्किंचन विद्यते।।
also *Agn.P.* 211.44[ab], *Var.P.* 99.61 *Br. P.* 83.21[cd]. *Pad. P.* VI.26. 3cd, 4ab.

128. *Gar. P.* II.42.3[ab].
नास्ति भूमिसमं दानं नास्ति भूमिसमो निधिः।

129. *Vāy. P.* II. 18.[ab].
जीवितस्य प्रदानाद्धि नान्यद्दानं विशिष्यते।

130. *Pad. P.* VI.27[ab].
पानीयदानं परमं दानानामुत्तमं सदा।

131. *Ska.P.* III. 3.3[cd].

132. *Agn. P.* 200.2[cd].

133. *Pad. P.* VI. 118.4[cd]; also *Lin. P.* II.40.1.

134. *Bh. P.* IV. 155.3.

135. *Lin. P.* II.44.1.

## Symbolic *Dāna*-s

### Dhenudāna and Merudāna or Parvatadāna —

The authors of the *purāṇa*-s attached paramount importance to a gift of cow and in this respect they have followed the popular tradition of the authors of the works on Dharmaśāstra.[136] The author of the *Bhaviṣya Purāṇa* considers a gift of a tawny cow as the most sacred and the most auspicious especially when its horns are decorated with gold., hoofs with silver, its udder with copper, when it is beautified with a garment, bells, ornaments, sandal-paste, flowers.[137] These details are exactly in consonance with the contents of the *Viṣṇu Dh. S.*[138] The same *purāṇa* elsewhere eulogises a gift of a thousand cows and states that it is able enough to help the donor to achieve the highest perfection.[139] The *Viṣṇu Dh. S.* streses the importance of a gift of a cow being delivered of her calf and states that such a cow is called Earth and a person who gives away such a cow to a Brāhmaṇa acquires the merit of making a gift of the whole earth.[140] The author of the *Bhaviṣya P.* incorporates the same norm and states that a giver of such a cow is honoured in the heaven for as many years as there are hair on the bodies of a cow and a calf.[141] The Śātātapa S. expects the donor to make a gift of a good natured milk yielding cow along with her calf.[142] The author of the *Bhaviṣya P.* has incorporated the same norm.[143] The

---

136. *Viṣṇu Dh. S.* 92.6-9; *Śatātapa S.* I.13.
137. *Bh. P.* IV. 161. 10, 65, 72.
138. *Viṣ. Dh. S.* 92.8-9.
139. *Bh.P.* IV. 159.13.
140. *Viṣṇu Dh. S.* 88.1-2.
    अथ प्रसूयमाना गौः पृथिवी भवति। तामलङ्कृतां ब्राह्मणाय दत्त्वा पृथिवीदानफलमाप्नोति।
    also *Atri S.* 326.
141. *Bh. P.* IV. 158. 3, 5.
142. Śatātapa S. I. 13[cd].
143. *Bh. P.* IV. 151.21.
    तरुणी रूपसंपन्ना सुशीला च पयस्विनी।
    न्यायार्जिता सवत्सा च प्रदेया श्रोत्रियाय गौः।।

works on Dharmaśāstra contain a few references to symbolic gifts such as the gifts of *śarkarādhenu*, *ghṛtadhenu*, *tiladhenu* and *ratnamayī dhenu* leading to concrete benefits.[144] The *purāṇa*-s abound in the accounts of such symobolic gifts. The author of the *Bhaviṣya P.* recommends gifts of *tiladhenu*, *jaladhenu ghṛtadhenu*, *lavaṇadhenu*, *suvarṇadhenu* and *ratnadhenu*.[145] While making a gift of *ghṛtadhenu*, pitchers filled with ghee are to be decorated with sandal paste, garlands. The feet of thos cow consist of sugarcanes, hoofs consist of gold, horns conist of aloe... and this symbolic cow is to be gifted to a Brāhmaṇa along with the recitation of incantations.[146] The idea behind the act of offering this symbolic cow is explained by the author himself stating that ghee *(ājya)* is lustre. It is the food of gods. The cow is a goddess made up of ghee. Such a *dāna* leads to the fulfilment of all desires and destruction of all sins.[147] It is difficult to say which *dhenu* was cheaper, the real one or the symbolic one and which *dhenudāna* was simpler, especially when the symbolic cow was to consist of gold or gems, as how precious were these things in those days cannot be known. However, it is certain that a gift of cow made of salt, jaggery or sesamum was much more cheaper and simpler and it appears that popularisation of symbolic gifts enabled the majority of people to follow the religious norm of making gifts. It is notworthy that besides direct references to symbolic gifts to *śarkarādhenu*, *ghṛtadhenu* mentioned earlier, the works on Dharmaśāstra contain indirect references to gifts which also can be regarded as symbolic gifts E.g. the *Viṣṇu Dh. S.* recommends a gift of the skin of an antelope covered with sesame to be made on the full moon day of the month of Vaiśākha, which was supposed to lead to the merit of gifting the ocean-girdled earth with all the forests and mountains. A gift of sesame, gold, honey, clarified

144. *Śatātapa S.* II.38, 39 and 49.
145. *Bh. P.* IV., Chapters 152-157; also *Agn. P. 210 for* guḍadhenu
146. *Bh.P.* IV. 154.2, 3, 7, 8[ab], 10
147. *Ibid*, IV. 154. 15,17.

butter in the skin of a black antelope was believed to be leading to the destruction of evils and the gift of the skin of an antelope was looked upon as the gift of earth.[148] The cocept of symbolic gifts in the *purāṇa*-s can be traced back to such references as well.

**Merudāna or Parvatadāna —**

Another type of symbolic gift mentioned in the *purāṇa*-s is that of a mountain *(merudāna* or *parvatadāna).* The *Matsya P.* lays down gifts of mountain made of a heap of grains. Grains are food. Food is to be honoured and hence identified with the goddess Lakṣmī and the god Janārdana. The author also says that this food is Brahmā, and life-breaths are stationed in food. Beings are born out of food. The world is sustained because of food.[149] Another such mountain glorified in this *purāṇa* is of salt heaped in the form of a mountain. Knowing the importance of salt the author says, "There is no flavour in any thing without a pinch of salt.... salt promotes health" and the mountain of salt was believed to protect the donor from the ocean of mundane existence.[150] Likewise the *Mat. P.* lays down many other types of *parvatadāna*-s such as *guḍaparvatadāna, suvarṇācaladāna, tilaparvatadāna, kārpāsaparvatadāna, ratnācaladāna, śarkarāśailadāna*[151] and they are said to be leading to different benefits. *Tilaparvatadāna* was supposed to yield happiness,[152] *kārpāsaparvatadāna* was supposed to take the donor to the region of Śiva,[153] *ratnācaladāna* was supposed to enable the donor to become an emperor, possessed of charm, health and excellent qualities.[154]

---

148. *Viṣṇu Dh. S.* 87.1, 8-10.
149. *Mat.P.* 83. 41-43.
150. *Ibid,* 84.78.
151. *Ibid,* Chapters 85-88, 90, 92.
152. *Ibid,* 87.4.
153. *Ibid,* 88.4.
154. *Ibid,* 90.10.

The concept of *parvatadāna* might have originated out of the mountain-cult that existed during the Ṛgvedic age. According to Dange S.S., the mountains were associated with divine element which is indicated by the term Indrāparavata occuring in the *Ṛgveda (RV.* III.53.1; X. 158.3; 45.3 etc.) and by the description of mountains as the sons of Prajāpati *(Mait. Sam.* I. 10.13, *Kāth. Sam.* 36.9).[155] *Dāna* of various things in the form of mountains, thus, had special significance of their own due to an idea of sanctity attached to them from ancient times.

**Types of Dāna —**

The *Bh. Gītā* describes three kinds of *dāna,* Sāttvika, Rājasa and Tāmasa among which Sāttvika *dāna* is regarded as the best of all these types[156] and the predominant element of the Primordial Matter (Prakṛti) is responsible for the differentiation. The *Garuḍa P.* mentions just the Sāttvika type or the *dāna* of pure quality and divides *dāna* into four categories - (i) *nitya* (or daily gifts), (ii) *naimittika* (or casual), (iii) *kāmya* (gifts given away with a desire to secure a special fruit and (iv) *vimala* (or pure). The *nityadāna* according to the *Garuda P.* is a gift of any article or cash to a Brāhmaṇa who does not do anything in return. The *naimittikadāna* is gifted by all good persons and something is given to scholars for wiping out sins. The gift made with a desire to have progeny, success, prosperity or heaven was termed as *kāmya* and gift made to a person with the knowledge of Brahman, with a *sāttvika* bent of mind just to please god is called *vimala* and is regarded as auspicious.[157] The author of the *Kūrma P.* also speaks of four types of *dāna,* viz. *nitya, naimittika, kāmya and vimala* and considers *vimala* to be the best of all the types and the details of these varieties are almost the same as those mentioned in the *Garuḍa P.*[158]

---

155. For more details of the mountain cult, see Dange S.S., *The Bhāgavata Purāṇa, Mytho-Social Study,* Delhi, 1984, pp. 183-187.

156. *Bh. Gītā* XVII. 22-24.

157. *Gar. P.* I.51.4-8.

158. *Kūr. P.* II. 26. 4-8.

### Mahādāna-s (great gifts)

The works on Dharmaśāstra enjoin supreme gifts *(atidāna-s)* such as cows, the earth (land) and learning that rescue the donor from all sins.[159] The authors of the *purāṇa*-s have enjoined great gifts *(mahādāna*-s) that were believed to be dispelling all sorts of ills and the effects of bad dreams. Thus, the *Matsya P.* lays down *tulāpuruṣadāna, hiraṇyagarbhākhyamahādāna,* Brahmānaṇḍadāna, *kalpavṛkṣadāna, gosahasradāna,* a gift of a golden milch-cow, a gift of a golden horse, a gift of a golden horse chariot, a gift of a golden elephant, that of a land with five ploughs, a gift of golden earth, a gift of the universal wheel, that of a *kalpalatā, a gift of seven seas, that of a ratnadhenu, a* gift of pot representing great elements.[160] The Agni P. states that the *mahādāna*-s are in all sixteen.[161] The advice to give away the *mahādāna*-s which were beyond the capacity of the common people may appear surprising, when the general leaning of the *purāṇa*-s was towards making the old religion simplified and practicable. However, the concept or the *mahādāna-s* seems to be a contribution of the Gupta period, which had a politico-religious significance. These great gifts were of immense significance because they were used by the regional Hindu kings to establish (or renew) their universal imperial sovereignty.[162]

Moreover, as shown by Acharya Kala on the basis of references to gifts such as the gift of entire treasurey at every fifth year at the time of *mokṣamahāpariṣad* at Prayag by Harshavardhana, a gift of thousands of cows by

---

159. *Br. S.* 18.

त्रीण्याहुरतिदानानि गावः पृथ्वी सरस्वती।
तारयन्ति हि दातारं सर्वात् पापदसंशयम्।।

*also Bh-P. IV. 151.18*[ab]

*160. Mat. P.* Chapters 275.289; also Lin.P. II. 29, 33, 35 and 38.

161. *Agn. P.* 210. 1-4.

162. Inden Ronald, "Ritual Authority and Cyclic Times in Hindu Kingship", *Kingship and Auithority in south Asia,* ed. by J.F. Richards, South Asian Studies, Univesity of Wisconsin, Madison Publication Series, No. 3, 1978, P. 38.

Samudragupta, which could be traced back to the *gosahasradāna* of the Puranic age, a gift in the form of an yearly grant of one hundred hons to meet the expenses of frankincense, lamp, sweeper... etc., the descriptions of the royal gifts mentioned in the *purāṇa*-s were not just the accounts of gifts presented by the authors with their usual Puranic style. They were significant royal customs adopted and followed by Indian kings in later times. It is important to note that such gifts were ultimately to be utilised in the interest of common people which indicates that the Puranic religion was in the interest of the masses in every respect.[163]

**Iṣṭāpūrta —**

*Iṣṭāpūrtadāna* is eulogised by the authors of the works on Dharmaśāstra. The *Viṣṇu Dh. S.* states that by digging a well, half of the sin is destroyed, by excavating a tank one reaches the region of Varuṇa and a giver of water enjoys perpetual satisfaction.[164] The *Likhitasmṛti* reflects a wide gap existing between the two classes, the class of the *dvija*-s and that of the non-*dvija*-s (*śūdra*-s) and considers *iṣṭāpūrta* as a common religion of the twice-born ones (*dvijāti*-s) and states that a *śūdra* is entitled to perform *pūrta* works but not the Vedic rites.[165] The author of the *Agni P.* also has glorified *pūrta dharma*. Thus, according to him, wells, lakes, temples, gift of food, gardens together constitute *pūrta dharma*. It enables one to achieve salvation. Similarly, gifts made during the time of the eclipses of planets and during the changes in the sun's movement from one zodiacal sign to another also is termed as *pūrta* and it enables the donor to reach the heavenly world.[166]

---

163. Fro more details, see Acharya Kala, *Thesis, Op. cit.*, pp.393-395.

164. *Viṣṇu Dh. S.* 91. 1-3.

165. *Likhita S.* 6.
इष्टापूर्ते द्विजातीनां सामान्यो धर्म उच्यते।
अधिकारो भवेच्छूद्रः पूर्ते धर्मे न वैदिके।।

166. *Agn. P.* 209.2,4.

**Pratimādāna (Gifts of Images) —**

Another striking feature of the Puranic concept of *dāna* forming a part of Puranic religion is the act of giving away images to Brāhmaṇa-s. Thus, according to the *Nārada P.*, an image of Gaurī along with that of her husband is to be made of gold, silver, copper or even earth and after worshipping it, it is to be gifted to the preceptor on the third day of the bright half of the month of Caitra.[167] The *Varāha P.* describes a number of vows and enjoins gifts of the images of animals such as a fish or a tortoise to be given away to a priest or a Brāhmaṇa and names these vows after these images. Thus, it enjoins a gift of an image of a fish to be given to a priest along with sandals, incense and cloth accompanied with the prescribed rituals and states that if the priest is wellversed in the Veda-s and the Upaniṣads, the resultant fruit will be many times more than when given to an ordinary person.[168] The same *purāṇa* also enjoins a gift of a gold-image of the Lord in the form of a tortoise and the vow is termed as Kūrmadvādaśīvrata.[169] The *Var. P.* also enjoins gifts of gold-images of god to be given to Brāhmaṇa-s. Thus, during the observance of Varāhadvādaśīvrata, to be performed on the twelfth day of the bright half of the month of Māgha, a gold-image of Viṣṇu is to be offered to a poor Brāhmaṇa learned in Veda-s and devoted to Viṣṇu.[170] Likewise a gold-image of Narasiṁha during the observance of Narasiṁhavrata,[171] a gold-image of Vāmana during the observance of Vāmanadvādaśīvrata,[172] a gold-image of Jāmadgnya during the observance of Jāmadagnyadvādaśīvrata[173] gold-images of Rāma and Lakṣmaṇa during the observance of Rāmadvādaśīvrata,[174]

167. *Nār. P.* I. 112. 2,3,6.
168. *Var.P.* 39.54-55.
169. *Ibid*, 40.7.
170. *Ibid*, 41.6-10, 13.
171. *Ibid*, 42.5-6.
172. *Ibid*, 43.5,7.
173. *Ibid*, 44.5
174. *Ibid*, 45.5.

a gold-image of the Lord Vāsudeva during the observance of Budhadvādaśīvrata[175] and a gold-image of Kalkin were to be given away to a Brāhmaṇa. The *Matsya P.* enjoins a gift of an image of Rohiṇī and the moon in gold along with white pearls, white clothes, milk..... etc. to a good Brāhmaṇa.[176]

Vipradakṣiṇā has always been a constituent part of *vratācaraṇa*.[177] During the observance of Ādityaśayanaśaṅkarārcana, a devotee was expected to give away a gold-lotus, eight fingers in length, made with eight petals and studded with jewels to a Brāhmaṇa along with bed-sheet, pillow, utensils, shoes, *cāmara*, a piece of mattress, garments, fruits, incense, bedstead, a cow with horns covered with gold and hoofs encased in silver along with her calf and a vessel-metal for milching the cow.[178] During the observance of Kāntivrata, and image of the moon with two digits in gold was to be worshipped for one year and at the end of the year was to be given away to a Brāhmaṇa and those who could not afford to do so, could also worship and give away a silver-image of the moon.[179] During the observance of Kṛṣṇāṣṭamīvrata, the devotee was expected to give away a cow, land, gold and cloth to the Brāhmaṇa-s who were expecially the devotees of Śiva.[180] The author of the *Agn. P.* combines the concept of *vrata* with the concept of *dāna* and names *vrata-s* after the articles offered at the time of the observance of *vrata*. According to the *Nār.P.*, while observing a vow on the fifth day of the bright half of the month of Bhādrapada in honour of the sages named Kaśyapa, Atri, Bhāradvāja, Viśvāmitra, Gautama, Jamadagni and Vasiṣṭha, seven cows fully bedecked with ornaments and clothes are to be given as gifts and the images of the seven sages made of gold are to be dedicated

175. *Ibid*, 47.3,5.
176. *Mat. P.* 57.20.
177. *Bh. P.* IV. 64. 26, also *Var.P.* 39.57, also *Ibid, 64.5,* Nār. P. *112.35-36,* Ibid, *112.42-44.*
178. *Mat. P.* 54.21-25.
179. *Var. P.* 57.2,5,10-12.
180. *Mat. P.* 56.5.

to Brāhmaṇa-s[181] It is needless to say that such gifts involved a great amount of expenditure and Brāhmaṇa-s were interested in keeping their own means of livelihood in tact through them.

**Simple Dāna-s (gifts) —**

The authors of the *Purāṇa*-s have also laid down very simple things that could be given away by the masses. The *Brahmāṇda P.* enjoins gifts of fragrant and fresh blue lotuses and Kalhāra flowers to propitiate the goddess Mahālakṣmī.[182] The *Garuḍa P.* enjoins a gift of betel leaves together with flowers for enhancing the delight of the residents of Yama's abode.[183] The *Varāha P.* enjoins a gift of water leading to eternal satisfaction,[184] the *Brahma P.* enjoins a gift of fruits and fragrant flowers.[185] The *Padma P.* lays down as simple gift as that of a lamp and states that it protects a hundred families.[186] The accounts of such simple gifts throw light on the fact that although the main objective of the authors of the *purāṇa*-s was to safeguard the interests of Brāhmaṇa-s these authors also provided common people every opportunity to follow religion, and consequently, Puranic religion became the religion of the masses.

**Dāna — as a part of Śrāddhakarma —**

*Dāna* was not just a part of *vratācaraṇa,* it was a part of *śrāddhakarma* as well. The author of the *Vāyu P.* enjoins a gift of a pitcher to be made at the time of performing *śrāddhakarma* whereby the donor was believed to be securing a cow yielding sweet milk.[187] The giver of bed

---

181. *Nār. P.* 114. 37ᵇ-39, 41, 45-46.
182. *Brahmāṇḍa P.* III. 4. 35. 89.
183. *Gar.P.* II. 31.18.
184. *Var. P.* 207. 47ᵃᵇ.
पानीयस्य प्रदानेन तृप्तिर्भवति शाश्वती।
185. *Br. P.* 216. 18.
186. *Pad. P.* VI. 121. 14ᵃᵇ.
दीपदानं महासेन कुलानां तारयेच्छतम्।
187. *Vāy. P.* II. 18.6; also *Brahmāṇḍa P.* I.16.7.

which is decorated with garlands of flowers was supposed to get excellent mansion. A person giving away gifts to ascetics was believed to be enjoying pleasures in the heavenly world, acquire pearls, lapis-lazuli, garments, various gems and divine vehicles.[188] The author of the *Bhahmāṇḍa P.* considers gifts in honour of manes as capable of conferring protection, leading to the heavenly world, bestowing long life, prosperity and auspicious charm. A giver of sandals at the time of performing *śrāddhakarma* was believed to be getting a beautiful vehicle, a giver of chappals to Brāhmaṇa-s a divine vehicle, a giver of an umbrella excellent mansion, a giver of pearls, lapis lazuli, garments and various gems, divine vehicles, a giver of fuel victory over his enemies in battle and fragrant garlands. One giving away desired articles to Brāhmaṇa-s was to have excellent memory and intellect. A giver of well-spread bed decorated with jewels was believed to be pleasing his forefathers and reaching the heavenly world. A person offering gifts with due faith was said to be attaining the fruit of Vājapeya sacrifice. A giver of silken garment and cotton garment was believed to be fulfilling his desires and attaining kingdom, heaven and the fruit of the performance of sacrifice. It was also believed that a person making gifts during *śrāddhakarma*-s would never suffer from grief.[189] In this respect, the authors of the *purāṇa*-s were seen to be continuing the traditional thought expressed by Atri that the gifts given away at the time of the performance of *śrāddhakarma*-s are excellent.[190]

**Gifts at various Holy Places —**

The authors of the *purāṇa*-s have attached great importance to various holy places having beautiful surrounding

---

188. *Ibid* II. 18.8-10.

189. *Brahmāṇḍa P.* I.16.8-11, 13, 22-23, 27ab, 31ab, 34ab, 35cd, 36ab, 43.

190. *Atri S.* 360ab.

and characterised by the sanctity of water flowing in their vicinity. Mere plunge into the water at these places was believed to be leading to the destruction of sins.[191] Equallly significant is the manner in which the authors of the *purāṇa*-s have sung the praises of the act of making gifts especially to the Brāhmaṇa-s at these holy places. Pilgrimage was another important constituent of the Puranic religion. The attention will be focussed on it in its relation with the changing social circumstances in the very next section of this chapter. Hence, there is no need to discuss it elaborately at this juncture. But since *dāna* at holy places is eulogised in the *purāṇa*-s time and again, it is necessary to discuss some of its aspects briefly.

In this connection, it is sufficient to state at this juncture that though the authors of the *purāṇa*-s tried to simplify religion by making people forget the importance of the performance of sacrifices, they were fully aware of the fact that sacrifice was an important means of their subsistence without which the survival of the class of Brāhmaṇa-s was endangered. Hence they tried to safeguard it by making frequent, earnest appeals to people to make gifts to them. For the same reason, the authors of the *purāṇa-s* kept on assuring people that the fruit secured through *dāna* was in no way inferior to that secured through the performance of sacrifice. The author of the *Bhaviṣya P.* e.g. states that the givers of land secure the fruit of the performance of Agniṣṭoma sacrifice.[192] According to the Garuḍa P., the merit accruing to one in offering protection to a poor Brāhmaṇa who is emaciated due to unemployment cannot be surpassed in sacredness even by performing a horse-sacrifice with the payment of sacrificial fees.[193] The author of the *Linga P.* considers a gift of goldhorse to be superior to Aśvamedha sacrifice.[194] The author of *Brahmāṇda*

---

191. *Mat. P.* 112.16.
192. *Bh. P.* IV. 164. 12-15.
193. *Gar. P.* II. 42.12.
194. *Ling. P.* II. 39.1.

*P.* states that a person giving gold-vessels, sesamum, sugarcanes, silver-vessels, a cow, fuel, fragrant flowers, a bed, a seat, a vehicle, a land while performing *śrāddhakarma* secures the fruit of the performance of Aśvamedha sacrifice.[195] A person who feeds Brāhmaṇa-s at the time of the performance of *śrāddha* rites and gives away silken cloth, fine-coloured cloth, woolen cloth, gold, and skin of an antelope to Brāhmaṇa-s obtains the fruit of the performanance of Vājapeya sacrifice,[196] fulfils all his desires, obtains kingdom and the heaven and acquires the fruit of the performance of sacrifice.[197] Knowing full well that Buddhism and Jainism were attracting the masses especially when people were disgusted with the rigidity, complexity and the expensiveness of sacrifices, the authors of the *purāṇa*-s replaced the institution of sacrifice by vows *(vrata*-s) and gifts *(dāna)* that had already become popular during the days of the works on Dharmaśāstra. However, even though the institution of sacrifice no longer retained its importnace, the objectives for which sacrifices were performed were still considered to be significant, *i.e.* obtainment of a son, destruction of sins, acquisition of wealth, merits and happiness etc, and the same were pursued through new means in the form of *vrata-s* and *dāna*. It is equally important to note that although the means with which these objectives were pursued changed, the socio-economic status of the class of Brāhmaṇa-s still remained high. At the same time, the authors of the *purāṇa*-s were successful in popularising Puranic religion by allowing the Śūdra-s and women to make gifts and achieve merits. The statements such as, as woman can get all her wishes fulfilled by giving away jaggery[198] or by donating a gold cow, women can reach the heaven and are worshipped by gods are sginificant in this re-

---

195. *Brahmāṇda P.* I.16.16-17, 19-20, 22-23, 25-26.

196. *Ibid,* I. 16.32[cd], 33, 34[ab].

197. *Ibid,* I.16.40.

सर्वकामानवाप्नोति राज्यं स्वर्गं तथैव च।

सर्वकामसमृद्धस्य यज्ञस्य फलमश्नुते।।

198. *Bh.P,* IV. 197. 26.

spect.[199] Similarly, while stating the account of a gift of a boar, the author of the *Bhaviṣya P.* is seen to be making conscious effort in throwing open the means of *dāna* for all the classes of society irrespective of *varṇa* or sex difference when he states, 'A gift of a boar could be made by the Brāhmaṇa-s, Kṣatriya-s, Vaiśya-s and Śūdra-s as well as by women.[200] A gift of a cow could be given away by the members of all the four classes[201] and Śūdra-s were assured that by giving a she-buffalo they will get their desires fulfilled.[202]

### Pilgrimage *(Tīrthayātra)*

*Tīrthayātra* was another significant part of the Puranic religion. Kane P.V. has throughly dealt with this topic.[203] Dange S.A. has dwelt on this aspect as one of the Puranic beliefs and practices[204] and Kumar Savitri has dealt with the Puranic lore of holy water places with special reference to the Skanda Purāṇa.[205] In this section this topic will be dealt with from the point of view of the relationship between religious change and social change.

As is rightly pointed out by Kane P.V., all religions have laid great emphasis on the sacredness of certain localities and have either recommended or enjoined with great insistence pilgrimages to them.[206] Rudhardt Jean has remarked: 'Whenever they are found, waters are often bound up with divine powers ... water fulfils a positive function. It bathes, dissolves and purifies. It symbolizes a gerative and life-giving quality very similar to creative power and is thus

199. *Ibid*, IV. 156. 24.
200. *Ibid*, IV. 194.21.
201. *Ibid*,, IV. 151.38.
202. *Ibid*, IV.162.16.
203. Kane P.V., *H. of Dh. S.*, Vol. IV, Pune, 1953, pp. 552-827
204. Dange S.A., *Ency. of Puranic Beliefs and Practices*, Vol. III, New Delhi, 1987, pp. 761-865.
205. Kumar Savitri, *The Puranic Lore of Holy Water Places*, New Delhi, 1983. pp. 1-319.
206. Kane P.V., *op. cit.*, p. 552

divine and sacralizing. It has a positive trait of conferring purity and immortality.[207] The descriptions of water presented in ancient Indian texts throw light on the same features of water. The *purāṇa*-s have continued the same tradition.

In India, the concept and the tradition of *tīrtha* are as old as the *Ṛgveda*. The word *tīrtha* occurs in the *Ṛgveda* and generally it appears to have been used in the sense of a road or a way. (RV.I.169. 6; I. 173. 11). At times, the same term is also used in the sense of a ford in a river (RV. VIII. 47.11). In *RV.* X.31.3. the word *tīrtha* could have been used in the sense of a holy place. The *Tait. S.* (VI. 1.1.1-2) has enjoined a bath for a sacrificer at *tīrtha* or a holy place. Language is a living phenomenon and it is but natural if the meanings of the words go on changing from time to time. For the same reasons, in the course of time, the term *tīrtha* could have been used in the sense of 'a locality or spot or expanse of water which gives rise to the accumulation of righteousness owing to its peculiar nature.'[208] The word *tīrtha* could be derived from the root *tṛ* meaning to cross over and may mean that sinful activities performed by an individual which are likely to form an obstruction in his course towards the yonder world or the heavenly world are crossed over or transgressed. It is pertinent to note in this connection that the Ṛgvedic seers regarded water to be pure and having cleansing and purifying trait. *Āpah:* are praised for their ability of cleansing man even from his moral guilt or the sins of violence (*RV.* I. 23.22; X.9.8. etc.). According to the seers to the *Ṛgveda*, the waters could bestow remedies and long life and even immortality upon human beings (*RV.* X. 95; 7; I. 23.19-21). They are described as conferring boons and wealth, excellent strength and immortality (X.9.5; 30.12). The Ṛgvedic seers regarded water as goddesses who helped the worshipper to become

207. Rudhardt Jean, (Tr. from French by Meltzer Erica), *The Ency. of Religion*, Vol. XV, Ed. by Eliabde Mircea, New Yourk, 1987, pp. 354-357.

208. Kane P.V., *op.cit.*, p. 553.

pure and cleansed (*RV.* X. 17.10). Holding these waters in high esteem, describing them as divine, pure and purifying and invoking them as goddesses, the Ṛgvedic seers have requested them to protect them.[209] The *Atharvaveda* also contains invocation in honour of water-goddesses. They are described as pure and purifying and have been requested to be auspicious towards the invoker (*AV.* I. 33.4). The *Tait. S.* (II. 6.8.3) identifies waters with all the goddesses (*āpo vai sarvāḥ devatāḥ)* and implies that all goddesses are deposited in them.

**The Concept of *Tīrtha* in the Works on Dharmaśāstra —**

Manu considers a Brāhmaṇa who is wellversed in the Vedas, to be a *tīrtha.*[210] Expressing the same view, Śatātapa expects *vipra*-s to undertake pilgrimage[211] and adds that they are moving pilgrimages void of water and granting all desires. Persons suffering from impurity (of sins) are purified by their wordlike water.[212] Recognising the importance of water, *Likhita S.* enjoins offering of libations of water unto the celestials and the *pitṛ*-s.[213] *Vyāsa S.* also enjoing bathing in tanks, wells and fountains and states that in cases where *tīrtha*-s would not be available or wherein ablution would not be practicable, one should bathe in the courtyard of a house with water enough to wet.[214] The *Śaṅkha S.* also considers *Kriyāsnāna* and *tīrthasnāna* to be very important

---

209. *RV. VII. 49.2.*

या आपो दिव्या उत वा स्रवन्ति
खनित्रिमा उत वा स्वयञ्जाः ।
समुद्रार्था याः शुचयः पावकास्ता
आपा देवीरिह मामवन्तु ।।

210. *Manu S.* III. 130.
211. *Śatātapa S.* I.28.
212. *Ibid*, I. 30.

ब्राह्मणा जङ्गमं तीर्थं निर्जलं सर्वकामिकम् ।
तेषां वाक्योदकेनैव शुध्यन्ति मलिना जनाः ।।

213. *Likhita* S. 8.
214. *Vyāsa S.* III.6-7.

and enjoins the performance of the rite of *ācamana* having dived in and out of water and the recommendation of invocation to the god Varuṇa to give one the sacred pool *(tīrtha)* for the expiation of all sins.[215] The *Śaṅkha S.* considers waters to be holy and enjoins people to seek their shelter,[216] recite the *mantra*-s beginning with *'hiraṇyavarṇa ......' 'śanno devī,' 'śanna apaḥ'* etc. recite Aghamarṣaṇa *sūkta* and the names of holy places and assures that by doing so, a bather acquires the merit of bathing at a sacred place.[217] The *Viṣṇu Dh. S.* also enjoins bathing in various *tīrtha*-s such as Puṣkara, Gayāśīrṣa, Akṣayavaṭa, Amarakaṇṭaka hill etc. with an assurance that bathing in such *tirtha*-s will free one from all sins.[218] Compared to the contents that glorify *dāna* or *vrata*-s, the verses that enjoin and applaud visits to holy places and bathing in them found in the works on Dharmaśāstra are less in number. Of course, the contents of the *purāṇa*-s show that the importance of *tīrtha*-s or holy places did not just depend upon the number. The tendency to eulogise them reached its climax in the days of the *Mahābhārata* and especially in the *purāṇa*-s so much so that the *tīrtha*-s were considered to be superior even to sacrifices. The *Mahābhārata* compares the act of performing sacrifices to the act of paying visits to pilgrimages and states that various implements, collection of materials, the coperation of priests, the presence of a wife are necessary for the performance of sacrifices and hence they can be performed only by princes and rich men and never by poor or helpless people.[219] The *purāṇa*-s have continued the same tradition by expressing almost the same ideas.[220] The author of the *Varāha P.* goes a step further and considers the fruit of bathing in the waters of holy places as superior

215. *Śaṅkha S.* VIII.2-3.
216. *Ibid*, VIII, $6^{cd}$.
217. *Ibid*, VIII. 8, 12, 14, 15.
218. *Viṣṇu Dh. S.* 85.3ff.
219. *Mbh. Vana* 82 12-15, $17^{cd}$.
also *Ibid, Anu.* 107.2-4.
220. *Mat.P.* 112.12-15 *Pad. P.* I.11.14-17; 49.12-15.

not only just to sacrifices but also to penance, meditation, as also self control[221] and glorifies the bather stating that he sees the past, present and future by just the circumambulations and reaches the world of Viṣṇu.[222]

**The Puranic Concept of *Tīrtha* —**

The author of the *Padma P.* throws light on the concept of *tīrtha* stating that just as certain parts of the body are regarded as the most sacred, similarly certain regions of the earth are considered to be the most sacred (especially) due to the wondrous qualities of the land, water or due to the fact that they have been resorted to by the sages.[223]

Conceptually, the holy places described and lauded in the *purāṇa*-s can be divided into three categories, though actual classification is a difficult task as it is quite possible that a specific holy place can fall under all these three categories. These categories are — (i) Those that eulcgise just the remembrances or visits to holy places. (ii) Those that applaud plunges or bathing into them. (iii) Those that glorify the act of making gifts or/and the performance of *śrāddhakarma*-s at them.

Likewise, as per the descriptions of the fruits conferred by paying visits to the *tīrtha*-s, they can be divided into three categories — (i) Those that lead to the acquisition of material pleasures and destruction or removal of all sins. (ii) Those that enable the visitors to reach the heaven or various other worlds such as Viṣṇuloka, Śivaloka etc. or even the final beatitude. (iii) Those that confer *yajñaphala* or are described as superior to various sacrifices.

---

221. *Var. P.* 152. 35.
न यज्ञैर्न तपसा न ध्यानैर्न च संयमैः।
न तत्फलं लभते स्नातो यथा विश्रांतिसंज्ञके।।
222. *Ibid*, 152. 36
223. *Pad.* VI.237.25-27.

Of course, certain *tīrtha*-s aimed at all these objectives[224] and in this respect the *tīrtha*-s are in no way different from the two other parts of religion, *i.e. vrata*-s and *dāna*.

It is indeed noteworthy that while eulogising various *tīrtha*-s, the *Mahābhārata* lays stress on the cultivation of moral and spiritual qualities. The authors of the *purāṇa*-s have continued the same tradition. Thus, according to the *Mbh.*, a person whose hands, feet and mind are under control, who is endowed with knowledge, penance and reputation reaps the fruit of pilgrimage. The author of the *Brahma P.* has incorporated the same verse.[225] According to the *Mbh.*, a person who has taken bath, one who has purified himself with self-control is a person who is pure internally as well as externally.[226] Continuing the same tradition the *Kūrma P.* states that a bath in the water of the river Narmadā will enable one to protect hundreds of families provided he has control over himself.[227] The author of the *Nārada P.* also states that one who is devoid of egotism, will reap the benefit of pilgrimage.[228] The *Brahma P.* goes a step further and states that pure mind, control over one's own sense organs are the (real) pilgrimages that lead one to heaven. Wicked mind can never become pure by bathing at holy places like a wine-pot which is never purfied even though it is washed hundred times with water. The places where a person lives with control over his senses are (for him) the holy places such as Kuruksetra, Puṣkara etc.[229] The author of the *Nārada P.* has stated that if a person enters a *tīrtha* after conquering

224. *Br. P.* 9.21.

तस्मात्पुण्यतमं तीर्थं वाराहं सर्वकामदम्।
तत्र स्नानं च दानं च सर्वक्रतुफलप्रदम्।।

225. *Mbh. Vana*, 82-9; *Br. P.* 23.2.

226. *Ibid, Anu* 108.9.

227. *Kūr. P.* III.83.11.

228. *Nār. P.* III. 62.14[ab].

अहंकारविमुक्तश्च स तीर्थफलमाप्नुयात्।

229. *Br. P.* 23, 3, 4, 6.

lust, fury, convetousness, there is nothing that is not attained by him through pilgrimage undertaken.[230]

**Simplification and Popularisation of Puranic Religion —** It has been already stated that the sacrificial texts glorified the institution of sacrifice and enjoined the performance of various scrifices as means leading to the fulfilment of various desires, enjoyment of various material pleasures and the opportunity to reach various worlds including the heaven. The Upaniṣads laid emphasis on the acquisition of the knowledge of the Highest Reality to free oneself from the chain of births and deaths and attain salvation. Knowing full well that these means were within the reach of a limted few and millions of people were unable to pursue *dharma* were likely to be led away by the new offshoots of the old Brahmanical relgion *i.e.* Jainism and Buddhism which were becoming more and more popular due to the simplicity of their principles, the authors of the *purāṇa*-s stressed the importance of visits to holy places as a means to attain material and spiritual benefits and thus, replaced the institution of sacrifice as also Brahmajñāna or Ātmajñāna. Thus, the *Varāha P.* states that bathing in Prayāga *tīrtha* leads to the merit of Agniṣṭoma sacrifice, a bather gets an opporutunity to reach the world of Indra and obtains happiness or by merely plunging into Kanakhala *tīrtha,* one is able to free oneself from all sins and enjoy pleasures in the heaven.[231] Similarly, according to the *Vāmana P.*, bath in waters of Somatīrtha leads to the fruit of Rājaśūya sacrifice[232] and bathing in Amṛtatīrtha leads to the attainment of Śiva's place and immortality.[233] According to the *Nārada P.*, just a casual visit to a holy place will enable the visitor

---

230. *Nār P.* II. 62. 18[cd], ef
    कामं क्रोध च लोभं च यो जित्वा तीर्थमाविशेत्।
    न तेन किञ्चिदप्राप्त तीर्थाभिगमनाद्भवेत्।।
231. *Var. P.* 152. 38-40;
    also *Nār.*[D]. II. 62.7[cd]. 9.
232. *Vām. P.* 20.4.
233. *Ibid.* 16.3[ab], 4[ab].

to fulfil all his desires and flourish in the heaven.[234] A visit to Sūryatīrtha, where the sun was worshipped by Bali is said to be removing all sins and bathing on Sundays, on the days of the sun's transit and on the days of the solar and lunar eclipses is said to be conferring the benefit of Rājasūya sacrifice.[235] A man bathing in Koṭitīrtha and propitiating the manes is believed to be liberating them all.[236] By bathing in Avimukta, one is said to be attaining salvation and one who puts an end to his life at this place is said to be reaching the world of god.[237]

Certain cities are considered to be holy and having the capacity of bestowing religious merits upon the vistors. Gayā, Prayāga, Vārāṇasī are prominent among them. The author of the *Matsya P.* identifies Vārāṇasī with Śiva as well as Brahmā and considers it to be the highest place and the highest abode[238] and states that a person meeting his death at Vārāṇasī is not reborn.[239] According to the *Vāyu P.*, the city of Gayā is the most prominent holy place and a person who visits this place is able to protect his parents. A person making a gift of food at Gayā purifies seven generations and a person performing *śrāddhakarma* at Gayā destroys sins caused by Brahmanicide, drinking liquor, theft and approaching the wife of one's own preceptor. Even the fruit secured by the performance of Aśvamedha sacrifice is much inferior to that secured by offering *piṇḍa*-s to forefathers at Gayā.[240]

---

234. *Nār. P.* II. 61.10.
    अज्ञानेनापि यस्येह तीर्थाभिगमनं भवेत् ।
    सर्वकामसमृध्दः स्वर्गलोके महीयते ।।
235. *Var. P.* 152. 55[ab], 56.
236. *Ibid,* 152.66.
237. *Ibid,* 152.33.
238. *Mat. P.* 180.77.
    एतदेव परं स्थानमेतदेव परं शिवम् ।
    एतदेव परं ब्रह्म एतदेव परं पदम् ।।
239. *Ibid,* 180.72.
240. Vāy.*P.* II. 43, 4[ab], 9[ab], 10, 11[ab], 12, 29.

An attempt at simplification of the Purāṇic religion in order to attract the masses is clearly discernible in statements such as a bath at Pippaleśvara will enable a person to get an opportunity of sharing the seat of Indra with him[241] or a bath in Śūlabhedatīrtha is able to confer the fruit of a gift of a thousand cows or a bath at Koṭitīrtha is able to confer the fruit of the performance of all sacrifices or a bath in the waters of Saṅgameśvaratīrtha is able to bestow the benefit of becoming a king, a visit to Bhīmeśvara enables one to become free from all sufferings and a bath in the waters of this *tīrtha* frees one from all sorrows.[242] A visit to Vimalatīrtha makes one's soul free from all sins and lead to the benefit of the performance of Vājapeya sacrifice and the attainment of the highest goal.[243] A bath in the waters of the holy place known as Hiraṇyākhya enables a sinful person to acquire the goal and a visit to Hiraṇyāsaṅgama confers the benefit of a gift of a thousand Kapilā cows, *tulāpuruṣadāna* and ten Aśvamedha sacrifices.[244] Of course the authors of the *purāṇa*-s expect pilgrims to be endowed with devotional feelings and faith while visting these holy places or bathing in sacred water. Thus, the *Nārada P.* states that the fishes stay in the sacred rivers like Gaṅgā etc. There are flocks of birds in a temple, but they are devoid of devotional emotions and hence they do not get any benefit from the *tīrtha* and the temple.[245]

The authors of the *purāṇa*-s were extremely keen on simplifying the old religion, so much so that they assured the masses that he who devoutly listens to the *purāṇa* at

---

241. *Pad. P.* III. 17.11, 14.
242. *Ibid,* III. 18.3, 8,55[cd], 56.28.
243. *Ibid,* III.25.37-38.
244. *Ibid,* VI. 2-3, 4, 9-11
245. *Nār.P.* II.62.19.
    गंगादितीर्थेषु वसन्ति मत्स्या देवालये पक्षिगणाश्च सन्ति।
    भावोज्झितास्ते न फलं लभन्ते तीर्थाच्च देवायतनाच्च मुख्यात्।।

Gaṅgādvāra with due observance of restraints attains eternal abode[246] or he who remembers Gaṅgādvāra even when he is far away attains good goal.[247] Yet another aspect of simplification is noticed when the authors of the *purāṇa*-s declare that a mere remembrance or the recitation of the names of certain *tīrtha*-s or the act of having just a look at certain *tīrtha*-s enables one to destroy all his sins[248] or a mere fast and the worship of the god with *bilva-patra* especially on Mondays at Indragrāmatīrtha lead to the three goals of human life, *i.e*, *dharma*, *artha* and *kāma*[249] or beholding the orb of the red sun at Bālātīrtha is believed to be enabling the pilgrim to attain Śūryaloka.[250] According to the author of the *Vāmana P.*, those who remember *tīrtha*-s and propitiate gods and bathe with faith attain final beautitude or a person remembering Kurukṣetra becomes holy internally as well as externally.[251]

## Holy Rivers

Along with the mention of certain holy places, the *purāṇa*-s also describe some rivers as pure and having purificatory traits and hence worth visiting. Among them, Gaṅgā, Narmadā, Godāvarī, Kāverī are the prominent ones. Praises of encomium have been showered upon the river Gaṅgā in the *Mbh.*[252] The Anuśāsanaparva of the *Mbh.* describes the adjecent regions of this river as wellknown for religious merits and the bathers in the sacred water of

---

246. *Nār. P.* II.66.53.
गंगाद्वारे पुराणं तु श्रुणुयाद्यश्च भक्तितः।
नियमेन महाभागे स याति पदमव्ययम्।।
247. *Ibid*, II.66.49.
248. *Pad. P.* III. 42.12.
प्रयागं स्मरमाणस्य सर्वमायाति संक्षयम्।
दर्शनात्तस्य तीर्थस्य नामसंकीर्तनादपि।।
249. *Ibid*, II. 151. 1, 13-14.
250. *Ibid*, III. 152. 27.28.
251. *Vām. P.* 12.5-6.
252. *Mbh. Vana*, 85.88-97.

the river are regarded as pure in spirit and superior even to those who perform sacrifices.[253] It is wellknown that the *Bh. G.* also considers this river as the best of all the streams (Srotasāmasmi Jāhnavī).[254] The *purāṇa*-s have continued the same tradition. The *Agni P.* states that the regions through which the river Gaṅgā flows are pure and a person resorting to the river Gaṅgā obtains the fruit of the performance of all sacrifices. She is the goddess (able enough) to remove all sins and the bestower of all the worlds and as long as one's bones (after one's death) are in the water of the river Gaṅgā, one remains in the heaven. Blind persons get an opportunity of becoming comparable to gods (after visiting the region of this river).[255] The sight, the touch, the act of drinking (the water of this river), the mention of the name of the river Gaṅgā purify hundreds and thousands of persons.[256] The river Narmadā also is praised by the authors of the *purāṇa*-s. Thus, the *Agni P.* states that the acts of making gifts, practising penance, recitation, or the performance of *śrāddhakarma*, in the vicinity of the river are indestructible.[257] The water of this river is described as holy, pure, adorned by foam, waves and able enough to make one free from sins. The river is also said to be having the capacity of purifying the three worlds.[258] The river is considered to be the best and able enough to protect all beings, movable as also immovable.[259] The river Godāvarī also is described as holy and able to

253. *Mbh. Anu,* 26.30-31.

254. *Bh. G.* X. 31.

255. *Agn. P.* 110. 1[cd]. 3, 4, 5[ab].

येषां मध्ये याति गङ्गा ते देशाः पावनाः वराः।
सकलाघहरी देवी सर्वलोकप्रदायिनी।
यावदस्थि च गङ्गायां तावत्स्वर्गे स तिष्ठति।।
अन्धादयस्तु तां सेव्य देवैर्गच्छन्ति तुल्यताम्।

256. *Ibid,* 110.6.

257. *Ibid,* 113, 5[cd].

258. *Pad. P.* III. 13.51,53[cd].

259. *Kūr. P.* II. 38.5.

remove all the sins. A person having bath in the waters of this river and satisfying one's forefathers is said to be becoming free from all sins and believed to the getting be fruit of a gift of a thousand cows.[260] The river Kāverī also is said to be capable of destroying sins.[261] A bath at the confluence of Kāverī and Narmadā and drinking of water of this river are supposed to lead to the fruit of Cāndrāyaṇa *vrata* and the bath in the waters of the river Dharmāvatī was supposed to lead one to the heaven.[262]

**Background of Mythological Accounts —**

The authors of the *purāṇa*-s are in the habit of glorifying these holy places with their usual Puranic style and while doing so, at times they present mythological accounts in order to stress therir importance. Thus, while glorifying Svānulomāyanatīrtha, the author of the *Vāmana P.* states that this is a place where excellent Brāhmaṇa-s got purified by uprooting the hair on their bodies by means of breath-control.[263] While presenting similar mythological account as a background to emphasise the importance of Nāradīyasaras it is stated that it was created by Nārada by digging the earth with a blade of grass. The *tīrtha* is important also because of the idol of Nārada established here and a Śivaliṅga established by Nārada himself.[264] Similar mythological account is presented regarding Koṭitīrtha of Rāmeśvara according to which Rāma killed Rāvaṇa and came to the mountain Gandhamādana at the bridge on the ocean. Rāma committed the sin of Brahmahatyā and hence he established a *liṅga* at this place. With a desire of washing it with fresh water, he dug the earth with the tip of his bow *(dhanuṣkoti)*. The tip entered the nether world where the course of the river Gaṅgā was flowing. Rāma pulled it up and the water of the river rushed up. At this place, Koṭitīrtha was established.[265] Rudrasaras located

260. *Ibid*, II.34.15.

261. *Ibid*, II. 34.16.

262. *Pad. P.* III. 16.6. $17^{cd}$.

263. *Vām. P.* 14. 47-48.

264. *Ska P.* I. 2.53, 15ff, *Ibid*, I. 52. 1, 2.

in Mahākālavana is glorified with the background of similar account according to which Brahmā's skull was attached to the palm of Śiva. He placed it in Mahākālavana. A terrible sound arose and the demon Halāhala approached the place in the form of a buffalo. The *gaṅa*-s of Śiva killed him immediately. From Brahmā's skull a number of mother-goddesses *(mātṛka*-s) came out. The place where the skull was placed got dimpled, turned into a lake and was known as Rudrasaras.[266]

**Dāna at various Holy Places —**

The concept of *dāna* as a component part of the Puranic religion is already discussed and it has been pointed out that *dāna* was a part of pilgrimage as well. The *purāṇa*-s contain many illustrations throwing light on this point. For instance, the *Kūrma P.* states that a gift of a lamp, ghee and Kapilā cow adorned with bells and ornaments offered on the fourteenth day of the month of Jyeṣṭha at Kapilātīrtha enables one to enjoy all material pleasures and reach the abode of Śakra, to enjoy pleasures in the company of Śakra and even if a donor has fallen from the heaven, he gets enjoyments and wealth.[267] *Dāna* at Prayāga, at the confluence of the river Gaṅgā and the ocean helps one in reaching the heaven.[268] Guḍadhenudāna at Bālātīrtha is said to be leading to the benefit of the performance of all sacrifices. A person suffering from affliction and disease is free from them, a person caught or imprisoned is freed and *piṇḍadāna* at this holy place is believed to be satisfying the forefathers.[269] Perhaps the simplest type of *dāna* to be made at holy places is enjoined in the *Padma P.* according to which one has to have a bath at Gotīrtha and please the mothers in the form of cows by offering *gavānhika* as a result of which one becomes free from the

265. *Ibid*, III.1.27.5-12.
266. *Ibid P.* V. 1.9.5-18.
267. *Kūr. P.* II.38.90-92, 94-95.
268. *Agn. P.* 11.12.
269. *Pad. P.* VI. 152. 30, 32.

debt one owes to mothers.[270] Sometimes, a visit to holy places or bathing in the waters of these places only serve the purpose of *dāna*. Thus, according to the author of the *Vāmana P.*, a visit to Kapilarhada-tīrtha and bath at this place along with the worship of deities and manes enable man to acquire the merit of making a gift of a thousand kine.[271]

**Vipradāna at Holy Place —**

The two other component parts of religion discussed in this section earlier, viz. vows and gifts replaced the institution of sacrifice which in the days of the sacrificial texts was highly laudable and which enabled Brāhmaṇa-s to enjoy a very high economic and social status. Innumerable details of the *vrata*-s and *dāna*-s stated by the *purāṇa*-s shed ample light on the fact that the authors of the *purāṇa*-s felt an utter need to wean the masses away from Jainism and Buddhism and make them forget the importance of various sacrifices. However, sacrifice was a significant and lucrative means of their livelihood. When it was shaken off, it was absolutely necessary to replace it tactfuly by some ohter means. It is already pointed out that the *purāṇa*-s stressed the importance of visits to holy places, bathing at these places and performing *śrāddhakarma*-s at these places in order to achieve merits and at times enjoined *dāna*-s at these places. Thus, they stated that a person making gifts to Brāhmaṇa-s as per rules at Kambutīrtha attains Viṣṇuloka by virtue of that holy place[272] or at Indragrāma, one should perform *śrāddhakarma*, and feed a Brāhmaṇa. Feeding one Brāhmaṇa is equivalent to feeding a thousand persons. One should give away gold, land,

---

270. *Ibid*, VI. 163.4.
तत्र तीर्थे नरः स्नात्वा दत्त्वा गोभ्यो गवाह्निकम्।
गोमातृणां प्रसादेन मातृणामनृणी भवेत्।।

271. *Vām. P. Saromāhātmya* 14.24, 29.

272. *Pad. P.* VI. 142. 2.
दत्त्वा दानानि विधिवद्ब्राह्मणेभ्यो विधानतः।
विष्णुलोकमवाप्नोति तीर्थस्यास्य प्रभावतः।।

garments as per one's capacity, should gift white milch-cow along with a calf.[273] In the same *purāṇa*, elsewhere it is stated that one who gifts a red cow (to Brāhmaṇa-s) reaps the fruit of the performance of all sacrifices, such a person never goes to hell, is free from disease and bondage[274] or one who has bath at Gotīrtha and one who gives away a milch-cow to the leading Brāhmaṇa-s attains Brahmapada.[275] The author of the *Vāmana P.* states that those who offer grains, boiled in milk and moistened with ghee do not have any more sins left in them and by feeding a Brāhmaṇa at Brahmodumbaratīrtha, one receives the favour of manes and gods who grant rare gifts of the world.[276] According to the *Brahmāṇḍa P.*, the discharger of a bull sanctifies twelve preceding and succeeding generations.[277] Likewise, the author of the *Nārada P.* states that by the not offering gold in gift and by not offering cows after visiting holy places, one becomes poor. [278]

**Pilgrimage as a Means for the Masses —**

Just as in order to popularise the old brahmanical religion, the authors of the *purāṇa*-s specifically mentioned that the *vrata*-s and *dāna*-s would be resorted to by all the sections of society irrespective of *varṇa* or sex difference, similarly, they thought it worthwhile emphasising the point that pilgrimage as a means of achieving merits could also be resorted to by all the sections of society. Thus, the *Padma P.* states that Pichumandaratīrtha is able to free one from disease. A person worshipping the sun with the recitation of twelve names of the sun (Āditya, Bhāskara, Bhānu etc.) will reap the fruit. Thus, a Brāhmaṇa will be rich and wellversed in the Veda-s in seven (con-

---

273. *Pad. P.* VI 151. 9[cd]-11[ab].
274. *Ibid*, VI. 152. 31[cd], 32[ab], cd.
275. *Ibid*, V.163.5.
276. *Vām.P. Saromāhātmya* 15.2,12.
277. *Brahmāṇḍa P.* III.19.15-19.
278. *Nār. P.* II. 62. 8[cd].

secutive) births, a Kṣatriya will get the kingdom, a Vaiśya will get wealth and a Śūdra will get devotion.[279] The authors of the *Matsya* and *Kūrma purāṇa*-s also have stressed the same point stating that Avimukta is the best cure for men of numerous *varṇa*-s, for men not (recognised as) belonging to any particular *varṇa* for Cāṇḍāla-s who are abhorred (by people) and for persons whose bodies are full of diseases and of aggrevated sins.[280] The *Vām.P.* goes a step further and incorporates one more point, *i.e.* Varṇāśrama difference also is never a bar for people resorting to this means and states that the persons of all the four *āśrama*-s protect seven generations of their families by bathing at holy places and persons belonging to the four *varṇa*-s and women achieve the highest goal.[281] While stating so, the *purāṇa*-s are undoubtely following the tradition of the *Mbh.*[282]

## Synthesis of Śaiva and Vaiśṇava Cults

Deliberate attempt to popularise Puranic religion is also noticed when the *purāṇa*-s aim at sythesising Śaiva and Vaiṣṇava cults even while eulogising the *tīrtha-s*. Thus, while glorifying the river Candrabhāgā, the *Padma P.* enjoins a bath, meditation and the worship of Śiva and states that the worshippers of Śiva are to be known as Śivarūpins. In the very next verse, obtainment of the abode of Viṣṇu glorified as the fruit secured by those who perform *śrāddhakarma* at this place.[283] The author of the *Vāmana P.* states that at Lokoddhāra *tīrtha*, Viṣṇu is perpetually present and the eternal god Śiva too is present there only and by propitating both these gods, by prostration, one obtains emancipation[284] and attracts the followers of both the cults.

---

279. *Pad. P.* VI. 158.12-13.

280. *Mat. P.* 184.66, *Kūr.P.* I.31.42.
नानावर्णा विवर्णाश्च चण्डाला ते जुगुप्सिताः।
किल्बिषैः पूर्णदेहाश्च प्रकृष्टैः पातकैस्तथा।।

281. *Vām.P.* 36. 78-79.

282. *Mbh. Vana.* 82.30-34.

283. *Pad. P.* 156. 3-4.

284. *Vām.P. Saromāhātmya* 14. 22
यत्र विष्णुः स्थितो नित्यं शिवो देवः सनातनः।
तौ देवौ प्रणिपातेन प्रसाद्य सनातनः मुक्तिमाप्नुयात्।।

**Norms to be Followed by the Pilgrims —**

It has been already pointed out that the *purāṇa*-s attach utmost importance to self-control and expect the pilgrims to be detached, to have control over their minds and sense-organs. Equally important according to them is the feeling of devotion to be cherished by the pilgiims in their hearts.[285] According to the Nārada Purāṇa, a person who maintains a householder's life is forbidden to visit holy centres by ancient authorities.[286] The author of this *purāṇa* expects a pilgrim to perform *śrāddha* with ghee for the welfare during pilgrimage[287] and to avoid the use of vehicles while visiting holy places and states that if a cow (or a bull) is used as a vehicle, pilgimage becomes fruitless... If one undertakes journey on foot, the pilgrimage leads to four times greater benefit. The author of this *purāṇa* allows pilgrims to use umbrella at the time of heavy downpour or scorching sunshine, use a staff as a prop if the path is thorny and allows the pilgrims to walk with shoes on if they are desirous of protecting their bodies.[288] A person whose father was alive was supposed to undergo *kṣaura* (shaving of the beard) rite after reaching the *tīrtha*. But one was not supposed to shave one's moustaches.[289] Though, by and large pilgrimage seems to be replacing the institution of sacrifice, according to the author of the *Nārada P.* when one's capacity to perform sacrifices comes to an end, a Brāhmaṇa should visit holy places and roam about the *tīrtha*-s.[290]

---

285. *Nār. P.* II. 62.20[ab].
भावं ततो हृत्कमले निधाय तीर्थानि सेवेत समाहितात्मा।

286. *Ibid.* II. 62.23.

287. *Ibid.* II. 62.27.

288. *Ibid.* II. 62.33-35.

289. *Ibid*, II. 62.53.

290. *Ibid*, II. 62.22[ab].
यज्ञाधिकारेऽप्यथवा निवृत्ते विप्र तीर्थानि परिभ्रमेच्च।

## Characteristics and Utilitarian Traits of Water Known in Modern Days and The Puranic Concept of Water

Kumar Savitri has referred to the fact that water enters the ground and passes through earth containing organic and mineral matter and may absorb mineral and exhange gases, hydrogene sulphide and methane and has also drawn attention to the points stated in Encyclopaedia of Britannica that carbonates, sulfates and clorides, iron, manganese and flourides may be acquired by water.[291] She has further stated that the climate of the world is tempered by the ability of water to soak and store the sun's heat and to release it slowly. The efficacy of water is increased by its contact with the sun's rays that directly penetrate the water whole day and shed abundance of elements such as helium, beryllium, jointly with boron, carbon, nitrogen diliem, phosperous, sulpher, calcium and iron.[292] On the basis of the information provided by the doctors at the Institute of Medicine, Naval Hospital, Bombay and the details given by Leopold in '*Water*'[293] she has pointed out that all these elements and to the healing curative and energy-giving aspect of water. River absorbs oxygen from the air and from the water weeds which release it during the process of photosynthesis. The laboratory experiments reveal that the Gaṅgā water contains Diatoms (a type of algae) which injenct other harmful bacteria and do not allow the growth of Bacillus Coli, causing diarrhoea etc. and allow water not to get spoiled for years. The *purāṇa*-s advise bath, sun-worship and meditation at some holy places. A continuous bath causes blood circulation. Many hot springs contain a large quantity of sulphur, phosphorous and inorganic salts. During the sun-drying, the ultra-voilet rays of the sun give vitamin D to the exposed body which also cure many skin-diseases, bone disorders. It is significant to

291. *Encyclopaedia of Britannica*, Vol. 19, p. 650.

292. *Ibid*, Vol. 17, p. 82.

293. For more details, see Kumar Savitri, *op. cit.*, pp. 1-4.

note in this conection that the authors of the *purāṇa*-s also have described water at holy places as curing and removing various sufferings and diseases. Thus, the author of the *Padma P.* states that those who visit Dhavaleśvara especially on Mondays are cured of their diseases and faults[294] or Picumandārkatīrtha is said to be removing diseases due to bath taken there.[295] However, one cannot state with certainty whether the authors of the *purāṇa*-s were aware of these scientific, utilitarian beneficiery qualities of water known to man in scientific era. The descriptions of purifying and sanctifying water at the holy places presented by the *purāṇa*-s seem to be more based on superstitions beliefs than on scientific knowledge, as visits to such places are mostly said to be leading to the destruction of sins, material pleasures, the attainment of various regions and even salvation. It is wellknown that superstitions belief is never based on scientific observation or scientific study of facts and hence it is likely to be false. Still it is agreed upon by all that when people regard certain things to be true, though in fact they may not be true, they do shape the behavioural patterns of people. For the same reason, eulogisation of the sanctity of water at holy places by the authors of the *purāṇa*-s might have induced people to visit these places in order to collect merits. Paying visits to holy places, at times worshipping divinities there, having bath in the water of these places and making gifts there were all simple religious modes popularised by the authors of the *purāṇa*-s in order to reattract the masses once again towards the old religion. The *purāṇa*-s popularised the old ancient Indian mythological belief that flowing water has curative efficacy due to its contact with the rays of the sun. For the same reason, the sacrificial waters also were collected from the flowing streams. A dip in the flow-

---

294. *Pad. P.* VI. 151. 15[ab].
तेषां रोगं तथा दोषं शमयेध्दवलेश्वरः।

295. *Ibid*, VI.158.7[a].
तीर्थं रोगहरं स्नानात्.........

ing water was believed to be leading to merit and the merit was doubled when the dip was at the confluence of two streams or two rivers.

In the words of Gupta A.S., 'In order to retain their authrotativencess and usefulness for the Hindu society, the Purāṇas had to keep pace with the vicissitudes through which the Hindu society had to pass owing to the varying political, religious and social conditions of India. Hence with the changes in the society, the Purāṇas, also underwent occasional revisions and redactions, but still they preserved in them traditions coming from the very early times.[296] When the survival of the old brahmanical religion and the society were endangered by the rise and popularity of Buddhism and Jainism, the *purāṇa*-s enthusiastically shouldered the responsibility of bringing about significant changes in the earlier fundamental principles and doctrines of Hinduism by turning people away from the pursuit of spiritual knowledge and the tedency to hanker after desired fruits through complex, complicated, rigid and difficult sacrifices involving tremendous expenditure by laying stress on the *vrata*-s, *dāna*-s and *tīrthayātrā*-s. Of course, as shown earlier, these three were not the innovative concepts introduced by these authors for the first time. They have been borrowed by them from other ancient works. But popularising them with an amazing zeal, the authors of the *purāṇa*-s brought about transformation in Hindu religion so as best to suit the changing needs of the time and the change in Hindu religion further brought about social change.

296. Gupta A.S., Introduction to *Vāmana Purāṇa*, Varanasi, 1968.

## CHAPTER — VIII

## MISCELLANEOUS

Besides the component parts discussed earlier, there are a few others, such as Karman doctrine or Karmavipāka theory, purificatory rites *(saṁskāra-s)*, the theory of incarnation, expiatory rites *(prāyaścitta-s)*, *śrāddhakarma-s* etc. which also formed parts of the Purāṇic religion. The authors of the *Purāṇa-s* have used the term *dharma* with a much wider perspective *i.e.* in the sense of duty as well and they discuss the duties of kings, women etc. Good conduct is regarded by them as the general duty or *sādhāraṇa dharma* of all human beings. Moreover, these authors have narrated a number of stories in order to attract the masses and many of them throw light on the Purāṇic concept of religion. In this chapter, the attention will be focussed on all such details.

### Dharma and Good Conduct —

Manu attached great importance to virtuous conduct. According to him, if the soul mainly practises virtue and vice is practised to a small degree, it obtains bliss in heaven and hence man should always fix his heart on the acquisition of merit.[1] According to Manu, *sattva* is the best of all the elements and *dharma* is the characteristic feature of *statva.*[2] The authors of the sacrificial texts or the Upanisads inculcated the importance of virtues.[3] The authors of the *purāṇa-s* also have emphasised the importance of virtuous conduct. Thus, the *Viṣṇu P.* states that a person of good conduct has conquered both the worlds, i.e. this

1. *Manu S.* XII. 20, 23[d].
2. *Ibid*, XII.38[cd].
3. Śat. Br. *I. 1.1.5*-
   स वै सत्यमेव वदेत्।

   *Tait. Up.* I.2.1- सत्यं वद। धर्मं चर।.......

   *Br. Up.* V. 2.3. तस्मादेतत् त्रयं शिक्षेद् दमं दानं दयामिति।

world and the yonder world.[4] The same author considers *dharma* as the best of the group of three *(trivarga)* and hence advises people to sacrifice *artha* and *kāma* at the altar of *dharma* as these two are said to be coming in the way of *dharma* which echoes similar thoughts expressed in the *Viṣṇu Dh. Sūtra.*[6] The same *purāṇa* elsewhere states that a person engaged in performing good deeds endowed with knowledge and modesty, who is wise, who never incurs sin even when behaving with persons committing sinful activities, one who speaks in a pleasing manner even in the company of the crooked ones, one whose heart is full of sympathy due to the feeling of friendship is ever entitled to achieve salvation.[7] Manu declard non-violence, truth, refraining from stealing, purity, selfcontrol as the principles of *Sāmāsika dharma.*[8] Yājñavalkya added forgiveness, straightforwardness, charity to the principles laid down by Manu. The *purāṇa*-s have incorporated these traditionally accepted norms of good conduct and have at times added a few more such as liberality, peace, penance,[9] tolerance, absence of pride, auspiciousness, pleasing talk, friendship, absence of desire, liberality, absence of jealousy.[10] According to the *Nār.P., dharma* springs from good conduct and activities devoid of good conduct lead to miseries.[11] Even a Brāhmaṇa appears to advantage by the

---

4. *Viṣ. P.* III. 11.2[cd]-
सदाचारवता पुंसा जितौ लोकावुभावपि।
5. *Ibid.* III. 11. 7[ab].
परित्यजेदर्थकामौ धर्मपीडाकरौ नृप।
6. *Viṣ. Dh. S.* 71-84.
7. *Viṣṇu. P.* III. 12.41
सदाचाररतः प्राज्ञो विद्याविनयशिक्षितः।
पापेऽप्यपापः परुषे ह्यभिधत्ते प्रियाणि यः।
मैत्री द्रवान्तःकरणस्तस्य मुक्तिः करे स्थिता।।
8. *Manu S.* X. 63.
9. *Vām. P.* 14.1-2.
10. *Br. P.* 114. 16-18.
11. *Nār.P.* I.15.54[c], 55[cd]-
आचारप्रभवो धर्मः
सदाचारविहीनानां धर्मा अप्यसुखप्रदाः।।

lustre of *Brahman* (only when) he is intent on following good conduct.[12] Even the *Mārk. P.* despises bad conduct and appeals to the masses to perform excellent deeds stating that a person performing evil activities does not live longer and hence one should strive to perform good deed (only).[13] The author of the *Bhāg. P.* has laid down principles of *sanātana dharma* such as truth, mercy, penance, purity, tolerance, observance, peace, control, non-violence, celibacy, sacrifice, concentration on one's own portion of study, straightforwardness, happiness, equal vision, service[14]...... which again throw light on the point that the authors of the *purāṇa*-s attached great importance to virtuous conduct.

### Puranic Dharma — a Wider Concept —

The authors of the *purāṇa*-s use the term *dharma* with a much wider perspective and impart valuable instructions even regarding the worldly dealings *(vyāvahārika dharma)* that will lead to the wellbeing of the masses. Thus, the author of the *Nār. P.* states that one's own kinsmen support him only as long as one earns money. *Dharma* (merit) and *adharma* (vice) only follow a man who goes to the yonder world, not his wealth, nor his sons, nor any of his kinsmen. Men who are nourished by means of wealth earned through *dharma* as well as *adharma* by a person consign him to flames and enjoy rich food soaked in ghee.[15]

### Appraisal of the *Śūdra*-s and Women —

Again, with a view to popularise and simplify religion,

---

12. *Nār. P.* I. 3. 78[ab].
    सदाचारपरो विप्रो वर्धते ब्रह्मतेजसा।
13. *Mārk. P.* 31. 8[abc].
14. *Bhāg. P.* VII.11.8; 9[a].
15. *Nār. P.* I. 42-43.
    यावदर्जयति द्रव्यं बांधवास्तावदेव हि।
    धर्माधर्मौ सहैवास्तामिहामुत्र चापरः।।
    धर्माधर्मार्जितैर्द्रव्यैः पोषिता येन ये नराः।
    मृतमग्निमुखे हुत्वा घृतान्नं भुञ्जते हि ते।।

the authors of the *purāṇa*-s declare that the *śūdradharma* or *strīdharma* is laudable Thus, while the author of the *Viṣṇu P.* states the *dvijāti*-s (the twiceborn ones) have to observe the vow of celibacy, study the *veda*-s and perform sacrifices by spending money. If these activities are performed in a wrong manner, they are likely to commit faults. They cannot even have food or drinks in keeping with their desires. They have to depend upon others for the sake of the performance of these activities but a *śūdra* entitled to perform *pākayajña* by waiting upon *dvijā*-s can secure victory over one's own worlds and is superior to other classes.[16] Yet, another simple reason as to why the *Śūdra-s* are considered to be good is the fact that they need not observe any (strict) rule regarding what is worthy of being eaten and what is worthy of being avoided, what is worthy of being drunk and what is not worthy of being relished.[17]

Likewise, the author declares the reason as to why women are to be considered to the superior (to men). Men have to perform sacrifices as per the rites laid down and give away gifts to the worthy with money acquired through righteous means and acquisition and protection of money involve great physical strain but women can reach asuspicious worlds by just waiting upon their husbands through deeds, mind and speech and being beneficial to them.[18]

**Strīdharma —**

Women of the Upaniṣadic period held philosophical discusssions. They were no longer praised by the authors of later works. Manu held that day and night women must be kept in dependence by the males of their families. The father of a woman protects her in childhood, her huband

16. *Viṣ. P.* VI. 2. 19, 21ab, 23.
17. *Ibid*, VI. 2.24.
भक्ष्याभक्ष्येषु नास्यास्ति पेयापेयेषु वै यतः।
नियमो मुनिशार्दूलस्तेनासौ साध्वितीरितः।।
18. *Ibid*, VI. 2. 25-28.

in her youth and her sons in old age and a woman is never fit to be independent.[19] Sacred texts do not lay down any sacramental rite for women. Women who are destitute of strength and destitute of knowledge of the Vedic texts are impure.[20] Women deliver babies they nurture them. Man's daily life is dependent on them.[21] Manu expected woman to control her thoughts, speech and acts and not to violate her duty towards her lord and dwell with her husband after his death as well and considers such a woman to be faithful (to her husband) *(sādhvī)*.[22]

The authors of the *purāṇa*-s also have expressed more or less similar traditional views regarding the duties of women. The *Bhaviṣya P.* states at one place that under all circumstances, a woman should carry out that which is beneficial to her husband through her mind, body and activites.[23] She should worship her husband and should not commit mistake in respect of activities to be performed for him.[24] According to this *purāṇa*, good character is the most important virtue of women and the author condemns women devoid of good character and intent on doing that which does not lead to the benefit of their husbands as worthy of being abandoned like 'Kālakūṭa' poison.[25] Again, following Manu's traditional views, the authors of the *purāṇa*-s also prohibited women from studying scriptures and held an extremely orthodox view regarding women's right to education. In fact, the *purāṇa*-s condemned women's right

---

19. *Manu S.* IX.2[ab], 3.
20. *Ibid*, IX.18.
21. *Ibid*, IX.27.
22. *Ibid*, IX.29.
23. *Bh. P.* I.14.27.
    तस्मात्सर्वास्ववस्थासु मनोवाक्कायकर्मभिः।
    हितं स्वाम्यनुकूलत्वं नारीणां तु विशेषतः।।
24. *Ibid*, I. 14.31[ab].
    एवमाराध्य भर्तारं तत्कार्येष्वप्रमादिनी।
25. *Ibid*, I. 8. 70.
    यास्तु विध्वस्तचारित्रा भर्तुश्चाहितकारकाः।
    त्याज्या एव स्त्रियः सद्भिः कालकूटविषोपमाः।।

to education by considering it to be useless.[26]

**Rājadharma —**

According to Manu, when creatures were without a king, they dispersed in all directions through fear and the Lord created a king for the procreation of this whole creation.[27] He identifies the rod of punishment with the king and regards the king to be the manager of affairs, the ruler and the surety for the four *aśrama*-s and obedience to the law.[28] He expects the king to get up early in the morning, worship Brāhmaṇa-s wellversed in the threefold sacred science and learned and follow their advice and believes that he who has conquered his own senses can keep his subjects in obedience.[29] According to Manu, a king should carefully shun ten vices springing from love of pleasure and the eight arising out of wrath which all end in misery and a king attached to the vices springing from love of pleasure loses his wealth and his virtue but he who is given to those arising from anger loses even his life.[30] Manu has devoted one full chapter for the discussion of the duties of a king.[31] According to him, a king should never retreat from the battlefield. He should always protect people, honour the Brāhmaṇa-s. He should strive to gain what he has not yet gained and carefully preserve what he has gained, should augment what he preserves and should bestow on worthy persons what he has augmented.[32] Manu expected a king to be ever ready to strike, with his prowess constantly displayed, his se-

---

26. *Ibid*, I.9.6.
    शास्त्राधिकारो न स्त्रीणां न ग्रन्थानां च धारणे।
    तस्मादिहान्ये मन्यंते तच्छासनमनर्थकम्।।
27. *Manu S.* VII.3.
28. *Ibid*, VII.17
29. *Ibid*, VII. 38, 44[cd].
30. *Manu S.* VII. 45-46.
31. *Ibid*, VII.
32. *Ibid*, VII. 88, 99.

crets constantly concealed and thought that a king should constantly explore the weakness of his foe. According to Manu, a king should plan his undertakings patiently meditating like a hero, should exhibit his strength like a lion, should snatch his prey like a wolf and should double his retreat like a hare.[33] Manu believed that just as the life-breaths of kings are destroyed by oppressing their kingdoms, and a king who governs his kingdom well easily prospers.[34] Among other important duties stated by Manu are the provision for the means of subsistence for the sake of a *śrotriya* in accordance with the sacred law and protection of the same and thinking of the six measures of royal policy viz. alliance, war, marching, halting, dividing the army and seeking protection.[35]

The author of the *Mārk.P.* expected the king to preserve the *varṇa* and *āśrama dharma*, to compel those who swerve from their own duty, to follow their *dharma*[36] and states that a king should have desire *(kāma)* under his control and should know six *guṇa*-s. Desire, anger, greed, pride, ego and delight are his enemies that lead to his destruction.[37] The *Agni P. presents a* thorough exposition on the duites of kings[38] including appointing the head of every village, for ten villages, hundred villages and an over all head and watching them daily through his spies to control any irregualrity through these heads and assures that the king would get wealth by protecting the state.[39] Among other noteworthy points to be remembered by the king are — avoiding sleeping during the day-time, strolling about idly, giving up censuring, cruel infliction of punishment and extravagance, destrtuction of mines, neglecting the care of the fort etc.[40] Even according to this *purāṇa*, a king should

---

33. *Ibid*, VII. 101-102, 105-106.
34. *Ibid*, VII. 112, 113$^{cd}$-
35. *Ibid*, VII 135, 160.
36. *Mārk. P.* 24.30.31.
37. *Ibid*, 24.10$^{cd}$, 14; also *Mat.P.* 216 -220, 222-228.
38. *Agn. P.* 223-225, 239.
39. *Ibid*, 224. 1-4
40. *Ibid*, 225. 4-6.

avoid passion, anger, haughtiness, pride, greed and arrogance and should win the love of citizens after having controlled the servants.[41] A king according to this *purāṇa*, would perish on account of modesty. He should learn three sciences, the science of administration, metaphysics and the science of wealth.[42] Among other duties of a king are mentioned the welfare and livelihood of the poor, destitute and old people; not to retreat from the battle, protection of subjects and giving away gifts to the *brahmins*. A king should arrange for the proper pursuit of the orders of the *varṇa*-s and *āśrama*-s. He should think about the wealth like a crane, conquer like a lion, pounce on the enemies like a wolf, dart forth like a hare and strike firmly like a boar. He should show vanity like a peacock, be faithful as a horse, speak pleasantly like a cuckoo, be suspicious like a crow...[43] Other significant duties laid down by this *purāṇa* include quick action, consistency, truthfulness, sevice to the aged, gratefulness, .... capactiy to exhibit valour, ...foresightedness, zeal, purity, generosity, modesty, virtuousness, eloquence, confidence, good memory, self-control, leadership, mastery over polity and the different branches of fine arts, capabality of facing an attack, capability of remedying all evils, knowledge of the principles of policymaking and war, capability of knowing the secret counsels in opportune time and place.[44] The king like the god of rain should be the sustainer of all good. He would take a part of the earnings from the sources of one's earnings, should employ efficient men to be in charge of all deeds, should protect eight things such as agricuturee, trade, fort, bridge, elephant, stable, mines, ocean and the abodes of the downcast and thus follow a good code of conduct.[45]

41. *Ibid*, 225.8.
42. *Ibid*, 225.22.
43. *Ibid*, 225.26-30.
44. *Ibid*, 239.2-12
45. *Ibid*, 239.43-45

**Simplicity —**

Simplicity is the hall-mark of the Purāṇic religion. It is specially adopted by the authors of the *purāṇa*-s in order to popularise religion, wean away those who were disgusted by the complicated and eleborate procedure of the ritualistic part of sacrificial texts and difficult metaphysical Upaniṣadic doctrines and therfore were likely to follow Jainism and Budhism.

**Importance of Faith *(śraddhā)*, Devotion *(bhakti)*, *Nāmamāhātmya* and *Japamāhātmya* —**

As stated earlier, the authors of the *purāṇa*-s tried to replace the institution of sacrifice by laying down the importance of comparatively simple activities such as observace of vows, making gifts or visiting holy places. But they also knew that some poeple were unable to perform even these activities and hence they tried to simplify religion by stressing the importance of faith, devotion. etc. Thus, the author of the *Nārada P.* states that all *dharma*-s (religions activities) performed faithfully lead to the fulfilment of one's cherished desires. Hari is pleased due to faith. Just as light is the cause of activities performed by all living beings, similarly devotion is the main cause of all achievements.[46]

The *Brahma P.* stresses the importance of the praise of Viṣṇu through the prayer for welfare, through which Viṣṇu is invoked with addresses such as the lord of the universe fulfilling the desires of people, the ocean of mercy, one who is favourably disposed towards his devotees, one who has lifted up the earth by his curved fangs, the guardian of quarters, the one and the only one, the all-pervading consciousness endowed with the supreme form which is devoid of positive and negative aspects... and states that

---

46. *Nār. P.* I. 4. 1 -2.
श्रद्धापूर्वाः सर्वधर्मा मनोरथफलप्रदाः ।
श्रद्धया साध्यते सर्वं श्रद्धया तुष्यते हरिः ।।
यथाऽऽलोको हि जन्तूनां चेष्टाकरणतां गतः ।
तथैव सर्वसिद्धीनां भक्तिः परमकारणम् ।।

he who reads, listens to and narrates the greatness of Viṣṇu, will shake off his sins and obtain the divine world and it is stated that this hymn despels sin and bestows pleasures and salvation.[47]

The *Nārada P.* lays down one thousand names of the Goddess Lalitā such a Kameśvarī, Bhagamālinī, Nityaklinnā, Bheruṇḍā Vanhivāsinī etc.[48] and says that these names afford the achievement of all objects. They yield the benefit of fourfold aims of life and he who repeats these names every day at dawn with pure mind becomes a Yogin, a knower of Brahman, a Śiva, Yogin and a knower of the Self. He who repeats them twice a day gains longevity, health and riches.. and by repeating them thrice a day man keeps the entire universe subservient... The recitation of these hundred names lead to the fulfilment of one's desire and more the number of times the names are repeated, greater is the fruit obtained by the devotee.

Again, according to the same author, a person repeating the names of the Goddess Lalitā achieves all objects and yields the benefit of fourfold aims of life, one repeating these names everyday at dawn becomes a *yogin* and a knower of Brahman a knower of the Self. He who repeats them twice a day gains longevity, health and riches and popularity among people. By repeating it thrice everyday, man keeps the entire universe subservient (to himself). By repeating it four times, his wish is fruitful... By repeating it sixteen times a day, a man becomes Maheśvara himself.[49] The same *purāṇa* elsewhere stresses the importance of utterance of *mantra*-s and declared that the *mantra*-s in honour of Viṣṇu enable people to attain their desired object and by the mere utterance of these *mantra*-s hosts of sins get dissolved.[50]

---

47. *Bra. P.* 46.59-60
48. *Nār. P.* I. 98.39, 163.
49. *Nār. P.* I.98.164-175.
50. *Ibid,* I.70.2[ab].

The *Liṅga P.* also presents a list of thousand names of *Śiva*[52] and states that he who reads them or listens to them attains the merit of the performance of the thousand sacrifices.[52] The author of the *Padma P.* emphasizes the importance of meditation of Viṣṇu and states that those who do not meditate upon Viṣṇu as the first Supreme being and the ruler and the great lord of all the worlds... go to hell.[53]

The authors of the *purāṇa*-s were so keen on simplifying religion that mere listening to the recitation of the *purāṇa*-s was believed by them to be enabling people to free themselves from the impacts of sinful deeds.[54] Even the author of the *Vāmana P.* held that by hearing and reciting the *purāṇa*-s with devotion, a man attains the world of Viṣṇu and can destroy sins.[55] Eulogising the act of *purāṇaśravaṇa* to the skies the author further states that diseases do not attack him, nor should poisons and magic have any effect on the body and family of one who hears the *Vāmana P.*[56] The listener attains the entire merit of the Horse-sacrifice (Aśvamedha) performed with the due payment of *dakṣiṇā* and of the gift of gold, land, horses, cows, elephants and chariots. A man or a woman hearing even a quarter verse becomes sanctified and the holiest in the world.[57] The recitation of this *purāṇa* will lead to the merit that accrues out of the gift of a jewel on the occasion of the eclipse of the sun and the moon by Rāhu, the merit of the gift of food to the hungry, good Brāhmaṇa and to one who tends the sacred fire.[58]

---

51. *Lin.P.* I. 64.
52. *Ibid*, I.64.172.
53. *Pad. P.* 96.11-13.
54. *Bh. P.* III.7.3.
   इतिहासपुराणानि श्रुत्वा भक्त्या द्विजोत्तमाः।
   मुच्यते सर्वपापेभ्यो ब्रह्महत्याशतं च यत्।।
55. *Vām. P.* 69.1[cd].2[cd].
56. *Ibid*, 69.2[ab].
57. *Ibid*, 69,3, 4[cd].
58. *Ibid*, 69.9.

Consecration of a well, lake etc. also was regarded as a holy deed through which the performer could achieve greatness in the world of Viṣṇu.[59] Mere meditation of Hari (Haridhyāna) was regarded as a means of the destruction of all sins. Thus, according to the author of the *Garuḍa P.*, meditation was the greatest *dharma*, greatest penance, greatest purity and *dhyāna* was supposed to lead to the destruciton of sins in a moment, sins that are usually destroyed by thousand *prāṇāyāma-s.*[60]

Again, knowing full well that *dāna*, *vrata-s* and pilgrimage as means of achieving merits connot be resorted to by every member of society, the authors of the *purāṇa*-s, have laid down activities such as planting of *tulasī*, sprinkling handful of water over it, giving away a delicate shoot of *tulasī* to a *brāhmaṇa* or bestowing it upon Śālagrama with which one could acquire merit or other benefits such as stay in the abode of Brahmā (Brahmāsadana) or in the abode of Viṣṇu[61] (Viṣṇusadana). Similarly, the worship of the banyan tree with three circumambulations and an incantation in honour of that tree is said to be leading to the destruction of sins[62] or the mere act of looking at the banyan tree, the householder could achieve the highest goal. Monier Williams M. has pointed out, 'Tree-worship.... was once common in Greece, France, Poland, Assyria and many other countries... and throughout a greater part of Asia a belief in a kind of divinity inherent in certain trees has always been a recognized element of the popular creed.[63] It is interesting to know how the *purāṇa*-s have followed this universal trend with a sole objective of simplifying religion and attract the masses.

---

59. *Gar. P.* I.222.22.
कूपवापीतडागादीनारामांश्चैव कारयेत्।
त्रिसप्तकुलमुद्धृत्य विष्णुलोके महीयते।।
60. *Gar. P.* I. 230.10ab. 19.
61. *Nār. P.* I.13.24, 29-31
62. *Br. P.* 54.12-15.
63. Monier-Williams M., *Brahmanism and Hinduism*, London, 1887, P.330.

**Importance of the *Mantra*-s (*mantramāhātmya*) —**

The authors of the *purāṇa*-s have emphasized the importance of various *mantra*-s. e.g. according to the *Nar. P.*, the eight syllabled *mantra 'Om namo Nārāyaṇāya'* in honour of Viṣṇu is supposed to lead to the acquisition of everything[64] and *mantra*-s in honour of Kṛṣṇa bestow worldly enjoyment and liberation.[65]

***Karmasiddhānta* and the Doctrine of Rebirth —**

The Karman doctrine and the doctrine of rebirth were inextricably woven together and the Karmasiddhānta was a part of the Vedic religion. According to the Śrauta tradition, the sacrificer performing sacrifices was entitled to get some unseen fruit *(apūrva)* and was able to achieve welfare after his death. This reflected Karmavipāka-siddhānta. Although the Ṛgveda does not contain any clear reference to the doctrine of rebirth, the heaven here is depicted as a reward for those that risk their lives in battle, bestow liberal sacrificial fees, practise rigorous austerity *(tapas)* and acquire merit for themselves through their offerings and pious gifts.[66] Addressing the departed one, the Ṛgvedic sage states in the same verse "May you be united with your body being endowed with beautiful lustre", which indicates that the departed soul was asked to come to the mortal world. His sin was believed to have been destroyed and good activities were said to be enbling him to be associated with new (good) body.[67] The sacrificial texts and the Upaniṣads have elaborated the same ideas through statements such as 'By holy deeds one becomes holy and by sinful deed one becomes sinful.[68] Whatever activity is performed by this one in this world, the fruit thereof is obtained by him (in the yonder

64. *Nār.P.* I.70.3-4
65. *Ibid*, I.80.5ab.
66. *RV.* X.14.8.
67. For more details see : Dange S.S., *Bauddha Dharma āṇi Tattvajñāna*, Pune, 1980, pp. 200-206.
68. *Br. Up.* III.2.13- पुण्यः वै पुण्येन कर्मणा भवति पापः पापेन।

world) and thereafter he comes down in order to perform activities once again.[69] He is what he is due to the deed he has performed.[70] The Mahābhārata contains numerous references to this doctrine in verses such as 'The fate of a person running fast follows him in the act or running, that of a sleeping person stands, that of a person walking or going moves. Whatever is done by a person in the past, the same is always enjoyed by him.[71] Somewhat similar idea is expressed in one of the Vedāntasūtra-s according to which the cycle of mundane existence goes on rotating according to its own rules and the Lord or the Creator is not to be blamed for the inequality and cruelty noticeable in this universe. The activities of the persons performed by them in their earlier life determined their fate.[72] In the *bhāṣya* upon the same *sutra,* Śaṅkrācārya describes three varieties of beings, *i.e.* some as experiencing extreme happiness *(atyantasukhabhājinaḥ)* and some as having the middling type of experience *(madhyamabhāgabhājinaḥ)* and states that Īśvara takes into consideration the merit and demerit cf persons while creating the world characterised by such an unequality.[73]

Belief in the doctrine of *karman,* was an important principle of Budhism and hence it propounded purity of mind, speech and deed. It is obvious that the Karman-doctrine was borrowed by Buddhism from the brahmanical faith. To give only one instance from the Buddhist faith of maintaining the *Karman-docrine,* a verse from the *Dhammapada* states, 'Neither in the sky, nor in the midst

69. *Ibid,* IV.4.6.
70. *Ibid,* IV.4.5.
71. *Mbh. Śānti* 181.8,9$^{ab}$, 10.
72. *Vedāntasūtra* II.1.34.
73. *Śāṅkarabhāṣya* on the *Vedāntasūtra* II.1.34.

of the ocean, there is nothing in this mundane existence having remained where one can escape the fruits of evil activities.[74]

The followers of Jainism also believe in the existence of eightfold activities and hold that the activities are related with the self and hence the self gets entangled in the mundane exstience and this is something that determines the good or bad fruit which is secured by the self.[75] Knowing full well the importance of the *karman* doctrine as a means which could induce people to perform excellent deeds in their lives, the authors of the *purāṇa*-s continued cherishing the same age-old popular doctrine.

Thus, the author of the *Varāha P.* declares the people who are sinful in thought, word and deed cannot commit offences[76] and further lays down thirty-three offences ranging from eating the tooth-stick or the king's food to drinking liquor[77] and states that he who is guilty of these will never see the Lord Viṣṇu.[78] The same *purāṇa* elsewhere lays down as list of sinful persons, liars, molesters of animals, women and children, killers of Brahmins, deceivers, the abstrinate, the ungrateful, those fond of the wives of others, those that outrage the modesty of maidens, defilers of Veda, those who harass people following the Vedic way of living, sacrificers on behalf of Śūdra-s, condemned Brāhmaṇa-s, performers of sacrifices for those who are ineligible... those

---

74. *Dhammapada* IX. 12.
न अन्तलिक्खे न समुद्दमज्झे।
न पव्वतानं विवरं पविस्स।
न विज्जती सेा जगतिप्पदेसो
यत्थट्ठितो मुञ्चेय्य पापकम्मा।।
75. For more details see : Dange S.S., *Jain Dharma āṇi Tattvajñāna*, Pune, 1980, pp.151-157.
76. *Var. P.* 179.3$^{ab}$.
77. *Ibid*, 179.3$^{cd}$-9.
78. *Ibid*, 179.10$^{cd}$.

who give up their mother and father or wife, those that have ill-will, hatred towards thir preceptors, those of bad conduct....the impure, the merciless, harassers, vow-breakers, sellers of *soma*,......speakers of falsehood, teachers of Veda for gaining money, ....those that steal others' wealth, assasinators, those justifying sinful actions,[79] those who do not observe vows out of ignorance..., those who defile sacred places...Presenting a philosophical discussion regarding the concept of sin and sinful persons, the author of this *purāṇa* states that when one is under the influnece of sin, one loses courage and even the sinless gets stupefied. One is also deprived of one's thinking faculty because of sin.[80] The *Garuḍa P.* also reflects the belief in the Karman-doctrine and states that a person afflicted by covetous thirst falls into hell and those who are freed of undue thirst, secure a residence in heaven.[81] According to this *purāṇa* a man has to experience the fruits of his action, auspicious or inauspicious.[82] Virtue is the cause of wealth, love and salvation. Hence one should be virtuous.[83] The same *purāṇa* elsewhere states that it is the virtue that triumphs and not evil. It is the truth that triumphs and not falsehood. It is the forgiveness that wins and not anger.[84] The author of this *purāṇa* induces people to follow the righteous conduct by creating a feeling of fear in their hearts stating that the sinners will have to undergo sufferings and the nature of suffering will be in accordance with the nature of sin. Thus, the author declares that if a person has been guilty of falsehood in speech, he becomes a stammerer, a teller of lies a dumb. The brahmin slayer

---

79. *Ibid*, 195.2$^{cd}$-13.
80. *Ibid*, 195.28-29$^{cd}$.
81. *Gar. P.* II. 12. 15.
82. *Ibid*, II.12.27$^{ab}$.
83. *Ibid*, II.12.31$^{cd}$.32$^{ab}$.
    धर्माच्च जायते ह्यर्थो धर्मात्कामोऽपि जायते।
    धर्म एवापवर्गाय तस्माद्धर्मं समाचरेत्।।
84. *Ibid*, II. 46.3.

is born consumptive of leprous, the wine addict becomes black-toothed.[85]

The Karman doctrine is always linked with the concepts of heaven and hell as also with the doctrine of rebirth. The authors of the *purāṇa-s* have continued the same tradtition. Accordingly, the *Garuḍa P.* states that bound by its own action the soul takes up body after body and undergoes a series of births ... Thus, do the birth and death of living beings rotate. The rise in the course is due to virtue and the fall is due to evil. The deityhood or manhood, the acts of benevolence and indulgence recur due to their previous *karman*. Whatever is observed is the fruit of action. If a person indulges habitually in evil actions due to passion, he will definitely fall into a terrible hell from which there is no escape.[86] The author of the *Brahmavaivarta P.* also stated that good deeds lead to the heavenly world and bad deeds lead to the hell.[87] Again, according to this *purāṇa* whether auspicious or inauspicious, the fruit of the *Karman* must be enjoyed. Enjoyment of *karman* purifies it and thereupon it leads to salvation.[88]

According to the author of the *Bhaviṣya P.*, one should know that people committing sinful activities reach dspicable gait, one should always perform holy deeds and avoid sins. By holy deeds one attains godhood and by sinful deed one reaches the hell.[89] Performers of auspicious deeds go to the abode of Yama through gental

---

85. *Ibid*, II.46.12.
86. *Ibid, 46.33-37.*
87. *Br. V.P.* II.85.47ab.
    स्वर्गं च सुकृतेनैव नरकं च दुष्कृतेन च।
88. *Ibid*, II.85.40.
89. *Bh. P.* I. 193.28.
    नीयंते देहिनः सर्वे ये मूढाः पापकारिणः।
    इति ज्ञात्वा नरः कुर्यात्पुण्यं पापं च वर्जयेत्।।
    पुण्येन याति देवत्वं पापेन नरकं व्रजेत्।।

path[90] but those who perform cruel deeds reach the abode of Yama through terrible southern path.[91]

**Eschatology —**

Some of the contents dealing with the Karman doctrine throw light on the ideas of the authors of the *purāṇa*-s regarding life after death which also formed a pat of the Puranic religion. Thus, the author of the *Garuḍa P.* held that at the threshold of Yama's city there exists the river Vaitaraṇī which is hundred *yojana*-s wide, impassable and foul smelling. A sinner is terrified because of this at the first sight. The river is full of putrid blood with sediments and marshy deposits of flesh. Having seen a sinner, it assumes the form of melted ghee in a vessel, abounding in worms and flesh and brought by vultures. The river is full of crocodiles, fishes... and the sinful people groan aloud and fall into it.[92] By presenting a horrifying description of this river, the author obviously tries to prevent people from performing sinful activities. The author holds that as a result of noble actions, one obtains pleasure, here and hereafter[93] and states that the creatures are parts and parcels of the Tıanscendental Self in the form of indivisible Śiva.. who is the lord of all-Self in the form of indivisible Śiva.. who is the lord of all-self luminous... The creatures are controlled by virtues and vices in the form of bliss and sorrow. They pass through four types of bodies in the order of their *karman* and leaving one body after another, a thousand times, taking birth in human form and acquiring

---

90. *Ibid*, I.192.4.
तत्र से शुभकर्माणः सौम्यचित्ता दयान्विताः।
ते नरा याति देवत्वं पापेन नरकं व्रजेत्।।

91. *Ibid*, I.192.8.
से पुनः क्रूरकर्माणः नरा पापरताः खग।
ते घोरेण पथा यान्ति दक्षिणेन यमालयम्।।

92. *Gar. P.* II. 47.2-6.

93. *Ibid*, II. 47.37cd.
सुकृतस्य प्रभावेण सुखञ्चेह परत्र च।

knowledge due to good acts one obtains release.[94] The author of the *Gar.P.* states that knowledge is of two kinds — one arising out of the study of scriptures and the other arising from discrimination, Śabdabrahma, according to this *purāṇa* is known from scriptures and Parabrahman from discrimination. The author holds that two words 'mine' *(mama)* and 'not mine' *(na mama)* signify bondage and release. By 'mine' the person is bound and by'not-mine' he is released and that is the right action which does not put one into bondage. That is the right knowledge which brings him release. All other actions are merely an artisanship.[95] However, according to this *purāṇa*, the city of the god of death is full of mansions, beautiful rows of buildings, having golden fort of spotless water, beautiful wells, lotusponds, also tanks and lakes.[97] There is a special entrance for gods, sages and others who perform good and virtuous deeds, which is a hundred hired gateway, ten *Yojana*-s in breadth and double that length... shining prominently and so tall as to appear as scraping the sky, highly lustrous and provided with several contrivances. Likewise, in the south, there is a gateway built of iron, highly hot, terrific in appearance, meant for all sinners and killers.[98] There is an assembly hall where justice is dispensed for the righteous as well as sinful, for good as well as bad, according to the store of result of actions performed and the judges decide the merit of actions.[99] Manu, Prajāpati, Parāśara Vyāsa, Atri, Auddālaki, Āpastamba, Bṛhaspati, Śukra, Gautama, Śaṅkha, Likhita, Aṅgiras, Bhṛgu, Pulastya, Pulaha and other law-givers are judges. Along with Yama, they think of the justice to be dispensed.[100] Near them, there is an eternal Kāla who is ordered by

94. *Gar. P.* II.48.6-9, 11-12.
95. *Gar.P.* II.49.91.94.
96. *Var.P.* 195.28-29.
97. *Ibid*, 196. 2-4, 6a.
98. *Ibid*, 196.1,3,6$^{b}$-8.
99. *Ibid*, 197.37.14$^{ab}$.
100. *Ibid*, 197.16$^{cd}$. 17-18$^{ab}$.

Dharmarāja to execute punishment, black in colour, with projecting cheek, erect hair and uncouth form, with ugly face, protruding cannies, full of anger, generating fear, holding a big can in his hand.[101] By the side of him, there is a respledent female form worshipped by Yama. She is the destroyer of the worlds and it is from her body that the opressing ailments and dreadful diseases arise.[102] The *Varāha P.* describes the god of death to be full of valour, but cruel and angry.[103] The same *purāṇa* elsewhere describes awful Vaitaraṇī river where hundreds of people in their curdled blood are beaten by numerous snakers wherein the sinful people get parched, sinking and vomitting with nobody to save them.[104] This Vaitaraṇī river has Śālmali tree in its vicinity, which is full of matallic nails.. having on its branches a large number of goblins and demons furiously hanging down.[105] The entire ground which is rugged and dark is strewn with iron nails and sinners are thrown on hard and burning rocks. Here cranes make showers of blood, bones and stones upon them.[106] The author of this *purāṇa* has presented a list of eight different hells, viz Tapta, Mahātapta, Mahāraurava, Raurava, Saptatāla, Kālasūtra, Andhakāra and Andhakārapara[107] and states that persons visiting these hells never get pleasures of senses, but experience only sorrow. The author has further presented an awful description of the earth which is full of hot and sharp nails and the sky covered with flocks of birds with fiery tongues. This place is said to be characterised by hunger and thirst.[108] The Rākṣasa-s are said to be thrashing the sinners, biting their lips in anger and exclaiming aloud.[109]

---

101. *Ibid*, 197.26-28.
102. *Ibid*, 197.33[cd]. 34[ab].
103. *Ibid*, 197.34[cd].
104. *Ibid*, 199.47. 49
105. *Ibid*, 199. 50-51.
106. *Ibid*, 199.1.5[cd], 37[cd], 38.
107. *Ibid*, 200. 1-2.
108. *Ibid*, 200.7¼10.
109. *Ibid*, 200.18.

Here, there is Vaitaraṇī of bitter water, fifty *yojana*-s long and five *Yojana*-s deep, deep in mud, full of skin, flesh and bones, having big scorpions with sharp teeth and owls, ferocious and poisonous with sharp tongues able enough to break bones.[110] Obviously, the purpose behind describing horrible and disgusting nature of these hells is to frighten the masses, to wean them away from sinning and to induce them to follow the path of righteous conduct. The performers of good deeds are assured that men of knowledge, those that stake their lives for the sake of their master, the liberal givers, those who look after comforts of their parents, those who make gifts of seasamum, cows, gold and land to Brahmins, those who perform sacrifices, observe Cāturmāsya, maintaining sacrificial fire, those who fulfil the wishes of their preceptors...who recite the Veda-s everyday, cultured persons; those who have full control over their senses... never go there.[111] With a view to induce the masses to perform meritorious deeds, the author of the *Padma P.* describes heaven as a place of various divine, meritorious charming pleasure-gardens, full of objects of desire and wishfulflling trees, aeroplanes attended by bands of clelestial nymphs and states that the wicked, cruel, ungrateful and proud people do not reach this place and describes hell as a place for those who are deluded by greed, those who have violated the norms of good conduct... religious hypocrites, ungrateful ones.[112]

### *Saṁskāra*-s and *Ātmaguṇa*-s

The authors of the works on Dharmaśāstra regard purificatory rites *(saṁskāra*-s) as sanctifying body and purifying sin in this life and even after death. Manu holds that the body is made fit for the union with Brahman by burnt oblations during (the mother's) pregnancy, by the ceremony

110. *Ibid*, 200. 28-30
111. *Ibid*, 207.25-29.
112. *Pad. P.* II. 95. 2ff.

to be performed after birth (*jātakarma*), by tonsure, by thread-ceremony. He believed that these rites can remove the sins of the twice-born men which they have derived from both the parents. The study of the Veda, the vows, burnt oblations, the recitation of sacred texts, the acquisition of the threefold sacred science, offering to the gods and manes, procreation of sons, great sacrifices, *śrauta* rites also purify body.[113] The *purāṇa*-s continue the same tradition. The *Agni P.* lays down forty-eight *saṁskāra*-s such as *garbhādhāna, puṁsavana, sīmantonnayana, jātakarma, nāmakaraṇa*[114] and eight *ātmaguṇa*-s. According to it, the *saṁskāraṣ* have ability to bestow material as well as spiritual benefits.[115] The authors of the works on Dharmaśāstra regard *saṁskāra* as a means of purifying body which needs to be protected as it is the abode of the soul. The main interest of the authors of the *purāṇa*-s was to popularise religion. That is why they attached significance to both the types of objectives, material and spiritual. Thus, for the same reason the author of the *Agni P.* has stated that a person purified with purificatory rites would obtain enjoyments and salvation.[116]

**Stories and Puranic Religion --**

Literary works and society are seen to act and react on each other. The *purāṇa-s* also bear out testimony to this observation. The *purāṇa*-s set about their task of reorientation of earlier religious concepts, ideologies and doctrines.[117] A history of all religions bears out that story is the best literary medium to attract the masses. No wonder, therefore, if the authors of the *purāṇa*-s also fabricated a variety of stories, cosmogonic, didactic, moral or ethical and sometimes even purely fictitious in nature so as best

113. *Manu S.* II. 26-28.

114. *Agn. P.* 32.2-6.

115. *Ibid*, 32.9, also *Mat.p.* LII. 8-9.

116. *Agn. P.* 32.12[ab].
संस्कारैः संस्कृतश्चैतैर्भुक्तिं मुक्तिमवाप्नुयात् ।

117. For more details see : Kane P.V., *H. of Dh. S.*, Vol. V, Pt. III, Pune, 1962, pp.913-914.

to suit their purpose of popularising and simplifying their religion. If classified into two major categories, *i.e.* religious and secular (say e.g. the stories of kings or sages), it is observed that those that outwardly appear to be secular also hint at some religious principle or the other. With simple and lucid style, ignoring at times, even the rules of grammar, the authors of the *purāṇa*-s go on narrating a number of stories, some of which are short, but some are inordinately, if not tediouly very long, so much so that sometimes they are unable to resist the temptation of linking a certain *ākhyāna* with another *upākhyāna* and thus are seen to be weaving a garland of interconnected stories. Thus, the story of the creator and his fascination for his daughter Gāyatrī is linked with the story of Madanadāha by Śiva. As already stated, the Karman doctrine and the doctrine of rebirth were closely related with each other and formed a vital part of the belief system of ancient people as also that of religion. The authors of the *purāṇa-s* retained the importance of these doctrines and narrated a number of stories to stress their importance. Thus, the author of the Mat. P.[118] preaches Karman doctrine through a cosmogonic story wherein Brahmā is shown to have experienced the truth of 'Reap as you sow' in the same birth. Brahmā created the *mānasaputra*-s and began to invoke Gāyatrī[111] who appeared in the form of a girl from half the portion of Brahmā's body. The creator was fascinated by her exquisite beauty. His *mānasaputra*-s began to express the feelings of humiliation and contempt at the attitude of the creator. But he did not heed in the least. He fixed his gaze at Gāyatrī. As she was circumambulating him, he felt shy of turning his head each time to her direction. He therefore, created four heads in order to stare at her. She, then, went to the heaven and Brahmā put on the fifth head right on top. This is how, he came to have five heads but thereafter he lost all his power that he had acquired by practising penance as he failed to control himself and fell into the snares of Cupid.[119] The importance of the age-

118. *Mat. P.* III.30-41, *Ibid*, IV.12.

119. *Mat. P.* III.30-41.

old dictum 'sinful deeds lead to sufferings' is, thus, very well stessed through the popular and appealing medium of story. The *Nārada P.* also contains a story of two brothers Yajñamālin and Sumālin. Owing to righteous conduct Yajñamālin could reach Viṣṇuloka and the younger brother was helplessly beaten by Yama's soldiers. Thanks to the power of the meritorious deeds that Yajñamālin shared with his brother that Sumālin was free from sins.[120]

Dharma in its wider sense meant virtuous conduct, righteous attitude or *mānavadharma*. The *purāṇa*-s abound in stories stressing its importance. Thus, the author of the *Nār. P.* explains how good men of calm minds perceive the good qualities present even in the offending fools and they do not offend them in return.[121] Similarly, according to the authors of the *purāṇa*-s, *dharma* was not just an ideal *puruṣārtha* to be pursued. It was also a matter to be practised. That is why, the author of the *Nārada P.* gives a valuable piece of advice regarding the ways of the world through the story of Gulika and Uttaṇka and states that the entire world is always under the influence of strong illusory power. One's own kiths and kins help one only as long as one earns money and merit and demerit accompany one only as long as one lives in this world but not when one leaves for the yonder world.[122]

The authors of the *purāṇa*-s narrate some of the famous mythological stories to stress the importance of certain principles. Thus, they story of Pralhāda is narrated[123] in order to stress the importance of the indestructible, eternal

---

120. *Nār.P.* I.36. 46-47.

121. *Ibid*, 37.33.

122. *Ibid*, I.37.39[ab], 42.

अहो बलवती माया मोहयत्यखिलं जगत्।
यावदर्जयति द्रव्यं बांधवास्तावदेव हि।
धर्माधर्मौ सहैवास्तामिहामुत्र न चापरः।।

123. *Bhāg. P.* VII. 2-10.

Lord named Brahmā as the support of all.[124] The *Viṣṇu P.* narrates the same story and states that the meditation of the Lord enables one to protect oneself from calamities and achieve the highest bliss.[125] Likewise, the story of Yayāti is narrated in order to stress the importance of righteous conduct and self-control through generalisation such as 'Thus desire is never fulfillled through enjoyment.. grains, barley, gold, beasts... are not sufficient even for one person. Hence having controlled senses, should give up (curb) thirst. If a person does not commit sin and has a non-discriminatory approach, all directions are full of pleasure for him.[126] Ajāmilopākhyāna stresses the importance of devotion and states how recitation of the name of Hari enabled Ajāmila to reach the highest abode.[127] The authors of the *purāṇa*-s have stressed the importance of pilgimage by narrating wellknown *ākhyāna*-s to appeal to the masses. Thus, the Saramākhyāna of the *Brahma P.* stresses the importance of the visit to Yamatīrtha-s[128] and the Purūravākhyāna of the same *purāṇa* emphasizes the importance of Urvaśītīrtha.[129] There are innumerable stories of the *vratamāhātmaya* in the *purāṇa*-s. The *śrāddha* ceremonies or *tarpaṇa* rites had for several years been a characteristic of Indian religion. The *purāṇa*-s narrated a number of stories to retain their importance.

Some of the stories bristle with the *subhāṣita*-s and reflect the Purāṇic concept of *sādhāraṇa dharma.* While narrating the story of Sāvitrī, the *Matsya P.* states that

---

124. *Ibid*, VII. 85[cd]. 86.
मत्तः सर्वमहं सर्वं मयि सर्वं सनातने।।
अहमेवाक्षयो नित्यः परमात्मात्मसंश्रयः।
ब्रह्मसंज्ञोऽहमेवाग्रे तथान्ते च परः पुमान्।।

125. *Viṣ. p.* I.20.34[cd].
तदा स भगवद्ध्यानात्परं निर्वाणमाप्तवान्।।

126. *Ibid*, IV. 10.23[a].24-25.

127. *Bhāg.P.* VI.1-2.

128. *Br. P.* 131.

129. *Ibid*, 171

the saints are the refuge of all, of the wicked as also of the good. There is no fear from poison, fire, snake, weapons as it is from the man who is inimically disposed towards the rest of the world without any cause. The good give up their lives for the sake of others and the wicked are ever ready to cause pain to others even at the sacrifice of their lives.[130] Considering *dharma* to be the best of all *puruṣārtha*-s, the author of the same *purāṇa* eulogises it stating that a group of three viz. *dharma*, *artha* and *kāma* are to be acquired by being born in this world. For a person who is bereft of *dharma*, *kāma* and *artha* are like a progeny of a barren woman. *Dharma* enables one to acquire wealth and to fulfil one's own desires. It is the *dharma* only that accompanies the embodied soul wherever it goes. Man's friends and relatives do not follow him. All other things excepting *dharma* perish with the body. The soul comes into existence by itself and leaves the body (without being accompanied by anything else or anybody else) such as his brother, friend, wife, son etc. *Dharma*, however, follows him (even at that time).[131]

It has been pointed out several times that due to the popularity of new religions the very means of subsistence of the priestly class was almost fatally threatened and the authors of the *purāṇa*-s endeavoured to keep the same in tact. That is why at the end of the *Mārk. P.*, it is stated that *kathāśravaṇa* or *purāṇaśravaṇa* would destory the sins of the listeners but an appeal is made to bestow gifts upon the Brāhmaṇa-s which is followed by an additional statement that *śravaṇa* without *dāna* (to Brāhmaṇa-s) would lead to no concrete benefit.[132]

---

130. *Mat. P.* 211. 2-4.

131. *Mat. P.* 212.3,4$^{ab}$.5 6$^{ab}$.

132. *Mārk. P.* 134. 20$^{cd}$.

श्रुत्वा तु पूजयेद्यस्तु पुराणं सप्तमं पुनः।
सर्वपापविनिर्मुक्तः पुनात्येव निजं कुलम्।।
श्रवणस्य फलावाप्त्यै दानैः संतोषयेद्गुरुम्।।

### The Theory of *Avatāras* or *Avatāravāda*

The term *avatāra* or descent is to be derived from the root avat*ṛ*—to come down and it indicated the coming down of the Lord from above in the form of a divine or human being.

Huttington Ronald explains the concept behind the term *avatāra.*[133] He states that *avatāra* signifies "the divine descent into earthly form" and symbolizes the passage from" the unconditioned to the conditioned, from the infinite to the finite, from eternity to the temporal sphere"[134] Dange S.S. has discussed at length the concept of incarnation.[135] The concept goes back to the Ṛgvedic *mantra*-s, when Indra is said to be *pururūpa* by his *māyā*-s.[136] Devasthali G.V. has shown how the first five of the famous ten incarnaions are mentioned or referred to in the stories of the Brāhmaṇa-texts.[137] It is interesting to note that the *Bh. Gītā* has led to the further development of the concept of incarnation, when it states that whenever there is decay of *dharma* and rise of *adharma*, the *Lord* embodies himself. He is born age after age for the establishment of *dharma.*[138]

The theory of incarnation suggests that—

(1) The various *avatāra*-s are the manifestations of the same Reality.

(2) One *avatāra* is followed by the next one and the

133. Huttington Ronald, "Avatāras and Yugas", *Purāṇa*, Vol. VI, No. 1, Varanasi, 1964, pp. 7-39.

134. *Ibid*, pp. 8-9

135. Mrs. Dange S.S., "Incarnations", *The Bhāgavata Purāṇa Mytho-social Study*, Delhi, 1984. pp. 233-258.

136. *RV.* VI. 47.18-

रूपं रूपं प्रतिरूपो बभूव

तदस्य रूपं प्रतिचक्षणाय।

इन्द्रो मायाभिः पुरुरूप ईयते।

युक्ता ह्यस्य हरयः शता दश।।

137. Devasthali G.V., *Religion and Mythology of the Brāhmaṇas*, Poona Uni. Pubn., Poona, 1965, pp. 8-10.

138. *Bh. Gītā* IV. 7-8.

theory thus is related with the doctrine of rebirth.

(3) The Lord manifests himself in any form and in any *yoni* so as to appeal to all kinds of people.

(4) The manifestation is just a part of the entire form of the Lord.

(5) The theory throws light on the concept of the evolution of the world according to which at the initial stage the beings that are small in size are created and at a later stage they are supposed to assume bigger forms.

Thus, the *Bhāg. P.* describes all the *avatāra*-s of the Supreme Lord, right from Varāha to Śrīkṛṣṇa[139] and imagines him to be Viśvabhāvana who is to be identified with Being (Sat) as also non-Being (Asat).[140] The same *purāṇa* elsewhere has related the incarnation of tortoise to the story of the churning of the ocean and states that the first incomprehensible tortoise held the mountain Mandara which was trembling due to the valour of the arms of gods and demons and which was revolving on its back.[141] The author of the *Brahma P.* considers *avatāra*, the act of descending as a great deed and states that whenever virtue dwindles down and evil increases, the Lord Viṣṇu takes incarnation by dividing his body into two in order to protect the gods, establish virtue and chastise the wicked and other enemies of *deva*-s. He is born in every Yuga for protecting the subjects.[142]

---

139. *Bhāg. P.* II.7; also XI. 4.

140. *Ibid*, II. 7.50.
सोऽयं तेऽभिहितस्तात भगवान् विश्वभावनः।
समासेन हरेर्नान्यदस्मात् सदसच्च यत्।।

141. *Ibid*, VIII. 7.10[abc].
सुरासुरेन्द्रैर्भुजवीर्यवेपितं
परिभ्रमन्तं गिरिमङ्ग पृष्ठतः।
बिभ्रत् तदावर्तनमादिकच्छपो।

142. *Br. P.* 72.2.-4
यदा यदा त्वधर्मस्य वृद्धिर्भवति भो द्विजाः।
धर्मश्च ह्रासमभ्येति तदा देवो जनार्दनः।।

According to the *Gar.P.*, the Lord Hari appeared as Viṣṇu, the repository of all virtuous deeds... The germ of all creation incarnated as Vāsudeva entered the womb of *māyā* and created *vāyu*. He entered the womb of Jayā and was born as Saṅkarṣaṇa.... Having created Mahat in subtle form, primary elements *(mahābhūta*-s), five organs of actions and five of knowledge, one mind, he was born as Aniruddha and then as Sanatkumāra... The Lord Viṣṇu became a hog, took the earth out of waters. He slew Hiraṇyākṣa, protected the pious and established rule of law over the earth. The Lord Hari incarnated himself as tortoise, supporting the Mandara mountain when it was being used by gods and *asura*-s for churning the ocean... The noble Lord incarnated himself as Nṛsiṁha and killed Hiraṇyakaśipu by tearing up his thighs with his nails. The lord was born as Vāmana to Aditi and Kāśyapa for restoring to Indra the land which had been usurped by Bali. Born of the sage Jamadagni, known as Paraśurāma who wanted to liberate the earth from the yoke of Kṣatriya-s who hated the Brāhmaṇa-s. He was also born as Vyāsa as the son of Parāśara and Satyavatī and as Kṛṣṇa as the son of Devakī and Vasudeva, killed Kaṁsa and his associate and protected the Pāṇḍava-s. In the Kali age, the lord was born as Buddha who deluded the *asura*-s and flouted the Veda-s[143] Regarding the incarnation that is yet to descend, the *Gar. P.* states that at the interval between Kalki and Satya age, the lord will be born in the house of Viṣṇugupta and slay the rulers who have turned thieves.[144] According to the *Garuḍa P.*, the incarnations of Viṣṇu, are twenty four beginning with Keśava and Saṅkarṣaṇa. Those beginning with Viśva are one thousand and those beginning with Para are innumerable and the Lord Viṣṇu is complete in all respects by virtue of strength, form and

---

अवतारं करोत्यत्र द्विधा कृत्वात्मनस्तनुम्।

साधूनां रक्षणार्थाय धर्मसंस्थापनाय च।।

143. *Gar. P.* III. 15.1-3, 5-16, 19-22, 25-26.

144. *Ibid*, III. 15.26.

qualities. He is eternal by virtue of his eternal qualities.[145] Making a reference to Buddhāvatāra[146] and the incarnation of Kalki,[147] the *Agni P.* has stated the incarntions of Viṣṇu at one place as innumerable as also ten in number.[148] The authors of the *purāṇa*-s are seen to be incorporating as many doctrines and theories as they could with a view to popularise religion. No wonder, therefore, if the theory of incarnation which was aleady popular among poeple was also incorporated by the authors of the *purāṇa*-s as a part of Purāṇic religion.

## Idol-worship and Temple-worship

As Dange S.A. has pointed out, the Veda-s, the Brāhmaṇa-s and the Upaniṣads do not contain any reference to temples. But the *Śrauta sūtra-s* and *Gṛhyasūtra*-s refer to them. The *Śānkh. Gr. S. (II.11.6)* and the *Kau. Gr. S. (III.7.21)* refer to a student observing the vow *mahānāmnī* and expect a student to observe fast in a temple. The *Mānava Gr. S.* (I.7.10) refers to the practice of a girl to be selected as a bride according to which out of eight kinds of balls of clay a bride was to select one and a ball made of earth brought from a temple was one of them. Even in primitive days, man was aware of the importance of natural powers and hence he started deifying them through symbols such as stones, moutains, trees, rivers and animals. In the course of time, man went on personifying divinities in human form. Dange holds that the custom of installation of idol and idol worshippig is non-Vedic. The Aryans observed non-Aryans observing this custom and they adopted it. The adoption of this custom by the Aryans is an indication of comprehensive nature of religion.[149] In the course of

145. *Ibid*, III. 15.29-30.
146. *Agn. P.* 16. 2-3.
147. *Ibid*, 16.8.
148. *Ibid*, 16.12.
149. For more details see Dange S.A., *Hindu Dharma āṇi Tattvajñāna, op. cit.*, pp. 309-316.

time, idol-worship and temple worship became important constituents of religion. Thus, the *Mahābhārata* contains references to an idol of Viṣṇu at Śāligrāma (II. 84. 24), to idols of Viśvesvara and the goddess of Śāligrāmatīrtha (III. 84.135) and to an idol of Dharma after touching which one was supposed to achieve the merit of Aśvamedha sacrifice (III. 84 102). This reference indicates that on the one hand, religion took a new turn because of the introduction of the practice of idol-worship, but the traditional importance of the instutition of sacrifice was not lost sight of.

The authors of the *purāṇa*-s continued the same tradition, primarily because it very well suited their purpose of simplifying religious modes by providing people with an opportunity to have a concrete object to focus their minds on and offer *arghya* consisting of eight things viz. curds, rice-grains, *kuśa,* milk, *dūrvā* gras, honey and mustard, fruits,[150] *candana,* camphor, saffron, forty lit up lights.[151] The same *purāṇa* makes a reference to the practice of consecration of idol and states that men of angry disposition, hypocrites, *liṅgin*-s should not undertake this act, a virtuous householder who is well accomplished in the Veda-s and is a Brahmaṇa should carry it out.[152] The *Brahma P.* also contains a reference to the instruction of making an idol of Kṛṣṇa with eyes as large as the petals of a lotus, having the scar of Śrīvatsa and Kausthubha Jewel, holding a conch, discus and iron club, an idol having the colour and lustre of the moon and cow's milk ... the idol of Viṣṇu having blue body, wearing yellow garments and having fierce and auspicious appearance.[153] The *Mat. P.* regards the coremonials of consecration as having the capacity of driving away ills.[154] The same *purāṇa* also makes a ref-

---

150. *Mat.P.* 267.1.

151. *Ibid,* 267. 20-22.

152. *Ibid,* 267. 31

नैतद्विशीलेन च दाम्भिकेन न लिङ्गिना स्थापनमत्र कार्यम्।
विप्रेण कार्यं श्रुतिपारगेण गृहस्थधर्माभिरतेन नित्यम्।।

153. *Bra. P.* 47. 41ff.

erence to the various sizes of the images of gods such as Rāma, Bali, Varāha, Narasiṁha as of ten *tāla*-s and that of Vāmana as of seven *tāla*-s. The images of Matsya and Kūrma may be made of as many dimensions as may appear beautiful. The image of Śiva as having bulky thighs and arms and having burnished gold colour... The image of Lord Śiva in dancing posture... the image of the lord with four and eight hands... and image of Bhairava with an aquiline nose, sharp teeth and formidable appearance[155] or an image of Ardhanārinaṭeśvara with the plaited hair of the Lord and with a crescent having the other half portion of the body in the form of an image of the Goddess Pārvatī with a *tilaka* mark on the forehead,[156] having in the right ear the serpent Vāsuki, in the left one an ear-ring, a mirror or a lotus in the left one[157] or the image of Gaṇeśa having the face of Gaṇeśa and the trunk of an elephant with three eyes, four arms, huge stomach, ears like those of an elephant, wearing a sacred thread, having a large and long tusk.. holding a *modaka* in this hand, having extensive shoulders, huge arms and feet full of bliss, riding a mouse....[158] or the image of the sun with beautiful eyes, seated in a chariot, holding a lotus, having seven horses and one *cakra* (wheel) in the chariot and a coronet beaming red on the head.[159]

The fact that the temple-worship was widely prevalent during the Purāṇic age is known from the statement from the *Agn. P.* that a person building a temple goes to the heaven and not to the hell.[160] The same *purāṇa* regards *pratimāsthāpana* as more beneficial and the fruit secured

154. *Mat. P.* 266. 68ab.
देवप्रतिष्ठाविधिरेष तुभ्यं निवेदितः पापविनाशहेतोः।
155. *Ibid*, 259. 1-2, 11, 13-14.
156. *Ibid*, 260. 1-2.
157. *Ibid*, 266.3-4[ab].
158. *Ibid*, 266. 52-55.
159. *Ibid*, 261. 1-2.
160. *Agn. P.* 38.34.

by the consecration of an image is believed to be endless. A wooden image is regarded as more meritorious than that of clay, that made of brick, that made of stone, and that made of Hemādri mineral. The authors of the *purāṇa*-s regarded the activity of preparing an image to be very important and thought that no sooner the activity of preparing an image began, that the sins performed in seven (earlier) births[161] will be destoyed. Similar references to the construction of temple occuring in the *Mat. P.* such as a temple having its building with four doorways, one in each direction and encircled by an enclosure wall[162] also throw light on temple-worship as a part of Purāṇic religion. Dange S.A. has discussed the details of temple-construction and its symblic significance.[163]

## Śrādhakarma

Kane P.V. has throughly dealt with the concept of *śrāddhakarma* with all its detail.[164] He derives the word *śrāddha* from *śraddhā* as firm faith or conviction that what is given to the *brāhmaṇa*-s for the benefit of the departed man or the fathers will reach him or them in some way.[165]. The belief in *śrāddhakarma*, thus, is closely associated with doctine of *karman* or rebirth. According to the *Nirṇayasindhu*, 'A *śrāddha* is a gift given to the *pitṛ*-s offered with faith and some auspicious exclamation (such as *svadhā* and followed by gifts to Brahmans.),[166] *Śrāddha*-s as acts of homage and as means leading to the welfare of the departed ancestors formed a significant part of the *smārta* religion. *Yājñavalkya* has dealt with the *srāddhakarman*-s elaborately. He has laid down rules re-

161. *Ibid*, 38. 31-33.
162. *Mat. P.* 254.1.
163. Dange S.A., *Encylopaedia of Puranic Beliefs and practices*. Vol. I., New Delhi, 1986, pp. 321-323.
164. Kane P. V., *H.of Dh. Ś.*, Vol. IV, Pune, 1953, pp. 334-551.
165. *Ibid*, p. 351
166. *Nirṇayasindhu*, q. by Monier-Williams M., *op. cit.*, p. 303.

garding the proper time for perfoming *śrāddhakarma*, has explained as to who are qualified and who are unqualified to perform *śrāddha*. He has stated the rules and the *mantra*-s for their performance, by giving the details regarding the type of food to be offered to the manes.[167] According to the *Yāj. S.*, *śrāddhakarma* leads to the material benefit such as the obtainment of a good daughter, good son-in-law, animals, excellent sons, success in gambling, agriculture.. and all desired objects.[168] According to the *Yāj. S.*, the propitiated, departed manes of men confer on them longevity, children, riches, knowledge, heaven, emancipation, pleasures and kingdom.[169] Even Uśanas held that if a *śrāddha* is performed with a view to fulfil certain desire on appropriate constellations, appropirate days of the month and days of the week, one reaches the heavenly world.[170] Uśanas speaks of the varieties of *śrāddha* such as *nitya* or daily, *kāmya* (performed with a particular objective) and *naimittika* or occasional.[171] Uśanas also has presented a list of persons qualified to perform *śrāddha* and has regarded Brāhmaṇa-s wellversed in the Veda-s....., knowers of religious rites or duties *(dharmajñāḥ)*, speakers of truth, observers of vows and rules, ... learned persons intent on performing *agnihotra*...., those interested in worshipping the preceptor, god and fire, those given to the acquisition of knowledge..., as persons qualified to perform *śrāddhakarma-s*.[172] Atri has praised *śrāddhadāna* stating that of all the gifts, that made at a *śrāddha* is an instrument of purification. Even a sin equal to (the Mount) Meru (in height) is purified through *śrāddhakarma*. *Śrāddhakarma* enables human beings to attain greatness in the heavenly world. To

167. *Yāj.S.* I. 217ff.

168. *Ibid*, I.262-264.

169. *Ibid*, I.260.

आयुः प्रजां धनं विद्यां स्वर्गं मोक्षं सुखानि च।
प्रयच्छन्ति तथा राज्यं प्रीता नृणां पितामहाः।।

170. *Uśanas. S* III. 113.

171. *Ibid*, III.115.

172. *Ibid*, IV. 2-6.

make gifts at a *śrāddhakarma* is undoubtely equal to the understanding of the meaning of all the scriptures, bathing at sacred places and the fruit of all the scriptures.[173]

Even in respect of the *śrāddhakarma*-s, the authors of the *purāṇa*-s are seen to be continuing the same tradition. Thus, the *Agni P.* states that one who performs the (annual) ceremony (in honour of manes) according to the prescribed rules reaches the heaven, gets progeny, radiance, land, strength, excellent sons, greatness, ... unimpeded sovereignty, trade, lordship, health, fame, plesaure, excellent state, wealth, learning, silver, cows, small cattle, horses and long life.[174] The *Viṣṇu Dharma-sūtra*-s stress the importance of the *śrāddha*-s to be performed on various asupicious asterisms such as Kṛttikā, Rohiṇī, Ārdrā, Punarvasu etc. leading to fruits such as residence in heaven, progeny, energy of Brahmā prosperous business, land etc. (respectively),[175] to be performed on various days of the month such as Pratipadā, Dvitīyā, Tīṛtīyā, etc. which are said to be enabling the performer of that *śrāddha* to have a house and a beautiful wife, daughter fulfilling the expectation of the father, desired objects etc.[176] The authors of the *purāṇa*-s continue the same tradition. Thus, the *Brahmāṇḍa P.* states that *śrāddha* performed on Pratipadā leads to the benefit of wealth, that performed on Dvitīya enables the performer of a *śrāddha* to become the lord of heaven, that performed on Tīṛtīyā will lead to the destruction of enemies and sins, that performed on Caturthī will enable the performer to know the loopholes of enemies, that performed on Pañcamī will lead to the benefit of the acquisition of a great amount of wealth.[177] The authors of the *purāṇa*-s also lay down the qualifications of *brāhmins* qualified to perform the *śrāddhakarma* and state that they should be the knowers of languages, expert in grammar, learned in the *purāṇa*-s and Dharmaśāstra,

173. *Atri. S.* 360, 357.

174. *Agn. P.* 163. 37-39; also *Mārk. P.* 390.1-7.

175. *Visdh-S.* 75. 8- 35.

176. *Ibid*, 75.36-50.

177. *Brahmāṇḍa P.* II. 3. 17. 10$^{cd}$-20.

those who have taken bath at holy places, those who have observed vows, those who observe the vow of truth, those who are interested in carrying out their duties, those who do not get angry, those who are not under the influence of greed.[178] The *Varāha P.* considers those who know six Vedāṅga-s, who worship three sacred fires, in the morning, at noon and in the evening at three *sandhyā*-s, who offer libations..., who worship five sacred fires, .... and who respect their parents — as fit for invitation at the time of the *śrāddha*-s.[179] This *purāṇa* also describes Brāhmaṇa-s who are not qualified to perform *śrāddha*-s e.g. those who trouble their friends, a priest conducting religious caremonies for all castes,...one who has married another man's wife, one who does not look after his parents, one who is born of or looked after by a Śūdra woman, the husband of a Śūdra girl, one performing idol-worship for the sake of others.[180]

Following the tradtion of the works on Dharmaśāstra, the Purāṇa-s also have laid down three varieties of *śrāddha* viz. *nitya, naimittika* and *kāmya* and state that no oblation, invocation or Viśvadeva worship is necessary for the sake of the performance of *nitya śrāddha. Naimittika śrāddha* is performed on the fourth, eighth day, each half month and on the days of the full and the new moon *(pārvaṇa)* days.[181]

That the status of the Śūdra-s was lower than that of the other three *varṇa*-s is indicated by somewhat stiff attitude that the authors of the *purāṇa*-s have shown towards them. The author of the *Var P.* states that Śūdra-s have different manes belonging to their own caste and they are not liberated.[182] However, he is liberal enough to allow Śūdra-s

---

178. *Ibid*, II. 3. 19. 22[cd], 23[ab], 24[cd], 25[cd], 26[ab].

179. *Var. P.* 14.2-3.

180. *Ibid*, 14.4-6.

181. *Mat. P.* 16.5.6[ab].

182. *Var. P.* 13.27.

ते तु तस्य पृथक् सन्ति पितरः शूद्रजातयः।
मुक्ताश्चेतनका ब्रह्मन्न दृश्यन्ते पितृष्वपि।।

to sacrifice for the manes with the sanction of the remaining theree castes.[183] The *Matsya P.* also reflects liberal ideology of its author when it allows Śūdra-s to perform the ordinary *śrāddha* and as the *vṛddhiśrāddha* with uncooked grain, and utternace of the formula of *namaḥ* instead of Vedic *mantra*-s.[184]

According to ancient tradition, *śrāddha* was supposed to nourish forefathers who bestowed nourishment and progeny upon the performers of the *śrāddhakarma*-s The *purāṇa*-s continued the same tradition.[185] However, they attached great significance to making gifts of *dāna*. In fact, *dāna* at the time of the performance of *śrāddhakarma*-s was another noteworthy feature of Purāṇic religion. The *Vāyu P.* devotes a whole chapter in describing various gifts such as a cover,... pitcher, .... bed, .... a place full of gems, .... food.... lustrous vessel or silver or gold vessel, a gift of cows, a gift of fuel to Brāhmaṇa-s[186] It throws light on the sole interest of the Brāhmaṇa-s to ensure their means of livelihood which as pointed out time and again was seriously threatened by the diminishing importance of sacrifices.

Although the authors of the *purāṇa*-s were interested in safeguarding the interest of the Brāhmaṇa-s and hence laid down various types of *dāna*-s to be made to them they were aware of the fact that the ability to make gifts differed from person to person. With a view to enable different sections of society to make gifts, they specifically laid down various alternatives, so that if the former alternative is

---

183. *Ibid*, 13.26[cd].
    वर्णत्रयाभ्यनुज्ञातः शूद्रः सर्वान्पितृन्यजेत्।
184. *Mat. P.* 17.70.
    एवं शूद्रोऽपि सामान्यवृद्धिश्राद्धेऽपि सर्वदा।
    नमस्कारेण मन्त्रेण कुर्यादामान्ततः सदा।।
185. *Vāy.P.* II. 31.
    श्राद्धानि पुष्टिकामाश्च ये करियन्ति मानवाः।
    तेभ्यः पुष्टिं प्रजाश्चैव दास्यन्ति पितरः सदा।।
186. *Vāy P.* II.18. 4-23.

difficult to resort to, the latter at least could be put into practice. Thus, the *Varāha P.* states that one who is rich can munificently offer jewels, garments, vehicles, all the wealth, well and pond to Brahmins, but one who is not so well-to-do can give meals at the proper time in accordance with his own means. If that is not possible, one can just offer Śāka leaves and a little money to Brāhmaṇa-s. In case that also is too difficult, one can offer to them a handful of dark sesamum and if that too is an impossiblity, one can give them a handful of water.[187]

The above details indicate that the practice of performing *śrāddhakarma* was one of the norms followed by Indian people which had its roots in the belief that those who please their forefathers through *śrāddhakarma*-s are benefitted. Although it is very difficult to state why a certain belief gets widespread, it is univesally agreed upon that the beliefs always have the capacity to shape the behavioural patterns of those who cherish them. It has been already stated that the authors of the *purāṇa*-s felt an utter need to introduce some changes in the existing *varṇa* systeṃ. They tried to lessen the tensions caused by *varṇa*-gradations, especially, because the members belonging to the lower *varṇa-s* were likely to follow other faiths. However, there was no need to introduce change in the extisting belief system that had culminated into the practice of performing *śrāddhakarma*. Hence the authors of the *purāṇa*-s continued stressing its importance.

## Prāyaścitta-s (Expiatory Rites)

Kane P.V. has thoroughly dealt with the concept of *prāyaścitta*-s.[188] The works on Dharmaśāstra discuss the issue of *prāyaścitta*-s from various points of view. The *prāyaścitta*-s reflect a belief system according to which sins committed by human beings lead to some conseqences and they can be expiated. These authors distinguish be-

187. *Var. P.* 13.51ff.

188. Kane P.V., *H. of Dh. S.*, Vol. IV, 1953, pp. 57-86.

tween grave sins (*mahāpātaka*-s) and and minor sins (*upapātaka*-s) and lay down various means of reducing the consequences of sins such as confession, repentance (*anutāpa*), *Prāṇāyāma*, *tapa*-s (austerity) *homa* sacrifice into the fire), *japa* (muttering), *dāna* (fifts), *upavāsa* (fasting), *tīrthayātra* (pilgrimage). And the *purāṇa*-s continue the same tradition. The *Agn. P. e.g.* enlists various offences and the ways to atone them. Thus, according to this *Purāṇa*, killer of a brahmin should live in forest for twelve years in a hut. One should seek alms carrying the skull of the dead person on a staff or one should throw oneself in the kindled fire thrice with head downwards in order to purify himself. Otherwise, one should perform Aśvamedha, Svarjit or Gosava or one should recite one of the *Veda*-s and walk one hundred *yojana*-s. Otherwsie, one should give away all his (wealth) to a Brāhmaṇa, learned in the *veda*-s. This leads to the destruction of impurity caused by great sins.[189] It is indeed surprising that when the importance of sacrifices was diminishing due to the consicous efforts undertaken by the authors of the *purāṇa*-s in order to simplify religion, the performance of sacrifices such as Aśvamedha, Svarjit was laid down as expiatory means to remove the stigma of sins. The *Varāha P.* lays down thirty three offences such as : false compulsions on elders, eating the food of an outcast, eating prohibited items of food, ... drinking liquor... and declares that he who is guilty of these offences will never see the Lord Viṣṇu.[190] It further lays down expiatory means e.g. an offence to an elder (or preceptor) can be removed by performing Cāndrāyaṇa and Parāka should be performed. If prohibited food is eaten, Cāndrāyaṇa, Parāka and Prājāpatya should be performed and a gift of cow and food should be made. For the offence of drinking liquor committed by the twice-born, the expiation of four Cādrāyaṇa-s and three Prājāpatya-s should be performed for twelve years. Bathing after due fasting in the Śaṅkaratīrtha

189. *Agn. P.* 169.1-4.
190. *Var.P.* 179.6-10.

in Gaṅgā in the middle of the year removes the effect of offences... The sins disapper by bathing there, by drinking water at these places, by carrying it, by speaking about it or thinking about it, also by hearing about it and seeing it.[191]

The concept of atonement of sins indicates an attempt on the part of man to distinguish between right and wrong, meritorious and sinful and the feeling of realisation that since sin leaves its bad impact upon human life, it must be necessarily removed. Although the beliefs that bad impact of sins can be removed through deeds such as stay in the forest, recitation of the *veda-s* or *vrata*-s such as Cāndrāyaṇa, Prājāpatya etc. are purely superstitions in nature, they made people realise the seriousness of the mistakes. *Prāyaścitta*-s, toned the moral fabric of Indian society. Knowing their utalitarian value, the authors of the *purāṇa*-s continued stressing their importance.

The above discussion once again throws light on the fact that the keen interest of the authors of the *purāṇa*-s was to appeal to the masses. With that purpose in view, they tried to incorporate as many doctines and rites such as Karman doctrine, the theory of *avatāra, śrāddhakarma*-s etc. as they could that had come down to them through popular tradition with the result that the Puranic religion became a mass religion in the true sense of the term.

191. *Var. P.* 179.14.16.17$^{ab}$. 22-24.

# CONCLUSION

Modern age is the age of rapid scientific and technological developments. Thinkers of modern era are prone to criticise the phenomenon of religion and deny its relevance to social facts and society. According to them religion based on superstitious belief hinders social progress. It is an obstacle that stands in the way of human welfare and human progress. Modern thinkers regard religion as the frozen thought of people that comes in the way of man's free development. Karl Marx maintained that religion is the "opium of people".[1] Although the above statements cannot be regarded as totally erroneous, the study of the Purāṇic religion leads to different findings. The analytical review of the Purāṇic religion indicates that this religion was definitely characterised by the functional aspect. It did serve some purpose in the Purāṇic age.

Although religion is always based on the superstitious belief, those who are characterised by such belief always have the yearning for the Divine and they aspire to unite with that Divine Spirit. The Purāṇic religion also reflects similar endeavour on the part of man which is reflected in his feelings, his moods, his behaviour, his beliefs and his actions.

As concluding remarks it can be stated that like any other religion, the Purāṇic religion also can be studied from various points of view, i.e. the historical, sociological, anthopological, psychological and philosophical which are not at all mutually exclusive, on the contrary, they are collectively exhaustive. All of them shape the phenomenon of religion in some way or the other and hence an intergrated analysis based on the synthesis of these points would throw light on the true nature of religion.

Like any other social phenomenon, religion is constantly in the state of incessant flux. Purāṇic religion appears

1. Marx Karl, *His life and work*, Otto Rühle (Tr. by Paul Eden and Cedar Eden), London, (Year of Pubn. not given) p. 57.

as a harbinger of change. It meets the challenge of change.

Purāṇic religion had its roots in the past and it can be studied in the light of the concept of social change. It is marked by both, change and continuity. On the one hand, the Purāṇa-s continued the earlier monistic and polytheistic traits of the Vedic religion and at the same time, by assimilating the views of various systems of philosophy readily available to them, they synthesised them all with the doctrine of absolute monism and gave a new turn to the old principles in order to attract the masses and to wean away large sections of society from getting attracted towards Buddhism and Jainism. The authors of the *purāṇa*-s, thus, carried out a very significant function of bringing together the followers of different philosophical systems and religious cults into a composite intergrated society.

As long as social life of Indian people was stable, there was no need to bring out any change. Thus, there was hardly any change in the *āśrama* system prevailing in the Purāṇic age. The existing *āśrama* system carried out an important function of leading to social order and social stability. However, knowing full well that many members of society were disgusted with the *varṇa*-differences and the hierarchical gradations caused thereby and hence were likely to get attracted towards Jainism and Buddhism, the authors of the *purāṇa*-s adopted liberal ideology and stated that the status of an individual was not just ascribed, it could also be achieved.

The nature of the divinities described and glorified in the *purāṇa*-s also indicates that social environment, values and beliefs of people were responsible for the change in religion. The Brāhmaṇa-texts glorified the institution of sacrifice and the Upaniṣadic seers hankered after the pursuit of the knowledge of the Highest Reality in order to achieve immortality and emphasized the monistic doctrine of beginningless, endless, indestructible abstract cause. Later Upaniṣads glorified deities such as Śiva, Viṣṇu. The authors of the *purāṇa*-s harmoniously blended the esoteric as well as exoteric aspects and laid down the worship of the personified gods, i.e. Brahmā, Viṣṇu and Śiva as the Creator, Preserver and the Dissolver of the world. whose functions were interchangeable and Highest Lord being only one, from the highest point of view, these can be regarded as the manifest forms of the unmanifest Lord. Introduction of the worship of idols is another attempt to simplify and popularise religion.

The fact that the changing social cirrcumstances bring about change in religion is revealed through the introduction of the observance of vows, importance of gifts and visits to holy places. Through these simple ways, the authors of the *purāṇa*-s could enable all the sections of society to follow religion and at the same time, by making incessant and frantic appeals to make gifts to Brāhmaṇa-s, could ensure their own means of livelihood.

Besides the details given above, the authors of the *purāṇa*-s have presented a number of other miscellaneous topics such as Karman doctrine related with the doctrine of rebirth, purificatory rites *(saṁskāra*-s*)*, the theory of incarnation *(avatāravāda)*, duties of kings, women, the *śrāddhakarma*-s etc. These doctrines or concepts were already popular among the people existing at that time. The authors of the *purāṇa*-s retained the same.

As concluding remarks it can again be stated that

(i) The Purāṇic religion is a product of an interaction of certain antecedent forces. The survival of Brāhmanism was threatened by the forces of new faiths, *i.e.* Buddhism and Jainism. Purāṇic religion was the need of the time and it was ably met with by the authors of the *purāṇa*-s.

(ii) The Purāṇic religion can be studied in the light of the concept of social change. Changing social circumstances do have their impact upon the phenomenon of religion as a result of which it undergoes changes. Indian society was disintegrated due to the fear lurking in the minds of some sections of society that in the absence of some ideal goal in the form of *dharma* they will have to grope in darkness. With an introduction of simple principles and doctrines that could be pursued by the majority of people, and by synthesising them with some of the old ones, the authors of the *purāṇa*-s transformed this religion into a mass-religion and

(iii) As the Puranic religion, thus carries out an important function, it can be described as a religion characterised by functional aspect.

In the words of Jamna Das Akhtar, "The authors of the Purāṇas played an important role in bringing the followers of the different religious cults into a composite Hindu society. ...India always had been a land of many people, many languages and many religious denominations. The interest of the country demanded all these sects should form the necessary parts of the Hindu society. The credit for doing this service must go to the authors of the Purāṇas. The authors of the Purāṇas created a sense of religious toleration among the followers of various cults and set their energies into motion create a solid and composite society.[2] ..."

2. "Introduction", *Matsya Purāṇam*, Ed. by Jamna Das Akhtar, Delhi, 1972, pp. vii-viii.

## APPENDIX

### PROBABLE DATES OF THE MAJOR PURĀṆA-S

To decide the dates of the Purāṇas has been a ticklish problem, for each Purāṇa has assumed an emormous size due to its earlier and later portions which are intermixed and cannot be demarcated easily. Hence there have been efforts to bring out the critical editions of the Purāṇas. All India Kashiraj Trust, Varanasi and the Oriental Institute, Baroda have been undertaking such projects, in the recent years.

Kane P.V. has rightly pointed put that some dates, particularly of ancient works are conjectural and disputed by several scholars.[1] Still broadly grouping the *mahāpurāṇa*-s into two categories, Kane has stated their probable dates. The same dates have been accepted while writing this thesis. Thus, some of the extant *purāṇa*-s such as *Vāyu*, *Viṣṇu*, *Mārkaṇḍeya*, *Matsya* and *Kūrma* are from 300 A.D. to 600 A.D. The *purāṇa*-s such as Agni, Garuḍa etc. are from 600 A.D. to 900 A.D.

According to De S. K., the chapter on the Alaṅkāra-s from the *Agn. P.* was composed in the 9th century A.D., after the period of Daṇḍin and Bhāmaha but before the period of Ānandavardhana.[2] According to Kane P. V., the *Agn. P.* was composed after the 7th century A.D. and the portion on poetics from the same *Purāṇa* might have been composed after the 9th century A.D.[3]

The *Varāha P.* must have been definitely composed much before 12th century A.D., since a number of verses from it are quoted in the *Dānasagara*, the work of Ballāḷasena,

1. Kane P.V., *H. of Dh. S.*, Vol. IV, Pune, 1953, p. ix. Also the cronological table given by Kane. Ibid, pp. ix.-xii.
2. De S.K. *History of Sanskrit Poetics*, Vol I, pp. 102-104.
3. Kane P.V. *The Sāhityadarpaṇa of Viśvanātha and the History of Sanskrit Poetics*, Bombay, 1951, pp. 3-5.

who flourisherd in the 12th century A.D. and the *Caturvargacintāmaṇi*, the work of Hemādri, who flourished in the 13th century A.D.[4]

Some writers like Colebrooke and Wilson regard the *Bhāgavata P.* to be a work of the 13th century A.D. Rāmānuja, who flourished in the 12th century does not revere this *purāṇa* much, which may lead to the inference that it might have been composed in the 10th century. However, it appears that the said *purāṇa* must have been composed much before Gauḍapāda i.e. 7th century, for he has quoted a verse (*Bhāg. P.* X. 14.4) in his commentary on the Uttaragītā and has stated 'this is said in the *Bhāg. P. (taduktam bhāgavate)*.[5]

The manuscript of the *Skanda P.* written in the 7th century is found in the library at Nepal. Similarly the script of this *purāṇa* written in 1008 is available at Calcutta. Hence it has to be borne in mind that a mere reference to the temple of Jagannātha does not lead to the conclusion that this *purāṇa* is a work of the 13th century.[6]

The *Brahmāṇḍa P.* was taken to the Bali islands in the 5th century and was translated in the native language. This translation is still available. This is a sure indication of the antiquity of this *purāṇa*.[7]

The *Brahma P.* refers to the Sun-temple at Konark, which was not built till 1241 A.D. Again there are descriptions of the holy places at Orissa. This indicates that most of the portion from this *purāṇa* might not have been composed before the 13th century.[8]

Most of the major *purāṇa*-s were composed from 300 A.D. as Kane P.V. has pointed out. The *purāṇa*-s had before them the deep-rooted tradition of the *gṛhyasūtra*-s and the *smṛti*-s. They respected it but did not follow it blindly,

4. Dange Sindhu S., *Bhāraīīya Sahityācā Itihāsa*, Maharashtra Grantha Nirmiti Mandal, Nagpur, 1975, P. 294.
5. *Ibid*, P. 291.
6. *Ibid*, p. 296.
7. *Ibid*, P. 298.
8. *Ibid*, p. 287.

since they wanted to propound the religion and faith of the ancient seers, to the masses, in consonance with the changed circumstances.

The *Bhaviṣya P.*, which contains the references to the British people, presents at times an amusing picture and shows how the work of making additions to the original *purāṇa* was going on for a long time.[9]

9. *Ibid*, p.293.

# BIBLIOGRAPHY

## (A) SANSKRIT TEXTS


Atharvaveda : Ed. by Vishva Bandhu Vishveshvarananda Vedic Research Institute, Hoshiarpur, 1960-64.

Ṛgveda Saṁhitā : Vaidika Samshodhan Mandal, Pune, 1933-51.

Taittirīya Saṁhitā : Ed. Weber, Albrecht, F. A. Brockhaus, Leipzip, 1871.

Vājaseneyi Saṁhitā : Ed. A. Weber, London, 1852.

Aitareya Brāhmaṇa : Pub. Apte Hari Narayan, Ānandasrama Sanskrit Series, Pune, 1896.

Śatapatha Brāhmaṇa : Ed. Śāstrī, Chinnaswāmī, Kashi Sanskrit Series, The Chowkhamba Sanskrit Series Office, Varanasi, 1937.

Bṛhadāraṇyaka Upaniṣad : Sri Ramakrishna Math, Madras, 1951.

Chāndogya Upaniṣad (6th ed.) : With the original text, word by word meaning, running tr. and copious notes by Swāhānanda, Sri Ramakrishna Math, Madras, 1984.

Chāndogya Upaniṣad (10th ed.) : With original passages, English rendering of each passage, copious notes by Swāmī Sarvānanda, Sri Ramakrishna Math, Madras, 1982.

Muṇḍaka Upanisad (10th ed.) : With original passages, English rendering of each passage, copious notes by Swāmī Sarvānanda, Shri Ramakrishna Math, Madras, 1982.

**Śvetāśvatara Upaniṣad** (8th ed.) : With original passages, English rendering of each passage, copious notes by Swāmī Tyagīsānanda Sri Ramakrishna Math, Madras, 1987.

**Nirukta** by Yāska : Ed. Pt. Mukunda Sharma, Nirnay Sagar Press, Bombay, 1930.

**Āpastamba Dharmasūtra** (3rd ed.) : Ed. Buhler G., Bombay Sanskrit Series, Bombay, 1932.

**Āpastamba Gṛhyasūtra** : Ed. Shintre, Shivaramashastri, with Marathi trans., Pub. Shintre, Shivaramashastri, Bombay, 1938.

**Baudhāyana Dharmasūtra** : Ed. A. Chinnaswami Shastri, Kashi Sanskrit Series, Benares, 1934.

**Gautama Dharmasūtra** : Ānandāśrama Press, Pune, 1932.

**Gobhila Gṛhyasutra** : Ed. Knauer, F., Commissionsverlag Von Simmel & Co., Leipzip, 1884-86.

**Kātyāyana Gṛhyasūtra** : Mantri Ramlal Kapur Trust, Bhalgadh, Sonipat, Haryana, 1983.

**Kauṣītaki Gṛhyasūtra** : Ed. Kunhan Raja C., with com. of Bahvatrāta, Madras University Sanskrit Series, No. 15, Madras, 1944.

**Mānava Gṛhyasūtra** : Ed. Priedrich Knauer, Commissionnaires de Pacademic, Imperiale des Sciences, St. Petersburg, 1897.

Pāraskara Gṛhyasūtra : Ed. Pathak, Shridharshastri, with Marathi trans., Patil Nidhi, Pune, Sake 1852.

Śāṅkhāyana Gṛhyasūtra : Ed. Sehgal, S.R., Munshiram Manoharlal, Delhi, 1960.

Vaikhānasa Dharmasūtra : Chowkhamba Sanskrit Series, Banares, 1932.

Varāha Gṛhyasūtra : Ed. by Raghu Vira, University of Punjab, Lahore, 1932.

Vedāntasūtra Brahmasūtrabhāṣya : Revised by Vasudeva Laksmanashastri, Panshikar, Nirnayasagar Press, Bombay, 1927.

The Kauṭilīya Arthaśāstra (2nd ed.) : Ed. Kangle R.P., University of Bombay, Bombay, Pt. I, 1970, Pt. II, 1972.

Aṅgiraḥ-saṁhitā : Ed. Dutt, M.N., *The Dharma Shastra* (T.D.S.), Vol. II, pp. 165-171, Cosmo Publications, New Delhi, 1979.

Atri-saṁhitā : Ed. Dutt, M.N., *T.D.S.*, Vol. II, pp. 181-214, Cosmo Publications, New Delhi, 1979.

Dakṣa-saṁhitā : Ed. Dutt, M.N., *T.D.S.*, Vol. II, pp. 291-309, Cosmo Publications, New Delhi, 1979.

Hārīta-saṁhitā : Ed. Dutt, M.N., *T.D.S.*, Vol. I, pp. 91-109, Cosmo Publications, New Delhi, 1978.

Likhita-saṁhitā : Ed. Dutt, M.N., *T.D.S.*, Vol. II, pp. 333-340, Cosmo Publications, New Delhi, 1979.

Manu-smṛti : Ed. by Sharma, Vasudeva, with comm. of Kullūkabhaṭṭa, Nirnayasagar Press, Bombay, 1920.

Parāśara-smṛti : Ed. Harihara, P., with Gujrathi

trans., Gujrathi Printing Press, Bombay, 1912.

**Saṁvarta-saṁhitā** : Ed. Dutt, M.N., *T.D.S.*, Vol. II, pp. 215-234, Cosmo Publications, New Delhi, 1979.

**Śaṅkha-saṁitā** : Ed. Dutt, M.N., *T.D.S.*, Vol. III, pp. 341-372, Cosmo Publications, New Delhi, 1979.

**Śatātapa-saṁhitā** : Ed. Dutt, M.N., *T.D.S.*, Vol. II, pp. 311-331, Cosmo Publications, New Delhi, 1979.

**Uśanaḥ-saṁhitā** : Ed. Dutt, M.N., *T.D.S.*, Vol. I, pp. 111-164, Cosmo Publications, New Delhi, 1978.

**Vasiṣṭha-saṁhitā** : Ed. Dutt, M.N., *T.D.S.*, Vol. III, pp. 425-466, Cosmo Publications, New Delhi, 1979.

**Viṣṇu-smṛti** : Ed. Krishnamacharya V., with Keśavavaijayanti of Nandapaṇḍita, The Adyar Library & Research Centre, Madras, 1964.

**Vyāsa-saṁhitā** : Ed. Dutt, M.N., *T.D.S.*, Vol. IV, pp. 467-488, Cosmo Publications, New Delhi, 1979.

**Yājñavalkya-smṛti** : Ed. Vasudev Laxman Sastri Pansikar, with Mitākṣarā of Vijñaneśvara, Nirnayasagar Press, Bombay, 1909.

**Smṛtīnām Samiccayaḥ** : Pub. Apte V.G., Ānandāśrama Sanskrit Series, Pune, 1929.

**Dhammapada** : Ed. Avadh Kishore Narayana Mahabodhi Sabha, Sarnath, Varanasi, 1946.

| | |
|---|---|
| Mahāpurāṇa-s | : |
| Agni Purāṇa | : Nag Publishers, Delhi, 1985. |
| Bhāgavata Purāṇa | : Geeta Press, Gorakhpur, Śake 2010. |
| Bhaviṣya Purāṇa | : Nag Publishers, Delhi, Year of Pub. not published. |
| Brahma Purāṇa | : Nag Publishers, Delhi, 1985. |
| Brahmāṇḍa Purāṇa | : Motilal Banarsidass, Delhi, 1985. |
| Garuḍa Purāṇa | : Nag Publishers, Delhi, 1984. |
| Kūrma Purāṇa | : Indological Book House, Varanasi, 1967. |
| Liṅga Purāṇa | : Motilal Banarsidass, Delhi, 1980. |
| Mārkaṇḍeya Purāṇa | : Nag Publishers, Delhi, Date of pub. not printed. |
| Matsya Purāṇa (Vols. I & II) | : Nag Publishers, Delhi, 1983. |
| Mastsya Purāṇa (ed.) | : Oriental Publishers, Delhi, 1972. |
| Nārada Purāṇa | : Nag Publishers, Delhi, 1984. |
| Padma Purāṇa (Vols. I, II & III) | : Nag Publishers, Delhi, Date of pub. not printed. |
| Skanda Purāṇa | : Nag Publishers, Delhi, 1982. |
| Vāyu Purāṇa | : Nag Publishers, Delhi, 1983. |
| Vāmaṇa Purāṇa (ed.) | : All India Kashirāj Trust, Varanasi, 1973. |
| Varāha Purāṇa | : Asiatic Society, Culcutta, 1893. |
| Viṣṇu Purāṇa | : Geeta Press, Gorakhpur, Sake 2045. |
| Devī Bhāgavata Purāṇa | : Nag Publishers, Delhi, 1986. |


## (B) ENGLISH & MARATHI BOOKS


| | |
|---|---|
| Baaren Th.P. Van & Drizvers H.J.W. (ed.) | : *Religion, Culture and Methodology,* Mounton & Co., Edinburg, 1973. |
| Bhandarkar R.G. | : *Vaiṣṇavism, Śaivism and Minor* |

| | | |
|---|---|---|
| | | *Religious Systems*, Oxford University Press, Bombay, 1913. |
| Brothers John | : | *Readings in Sociology of Religion*, Pergamon Press, Oxford, 1967. |
| Caird John | : | *An Introduction to the Philosophy of Religion*, James Maclehose & Sons, Glasgo, 1910. |
| Charlesworth M. J. | : | *Philosophy of Religion : The Historical Approaches*, Macmillan, London, 1972. |
| Chowdhari Nirad | : | *Hinduism*, B. I. Publications, New Delhi, 1979. |
| Danielou Alain | : | *Hindu Polytheism*, Routledge and Kegan, London, 1964. |
| Dange S. A. | : | *Hindu Dharma āṇi Tattvajñāna* (Marathi) Shrilekhan Vachan Bhandar, Pune, 1973. |
| Dange Sindhu S. | : | *Bauddha Dharma āṇi Tattvajñāna*, (Marathi) Continental Prakashan, Pune, 1980. |
| Dange Sindhu S. | : | *Jaina Dharma āṇi Tattvajñāna*, (Marathi) Continental Prakashan, Pune, 1980. |
| Dange Sindhu | : | *The Bhāgavata Purāṇa : A Mytho-Social Study*, Ajanta Publication, New Delhi, 1984. |
| Dange Sindhu S. | : | *Myths of Creation*, (ed.), Bombay University Publication, Bombay, 1987. |
| Dange Sindhu S. | : | *Puranic Etymologies and Flexible Forms* (some glimpses), Viveka Publications, Aligarh, 1989. |
| De S.K. | : | *History of Sanskrit Poetics*, 2nd Revised edition, K.L. Mukhopadhyay, Calcutta, 1960. |
| Deussen Pual | : | *The System of Vedānta*, O. C. |

Pub. Co., Chicago, 1912.

Devasthali G.V. : *Religion and Mythology of the of the Brāhmaṇas*, Bhau Vishnu Ashtekar Vedic Series, Vol. No. 1, University of Poona. Poona, 1965.

Dutt M.N. : *Viṣṇu Purāṇa*, (ed.) Ess Ess Publications, Delhi, 1978.

Feaver Claton & Horosz Williams : *A Religion in Philosophical and Cultural Perspective . A new approach to the philosophy of Religion through cross-disciplinary studies* (ed.), Princeton D. Van Nostrand Co., Inc., 1967.

Ferm V. : *Religion in Transition*, (ed.) George Allen and Unwin Ltd., London, 1937.

Geertz Clifford : *Anthropological Approaches to the Study of Religion*, Traistock Publications, London, 1965.

Ghurye G.S. : *Caste, Class and Occupation*, Popular Book Depo., Bombay, 1961.

Gillin J.P. : *An Introduction to Sociology*, The Macmillan Co., New York, 1963.

Gonda J. : *Vaiṣṇavism and Śaivism : A Comparison*, Munshiram Manoharlal Publishers Pvt. Ltd., New Delhi, 1976.

Hault Thomas Ford : *The Sociology of Religion*, Dryden Press, New York, 1958.

Holuves Edward : *Introduction to the Philosophy of the Upaniṣads*, George Allen & Unwin Ltd., London, 1924.

Hopkins E.W. : *Handbook on the History of Re-*

*ligion*, Vol. I, Grinn & Co., Boston, 1895.

Horton Paul & Hunt Chester L : *Sociology* Mc Grew Hill Kogakusha Ltd. Tokyo, 1976 (First published in 1964)

Hume R.B. : *The Thirteen Proncipal Upaniṣads*, Coeffrey Cumberlege, Oxford University Press, London, 1921.

Joshi J.V. : *Hindu Dharmāce Tattvajñāna*, (Marathi) Continental Prakashan, Pune, 1975.

Jung C.G. : *The Collective Works of C.G. Jung*, Vol. II, Routledge and Kegal Ltd., London, 1958.

Kane P.V. : *Sāhityadarpaṇa of Viśvanātha and the History of Sanskrit Poetics*, (3rd ed.) pub. Kane P.V. Bombay, 1951.

Kane P.V. : *History of Dharmaśāstra*, Bhandarkar Oriental Research Institute, (BORI), Pune —
Vol. I, Pt. I - 1968.
Vol. II, Pt. II - 1941.
Vol. III - 1962.
Vol. IV - 1953.
Vol. V, Pt. I - 1962.
Vol. V, Pt. II - 1962.

Kumar Pushpendra : *Śakti Cult in Ancient India*, Bharatiya Publishing House, Varanasi, 1974.

Kumar Savitri : *The Puranic Lore of Holy Water Places*, Munshiram Manoharlal Publishers Pvt. Ltd., New Delhi, 1983.

Macdonell A.A. : *Vedic Mythology*, Indological House, Varanasi, 1963.

Malefift A.D.W. : *Religion and Culture*, The Macmillan Co., New York, 1897.

Max Müller K.M. : *Introduction to the Science of Religion*, Longamans, Green & Co., London, 1897.

Merton R.K. : *Social Theory and Social Structure*, Amerind Publishing Co. Pvt. Ltd., New Delhi, 1972, (Published by arrangement with the original publisher, The Macmillan Co., New York).

Monier-Williams Monier : *Brahmanism and Hinduism*, John Murray, London, 1887.

Monier-Williams Monier : *Hinduism*, Rare Books, Delhi, 1971.

Nottingham Elizabeth : *Religicn : A Sociological Review*, Random House, New York, 1971.

O Dea Thomas & O Dea Janet Aviad : *The Sociology of Religion*, (2nd ed.), Prentice Hall, Inc., 1983.

Otto Rühle : *Karl Marx, His Life and Work*, (tr. by paul Eden and Cedar Eden) George Allen and Unwin Ltd., London, Year of pub. not given.

Parsons Tolcott : *Theories of Society : Foundations of Modern Sociological Theory*, The Free Press, New York, 1961.

Pickering S. T. : Durkheim's Sociology of Religion, Routledge and Kegan Paul, London, 1984.

Radhakrishnan S. : *Eastern Religions and Western Thought*, Clerindon Press, Oxford, 1939.

Radhakrishnan S. : *Religion and Society*, George Allen & Unwin Co. Ltd., London, 1948.

Ram Gopal : *India of Vedic Kalpaūtras*, (2nd ed.), Motilal Banarsidass, Delhi, 1989.

Selbi : *The Psychology of Religion*, Clarendon Press, Oxford, 1924.

Seth Surabhi : *Religion and Society in the Brahma Puraṇa*, Sterling Publishers Pvt. Ltd., New Delhi, 1979.

Srinivas M.N. : *Caste in Modern India*, Asia Publishing House, Bombay, 1970.

Shinivas M.N. : *Religion and Society among the Coorgs of South India*, Clarendon Press, Oxford, 1952.

Srivasthava V.C. : *Sun Worship in Ancient India*, Indological Publication, Allahabad, 1972.

Tiele C.P. : *Elements of Science of Religion*, Pt. II, Ontological William Blacwood & Sons, Edinburg, 1898.

Weber Max : *Religion of India : The Sociology of Hinduism and Buddism*, Free Press, Clencoe, Illionois, 1958.

Wilson : *Viṣṇu Purāṇa* (ed.) Kunthipustak Prakashan, Calcutta, 1961.

Winternitz : *History of Indian Literature*, Vol. I (2nd ed.), Oriental Books Reprint Corporation, Delhi, 1972. (First pub. in 1877, by the University of Calcutta).

Yinger Milton : *Religion, Society and the Individual*, The Macmillan Co., New York, 1957.

Yinger Milton : *The Scientific Study of Religion*, Macmillan Co., London, 1970

## (C) RESEARCH PAPERS AND THESIS


Dange Sindhu S. : "The Principle of Jātyutkarṣa in the Social Evolution", *Ajaya-Sri (Prof. Ajaya Mitra Shastri Fel. Vol.)*, Vol. II, Sandeep Prakashan, Delhi, Feb., 1989.

Huttington Ronald : "Avatārās and Yugas", *Purāṇa*, Vol. VI, No. 1, All India Kashiraj Trust, Varanasi, 1964.

Acharya Kala D. : *Puranic Records of Gifts*, Thesis, University of Bombay, Bombay, 1985.


## (D) ENCYCLOPAEDIA


**Encyclopaedia of Britannica** : Willian Benton, Publisher (The University of Chicago), Inc, 1973. (First pub. in 1768).

**Encyclopaedia of Puranic Beliefs and Practices** : Dange S.A., Navrang, New Delhi, Vol. I, 1986, Vol. II, 1987, Vol. III, 1987, Vol. IV, 1989, Vol. V, 1990.

**Encyclopaedia of Philosophy** Vol. II, : ed. Paul Edwards (ed in Chief), Collier Macmillan Publishing Co. New York, 1967.

**Encyclopaedia of Religion** : ed. Mircea Eliade, (ed. in Chief) Macmillan Publishing Co., New York, Vol. II, 1987, Vol. IV, 1987, Vol. V, 1987.

**Encyclopaedia of Religion and Ethics** : ed. Hastings James (ed. in Chief), T. & T. Clark, Edinburgh, Vol. IV, 2nd ed. 1935 (first pub. 1911),

| | | |
|---|---|---|
| | | Vol. X, 4th ed. 1956 (first pub. 1918). |
| International Encyclopaedia of Social Sciences, Vol. XIII | : | ed. David Sills, Macmillan Co. & Free Press, Inc, 1968. |

## (E) DICTIONARIES AND KOŚA-S

| | | |
|---|---|---|
| **Bhāratīya Saṁskriti, Kośa,** Vol. IV (Marathi) | : | ed. Joshi Mahadevashastri and Hodavar Padmaja, Mahārashtra Samskriti Mandal, Pune, 1967. |
| **Mahārashtra Śabdakośa,** Pt. IV (Marathi) | : | ed. Date Y.R., Mahārashtra Kośamaṇḍala Ltd., |
| **Marathi Vyutpattikośa Aitihasika and Taulanika** | : | ed. Kulkarni K.P., Dhavle Publication, Bombay, 1946. |

# INDEX